THE FEAR OF TOO MUCH JUSTICE

THE FEAR OF TOO MUCH JUSTICE

Race, Poverty, and the Persistence of Inequality
in the Criminal Courts

STEPHEN B. BRIGHT AND JAMES KWAK

THE
NEW
PRESS

NEW YORK
LONDON

Requests for permission to reproduce selections from this book should be made through our website: https://thenewpress.com/contact.

Published in the United States by The New Press, New York, 2023
Distributed by Two Rivers Distribution

ISBN 978-1-62097-025-6 (hc)
ISBN 978-1-62097-804-7 (ebook)
CIP data is available

The New Press publishes books that promote and enrich public discussion and understanding of the issues vital to our democracy and to a more equitable world. These books are made possible by the enthusiasm of our readers; the support of a committed group of donors, large and small; the collaboration of our many partners in the independent media and the not-for-profit sector; booksellers, who often hand-sell New Press books; librarians; and above all by our authors.

www.thenewpress.com

Book design and composition by Bookbright Media
This book was set in Bembo

Printed in the United States of America

10 9 8 7 6 5 4 3 2 1

For Patricia and Robert H. Bright Jr.,
Inkyung and Nosup Kwak,
and all the people who have ever worked for the
Southern Center for Human Rights

The mood and temper of the public in regard to the treatment of crime and criminals is one of the most unfailing tests of the civilisation of any country. A calm and dispassionate recognition of the rights of the accused against the State, and even of convicted criminals against the State, a constant heart-searching by all charged with the duty of punishment, . . . and an unfaltering faith that there is a treasure, if you can only find it, in the heart of every man—these are the symbols which in the treatment of crime and criminals mark and measure the stored-up strength of a nation, and are the sign and proof of the living virtue in it.

—Winston Churchill, address to the
House of Commons, 1910

Contents

Foreword

Stephen Bright was a teenager living on a farm in rural Kentucky near the western edge of Appalachia when the United States Supreme Court announced its historic ruling in *Gideon v. Wainwright*. The 1963 decision declared that poor people accused of a crime have a right to counsel when their life or liberty is threatened by the state or federal government. The monumental judgment came amidst a wave of transformative civil rights decisions that fundamentally changed America—and shaped the life of Steve Bright.

Even before he left the farm, Steve was nurturing convictions about the plight of the poor and the marginalized that were rooted in his relationships with people in great need. He attended the University of Kentucky at a time of unprecedented student activism and political protest. An outspoken student leader, Steve championed reforms and change. It was a turbulent time when many courageous young people believed that fighting the war on poverty and inequality in the United States should be the priority, not combat abroad. Steve's willingness to address often-ignored issues drew criticism and disdain from many, but Steve simply became more determined.

Steve took with him to law school his belief that inequality and injustice are perverse obstacles in the lives of too many people, and put his beliefs into action as a lawyer at Legal Services in Appalachia. By the time he arrived in Washington, DC, to join the premier public defender program in the country in 1976, Steve had become an attorney with unsurpassed dedication and commitment to fighting for the poor and indigent.

In the decades leading up to *Gideon*, defense lawyers often were appointed to represent disfavored defendants for the express purpose of facilitating quick and efficient convictions. *Gideon* created a new constitutional paradigm that reshaped the role of defense counsel in the criminal legal system, but no one knew what kind of lawyering would actually emerge.

A handful of people argued that *Gideon* required constitutionally appointed lawyers and public defenders to be totally committed to their clients, and zealously and passionately to defend their clients' rights. This kind of lawyering was expected for rich, powerful, and high-profile defendants, but it was not the model for poor people accused of crimes. Many legal professionals and scholars believed that "client-centered" lawyering was impractical for poor defendants; only the wealthy could afford or expect that level of legal advocacy. Steve Bright was among a handful of post-*Gideon* architects who were persuaded that indigent defendants are entitled to the best defense possible. He was determined to achieve outstanding advocacy for every person he represented, and he chose to represent only indigent people. It is this philosophy, coupled with his remarkable talent, that has made Steve Bright one of America's greatest defenders of the poor, the accused, and the condemned.

I went to work with Steve while I was a law student in the early 1980s. By the time we met, he had become a highly respected and seasoned trial attorney who had accepted the daunting responsibility of building a new resistance to the recently revived effort to execute people in America. He took over what was then called the Southern Prisoners Defense Committee in Atlanta, Georgia, at a time when few lawyers anywhere in the country were working full time to represent people facing execution. With little funding and great opposition, Steve led a national effort to represent indigent people on death row, while an intensifying fervor to execute people was spreading across the South.

Death penalty work in the 1980s meant long days, late nights, lots of stressful emergencies, and tense, unnerving litigation before scheduled executions. The work was frantic, chaotic, desperate, and constant. You never knew from one day to the next where an execution date would emerge that required immediate attention. We worked in Georgia, Virginia, North Carolina, South Carolina, Florida, Louisiana, Mississippi, Alabama, Texas, and Arkansas, where just a decade earlier intense battles to resist racial integration and civil rights had raged.

The death penalty is a potent vestige and symbol of the Old South, embodying the region's deep commitment to racial hierarchy, disdain for "outside agitators," and contempt for federal oversight. As this extraordinary book makes clear, capital punishment is disproportionately imposed on Black people accused of crimes against white people. In the 1980s, it was not uncommon for prosecutors and judges freely to use racial slurs and overt racial bigotry to ensure Black defendants were convicted and condemned.

Black people were typically tried by all-white juries even in counties with large Black populations. Poor white and Black people accused of crimes were often defended so ineffectively that trials lasted less than a day. When we challenged these clearly unfair and unreliable proceedings, many state officials were outraged. We frequently went into courtrooms that were overtly hostile, discriminatory, and menacing. But Steve never backed down. Despite the threatening stares and animosity we encountered, he fearlessly and skillfully argued on behalf of his clients in his booming, powerful voice. He refused to be silenced.

I am a product of *Brown v. Board of Education.* I started my education in a "colored school," where civil rights lawyers ultimately forced an end to racial segregation. That lawyers had the power to protect disfavored and marginalized people by enforcing their rights under the law captivated me. These lawyers could achieve things the political process could not, and that was exciting. When I started Harvard Law School in 1981, I had never met a lawyer, but I was persuaded that the rule of law might create justice for the poor and people of color that could not be achieved outside of a courtroom.

During my first year of law school, I began to doubt whether becoming a lawyer made sense. Almost everyone I met seemed to have a more abstract, less practical notion of what lawyers could and should do to help the poor and most vulnerable people in society. The curriculum and discourse often seemed focused on the powerful and the privileged. I began to fear that the generation of lawyers who came into my racially segregated community and changed things when I was a child were no more.

Meeting Steve Bright changed things for me. Steve revived a hope that I could make a difference as an attorney in the lives of people who were unfairly discarded, oppressed, and condemned. His passionate commitment to fighting for the condemned was energizing and deeply compelling. I became one of many young lawyers and law students who have been influenced and encouraged by Steve Bright to challenge the justice deficit in our country.

Today, nearly forty years later, Steve is still teaching, inspiring, and motivating students and lawyers to do the kind of justice work that can save lives and revive hope. It's appropriate that his co-author, respected law professor James Kwak, was himself a student of Steve's.

In many ways, this book continues Steve's work and legacy. It documents the extraordinary effort needed to confront a legal system that treats you better if you are rich and guilty than if you are poor and innocent. It calls all of us to reckon with our long history of racial injustice and inequality, to educate ourselves about the multitude of flaws and failures that must be addressed in our courts. Above all, it reveals the heart of a man who has much to teach anyone who cares about justice.

The Fear of Too Much Justice documents the inequality that continues to infect our criminal legal system. It provides an urgently needed analysis of our collective failure to confront and overcome racial bias and bigotry, the abuse of power, and the multiple ways in which the death penalty's profound unfairness requires its abolition. You will discover Steve Bright's passion, brilliance, dedication, and tenacity when you read these pages.

But there is something else I hope you'll discover about Steve: his extraordinary generosity and compassion. We don't often speak of generosity as a trait of great lawyers, advocates, and teachers. Lawyers who represent people on death row, people who have been convicted of terrible crimes, are often tempted to become cynical. We are required to witness a lot of cruelty, pain, and animosity when we fight a state that is intent on executing a human being. In the face of overwhelming layers of inequality, it's critical that our life and work be fueled by hopefulness. It's one of the most important lessons I learned from Steve.

In 1985, after two internships, I returned to SPDC—now the Southern Center for Human Rights—as a full-time lawyer. My annual salary was $14,000. I had student loans to pay and did not come from a family with means, and I simply could not afford a place to live in Atlanta. So Steve invited me to sleep on his couch. He lived in a small "shotgun" apartment in Grant Park, a duplex with one bedroom, a living room, bathroom, and kitchen. "Humble" is perhaps the most polite way to describe Steve's living quarters, although I fully acknowledge that I gratefully stayed there for a year and a half without complaint.

We worked from very early in the morning until late at night every day. We would take evening meal breaks and seek out cheap food at various inexpensive Atlanta diners and food trailers. We talked constantly about the law, legal strategy, race, poverty, and the bigotry and abusive politics that had condemned so many of the people we fought to serve. Steve had an amazing ability to discuss difficult issues with humor, compassion, wit, and wisdom. He never expressed bitterness, only his deeply held hope for more justice. It is totally appropriate to characterize the lawyering that Steve organized, modeled, and inspired as heroic; he is certainly one of my heroes.

What you will learn about our legal system in these pages should anger you. But this book calls for more than anger. The authors are calling on us to fight for justice. I've come to believe that without compassion and generosity, there can be no justice. We are truly fortunate to have these writings and the extraordinary Steve Bright to guide us in our understanding of what justice requires. He is generously preparing us for the work that remains—the rest is up to us.

Bryan Stevenson

THE FEAR OF TOO MUCH JUSTICE

1

The Myth of the Adversary System

The Law is a mighty machine. . . . Woe to the unfortunate
man who, wholly or in part innocent, becomes entangled
in its mighty wheels, unless his innocence is patent or his
rescue planned and executed by able counsel. The machine
will grind on relentlessly and ruthlessly, and blindfolded
justice does not see that the grist is sometimes stained with
blood.

—*Edward Johnes, 1893*[1]

Glenn Ford, a Black man, was sentenced to death for a crime he
did not commit. He was convicted of robbing a jewelry store
and murdering its white owner, Isadore Rozeman. Ford had occa-
sionally done yard work for Rozeman. That made him a suspect.

To represent Ford at his death penalty trial, a Louisiana judge
selected two lawyers from an alphabetical listing of members of the
local bar association. One specialized in oil and gas law and had never
tried a case. The other had been out of law school for only two years
and worked on slip-and-fall cases.

Ford was tried in the Caddo Parish Courthouse in Shreveport in
1984. As is common in the South, a monument to the Confederacy
stood in front of the courthouse. It was thirty feet high and featured a young Confederate soldier holding a rifle, surrounded by
busts of Robert E. Lee, Thomas "Stonewall" Jackson, and two other

Confederate generals. The pedestal was inscribed "Lest We Forget," and, below that, "Erected by the United Daughters of the Confederacy. 1905, Love's Tribute to Our Gallant Dead." The Third National Flag of the Confederacy flew from the monument.[2]

Prosecutors failed to pursue—or disclose to the defense lawyers—leads that would have demonstrated Ford's innocence. During jury selection, the prosecution used its peremptory strikes to remove all the prospective Black jurors, and, with no murder weapon or eyewitnesses, relied upon "experts" of dubious credibility to prove its case. Ford's lawyers had no money for investigators or experts to rebut the prosecution. They also did not know how to subpoena witnesses who could have helped convince the jury to spare Ford's life. The all-white jury convicted Ford and sentenced him to death.

After thirty years of fighting Ford's attempts to appeal his conviction, prosecutors admitted that they did not have a case against him. He was released on March 11, 2014, and given $20. Ford was sixty-four when he was released. He died of lung cancer the following year.[3]

A.M. "Marty" Stroud, the chief prosecutor in the case, apologized to Ford and the community in a letter to a Shreveport newspaper. He admitted that the evidence that eventually exonerated Ford was so strong that, had it been disclosed during the investigation of the crime, Ford would not have been arrested. "In 1984, I was 33 years old," Stroud wrote. "I was arrogant, judgmental, narcissistic and very full of myself. I was not as interested in justice as I was in winning." Stroud said that he did not question the unfairness of Ford being represented by inexperienced lawyers or think much about the discrimination involved in striking Blacks so that Ford was tried by an all-white jury.[4]

Ford's trial was a complete breakdown of the process for determining guilt and punishment. There was no adversary process. The judge's appointment of lawyers who did not know what they were doing left Ford defenseless. The exclusion of Black people from the jury put the fate of Ford, a Black man accused of the murder of a white man, in the hands of an all-white jury in a courthouse where the Confederacy was celebrated. Yet for over thirty years state and federal courts upheld his convictions and death sentence, finding no legal error in the case. The prosecutors' belated recognition of his innocence saved him from an execution that the courts would have allowed.

Such breakdowns—caused by unchecked prosecutorial power, inadequate lawyers for the accused, biased or indifferent judges, and racial discrimination—occur far more often than is generally acknowledged. The same year that Ford was released, North Carolina released two Black men, Henry McCollum and Leon Brown, after DNA testing established their innocence and revealed that a serial rapist and murderer was the actual perpetrator of the murder they had been convicted of. The two men, intellectually disabled half brothers, were initially sentenced to death and had spent thirty years in prison.[5] In recent years, DNA testing has established the innocence of three Black men—Kennedy Brewer, Eddie Lee Howard Jr., and Sherwood Brown—sentenced to death in Mississippi because of unreliable testimony by a dentist that bite marks connected them to the murders. In Brewer's case, the bite marks turned out to be insect bites. He was released in 2008 after fifteen years in custody. Howard was released in 2020 and Brown was released in 2021; each spent twenty-eight years in custody.[6] Another Black man, Paul Browning, spent thirty-three years on Nevada's death row before being released in 2019. A federal appeals court described his trial as "a mixture of disturbing prosecutorial misconduct and woefully inadequate assistance of counsel."[7]

There are many others. Between 1973 and the end of 2020, 185 people *sentenced to death* were found not to be guilty of the crimes for which they were sentenced. Thirteen of them spent thirty years or longer in prison; twelve of the thirteen were Black.[8] The criminal courts have repeatedly failed in their most fundamental responsibility—separating the guilty from the innocent—in the cases with the highest stakes.

Americans were once assured that the courts protected innocent people from being convicted. The revered federal judge Learned Hand said in 1923 that the possibility of an innocent person being convicted was an "unreal dream."[9] But DNA testing has repeatedly exonerated people convicted of crimes and identified the actual perpetrators. Others have been exonerated after their cases were thoroughly investigated by innocence projects, other public interest legal programs, public defenders, pro bono lawyers from law firms, journalists, law students, or conviction integrity units—divisions of prosecution offices that investigate claims of wrongful convictions. The National Registry of Exonerations reported in 2021 that over 2,800 people convicted of all types of crimes have been found not to be guilty. They had collectively served over 25,000 years in prison.[10]

The conviction of innocent people, although the most striking failure of the criminal legal system, is only the tip of the iceberg. The courts are failing in another essential obligation: to provide fair and equal treatment to all people. The fates of people accused of crimes often depend less on what they did than on the whims of prosecutors; their choice to exercise their right to a trial instead of taking a plea deal; the assignment of incompetent or overworked attorneys to defend them; their race and the victims' race; the political motives of elected judges and prosecutors; and the exclusion of members of their race from juries.

A person charged with murder was much more likely to be sentenced to death and executed if prosecuted in Harris County, which includes Houston and its surroundings, between 1979 and 2000, than if prosecuted at any time in any other county in the country. Between 1982 and late 2022, 131 people who had been sentenced to death in Harris County were executed, more than in the *states* with the second and third highest number of executions: Oklahoma, with 118; and Virginia, with 113. (Texas executed 574 during that period.) Another seventy-two people sentenced to death in Harris County are on death row waiting to be executed.[11]

The reasons why this single county generated so many death sentences and executions are as obvious as the injustices in Glenn Ford's case. District Attorney Johnny Holmes Jr. aggressively sought the death penalty during his tenure from 1979 to 2000.[12] Houston's judges, many of them former prosecutors from Holmes's office, repeatedly assigned notoriously bad lawyers to represent people facing the death penalty. Some judges assigned capital cases to lawyers who made contributions to the judges' electoral campaigns. One lawyer, who was once jailed for neglecting a client's capital case, suspended from practice on another occasion, and reprimanded by the bar several times for professional misconduct, represented sixteen people who were sentenced to death.[13] Another hurried through trials like "greased lightning" without much questioning of witnesses or making objections; he fell asleep during trial in two of the ten cases in which his clients were sentenced to death.[14] Other lawyers missed deadlines for obtaining federal court review of their cases.[15]

During the final years of Holmes's tenure, the death penalty was more likely to be imposed against Black defendants and in cases involving white victims.[16] After he left office, the frequency of death sentences declined by more than half under his successor, Charles Rosenthal. The district attorneys after Rosenthal seldom sought the death penalty. In modern history, in 85 percent of all U.S. counties no case resulted in an execution. The majority of executions originated in only 2 percent of all counties.[17]

The courts accept—and are often responsible for—inadequate lawyers for people accused of crimes. In 2004, the American Bar Association reported that "the fundamental right to a lawyer that Americans assume appl[ies] to everyone accused of criminal conduct effectively does not exist in practice for countless people across the United States." Another report found that, in juvenile courts, "countless children" are "prosecuted and convicted every year without ever seeing a lawyer."[18]

In the same Louisiana parish where Glenn Ford was represented by an oil and gas lawyer at his capital trial, lawyers who specialize in tax, real estate, insurance, and adoption were drafted by judges, without compensation, to represent poor people accused of serious crimes.[19] In other places, lawyers have been asleep, intoxicated, under the influence of drugs, and suffering from serious mental illness while supposedly defending their clients.[20] Sometimes people accused of crimes languish in jail without any lawyer at all. Many defense lawyers have such immense caseloads and so little time for each case that it is impossible for them to represent their clients effectively.[21]

The inevitable result of representation by incompetent or overworked attorneys—or the lack of any representation—is the mass production of guilty pleas. The overwhelming majority of criminal cases—97 percent of federal convictions and 94 percent of state convictions—are resolved with guilty pleas.[22] Those pleas are dictated by prosecutors who control the information provided by law enforcement agencies, the charges brought against people accused of crimes, and the sentences that those people will receive. In some places, people in handcuffs and leg irons are herded into the courtroom and placed in the jury box and the front rows of the gallery. Often so many of them are people of color that it looks as if a slave ship has docked outside the courthouse. They wear jumpsuits—often orange, but sometimes with old-fashioned black-and-white stripes. One or more court-appointed attorneys walks down the line, often meeting their "clients" for the first time. In these brief, non-confidential conversations, the lawyers explain that the prosecutor will drop some of the charges or recommend a lighter sentence if the client pleads guilty, but will insist upon a severe sentence if the client exercises his right to trial.

Once this caricature of zealous representation is completed, the judge takes the bench. In some courtrooms, the people charged with crimes are brought before the judge in groups to enter their guilty pleas. A 2016 investigation found that in one court in Louisiana, groups of up to fifty people—almost all Black—entered guilty pleas simultaneously on "felony plea day," after speaking to their lawyer for about thirty seconds each.[23] In other courtrooms, judges accept one guilty plea after another, speaking so rapidly it is hard to understand them, in order to accept pleas as fast as possible. The judge tells those pleading that they are giving up their constitutional rights and asks them if they understand. The lawyer may prompt them to say that they do. The judge asks them whether they are guilty. If they hesitate, the lawyer may prompt them to say they are. Some of them are not guilty but are pleading guilty in order to be released from jail. At some point, the judge asks those pleading guilty if they are satisfied with their lawyers. They are prompted to say that they are, even though many have little or no understanding of what has just happened.

In some places, this system is called "McJustice." In others, it is known as "meet 'em and plead 'em." As one public defender said after standing beside seventeen people as they entered guilty pleas: "I met 'em, pled 'em, and closed 'em—all in the same day."[24] Everyone involved knows that those pleading guilty have had no real representation by a lawyer and have been granted no real legal process. "Meet 'em and plead 'em" is not about justice; it is about processing people through courts and satisfying the legal requirements for guilty pleas in order to cover up the breakdown of the system.

A system that resolves the overwhelming majority of its cases through pleas is not equipped, in the few cases that go to trial, to decide whether someone is guilty or innocent. In the absence of a capable lawyer, a person accused of a crime is virtually defenseless against a prosecutor who can call on the assistance of law enforcement agencies and has ample resources for investigation, expert witnesses, and other expenses. Nor is the system equipped, in assessing the accused person's culpability and imposing sentences, to treat those found guilty as individuals.

These deficiencies are not universal. In some places, poor people accused of crimes can consult with lawyers and make informed assessments of their cases before deciding whether to plead guilty or ask for a trial. The lawyers investigate the cases and provide competent representation if they decide to go to trial. But only a few states and a few counties provide the funding, independence, and structure that enable capable, caring, and dedicated lawyers to handle reasonable workloads and represent their clients competently. Most refuse to provide the funding necessary to provide competent representation for poor people, which could frustrate efforts to convict them, collect fines and fees from them, or send them to jail or prison.

Instead, many states and municipalities have attempted in recent decades to extract ever-increasing amounts of money from poor people accused of crimes, who are often already deep in poverty. Police are encouraged—and sometimes required—to patrol for minor traffic offenses to generate revenue for local governments. States, counties, and cities impose long lists of fees on people hauled into court for misdemeanors. Private probation companies profit by charging monthly fees and using the threat of jail to squeeze as much cash as possible out of people with no money to spare.

When Hills McGee appeared in court in Augusta, Georgia, on charges of public drunkenness and obstruction of the law enforcement officer who arrested him, he was told he had to pay $50 to apply for a public defender. McGee, whose sole source of income was a Veterans Administration disability payment of $243 per month, was unable to pay the fee. No one told him that the fee could be waived if he could not afford it. He pleaded guilty without a lawyer. The judge fined him $200 plus $70 in fees and surcharges, which McGee also could not pay. The judge ordered him to pay the fine in installments to a private probation company, which charged an enrollment fee of $15 and a $39 monthly service charge. McGee could not afford the monthly payment of $61.50, but he did his best. A year later, having paid $552, he was jailed for failure to pay off all of his fines and fees.[25]

Race is a key determining factor in many criminal cases. The courts tolerate discrimination that is not acceptable in any other area of American life. In at least five capital cases in Georgia, defense lawyers referred to their own clients with racial slurs before the jury.[26] Convictions have been upheld in cases where jurors used racial slurs and admitted that they had racist attitudes.[27] Many courtrooms look no different today than in the 1950s. The judge, the prosecutor, the court-appointed lawyer, and the jurors are all white, even in communities with substantial Black or Latino populations. The jurors are white because many prosecutors routinely strike people of color in jury selection, as happened in Glenn Ford's case. In 1986, the Supreme Court held that lawyers are not allowed to strike potential jurors on the basis of race, and that a lawyer who exhibits a pattern of striking people of a particular race must give race-neutral reasons for the strikes.[28] However, discrimination remains rampant. Prosecutors often give reasons that are trivial, such as a juror's haircut or facial expression or clothing. Prosecutors in Philadelphia were taught to question Blacks "at length" during jury selection and "mark something down that you can articulate later" as a reason for striking them.[29] Many prosecutors have lists of reasons and read off one or two. In most instances, the judge accepts the reasons and allows the strikes. This is a charade. Everyone watching knows that the real reason for many of the strikes is the potential juror's race.

The treatment of Glenn Ford, Hills McGee, and many others is at odds with bold declarations, from the Supreme Court on down, that the Constitution guarantees fairness and equality to people accused of crimes. The survival of the all-white jury and the continuing incarceration of people solely because they are poor are two of many examples of the Supreme Court's failure to live up to these constitutional requirements. While the Court has often denounced practices such as racial discrimination in jury selection and the imprisonment of poor people without consideration of their financial capacity, it has often seemed afraid to actually require equal justice for all.

In 1987, the Supreme Court addressed the question whether states could continue to execute people despite significant racial disparities in capital sentencing. Lawyers for Warren McCleskey, a Black man who had been sentenced to death in Georgia for the murder of a white police officer, presented sophisticated statistical studies proving what was obvious to people who closely observed Georgia's criminal courts: that prosecutors sought the death penalty primarily in cases where the victims were white, even though Black people were the victims in over 60 percent of murder cases in the state, and that death was more likely to be imposed in cases involving white victims and Black defendants.[30] This was nothing new. Race has always mattered in capital and other criminal cases in Georgia—all the way back through the era of Jim Crow and, before that, slavery.

The Supreme Court rejected McCleskey's claim by a 5–4 vote. Justice Lewis Powell said in his opinion for the majority, "Disparities in sentencing are an inevitable part of our criminal justice system." If the Court were to recognize discrimination in death sentences, he wrote, it "could soon be faced with similar claims as to other types of penalty," pointing out studies showing racial disparities in sentences for other crimes. Furthermore, if the Court recognized discrimination against Blacks, it would invite challenges claiming discrimination against other minority groups or discrimination on other bases such as gender and even "the defendant's facial characteristics, or the physical attractiveness of the defendant or the victim."[31]

In dissent, Justice William Brennan described Justice Powell's concerns as "a fear of too much justice." He gave the majority of the Court the benefit of the doubt, saying that it would surely recognize that disproportionate sentencing was unconstitutional if confronted with "striking evidence."[32] But the majority had failed to do just that in McCleskey's case.

This was not the first time that the Court and Justice Powell had expressed the fear that addressing injustice would lead to too much justice. When the Supreme Court struck down the death penalty in 1972 because of arbitrariness and discrimination in its infliction, Justice Powell dissented. He responded to evidence of discrimination by arguing, "The same discriminatory impact argument could be made with equal force and logic with respect to those sentenced to prison terms. . . . If discriminatory impact renders capital punishment cruel and unusual, it likewise renders invalid most of the prescribed penalties for crimes of violence."[33]

In 1976, the Court held that lawyers for James Ross Jr. and two other Black men accused of armed robbery and assault and battery against a white security guard had no right to ask during jury selection whether prospective jurors believed that a white person is more likely to tell the truth than a Black person. If such questioning were allowed, Justice Powell wrote for the majority, it could not be limited to racial prejudice, but would apply whenever "questioning about ethnic origins was sought, and its logic could encompass questions concerning other factors, such as religious affiliation or national origin."[34]

That was a very different approach than the Supreme Court had taken forty-five years earlier. In 1931, in *Aldridge v. United States*, the Court overturned a conviction where counsel for a Black man had not been allowed to question prospective jurors about racial bias. Chief Justice Charles Evans Hughes observed that if potential jurors were asked about racial prejudice and "found to be impartial, no harm would be done in permitting the question, but if any one of them was shown to entertain a prejudice which would preclude his rendering a fair verdict, a gross injustice would be perpetrated in allowing him to sit." Chief Justice Hughes rejected the argument that "it would be detrimental to the administration of the law" to allow such questions. "It would be far more injurious to permit it to be thought that persons entertaining a disqualifying prejudice were allowed to serve as jurors and that inquiries designed to elicit the fact of disqualification were barred," he wrote.[35] But in 1976, in the case of James Ross Jr., the Court held that *Aldridge* applied only to the federal courts—seeing no problem with the "gross injustice" of allowing a person with racial prejudice to sit on a jury in the state courts.[36] Five years later, the Court held that such questioning was not required in most federal cases.[37]

The fear of too much justice helps explain the ineffective responses of federal, state, and local governments to the systematic failures that have led to the conviction of innocent people and the unequal treatment of racial minorities and the poor in the courts. In the 1950s and 1960s, the Supreme Court recognized that there "can be no equal justice where the kind of trial a man gets depends upon the amount of money he has."[38] The Court held that poor people accused of crimes have a right to a lawyer at trial and on appeal, as well as a transcript of their trials.[39] However, over a half century later, many poor people today receive no meaningful representation because, in the 1980s, the Supreme Court held that the purpose of the right to a lawyer is only to ensure some minimal level of fairness, and that any lawyer is "strongly presumed to have rendered adequate assistance." And even when a lawyer fails to provide adequate representation, a judge may uphold a conviction based on the belief that the deficient representa-

tion did not make a difference.[40] For people represented by incompetent lawyers, this replaced trial by jury with trial by judges—judges
on reviewing and appellate courts who, because they did not see the
witnesses at trial and participate in jury deliberations, could not possibly know the impact of a lawyer's incompetence on the outcome of
a case.

As one federal appellate court judge observed about the Supreme
Court's standard of representation,

> The Constitution, as interpreted by the courts, does not
> require that the accused, even in a capital case, be represent-
> ed by able or effective counsel. . . . Consequently, accused
> persons who are represented by "not-legally-ineffective"
> lawyers may be condemned to die when the same accused,
> if represented by *effective* counsel, would receive at least the
> clemency of a life sentence.[41]

This low standard of representation is why many governments can
avoid spending the money necessary to ensure adequate representation for poor people accused of crimes.

There is also fear of the potential consequences. Zealous representation by competent lawyers with reasonable caseloads slows down
the machinery of plea bargaining, conviction, sentencing, imprisonment, and execution. Prosecutors have more difficulty obtaining
convictions of poor people. More people are released pending trial,
more negotiate better plea bargains, and more insist on going to trial.
Defense attorneys with sufficient time and resources to investigate
cases, demand information from the prosecution, and consult with
experts are able to contest charges effectively.

However, neither the cost nor the consequences justify tolerating
the injustices occurring in the criminal courts. Americans no longer
have the luxury of believing, as they may have once, that the courts

are properly and reliably deciding the issues presented to them. As discussed earlier, DNA testing has conclusively established that many people convicted in the courts, including some sentenced to death, were completely innocent. Only a small percentage of cases have evidence that can be subject to DNA testing, and in cases where DNA testing is not possible, there is no reason to believe that the error rate is different. The conviction of so many innocent people is unacceptable in a system that condemns people to death and prolonged deprivation of their liberty.

Cell phones and surveillance cameras have made it impossible to ignore the injustices that pervade policing and prosecution. Prosecutors did not charge three Georgia men in the 2020 killing of Ahmaud Arbery until a cell phone video of the shooting was disclosed; they were later convicted of murder. In 2015, a judge in Chicago ordered the release of a police dash cam video that prosecutors, police, and other officials had refused to disclose for over a year. It led to the conviction of police officer Jason Van Dyke for killing a seventeen-year-old Black youth, Laquan McDonald. It was because of a cell phone video that police officer Derek Chauvin was convicted of the 2020 murder of George Floyd in Minneapolis. These incidents have led to concern about policing practices, but there is an equally urgent need for attention to how people are treated in the courts after they are arrested.

This book examines some of the many ways in which different parts of the criminal legal system—thousands of federal, state, local, and tribal law enforcement agencies, courts, prosecutors, public defense programs, and other agencies that operate independently of each other—fail to deliver justice to poor people accused of crimes. In each case, we show how the system fails to live up to the values of equality and justice. But we also show some of the places where those values are being realized: in public defender offices that provide representation as good as or better than what wealthy people receive;

in jurisdictions that require full disclosure to defense lawyers of all information regarding a crime; in places that have eliminated cash bail for minor offenses and abandoned the pursuit of fines and fees to raise revenue; in state courts that have prohibited discrimination in jury selection and ended the death penalty because of racial discrimination; and in restorative justice processes that bring victims and offenders together to deal with the aftermath of a crime and reach reconciliation instead of insisting on retribution in the form of excessive sentences that destroy individuals, families, and communities.

The problems of the criminal legal system are rooted in the problems of our society—in racism, in poverty, in the concentration of political power, and in widespread indifference to our fellow human beings—and cannot be solved overnight. But we know how to start addressing them: by taking seriously the ideals our legal system claims to uphold. As a society, we cannot in good conscience proclaim that justice should be blind—that it should not depend on the color of a person's skin, the amount of money one has, or the place where one is accused of a crime—and then shy away from the consequences of that principle. It is never wrong to remedy discrimination; the fact that it may open the door to other claims of discrimination can only advance the cause of justice. Virtually everyone agrees that people accused of crimes should be represented by competent lawyers, that prosecutors should serve the public good, that judges should be impartial, that people should not be jailed simply because they are poor, and that all people should be equal before the law. The first step is to demand a criminal legal system that lives up to its own ideals.

2

The All-Powerful Prosecutor

While the prosecutor at his best is one of the most benefi-
cent forces in our society, when he acts from malice or
other base motives, he is one of the worst.

—*Attorney General Robert H. Jackson, 1940*[1]

It is the prosecutor, not the judge, who effectively exercises
the sentencing power, albeit cloaked as a charging decision.

—*Judge Jed S. Rakoff, 2021*[2]

Paul Lewis Hayes was charged in Kentucky with forging an $88
check. Kentucky law set the punishment for forgery at two to
ten years in prison. The prosecutor offered to recommend a sentence
of five years if Hayes would plead guilty and "save the court the
inconvenience and necessity of a trial." But if Hayes turned down
the offer, the prosecutor threatened to charge Hayes, who had two
prior convictions, under Kentucky's Habitual Criminal Act, which
provided for a mandatory sentence of life imprisonment.

Hayes claimed innocence, turned down the offer, and went to trial.
The prosecutor charged Hayes under the Habitual Criminal Act, a
jury found Hayes guilty, and he was sentenced to life in prison. As
Supreme Court Justice Lewis Powell observed, "Persons convicted of
rape and murder often are not punished so severely."[3] Not long after-

ward, the Kentucky legislature changed the law so that someone in Hayes's situation would receive, at most, a sentence of ten to twenty years.[4] But the new law did not apply to Hayes.

The U.S. Supreme Court found nothing wrong with prosecutors punishing Hayes with life imprisonment for exercising his right to a trial. Justice Potter Stewart said in the Court's opinion that the prosecutor's tactics were simply part of the "give-and-take" of plea bargaining. Justice Harry Blackmun pointed out in dissent that the prosecutor had determined that the state's interests were served with a sentence of five years. The purpose of the life sentence was solely to punish Hayes for going to trial.[5] This is the "trial penalty": a more severe sentence that a defendant receives for going to trial.

The trial penalty can be the defendant's life. A prosecutor may seek the death penalty not because of a belief that justice requires it, but as a bargaining chip to obtain a guilty plea and a sentence of life imprisonment. This usually works because most people will not risk the possibility of a death sentence. But if a defendant exercises his right to trial, the prosecutor can make good on the threat and seek the death penalty.

Kelly Gissendaner and Gregory Owen were charged with the murder of Gissendaner's husband, Douglas Gissendaner. District Attorney Danny Porter gave each an offer to plead guilty in exchange for a sentence of life imprisonment with the possibility of parole after twenty-five years. Owen, who had carried out the murder, accepted the offer and testified against Kelly Gissendaner. Her lawyers, arguing that she was less culpable than Owen, said she would accept a sentence of life imprisonment with parole eligibility (not a guarantee of release) after fourteen years instead of after twenty-five. District Attorney Porter rejected the counteroffer. Kelly Gissendaner went to trial because of the disagreement over eleven years of parole eligibility. A jury convicted her and sentenced her to death in 1998.

In prison awaiting execution, Gissendaner converted to Christianity, earned a degree in theology from Emory University, and ministered to other women at the prison, including counseling some who were suicidal. Guards said that she was a powerful and positive influence in their lives and the lives of their children. As her execution drew near in 2015, Pope Francis, the former chief justice of the Georgia Supreme Court, and the Gissendaners' three children were among many who urged the state's board of pardons and paroles to commute her death sentence to life imprisonment. The board refused. She managed to get halfway through the second verse of Amazing Grace before lethal drugs ended her life.[6]

In another case, District Attorney Porter charged Eman and Tiffany Moss with killing Eman's ten-year-old daughter, Tiffany's stepdaughter, by starvation. Porter offered them life imprisonment without the possibility of parole in exchange for guilty pleas. Eman accepted the offer and testified against Tiffany. Tiffany rejected not only the plea offer, but also legal representation. She sat silently at the defense table during trial, offering not a word. Porter told the jury, "There are some crimes that are so horrible, so heinous, the only balance you can pay is with your life. Justice demands the proper payment." But he knew better. He had offered Tiffany a sentence of life imprisonment without parole, just as he had accepted that sentence for Eman. He sought death because she rejected the plea offer.[7] The jury sentenced her to death.

These cases illustrate the enormous power of prosecutors. They decided what to charge, what plea bargains to offer, and what sentences would be imposed. They did so completely independently, without regard for the practices of other prosecutors and with no oversight or accountability. They were not required to obtain a judge's approval for their decisions. To convict Gissendaner and Moss, the prosecutor also exercised the extraordinary power to reward witnesses for their testimony. It is not unusual for the most culpable person to get a less severe sentence than another participant in the crime by testifying for the prosecution.

The person exercising this enormous power is usually a white man chosen in an election that received little public attention. Ninety-five percent of the 2,442 elected prosecutors across the country in 2019 were white; 73 percent were white men, even though white men make up only 31 percent of the population.[8] Prosecutors are elected in forty-five states, and the vast majority run unopposed. No other place in the world elects prosecutors.

A "System of Pleas"

The criminal legal system is supposedly an adversary system premised on the "principle that truth—as well as fairness—is best discovered by powerful statements on both sides of the question."[9] For an adversary system to work, there cannot be significant disparities between the power and resources of the prosecution and the defense. In fact, the disparities could hardly be any greater. Prosecutors have enormous advantages over people accused of crimes and their lawyers. Almost all cases are not resolved by a neutral factfinder—a judge or jury—but by prosecutors in what the Supreme Court has described as "a system of pleas, not a system of trials."[10] Plea bargaining, the Court has said, "is not some adjunct to the criminal justice system; it *is* the criminal justice system."[11]

Prosecutors usually make the initial charging decision based on information gathered by law enforcement agencies. They can gather more information through investigations, interviews with witnesses, and consultations with experts. They can compel witnesses to testify in secret grand jury proceedings. A poor person accused of a crime may have only an overworked lawyer—if any lawyer at all—who may lack the resources for an investigator or for the expert consultations that are necessary in many cases.

Federal prosecutors spent four and a half years reviewing thousands of documents before charging three people with mail fraud relating to a complicated check-kiting scheme. Two of them agreed to testify for the prosecution. The third was assigned a real estate lawyer who had never tried a case and was given twenty-five days to prepare for trial. Not surprisingly, the defendant was convicted and sentenced to twenty-five years in prison. A federal appellate court held that, under the circumstances, the lawyer could not competently defend him. The Supreme Court reversed, observing that every experienced lawyer "once tried his first criminal case," suggesting that the prosecution's investigation "simplified the work of defense counsel," and speculating that the lawyer's real estate experience might have been more helpful than experience in criminal cases.[12] Several years later, a lower court determined that the evidence was insufficient to establish mail fraud and dismissed the charges.[13]

Prosecutors may overcharge in order to increase their bargaining power. A single act can often be charged under numerous overlapping statutes with different penalties. The prosecutor's choice of which charges to accept as part of a plea bargain usually determines the sentence. For example, prosecutors may charge a person who assaulted someone with "aggravated assault," a felony punishable by years in prison, or "simple assault," a misdemeanor. According to law professor John Pfaff, prosecutors' increasing propensity to bring felony charges is a major factor behind the vast increase in incarceration rates in recent decades.[14] Prosecutors also choose whether to charge someone arrested for a minor act with a misdemeanor or not to charge him at all.

Prosecutors decide who is sentenced to death. Prosecutors are never *required* to seek death, but they may seek it if they allege that a murder involved "aggravating circumstances," which are defined very broadly; for example, a common aggravating circumstance is that the murder occurred during the commission of another felony. They also decide whether to offer a plea bargain. Most prosecutors never pursue the death penalty. The ones who do usually make the offer that Kelly Gissendaner and Tiffany Moss received: to plead guilty in exchange for a prison sentence, usually life imprisonment without the possibility of parole.

In the federal courts, the U.S. attorney general must approve any death penalty prosecution upon the recommendation of a committee that reviews all such cases.[15] But the overwhelming majority of death sentences are imposed in state courts. No state that allows capital punishment has statewide standards for when the death penalty should be sought (other than the requirement of establishing an aggravating circumstance). Practices vary from one prosecutor's office to another and within the same office when one district attorney is replaced by another.

As a result of this variation, a minority of states and counties are responsible for most death sentences and executions. Since the reinstatement of the death penalty in 1976, more than 80 percent of executions have been carried out in the South, with 58 percent in Texas, Virginia, Oklahoma, and Florida.[16] As of 2007, fourteen counties, which together include less than 5 percent of the nation's population, were responsible for 53 percent of all executions since 1976.[17]

Johnny Holmes Jr. singlehandedly made Harris County the death penalty capital of America, but recent Harris County district attorneys seldom seek death. Philadelphia has had a similar experience. From 1986 to 2009, under District Attorneys Ronald Castille and Lynne Abraham, the office obtained 155 death sentences. The number declined to less than one a year after 2010 under Seth Williams.[18] Since his election in 2017, Larry Krasner, as promised in his campaign, has not sought the death penalty at all.

Even when the death penalty is not an option, prosecutors decide whether to seek sentencing enhancements or mandatory minimums for factors including prior convictions, using a firearm in the commission of a crime, or committing a crime near a school. Many states have "three strikes" laws that provide for a more severe sentence for a person convicted for the third time. Until it was modified in 2012, California's three-strikes law provided for a sentence of twenty-five years to life for anyone convicted of a third felony if the two prior felonies were classified as "serious" or "violent." The Supreme Court upheld life sentences obtained under this law for a person whose third felony was stealing $150 worth of videotapes and another who stole some golf clubs.[19]

The federal government and some states have adopted sentencing guidelines—rules that set out a minimum and maximum sentence on the basis of the crime's characteristics and those of the person accused. This system gives prosecutors additional tools to dictate punishments. Under the federal guidelines, a defendant's acceptance of responsibility by pleading guilty reduces the sentence by 25 to 35 percent—effectively codifying the trial penalty. Prosecutors can grant an additional 50 percent reduction for providing "substantial assistance in the investigation or prosecution of another."[20] Sentencing enhancements, mandatory minimums, and factors that increase sentences under the guidelines give prosecutors "weapons to bludgeon defendants into effectively coerced plea bargains," in the words of federal judge Jed S. Rakoff.[21]

Prosecutors have complete discretion in deciding what plea offers to make to defendants. Prosecutors may offer to stop seeking the death penalty or another enhanced sentence, reduce the charges, agree to a specific sentence, or make other concessions in exchange for a guilty plea and waiver of any appeals. A plea offer may require a defendant to disclose information, to testify against a co-defendant or a defendant in another case, or to assist the prosecution in some other way. Prosecutors may insist upon a "fast track plea," which requires the defendant to plead guilty and waive indictment, trial, and an appeal promptly after being charged.[22]

The trial penalty is a fundamental part of this system. As the Supreme Court has observed, people who

> take their case to trial and lose receive longer sentences than even Congress or the prosecutor might think appropriate, because the longer sentences exist on the books largely for bargaining purposes. This often results in individuals who accept a plea bargain receiving shorter sentences than other individuals who are less morally culpable but take a chance and go to trial.[23]

Consequently, some of the people serving the most prison time received their sentences simply because they exercised their right to trial. Innocent people are punished with severe sentences if they go to trial but cannot convince juries of their innocence—often because of other structural advantages enjoyed by the prosecution.

Judge Rakoff, who was a prosecutor and a defense lawyer before becoming a federal judge, gave this example:

> The prosecutor can agree with the defense counsel in a federal narcotics case that, if there is a plea bargain, the defendant will have to plead guilty only to the personal sale of a few ounces of heroin, which carries no mandatory minimum and a guidelines range of less than two years; but if the defendant does not plead guilty, he will be charged with the drug conspiracy of which his sale was a small part, a conspiracy involving many kilograms of heroin, which could mean a ten-year mandatory minimum and a guidelines range of twenty years or more.[24]

In drug cases over the course of the 2010s, Rakoff noted, the average sentence for people who accepted plea offers was five years, while those who went to trial and were found guilty received more than fifteen years.[25] An analysis of convictions in all types of federal cases found that defendants convicted at trial received prison sentences that were 64 percent longer than what they would have received if they had resolved their cases with guilty pleas.[26]

Given this vast amount of power, an overzealous prosecutor may demand an unreasonable resolution of a case—insisting, for example, on a conviction despite serious questions of innocence, or prison time instead of diversion or probation for a first-time offender. People accused of crimes have little or no negotiating power. Judges are precluded from participating in plea bargaining in most jurisdictions, so a defense lawyer can only appeal to the prosecutor to make a better offer, but has little leverage. Moreover, resorting to a jury trial is often not a real option because the disagreement is not about guilt or innocence, but about the fairness of the sentence.

When cases are resolved with plea bargains, there is a limited proffer of the facts of the crime. The judge may know nothing more than what the prosecutor and defense lawyer tell her, typically in the most conclusory terms. The main concern when a plea is taken is whether the defendant understands what he is doing and whether he has made a voluntary decision to plead guilty.

As summed up by Judge Rakoff, "The Supreme Court's suggestion that a plea bargain is a fair and voluntary contractual arrangement between two relatively equal parties is a total myth. . . . One party can effectively force its will on the other party."[27] According to federal judge Gerard E. Lynch, "the prosecutor acts as the administrative decision-maker who determines, in the first instance, whether an accused will be subject to social sanction, and if so, how much punishment will be imposed."[28]

Because of the prosecution's advantages at trial, even innocent people plead guilty instead of risking the death penalty or a long prison term. Most courts allow defendants who insist they are innocent to enter a plea of guilty without contesting the case against them.[29] The National Registry of Exonerations reports that, as of 2015, 15 percent of people who had been exonerated—261 of 1,702—pleaded guilty.[30] Eight percent of them pleaded guilty to murder, including Russell Weinberger, an intellectually disabled man prosecuted in Philadelphia. In order to avoid the death penalty, he agreed to accept a sentence of fifteen to thirty years and testify against his friend, Felix Rodriguez. Weinberger's testimony helped convict Rodriguez of second-degree murder at a trial in 1985. Rodriguez was sentenced to life imprisonment without the possibility of parole. However, in 2001, two other men confessed to the murders. Twenty-one years after their arrests, Weinberger and Rodriguez were sentenced to the time they had served and released.[31]

Another case was that of Johnny Lee Wilson, a mentally impaired man accused of murdering a seventy-nine-year-old woman found dead in her home in Missouri in 1986. Wilson pleaded no contest in 1987 to a charge of first-degree murder to avoid the death penalty. He was sentenced to life imprisonment without the possibility of parole. A year later, a person in prison for a similar crime—committed sixteen days after the murder of the seventy-nine-year-old woman—admitted killing her as well. In 1995, Governor Mel Carnahan pardoned Wilson, saying it was clear that he did not commit the crime.[32]

Justice requires that people accused of crimes be allowed to exercise their right to a jury trial without being punished with a sentence that is completely out of proportion to their crimes. But because of the trial penalty, a trial by jury—the "gold standard of American justice"—is virtually nonexistent.[33]

Testimony on Demand

In the very few cases that go to trial, prosecutors have the extraordinary advantage of being able to reward witnesses for their testimony, as occurred in the cases of Kelly Gissendaner and Tiffany Moss. "No practice is more ingrained in our criminal justice system than the practice of the government calling a witness who is an accessory to the crime for which the defendant is charged and having that witness testify under a plea bargain that promises him a reduced sentence," a federal court of appeals observed. "It is difficult to imagine a greater motivation to lie than the inducement of a reduced sentence."[34] Only prosecutors can reward witnesses for their testimony. Any other lawyer who rewards a witness for testimony would be guilty of bribery and witness tampering.

Prosecutors routinely reward accomplices for their testimony; for example, they cut deals with "little fish" to prosecute "big fish" in conspiracy cases. However, they also cut deals with people who know nothing about a crime but claim that they heard a person accused of the crime admit guilt—usually in a jail cell. Despite the dubious credibility of these "jailhouse snitches"—who are known to be "con artists, congenital liars, and practiced fraudsters"—prosecutors use their testimony to obtain convictions.[35] In some cases, the prosecution has little to no other evidence of guilt.

Prosecutors and police reward snitches by dismissing or reducing the charges against them, granting them immunity from prosecution, releasing them from jail, paying them money, asking judges for lighter sentences, urging parole boards to release them, and putting them in witness protection programs. Some snitches have even been allowed to carry on with criminal activities, and others have been rewarded with drugs, alcohol, and sex.[36] The practices of using snitches are secret and unregulated. As a result, jurors are ill equipped to assess the credibility of these individuals.

Typically, prosecutors and police informally suggest, but do not promise, that jailhouse informants will be rewarded if prosecutors are pleased with their testimony. The informant testifies to the jury that he is not getting anything for his testimony, but he knows that he can expect something in exchange—and the more satisfied the prosecutor, the bigger the reward. The informant has a compelling incentive to say what the prosecutor wants to hear.[37] And the prosecutor must reward the informant in order to encourage other informants in other cases.

In seeking the death penalty for Samuel Bonner in California in 1983, prosecutor Kurt Seifert relied on the testimony of a jailhouse snitch, Michael Hayes, that Bonner had admitted shooting the victim to Hayes. Bonner was convicted and sentenced to life in prison. At a separate trial of Bonner's co-defendant, Watson Allison, Seifert argued that *Allison*, not Bonner, had fired the fatal shots and that Bonner was only the getaway driver. Allison was convicted and sentenced to death. Hayes, the jailhouse snitch, had also been charged with murder but, as a reward for his testimony, was allowed to plead guilty to manslaughter and sentenced to just four years in prison. Hayes already had an extensive history of trading testimony for leniency in Kentucky, but prosecutors there had stopped using him because of his repeated dishonesty. Many years later, Judge Daniel Lowenthal observed that Hayes began lying as soon as he took the witness stand in Bonner's case, starting with his name. "His name is Charles Jones," the judge said. "Everything thereafter appears to have been a lie as well." The judge concluded, "That the death penalty was sought against someone based on testimony that was known to be false is horrifying and shocks the conscience." Bonner was released in 2019 after thirty-seven years in prison. Judge Lowenthal declared Bonner factually innocent in 2020.[38]

The pervasive use of informants is a significant source of wrongful convictions. Would-be informants look for the information they need to fabricate the believable, incriminating testimony that police and prosecutors want. To create a credible confession, informants need only some basic details about a case, which they can get from media reports, the legal papers of people awaiting trial, jailhouse gossip, and official sources such as law enforcement officers.[39]

In 1989, Leslie Vernon White, a prolific jailhouse informant in Los Angeles, demonstrated for the media how he used the telephone at the jail to call government agencies and, posing as a bail bondsman, a prosecutor, and a police officer, obtain information that he used to create detailed false confessions. He also arranged to be placed in proximity to defendants in order to establish an opportunity to "hear" their confessions. White—a convicted kidnapper, robber, and car thief—had testified or offered to testify in more than a dozen cases, including six homicide cases, and had received in return money, furloughs, and a letter recommending parole. He admitted lying in multiple cases.[40]

In response to the revelations, a grand jury investigated the use of jailhouse informants in Los Angeles and found an "appalling number of instances of perjury or other falsifications to law enforcement."[41] At any one time, as many as eighty to ninety inmates at the Los Angeles County Jail were classified as informants, and they had been involved in as many as 250 cases over a ten-year period.[42] Among the grand jury's findings: informants manufactured false testimony and lied about receiving benefits for their testimony; in some high-profile cases, as many as sixteen to twenty informants offered to testify that the defendant had confessed to them; individual informants testified after being described as "a pathological liar," "a real flake," and "an acknowledged liar and perjurer"; and violent offenders, including one considered a "danger to the health and safety of others," were released in exchange for their testimony and later arrested for violent crimes.[43] Public defender Scott Sanders discovered similar abuses in neighboring Orange County in 2013. After his investigation, convictions were set aside in more than a dozen cases, including several murder cases.[44]

Paul Skalnik built a career as an informant for prosecutors. In 1981, after several convictions in Florida and Texas, he was facing five years in prison for grand theft in Florida. Skalnik called prosecutors and offered information on three defendants accused of murder. Over the next eleven months, Skalnik testified in several drug and murder cases that the defendants had admitted their crimes to him. Prosecutors were so pleased that they recommended a sentence of probation for Skalnik that was accepted by the judge. Skalnik was later arrested for theft, forgery, and other crimes. Each time he offered prosecutors testimony in exchange for getting out of jail, helping them win convictions in scores of cases, including at least eighteen murder cases, and death sentences in four of those cases. Even though he was well known as a snitch, he testified that other people spontaneously admitted their guilt to him, even adding lurid details. Each time, he claimed that he had not been promised anything for his testimony.[45]

In 1988, Skalnik was arrested in Texas for forgery. When he tried to trade testimony for lenient treatment, a prosecutor rejected him, writing in a memo that he was "a BIG con artist." After being returned to Florida, Skalnik revealed that Florida prosecutors had worked with him to fool jurors and promised him favorable treatment in return for his false testimony.[46] The Florida prosecutors, who had repeatedly asked jurors to believe Skalnik, now said that his accusations ranged from "gross exaggeration to preposterous fabrication." Skalnik then did another about-face, disavowing his own accusations against the prosecutors. Even though he was exposed as a fraud, it made no difference for the people he had helped send to prison and death row. One man sentenced to death, James Dailey, challenged the reliance on Skalnik's testimony. The Florida Supreme Court rejected his challenge, saying, "Skalnik disavowed the accusations [against the prosecutors] . . . and unequivocally stated that they were false"—as if he were someone to be believed. It also noted that the prosecutor "testified that she believed Skalnik's testimony to be truthful at the time of trial."[47] Skalnik was never prosecuted for perjury.

In addition to helping convict innocent people, the leniency provided to informants denies justice to the victims of their crimes and threatens public safety. Skalnik had been arrested for molesting a twelve-year-old in 1982, but prosecutors dismissed the charges, rewarding him for his testimony. Ten years later, he was arrested for the sexual assault of a fifteen-year-old girl.[48]

District Attorney Doug Evans presented the testimony of Odell "Cookie" Hallmon at four of Curtis Flowers's six trials on charges of murdering four people in a furniture store in Mississippi in 1996. While in jail in 2001 on armed robbery and gun and drug charges, Hallmon told a prosecution investigator that Flowers had confessed to him that he had committed the murders.[49] A week after joining the prosecution, Hallmon's robbery charge was dismissed; in 2002, he pleaded guilty to having been a felon in possession of a firearm and was released two weeks later. He was arrested on drug, robbery, and assault charges in January 2003, but the charges were dropped. In April that year, he fired shots at several people. Several months later he was arrested and returned to prison for violating his probation.[50]

Evans called Hallmon—an admitted perjurer with a rapidly expanding criminal record—as the prosecution's star witness at Flowers's trial in 2004. Hallmon testified that Flowers had confessed to him that he had committed the murders. The jury convicted Flowers and sentenced him to death. Eight months later, the charges against Hallmon of shooting at people were dismissed and he was released from prison. A few months later, he was caught with cocaine and a stolen gun. Hallmon faced up to forty-six years in prison, but, in a plea deal, he was sentenced to fourteen years in prison and five years on probation. He served just over eight years of the sentence.[51]

Flowers's convictions were reversed on appeal. Hallmon testified at three more trials that Flowers had admitted the killings. The juries could not reach a verdict in two of the trials, but Flowers was convicted in the final trial and sentenced to death. Hallmon was released from prison in 2013. The next year, he was arrested for trying to run over a deputy sheriff, and, in 2016, he was arrested for armed robbery and assault, but he was released both times. Finally, in April 2016, Hallmon shot four people, killing three, including his former girl-friend. Within two weeks, District Attorney Evans allowed Hallmon to enter guilty pleas and be sentenced to life imprisonment without the possibility of parole.[52]

Back in prison, Hallmon told American Public Media that his testi-mony against Flowers was "make believe" and that he had testified to get charges against him dismissed.[53] In 2019, the U.S. Supreme Court reversed Flowers's conviction at his last trial because D.A. Evans had discriminated during jury selection by striking African Americans from the panel.[54] Evans recused himself from the case. The Missis-sippi attorney general dismissed the charges against Flowers for lack of evidence, and he was released after almost twenty-three years in custody.[55] We only know as much as we do about Hallmon and his role in Flowers's convictions because of exceptional reporting by the American Public Media podcast *In the Dark*.

Although Hallmon testified that he received nothing in exchange for his testimony, he was repeatedly freed as he committed one crime after another. Hallmon finally killed three people and attempted to kill his own son—an extraordinary price in blood and suffering for testimony wholly lacking in credibility. As Michael Gross, a police officer and jailer in the community where the crimes occurred, said, "They created a monster, the state of Mississippi did. That's what I said, with Odell Hallmon. They created a monster."[56]

The use of jailhouse snitches has resulted in many other disastrous miscarriages of justice. In 1988, Ron Williamson and Dennis Fritz were convicted of murder and rape in Oklahoma primarily on the basis of the testimony of jailhouse informants. They were released twelve years later after DNA testing then established that the crimes had been committed by *one of the jailhouse informants*.[57] Over one hundred people convicted of murder in cases in which informants testified for the prosecution have been exonerated; in one-fourth of those cases, the innocent person was sentenced to death.[58]

Courts have generally not allowed defendants to present expert testimony about how informants trade testimony for leniency.[59] Absent rare admissions by snitches, relentless investigations by lawyers or journalists, or DNA evidence of innocence, the false testimony of many jailhouse informants would never have come to light. All of those things are missing in the vast majority of cases. Jailhouse snitches often testify in high-stakes cases in which there is little other evidence of guilt. Admitting their testimony risks the conviction and, in some cases, the execution of innocent people and the continued lawlessness of people like Paul Skalnik and Cookie Hallmon.

Some states have adopted measures to address this problem, but they are inadequate to prevent serious miscarriages of justice. Rocky Eugene Dodd was sentenced to death after Kenneth Bryant, a jailhouse snitch, testified that Dodd had admitted two murders to him. In 2000, the Oklahoma Court of Criminal Appeals reversed the convictions because Dodd's lawyer had not been allowed to question Bryant about a letter he wrote to the prosecutors in which he said, "The testimony from me in this case about a confession that you both asked & wanted from me—you'll not get—because as you very well know—there wasn't one."[60] The Court held that prosecutors must disclose to the defense any statements allegedly made by the defendant to an informant, the time and place of the statements, any benefits the informant received, the informant's criminal record, other cases in which the informant offered to testify, and any recantations by the informant. The Court also ordered that juries be instructed that they should weigh the testimony of an informant with greater care than the testimony of an ordinary witness.[61]

Several other states have adopted similar requirements. However, in the absence of comprehensive records, prosecutors may be unaware that informants testified for other prosecutors or even in other states.

After a prosecutor presented the testimony of a jailhouse snitch in a Virginia murder trial, the prosecuting attorney in another district notified the defense lawyer that the snitch was "well-known to prosecutors for giving false testimony." The prosecutor trying the case said that he was not aware of the snitch's questionable credibility.[62] After the release of the grand jury report on the abuses in Los Angeles, the city's district attorney created a central index of jailhouse informants.[63] Connecticut and Texas have established similar systems.[64] Without such record keeping, individual prosecutors may not know about the snitches they are calling as witnesses and cannot disclose to defense lawyers critical information about their credibility.

Several states have policies of using jailhouse informants only when there is corroborative evidence against the defendant, but that evidence may be minimal and unreliable.[65] The Los Angeles district attorney adopted a policy allowing the use of jailhouse informants only when there is "strong corroborative evidence" of the defendant's guilt and approval by the Jailhouse Informant Committee.[66] Of course, if strong evidence exists to establish a person's guilt, there is no need for an informant. The office realized that the need for informants was not so great after all. A 2008 report found that the committee rarely approved the use of in-custody informants; fewer than six a year were approved during the 1990s, and none had been approved during the twenty months prior to the report's release.[67]

A few states, including Connecticut, Illinois, and Nevada, require judges to hold pretrial hearings at which the prosecution must show that a jailhouse informant's testimony is sufficiently reliable to be admissible.[68] But a good con artist may be able to con the prosecutor, judge, and jury. Even when all the rewards for testifying are disclosed, it is impossible to tell whether an informant is telling the truth. Prosecutors, judges, and juries believed Paul Skalnik—who also married eight women and scammed many other people out of their money. As federal appellate judge Stephen S. Trott warned, "Sometimes these snitches tell the truth, but more often they invent testimony and stray details out of the air."[69] The only way to ensure justice is to simply not allow their testimony.

Information and Justice Withheld

Prosecutors have another advantage: their exclusive access to most of the information gathered in investigations by law enforcement agencies and their own offices. When a crime occurs, law enforcement agencies interview witnesses, process the crime scene, and continue collecting and analyzing evidence to build a case. The prosecutor decides which evidence and witnesses—and what version of events—to present at trial. As Professor Bennett L. Gershman has observed, "The prosecutor's institutional role in controlling access to information relevant to a defendant's guilt, and the prosecutor's ability to withhold evidence that might prove a defendant's innocence . . . dramatically distort[] the ability of the adversary system to function fairly and properly."[70]

Except for evidence favorable to the defendant, which we discuss below, federal prosecutors and many state prosecutors are generally not required to give the defense the names of witnesses or reports from law enforcement agencies before trial. Before the trial, they must disclose only statements made by the defendant, the defendant's criminal record, the results of scientific tests, and a summary of any expert opinions, and allow the inspection of any physical evidence they intend to introduce.[71] This is different from civil cases, in which lawyers for each side disclose the names and addresses of their witnesses, exchange documents and expert reports, and question each other's witnesses at depositions. As federal judge H. Lee Sarokin and attorney William E. Zuckerman have observed, "Where money is involved, all parties receive all relevant information from their adversaries upon request; but where individual liberty is at stake, such information can be either withheld by the

prosecutor or parcelled out at a time when it produces the least benefit to the accused."[72]

Because of this lack of disclosure, an innocent person accused of a
crime may know nothing about the prosecution's case against him.
Yet the prosecutor may give him very little time to decide whether
to accept a plea offer. If he declines the offer, he may suffer "trial
by ambush": presentation of evidence that he is unprepared to contest. Much relevant evidence may never come to light because, as
Professor Richard Rosen has observed, "evidence that may allow an
innocent defendant to prove innocence—names of other suspects,
physical evidence not used at trial, and leads that did not pan out—
are often considered the private property of the prosecution."[73]

Prosecutors are required to disclose to the defense any evidence in
the possession of the prosecution or law enforcement agencies that is
favorable to the defense, such as evidence of innocence or evidence
regarding the credibility of a prosecution witness. This is known as
the *Brady* rule, after the 1963 Supreme Court case *Brady v. Maryland.*[74]
A few years after that decision, the Supreme Court set aside Lloyd
Eldon Miller's conviction and death sentence for the sexual assault
and murder of a child in Illinois. At Miller's trial, the prosecutor
introduced a pair of men's undershorts with reddish-brown stains,
argued that they belonged to Miller, and presented the testimony of
a chemist who said that the stains were blood of the victim's type.
However, Miller's lawyers proved after the trial that the reddish-
brown stains were not blood, but paint—and that the prosecutor had
known at trial that they were paint. Because "the prosecution deliberately misrepresented the truth," the Court unanimously held that
Miller was entitled to a new trial.[75]

However, the prosecution's failure to disclose evidence favorable
to the defense can become an issue only if the defendant discovers
the evidence after trial. It is impossible to know how often prosecutors fail to reveal evidence that is never discovered. When evidence

is discovered, the Supreme Court has made it difficult for a person to get a new trial—even when the defense asked for the evidence before trial and was told by prosecutors that it did not exist.

Before Hughes Anderson Bagley's federal trial on narcotics and firearms charges, his lawyers moved for the disclosure of "any deals, promises or inducements" made to prosecution witnesses. The prosecution provided affidavits of its two principal witnesses containing statements that they provided information to the Bureau of Alcohol, Tobacco, and Firearms "without any threats or rewards, or promises of reward having been made to [them] in return for it." After being convicted on some of the charges, Bagley discovered through requests under the Freedom of Information Act and the Privacy Act that, before trial, both witnesses had signed contracts with the Bureau promising them, in exchange for information about Bagley, "a sum commensurate with services and information rendered." The case against Bagley depended entirely upon the credibility of the two witnesses.[76]

In reviewing the case, the Supreme Court held that Bagley was entitled to a new trial only if he could show there was "a reasonable probability that, had the evidence been disclosed to the defense, the result of the proceeding would have been different."[77] Justice Thurgood Marshall dissented, arguing that the reasonable probability standard does not ensure that evidence favorable to the defense will be disclosed. It is impossible to know what evidence might create a reasonable doubt that would result in a verdict of not guilty. This invites the prosecutor—a "zealous advocate" for conviction—"to gamble, to play the odds, and to take a chance that evidence will later turn out not to have been potentially dispositive."[78]

Justice Marshall's concern that prosecutors would try to "play the odds" has been borne out in practice. According to Professor Gershman, prosecutors enjoy "an extraordinarily wide berth to conceal favorable evidence from the defense" in the hope that the suppression will not be discovered or, if it is discovered, "that an appellate court reviewing the conviction will conclude that there is no 'reasonable probability' that the evidence would have changed the result."[79] Despite pervasive failures to disclose exculpatory evidence, courts have failed to enforce the *Brady* rule, and prosecutors who violate it rarely face discipline.[80]

An egregious violation of the *Brady* rule resulted in the conviction and death sentence of Robert Henry McDowell in North Carolina. The only direct evidence against McDowell, a Black man, was the testimony of fourteen-year-old Patsy Mason, who identified McDowell from a photograph as the person who attacked her and Carol Ann Hinson, a member of her family, with a large knife at their residence in the middle of the night, killing Hinson. The prosecution did not disclose to McDowell's attorney that Mason initially told law enforcement authorities that the perpetrator was white, or that two of Mason's cousins reported seeing a "white/male," knife-wielding intruder near the house on the night of the attack. Remarkably, the North Carolina courts upheld the conviction and death sentence. However, a federal court of appeals reversed McDowell's conviction because the evidence could have created a reasonable doubt in the minds of the jurors.[81]

In 1998, Alan Gell was sentenced to death for a robbery and murder allegedly committed on April 3, 1995, based on the testimony of fifteen- and sixteen-year-old girls who admitted involvement in the crime and pleaded guilty to second-degree murder. In 1996, however, the North Carolina legislature had adopted a law requiring the state, in the cases of people sentenced to death, to disclose the complete files of its investigation and prosecution.[82] Those files contained a recording in which the fifteen-year-old witness said that she needed to "make up a story" regarding the murder. The files also contained statements of eighteen witnesses who said they had seen the victim alive after April 3—which meant that Gell could not have committed the crime because he was either out of the state or in jail from that date until the discovery of the victim's body on April 14. The trial judge had ordered the prosecution to produce these statements, but the prosecutors did not comply. After the prosecution files were disclosed to defense counsel, a judge granted Gell a new trial, and he was acquitted—after nine years in prison, half of it on death row.[83]

The convictions in the cases of nine other people sentenced to death in North Carolina were reversed within ten years of the passage of the 1996 law requiring full disclosure after death sentences. The cases demonstrated that full disclosure is necessary to enforce the *Brady* rule. "For a prosecutor who has reached the conclusion that the accused is guilty," Professor Robert P. Mosteller observes, "there can be no true exculpatory evidence," so the prosecutor tends to make the "close calls in favor of convicting the guilty." Requiring disclosure of all the evidence in the prosecution's file eliminates difficult, subjective decisions about what evidence is favorable to the defense.[84] That was accomplished in North Carolina by another law, passed in 2004, that requires prosecutors to disclose the files of the prosecution and investigative agencies *before trial* in all felony cases.[85] In return, defense attorneys must provide prosecutors with witness lists and the grounds on which they plan to defend their client.[86]

In Texas, the exoneration of Michael Morton in 2011 prompted a major revision of its disclosure laws. Morton was convicted of murdering his wife, Christine, and spent almost twenty-five years in prison before the disclosure of evidence that had been withheld by the prosecutor established his innocence and the identity of the killer. The evidence included the results of DNA tests, a statement by Morton's three-year-old son that a "monster"—not his father—had committed the crime, statements by neighbors that a suspicious green van was parked behind the house at the time of the murder, and a bandanna, found near the home, that was stained by Christine's blood and contained a hair from the actual killer.[87] DNA tests on the bandanna revealed that the murder was committed by Mark Alan Norwood, and he was convicted in 2013; the tests also linked Norwood to a similar murder that occurred two years after the murder of Christine Morton.[88]

The Morton case dramatically illustrated the need for greater disclosure of information to defendants before trial. In response, the Texas legislature passed the "Michael Morton Act," requiring disclosure of offense reports and other information—whether or not favorable to the defense—in the possession of the state or any person under contract with the state.[89]

The convictions of Robert Henry McDowell, Alan Gell, and Michael Morton were not isolated incidents. A report by the National Registry of Exonerations found that failure to disclose exculpatory evidence played a role in the convictions of more than a thousand people who have since been exonerated—44 percent of all the exonerations from 1989 to 2019.[90] Of course, this excludes additional cases where prosecutors failed to disclose exculpatory evidence that was never uncovered.

Full exploration of all the facts—regardless of whether a prosecutor thinks they are exculpatory—is required for fair and reliable outcomes. The American Bar Association has advocated such broad disclosure since 1970.[91] Florida has required disclosure of witnesses' names, addresses, and statements and allowed the defense to take depositions of witnesses since 1968.[92] The Florida Supreme Court found that depositions ensure "fairness and equal administration of justice."[93] New Jersey has required disclosure of "persons whom the prosecutor knows to have relevant evidence or information" since 1973.[94] Other states have recently adopted similar measures in response to concerns about wrongful convictions. By 2020, over half of the states instituted requirements to disclose the names and addresses of prosecution witnesses and any recorded statements; some also require disclosure of all persons with information about the case.[95] However,

full disclosure remains "too much justice" for the federal government and about twelve states that maintain very limited disclosure
practices.[96] Only a few states allow depositions in criminal cases.[97] It
should not take more miscarriages of justices to bring about reform
in jurisdictions that still conduct "trial by ambush" and risk verdicts
based on a partial or speculative presentation of the facts.

The Failure to Preserve Evidence of Innocence

In addition to failing to disclose information regarding innocence or
the credibility of witnesses before trial, prosecutors and law enforcement agencies sometimes after a trial destroy or fail to preserve evidence such as recordings of 911 calls, videotapes, reports of witness
interviews, and items collected at crime scenes. Since 1989, at least
375 people convicted of crimes have been later exonerated by DNA
testing.[98] But this has been possible only in cases where biological
evidence existed and was preserved.

The Supreme Court addressed what preservation is required in the
case of Larry Youngblood, who was convicted of kidnapping and
sexually assaulting a ten-year-old boy in Tucson in 1983.[99] The victim, who usually wore glasses but was not wearing them at the time
of the assault, identified Youngblood from six photographs shown to
him by police. Such identifications are often mistaken; 69 percent of
the convictions later overturned through DNA evidence involved
eyewitness identifications.[100] The victim said that the man who
assaulted him was a Black man with a bad right eye. Youngblood was
a Black man with a bad left eye.

The police had collected the victim's underwear and T-shirt after
the assault, and when they were tested fifteen months later, a crimi-
nologist found semen stains on them. Because the police had failed to
refrigerate the clothes, however, it was not possible to determine the
blood group of the assailant with the testing available at that time.
The Arizona Court of Appeals found that the failure to preserve the
evidence denied Youngblood a fair and reliable trial and reversed

his convictions.[101] However, the U.S. Supreme Court reversed the Arizona court in 1988, holding that the failure to preserve evidence denies a defendant a fair trial only if the police acted in bad faith in failing to preserve the evidence.[102] "The Constitution requires that criminal defendants be provided with a fair trial, not merely a 'good faith' try at a fair trial," Justice Blackmun wrote in dissent. Youngblood was denied a fair trial "by what may have been nothing more than police ineptitude."[103]

Twelve years later, Youngblood's lawyers obtained newly available, more sophisticated DNA testing of the semen stains, which showed that Youngblood was innocent. The DNA profile from the new test matched the profile of Walter Cruise, who had two prior convictions for sexual abuse of children and was serving time in Texas. Cruise pleaded guilty to sexually assaulting the victim and was sentenced to twenty-four years in prison. After learning that DNA evidence exonerated Youngblood and implicated someone else, David Leon, the victim of the crime, ended his life by stepping in front of a freight train in Tucson.[104] Dr. Edward Blake, a forensic scientist, described the decision in *Youngblood* as "a flawed legal precedent that stands on the shoulders of an innocent man."[105] Instead of requiring that police collect, maintain, and properly preserve evidence to ensure fair trials, the *Youngblood* decision increases the risk of wrongful convictions.

The Supreme Court went further in 2009, holding that even if evidence has been preserved, a person convicted of a crime does not have a constitutional right to DNA testing of the evidence, even at his own expense.[106] Chief Justice John Roberts's opinion clearly betrayed the fear of too much justice; if a person had a right to DNA testing, he cautioned,

> we would soon have to decide if there is a constitutional obligation to preserve forensic evidence that might later be tested. If so, for how long? Would it be different for different types of evidence? Would the State also have some

obligation to gather such evidence in the first place? How much, and when?[107]

The answers to these questions seem obvious in light of what happened to Larry Youngblood, but Chief Justice Roberts and four other justices were afraid to address them.

Many people convicted of crimes they did not commit will never have a chance to prove their innocence because evidence has been destroyed. In 1997, Texas governor George W. Bush pardoned Kevin Byrd, who had spent twelve years in prison for sexual assault before being exonerated because his DNA did not match the evidence preserved in the rape kit. Bush predicted that Byrd would be the "first of many" whose cases would be reexamined with new DNA technology. However, that same week, evidence custodians began to destroy rape kits in the Harris County Clerk's Office, asserting a shortage of storage space.[108] Other jurisdictions, including New York and New Orleans, have also engaged in the systematic destruction of rape kits.[109] As Professor Cynthia Jones has written, "destroying biological evidence, with full knowledge of its potential use to exonerate the wrongly convicted, is a cruel and callous injustice."[110]

All fifty states, the District of Columbia, and the federal government have statutes that govern access to DNA testing for people convicted of crimes, although many have severe limits on those individuals' ability to obtain testing. However, DNA evidence is only one type of evidence that could show a defendant's innocence, and is only relevant in certain types of cases. A better way to prevent wrongful convictions is to require full disclosure of all evidence by the prosecution before trial.

The Rewards of Misconduct

In 2017, the Supreme Court affirmed convictions obtained at trial despite the prosecution's failure to disclose evidence that, according to Justice Elena Kagan's dissent, would have changed "the whole tenor of the trial."[111] At the 1984 trial, prosecutors presented evidence to show that ten defendants were part of a group that robbed and murdered a woman. The case was based on the testimony of two participants who pleaded guilty and testified against the remaining defendants, two people who admitted they were high on PCP at the time of the crimes, and several other witnesses, many of whom had various motives to testify falsely and had made numerous inconsistent statements.[112] No physical evidence tied any of the defendants to the crimes. The jury convicted eight of the defendants.

Over twenty-five years later, the defendants learned that the prosecution also "knew about but withheld the evidence of an alternative perpetrator" committing the crimes.[113] A witness had seen two men acting suspiciously near the victim's body before running away, but the prosecution did not disclose their names before trial. One of them, James McMillan, assaulted and robbed two other women in the same neighborhood in the weeks after the murder. He had been arrested by the time of trial. The prosecution also withheld statements of witnesses saying that one or two perpetrators carried out the attack—not a group. And the prosecution "suppressed a raft of evidence discrediting its investigation and impeaching its witnesses." If the jury members had been able to consider the evidence that McMillan, a man known to assault women, could have committed the crimes, they could have been far less certain that eight of the defendants were guilty.[114] Nevertheless, the Court credulously accepted the prosecution's assurance that it had adopted a "generous policy of discovery" and recognized that a "prudent prosecutor's better course is to take care to disclose any evidence favorable to the defendant"—while upholding convictions where prosecutors did just the opposite.[115]

Most courts take a similar approach to another prosecutorial tactic: improper closing arguments, often intended to inflame the jury or give it information that is inadmissible at trial. Courts usually respond by condemning the arguments but rewarding prosecutors by upholding the convictions. In a 1974 opinion by Justice William Rehnquist, the Court held that an improper closing argument requires reversal of a conviction only if it rendered the trial "fundamentally unfair."[116] This subjective standard allows judges to affirm convictions even where prosecutors engage in egregious misconduct in their closing arguments.

In 1986, the Supreme Court upheld the conviction and death sentence of Willie Jasper Darden, even while acknowledging that the closing argument by the Florida prosecutors "deserves the condemnation it has received from every court to review it."[117] Darden, a Black man, was tried for the robbery and murder of a white man in a furniture store. The prosecution's case depended on the testimony of the victim's widow, who identified Darden as the perpetrator at a hearing where he was the only Black man present, and that of a sixteen-year-old employee, who identified Darden from an array of six photographs shown to him by police.[118] Darden testified on his own behalf and denied any involvement in the crime.

Ethical rules prohibit lawyers from expressing their personal opinions about guilt or innocence or the credibility of witnesses, and making arguments that inflame the passions or prejudices of the jury or divert the jury from its duty to decide the case on the evidence.[119] Nevertheless, one prosecutor in Darden's case told the jury he was "as convinced as I know I am standing before you today" that Darden was guilty.[120] He called Darden an "animal" who "shouldn't be out of his cell unless he has a leash on him." He told the jury that he wished the victim had blown Darden's face off with a shotgun, adding, "I wish that I could see him sitting here with no face, blown away by a shotgun." He told the jury that he wished Darden had killed himself.[121] Another prosecutor told the jury to disregard Darden's testimony because, "if I am ever over in that chair over there, facing life or death, life imprisonment or death, I guarantee you I will lie until my teeth fall out."[122]

Justice Powell, writing for the Supreme Court majority, acknowledged that the arguments "undoubtedly were improper," but held that they did not deprive Darden of a fair trial because the evidence of guilt was "overwhelming."[123] Justice Blackmun, in dissent, said the majority had failed to consider ethical standards governing prosecutors and accepted "a level of fairness and reliability so low it should make conscientious prosecutors cringe." He found the evidence of guilt far from overwhelming, as the case depended on the testimony of three witnesses: two who made questionable identifications of Darden, and Darden himself, who proclaimed his innocence.[124] Justice Blackmun also pointed out the Court's disturbing pattern of condemning "clearly improper prosecutorial misconduct" in closing argument while affirming convictions obtained via that same misconduct. The Court, he said, "must do more than wring its hands."[125]

Prosecutors know that the highest price they are likely to pay for an improper closing argument is what one judge called a "ritualistic verbal spanking"—and they act accordingly.[126] In California from 1997 to 2009, appellate courts found prosecutorial misconduct in 707 cases (which does not include the many cases that were never appealed). Those same courts overturned only 159 of the convictions that were illegally obtained; only six prosecutors were disciplined by the California State Bar for misconduct in a criminal case.[127] A study of 2,400 cases in the entire country in which prosecutorial misconduct led to the conviction of a person who was later exonerated found that the prosecutors responsible were disciplined only 4 percent of the time.[128]

Juan Martinez, a deputy county attorney in Maricopa County, Arizona, continued to engage in misconduct after being repeatedly cited for it—without being reversed. In 2020, the Arizona Court of Appeals upheld the conviction of Jodi Arias for first-degree murder after a 67-day trial despite finding that "prosecutorial misconduct

undeniably permeated this case" and "a pattern of intentional misconduct saturated the trial."[129] Martinez ran roughshod over defense
attorneys, witnesses, and even the judge. He was hostile, combative,
and belligerent in questioning witnesses, used "innuendo to intimidate and malign" witnesses, repeatedly suggested during his questioning of a psychologist that the witness had romantic feelings for
Arias, engaged in self-promoting conduct with the media, argued
that the defense experts were unethical liars, and appealed to the
jurors' passions in a way that "unquestionably exceeded permissible
bounds." In closing argument, Martinez argued that Arias had personally wronged the jurors because she had "looked at each and every
one of [them]" and "lied to [them]" when testifying. He also insinu-
ated that the jurors would be complicit if they failed to convict.[130]
One Court of Appeals judge called Martinez's conduct "sickening"
and "childish."[131]

The Court of Appeals found that the misconduct was "egregious,"
and that the judge should have taken stronger measures—such as
holding Martinez in contempt.[132] Nevertheless, the court concluded that "Arias was not deprived of a fair trial." Although the trial
could hardly have been more unfair, the court decided that Martinez's misconduct did not matter because, it believed, Arias was guilty
anyway.[133] But a person accused of a crime is entitled to a fair trial,
not an appellate court's judgment that the evidence would have persuaded a jury to convict if there had been a fair trial. Nevertheless,
although the Arizona Supreme Court had observed that Martinez's
"misbehavior has been repeatedly noted in prior cases," the Court
of Appeals invoked "the well-established principle that we do not
'reverse convictions merely to punish a prosecutor's misdeeds or to
deter future misconduct.'"[134]

Instead, the Court of Appeals referred Martinez to the Arizona
State Bar for possible disciplinary action.[135] The bar filed a disciplinary complaint against Martinez based on courts' findings of miscon-

duct in five different cases. The Arizona Supreme Court found that his repeated improper arguments to juries were "inexcusable given his substantial experience as a prosecutor and repeated court warnings to cease such conduct."[136] It imposed a reprimand—a light punishment for routinely disregarding judges. Martinez did lose his job, but for other reasons: a complaint filed with the bar alleged that he leaked confidential information during the Arias trial, lied to state bar investigators, and sexually harassed women employees in the Maricopa County Attorney's Office. He agreed to be disbarred two days after a hearing had been scheduled on the complaint.[137]

Not all courts have tolerated such misconduct. For example, the Washington Supreme Court reversed a murder conviction because the prosecutor alleged in closing argument a "code" that "black folk don't testify against black folk" to attack the credibility of Black witnesses, and referred to the police as "po-leese" in questioning Black witnesses in order to draw attention to their race.[138] It reversed another conviction because a prosecutor used presentations containing slides that were racially inflammatory.[139]

Turning the Tables

The prosecutor is clearly the most powerful actor in the criminal legal system. In the past decade, a number of people across the country have attempted to use the power of the prosecutor's office to bring about transformational change in the criminal legal system. Their objectives have included the elimination of cash bail for many cases, decriminalization of marijuana possession and other minor offenses, greater use of diversion and alternatives to incarceration, the treatment of addiction as a health problem, an end to prosecutions of children in the adult system, and abandonment of the death penalty.

Candidates running as "progressive prosecutors" have won office in many districts around the country, although they vary in the degree of change they represent. Scott Colom, a Black man, was

elected district attorney in northeast Mississippi in 2015 on a plat-
form that included reducing incarceration and expanding the use of
rehabilitation services for drug offenses. He defeated a white man
who had been elected to the office six times over twenty-five years.
In office Colom has expanded the use of alternative sentencing programs and created a civilian panel to determine when to seek the
death penalty.[140]

The next year, progressive Black women were elected to the chief
prosecutor's offices of Chicago, St. Louis, and Orlando. Kimberly
Foxx defeated a two-term incumbent to become Cook County state's
attorney. Her office declined to pursue almost three thousand felony
cases that would have been pursued in the previous administration.
The office also dismissed the cases of dozens of people who had been
convicted based on the testimony of a corrupt police officer.[141] Foxx
decided not to pursue the prosecution of Arthur Brown, after a judge
set aside his convictions for murder and arson, because of concerns
about the fairness of his previous trials and whether he was guilty.
Brown had been in prison almost thirty years.[142]

In St. Louis, Kimberly Gardner reduced prosecutions of minor
marijuana offenses and refused to pursue cases that depended on the
testimony of police officers whose credibility was in question. She
also sought to overturn the murder conviction of Lamar Johnson,
who had served twenty-five years in prison, after her office determined that he was innocent.[143] However, the Missouri attorney general opposed her efforts and the state supreme court held that Gardner
did not have the authority to challenge the conviction.[144] In Orlando,
Aramis Ayala announced that her office would never seek the death
penalty—prompting Governor Rick Scott to issue executive orders
removing murder cases from Ayala's office to another district.[145] The
Florida Supreme Court upheld the governor's action.[146]

Larry Krasner, a civil rights lawyer who was elected as Philadelphia's district attorney in 2017, promised never to seek the death pen-

alty. In office, he urged the Pennsylvania Supreme Court to declare the death penalty unconstitutional and stopped contesting appeals by many people on death row. Krasner ordered lawyers in the office to seek plea deals that generated the least amount of prison time. The office also stopped seeking cash bail for a number of nonviolent offenses, stopped prosecuting marijuana possession cases, and reduced the length of probation sentences it requested.[147] Krasner established a conviction integrity unit, whose work resulted in twenty-one exonerations during his first term. According to his office, "In 20 [of the 21] cases, prosecutors withheld evidence they were ethically and constitutionally required to disclose. In 15 cases, police committed egregious misconduct."[148] The changing tide has even touched Harris County, Texas, where District Attorney Kim Ogg—who continues to seek the death penalty on occasion—agreed to life sentences for three men who had been sentenced to death: Bobby Moore, who is intellectually disabled; Duane Buck, whose sentencing proceedings were tainted by racial prejudice; and Raymond Riles, who is severely mentally ill.[149]

Candidates with progressive views were elected in 2019 and 2020 in Los Angeles; San Francisco; New Orleans; Austin, Texas; and Columbus, Ohio. George Gascón, upon being elected district attorney in Los Angeles, issued a directive that the office would no longer seek the death penalty.[150] He also directed that the office would no longer: request cash bail for misdemeanors or for non-serious or nonviolent felony offenses; transfer children to adult court; seek certain sentencing enhancements such as those available under the state's three-strikes law; or appear at parole hearings to oppose parole. He promised a comprehensive review of sentences with a goal of resentencing twenty thousand people.[151]

The changes that these prosecutors have brought about show the extraordinary power that prosecutors have regarding how society responds to crime. Depending on the election of progressive prosecutors, however, is an imperfect solution to the problems that beset the criminal legal system. Justice should not be subject to the tides of politics or the electoral district in which a crime occurs. Progressive prosecutors have also faced significant opposition. George Gascón in Los Angeles has faced multiple recall election campaigns, and Chesa Boudin in San Francisco was recalled in 2022.

In a 2019 speech to the Fraternal Order of Police, then attorney general William P. Barr lamented "the emergence in some of our large cities of District Attorneys that style themselves as 'social justice' reformers, who spend their time undercutting the police, letting criminals off the hook, and refusing to enforce the law."[152] Three reform prosecutors, Parisa Dehghani-Tafti of Virginia, Mark Gonzalez of Texas, and Wesley Bell of Missouri, replied in an op-ed in the *Washington Post*:

> Not every social problem should be criminalized. We shouldn't use cash bail to keep poor people in jail when similarly situated but wealthier people can pay to go home. We should aim to help victims recover from the trauma of crime and listen to what will help them heal, instead of using their pain to obtain the harshest possible sentences.
>
> We believe that the default approach to children who make mistakes should be diversion and education rather than incarceration. People suffering from mental illnesses or substance-use disorders should be offered treatment rather than jail. . . .
>
> We also believe that no system can achieve justice if it tolerates racial and class disparities. Citizens returning from incarceration should be afforded the right to vote and to be productive members of our community. And the death penalty has no place in a civilized society.[153]

These are key principles that should guide our entire criminal legal system. They should be observed everywhere, not only in jurisdictions progressive enough to elect a prosecutor who believes that there is no such thing as too much justice. The awesome powers of the prosecution must be brought into balance through measures such as requiring full disclosure of information and preservation of evidence, restricting the extent to which prosecutors can punish people who exercise their right to trial, prohibiting the use of jailhouse informants, reversing convictions when prosecutors engage in egregious misconduct in closing arguments, and, as we discuss in the next chapter, ensuring that all people accused of crimes are represented by competent and dedicated attorneys.

3

A Poor Person's Justice

There can be no equal justice where the kind of trial a man gets depends on the amount of money he has.

—*United States Supreme Court,* Griffin v. Illinois, *1956*[1]

Of all the rights that an accused person has, the right to be represented by counsel is by far the most pervasive for it affects his ability to assert any other rights he may have.

—*United States Supreme Court,* United States v. Cronic, *1984*[2]

The saga of James T. Fisher Jr. began on December 12, 1982, when Terry Neal, a white man, was stabbed to death with a broken wine bottle in his apartment in Oklahoma City. Fifteen-year-old Fadjo Odell Johnson, who had been seen getting into a car with Neal that night, claimed that an older man named "James" had been with them—and had killed Neal. Both Johnson and Fisher, who was an adult, were Black. Two witnesses told police that they had seen two Black men in Neal's car the night of the murder, but the older of the two had gotten out of the car, and Neal had driven off with the younger one. After being questioned, Johnson fled to Houston, but he was arrested there, brought back to Oklahoma City, and kept in custody until the trial. Although Johnson was initially charged with the murder, District Attorney Bob Macy decided to charge Fisher and seek the death penalty. He dropped the charges against Johnson, who became his main witness against Fisher.[3]

At trial, Johnson testified that Neal had picked Fisher and him up in an area of Oklahoma City known to be frequented by homosexual prostitutes and then had taken them back to his apartment. Johnson claimed that Fisher and Neal started arguing after having sex, and Fisher hit Neal with a wine bottle and then stabbed him in the neck with the broken bottle. Johnson's testimony contradicted two different accounts he had previously given.[4]

Fisher was represented by Melvin Porter, a state senator who was juggling at least twenty-five criminal cases in the month that Fisher was tried, including another capital murder case he tried the week before Fisher's trial. The judges were well aware that Porter was so busy that sometimes he would leave during jury deliberations in one case to begin trying another. Such a busy lawyer would not be able to prepare for a capital trial without a second lawyer and a couple of investigators to interview witnesses, gather information about the crime, and investigate aspects of Fisher's life that could be a basis for arguing against the death penalty. But Porter did not ask for an investigator, explaining later that it was "an unwritten rule in Oklahoma County that you would not ask for investigative assistance when you were court-appointed."[5]

More remarkably, Porter was prejudiced against his client. He thought Fisher was homosexual and later said that homosexuals "were among the worst people in the world." He also later admitted that he resented Fisher's refusal to accept an offer to plead guilty before trial to avoid the death penalty.[6] He made no effort to conceal his distaste for Fisher during trial.

Porter made no opening statement or closing argument at either the guilt-innocence phase or the penalty phase of the trial. Because he was unprepared, a federal court observed years later, "the examination of Mr. Fisher and the other witnesses read more like first-time interviews conducted during discovery than the presentation of a defense at a capital murder trial. As a result, Mr. Porter elicited testimony . . . that, far from assisting in Mr. Fisher's defense, was highly detrimental to it." He called only one witness—Fisher. But then Porter "badgered Mr. Fisher, elicited damaging and irrelevant testimony through entirely inappropriate questions, and was generally hostile towards his own client." His questions were "irrelevant, abusive, and appeared designed to leave the jury with the impression that Mr. Fisher was a lying intravenous drug addict."[7] Although the case rested on Johnson's word against Fisher's, Porter indicated that he believed Johnson. He did not bring out that Johnson's trial testimony was contradicted by his previous statement to his school principal that he did not see the stabbing. He did not even ask Johnson whether he agreed to testify in exchange for the state dropping the murder charge against him. At the penalty phase, where the jury could hear anything about Fisher's life to help it decide whether to impose the death penalty, Porter uttered only *nine words*. Four were "judicial pleasantries," and the other five formed an objection overruled by the judge.[8]

On appeal, the Oklahoma Court of Criminal Appeals said it was "deeply disturbed" by Porter's "lack of participation and advocacy during the sentencing stage"—but not disturbed enough to reverse the conviction or sentence.[9] It was not until eighteen years after the trial that a federal court of appeals ruled that Fisher had been denied his right to counsel and ordered a new trial. It found that Porter was "grossly inept," "sabotaged his client's defense," and showed "actual doubt and hostility" toward his client and "sympathy and agreement with the prosecution."[10]

Fisher's case was returned to Oklahoma City for a new trial. But the lawyer assigned to defend him at his second trial, Johnny Albert, was drinking heavily and abusing cocaine. According to Albert's colleagues, he was "neglectful of his cases," and spent "less time working on cases and more time drinking beer and playing pool during work hours."[11] Within a year of Fisher's trial, Albert was arrested for failing to show up for court at least seven times, held in contempt for failing to enter a substance abuse treatment program, and suspended from the practice of law for his irresponsible representation of clients. His sobriety and competence were challenged in the cases of three other people he represented who were sentenced to death.[12]

Before the trial, Albert was given eighteen boxes of documents that had been collected during the challenge to Fisher's first conviction, but he hardly looked at them. He did no investigation, even though an investigator was assigned to work on the case. At a hearing in March of 2004, Albert called Fisher a "little bitch" and asked sheriff's deputies to remove Fisher's handcuffs so he could "kick his ass right now."[13] At trial, Albert did not point out the contradictions in Johnson's statements, the fact that he had fled to Houston, or that he had been convicted of assault and battery since Fisher's first trial. He did not bring to the jury's attention the two witnesses who said that Terry Neal drove off with the younger of the two men who got in his car.[14]

Albert's representation was so bad that the Oklahoma Court of Criminal Appeals in 2009 held that Fisher had again been denied his right to counsel and set aside his conviction. But, instead of a third trial, prosecutors agreed to release Fisher if he would plead guilty to first-degree murder and agree to be banished from Oklahoma. After his experience with two court-appointed attorneys, it is no surprise that Fisher accepted the deal. After entering a guilty plea and receiving a suspended sentence, he promptly left the state.[15]

The representation provided to James Fisher in two capital trials was a disgrace. Two judges presided over trials in which the incompetence of his lawyers could not have been any more complete or obvious. Two district attorneys took advantage of that incompetence to obtain death sentences. If Fisher had been represented by a competent lawyer at his first trial in 1983, it is likely that he would not have been found guilty and would not have spent a day on death row. If Melvin Porter and Johnny Albert were the best lawyers that Oklahoma could provide for Fisher and other capital cases, it is doubtful that it was providing any better lawyers for people accused of less serious crimes.

Because he was poor, Fisher had no control over the lawyers appointed to represent him at any stage of the proceedings. He was spared execution only because he had the good fortune to be well represented on appeal by lawyers from public defender offices who challenged his convictions. But many people convicted in violation of the Constitution are not so fortunate. Some are assigned inept lawyers who fail to challenge constitutional violations; some courts fail to provide lawyers even when defendants are entitled to them; and the Supreme Court has held that there is no right to a lawyer at the later stages of review. This system resembles a lottery in which the fate of a person accused of a crime depends upon whether he is lucky enough to be assigned a competent lawyer at each stage of the process.

The Promise of Equal Justice for All

Of all the rights accorded a person accused of a crime, the most fundamental is the right to a lawyer; every other right depends upon it.[16] In an adversarial justice system, an able and dedicated defense attorney, with the resources to properly investigate and prepare a defense and the ability to protect the legal rights of the accused person, is critical to a just result. An accused person's rights are only those that his lawyer asserts. An accused person's assessment of the prosecution's case is only as good as his lawyer's investigation. The experts who testify for an accused person are the ones that his lawyer realizes are needed and obtains the funds to retain. An accused person without an able lawyer stands alone and virtually defenseless against the prosecution. But most people accused of crimes—about 80 percent—cannot afford an attorney. Like James Fisher, they are dependent upon the court to provide a lawyer.

The right to a lawyer for a poor person accused of a crime was recognized by the U.S. Supreme Court in 1932, but only for capital cases.[17] In 1931, nine young African Americans were charged with raping two white girls in a train car at a time when the crime could be punished by death—and when Black men suspected of raping white women were often lynched. The defendants were young, ignorant of the law, and illiterate. Their lawyers were not selected until the morning of the first trial, which started nine days after their arrests; one lawyer was under the influence of alcohol and the other was senile. The nine Black youths went on trial with no preparation and "less than a half-hour interview with their lawyers."[18] Eight were sentenced to death; the trial of the ninth, who was only thirteen, resulted in a mistrial. In *Powell v. Alabama*, the U.S. Supreme Court set aside the convictions, holding that "in a capital case, where the defendant is unable to employ counsel, and is incapable adequately of making his own defense because of ignorance, feeble-mindedness, illiteracy, or the like, it is the duty of the court, whether requested or not, to assign counsel for him as a necessary requisite of due process of law."[19]

The Supreme Court expanded the right to a lawyer in 1938 when it held that the right to the "Assistance of Counsel" in the Sixth Amendment requires that lawyers be provided to poor people charged with crimes in the federal courts.[20] (Previously, the right had meant only that a person who could retain a lawyer had a right to be represented by that lawyer.) However, in 1942, the Court held that people charged with crimes in state and local courts were entitled to a lawyer only if necessary for a fair trial. It held that Smith Betts, a forty-three-year-old farmworker, did not have the right to a lawyer at his robbery trial in Maryland because he was a man of "ordinary intelligence" who had some familiarity with court procedure from pleading guilty in an earlier case, and the "simple issue" at the trial was "the veracity of the testimony for the State and that for the defendant."[21]

For the next twenty years, people who were denied a lawyer in state and local courts petitioned for new trials, arguing that they did not have a fair trial without a lawyer. One of them was Clarence Earl Gideon, who was convicted of breaking into a pool hall in Panama City, Florida, in 1961. At his trial, he asked the judge to provide him a lawyer, but Florida law allowed judges to appoint counsel only in capital cases.[22] Gideon was convicted and sentenced to serve five years. In prison, he hand-wrote a petition to the U.S. Supreme Court arguing that the judge's refusal to provide him with an attorney deprived him of his right to due process. The Supreme Court accepted his case and appointed a prominent lawyer, Abe Fortas, to represent him. The brief filed on behalf of Gideon described the need for counsel:

> In the absence of counsel an accused person cannot determine whether his arrest is lawful; whether the indictment or information is valid; what, if any, preliminary motions should be filed. He cannot accurately evaluate the implications of a plea to a lesser offense, and he is at a loss in discussions with the prosecuting attorney relating to such a plea.
>
> The indigent, apart from all other considerations, has probably been in jail from the time of arrest because of inability to furnish bail. How can he prepare his case? And how unreal it is to suppose that a layman can [question prospective jurors during jury selection], or cross-examine the prosecution's witnesses, or interpose objections to incompetent and prejudicial testimony.[23]

In 1963, the Supreme Court agreed, holding in *Gideon v. Wainwright* that the right to counsel applies to felony cases—those punishable by more than a year in prison—in state courts. Gideon was granted a new trial; provided with a court-appointed lawyer and a proper defense, he was found not guilty and released.[24]

The Supreme Court extended the right to counsel to more cases in the following decade. In 1967, the Court held in *In re Gault* that children are entitled to counsel in delinquency proceedings. At the time, over 600,000 came before juvenile courts each year; only a small percentage were represented by lawyers.[25] Five years later, in *Argersinger v. Hamlin*, the Court held that anyone facing *any* loss of liberty as punishment is entitled to a lawyer.[26]

The Court acknowledged that its decision in *Argersinger* created an immense challenge for state and local governments, which handled between 4 and 5 million misdemeanor cases and 40 to 50 million traffic cases each year.[27] Although lawyers were not required for many of those cases,[28] they were required for a very substantial number of cases in which prosecutors sought a sentence of jail time or judges considered such a sentence. This burden grew even greater as a result of the so-called wars on crime and drugs fought by successive presidents, beginning with President Lyndon Johnson's creation of the Law Enforcement Assistance Administration in 1968 to fund crime control projects. More people were sent to prison in the next twenty years than in the entire century before.[29] In 1972, when *Argersinger* was decided, there were 200,000 people in prisons and jails in the United States; today there are almost 2 million.[30]

Shortly after *Gideon* was decided, *New York Times* reporter Anthony Lewis wrote:

> It will be an enormous social task to bring to life the dream of *Gideon v. Wainwright*—the dream of a vast, diverse country in which every man charged with crime will be

capably defended, no matter what his economic circumstances, and in which the lawyer representing him will do so proudly, without resentment at an unfair burden, sure of the support needed to make an adequate defense.[31]

Unfortunately, our country has failed at this task more often than it has succeeded.

The Promise Broken

Samuel Moore was arrested on December 23, 2001, for loitering, and confined in the Crisp County Jail in Cordele, Georgia.[32] Nine months later, he was still in jail and had not seen a lawyer or a judge. He made a written demand for a lawyer on September 11, 2002. Three days later, the district attorney dismissed all charges against him—but neither Moore nor the jail was told, so he stayed in jail. In October, a judge appointed a lawyer to represent Moore—but the lawyer never contacted him. On January 8, 2003, an investigator for a civil rights organization found out about Moore and asked to see him. He was released the next day—more than twelve months after his arrest.

Georgia created a statewide public defender program in 2003. However, in 2022, it was discovered that a person charged with shoplifting had been in jail in Atlanta without a lawyer since 2018, that a child charged with drug possession had been locked up without a lawyer in another county since 2020, and that hundreds of people charged with crimes were in jails around the state without lawyers.[33]

These cases are not unique. Many people who are arrested do not see a lawyer for weeks or months—or at all. One national study in 2009 found that in many misdemeanor cases—punishable by up to a year in jail—judges encouraged defendants to plead guilty without counsel, and prosecutors talked directly with defendants and convinced them to plead guilty, again without counsel. As of 2009, in a large majority of counties in Texas, fewer than 20 percent of defendants in misdemeanor cases punishable by imprisonment were appointed lawyers.[34] A 2011 study found that one-third of defendants in misdemeanor cases in Florida were not represented by counsel. In Kentucky, only 30 percent of people accused of misdemeanors were represented by counsel in 2011. Half of all guilty pleas in Michigan in 2015 were entered by people without lawyers.[35] The National Juvenile Defender Center said in a 2016 report, "It is an open secret in America's justice system that countless children accused of crime are prosecuted and convicted every year without ever seeing a lawyer."[36]

In many places, poor people are charged a fee to be represented by a lawyer. Public defender fees, which can be as high as $200, are used in most states to try to get the poor to pay for legal assistance they cannot afford.[37] These fees may be waived in some states, but defendants are often not informed of this possibility. In Florida, the only way to avoid a minimum $50 fee is to forgo representation. In Louisiana, a $45 fee is paid to the public defender's office only by its clients who are convicted—creating the perverse incentive that the office gains financially by losing cases.[38]

The Supreme Court recognized in *Powell v. Alabama* that the most critical time for people accused of crimes is "from the time of their arraignment until the beginning of their trial, when consultation, thorough-going investigation and preparation [are] vitally important."[39] Yet poor defendants may sit in jail for months before getting a lawyer despite a 2008 Supreme Court holding that they are entitled to counsel "within a reasonable time" after "the initiation of adversary judicial proceedings."[40]

Jacqueline Winbrone was arrested in September 2007 for possession of a firearm in her car. Unable to come up with $10,000 in bail, she tried to contact her appointed attorney to get her bail reduced—without success. Winbrone was the sole caretaker for her husband, who required frequent dialysis treatment. Without her to look after him, he died. Still unable to contact her attorney, she could not attend his funeral. In November, after writing to the court, she was released from jail; the charge against her was later dismissed.[41]

Again, this is not an isolated case. Diego Morin, facing the death penalty in Del Rio, Texas, asked for a lawyer the day after his arrest. He did not get one for over eight months.[42] Eric Wyatt was arrested in March 2014 in Ben Hill County, Georgia, and charged with failing to return a borrowed truck on time. But Wyatt had already been convicted of the crime in another county three years earlier and had served time in jail. For three months after his arrest he tried to talk to a public defender to explain the mix-up, but could never get more than five minutes. Then he was hauled into court, where a public defender recommended that he plead guilty and receive a twenty-year sentence. "Are you serious?" Wyatt responded. "I've already served time for this!" Eight days later the prosecutor dismissed the charges.[43]

Many poor people spend more time in jail waiting for the appointment of a lawyer than they would spend if found guilty and sentenced.[44] Some jurisdictions have "jail clearing days," when people in this situation can plead guilty and be sentenced to time served. Innocent people plead guilty to get out of jail—and then face a lifetime of restrictions imposed on them because of their convictions.[45]

When poor defendants are appointed lawyers, they may have their assistance for only a matter of minutes. Reontay Miller, a seventeen-year-old Black student charged with stealing a go-cart, asked for a lawyer when he appeared in court in Cordele, Georgia, in March 2012. He did not speak to an attorney, but an investigator from the public defender office advised him to plead guilty. Later that morning Miller was in a group of people who pleaded guilty together. The judge asked them if they were satisfied with their attorney's services. Miller looked around, confused, and said, "I don't have one." A public defender standing nearby volunteered that he represented Miller, but said nothing on his behalf. The judge sentenced Miller to five years' probation, a $300 fine, and $500 restitution—and imposed a $50 public defender fee.[46]

Many poor defendants do not see a lawyer until the court proceeding in which their cases are resolved—often some version of the "meet 'em and plead 'em" ritual described earlier. The Florida Supreme Court, describing the "meet and greet" procedures that were routine in Miami, concluded that "the public defenders serve 'as mere conduits for plea offers.'"[47] A federal court found that representation of poor people accused of crimes in two municipalities in the state of Washington "amounted to little more than a 'meet and plead' system," and people accused of crimes "had virtually no relationship with their assigned counsel and could not fairly be said to have been 'represented' by them at all."[48]

Well over 90 percent of criminal cases are resolved with guilty pleas. In the few cases that go to trial, many poor people accused of crimes are, like James Fisher, saddled with lawyers who lack the competence, time, and resources to defend them properly. Robert Wayne Holsey, a Black man, was represented by a lawyer who drank a quart of vodka every night of his death penalty trial in Georgia. The judge assigned Holsey a second lawyer who had no experience in defending capital cases. She was given no direction by the alcoholic lawyer except during trial, when she was told to cross-examine an expert on DNA evidence and give the closing argument at the penalty phase. She lacked the knowledge and experience to do either. The lawyers failed to find and present evidence that could have convinced the jury to impose a sentence of life imprisonment instead of death. As a federal appeals court judge pointed out later, Holsey was intellectually limited, and as a child had been "subjected to abuse so severe, so frequent, and so notorious that his neighbors called his childhood home 'the Torture Chamber.'"[49] Holsey received the death sentence. After the trial, the alcoholic lawyer was disbarred, prosecuted, convicted, and sent to prison for stealing client funds.[50]

Judy Haney was accused of arranging the murder of her husband who had abused her and her children. Her court-appointed lawyers at her capital trial in Talladega County, Alabama, did not get hospital records that documented the injuries that Haney and her daughter had suffered and that would have corroborated their testimony about the physical abuse. One of her lawyers came to court so drunk that the judge held him in contempt and sent him to jail. The next morning, the lawyer and Haney were both produced from jail. The trial resumed, and the death penalty was imposed a few days later.[51]

In Houston, the longtime death penalty capital of the United States, judges often assigned incompetent lawyers to represent people facing capital charges. One lawyer, Jerry Guerinot, had twenty clients sentenced to death owing largely to his "failure to conduct even rudimentary investigations."[52] Judges repeatedly appointed Ronald Mock despite his poor performance in capital cases and even though the Texas State Bar publicly reprimanded him twice and placed him on probation three times. Sixteen of Mock's clients were sentenced to death before the bar suspended him from practice.[53] Joe Frank Cannon, who was known for trying cases like "greased lightning," had ten clients sentenced to death. Cannon was one of two lawyers appointed to represent Carl Johnson, who was charged with capital murder in the course of a 1978 armed robbery in Houston. The other was less than a year out of law school and had never tried a death penalty case. Cannon slept during parts of jury selection and witness testimony. Johnson was sentenced to death. Four years later, Cannon was appointed to represent Calvin Burdine, who was also accused of capital murder in the course of an armed robbery. Again, Cannon fell asleep repeatedly during the trial. Burdine received the death sentence.[54] A federal court set aside Burdine's conviction because Cannon was his only lawyer. However, it upheld a death sentence in another case in which the defense lawyer slept because there was a second lawyer on the case.[55]

Supreme Court Justice Ruth Bader Ginsburg said in 2001, "I have yet to see a death case, among the dozens coming to the Supreme Court on eve of execution petitions, in which the defendant was well represented at trial."[56] However, defendants in criminal cases are supposed to be protected from unfair trials by the appeals process. Someone convicted in a state court can appeal directly to a higher state court; many states have two appellate courts, one an intermediate court and the other the supreme court. If unsuccessful on appeal, he can initiate what are called "post-conviction proceedings" in a state trial court and appeal an adverse ruling. Every state provides some type of process in which a convicted person can challenge his conviction and sentence for reasons that were not available at the time of the trial or the initial appeal, such as jury misconduct, denial of a competent lawyer at trial, or the prosecution's failure to disclose exculpatory evidence. Finally, a convicted person can file in federal court a "petition for a writ of habeas corpus," which invokes review by federal trial and appellate courts, which have the power to set aside a conviction or sentence obtained in violation of the U.S. Constitution. This stage of review is also referred to as "federal post-conviction review."

With the exception of the automatic appeal that typically follows an initial death penalty sentence, there is one crucial requirement for all of these appeals: they must be filed on time. At least six people have been executed in Texas without any federal habeas corpus review because their lawyers missed the deadline.[57] Jerome Godinich filed petitions after the deadline on behalf of two people under death sentence in Texas. Despite newspaper coverage in 2009 of his failure to file on time, judges in Houston continued appointing him to cases. In 2018, Godinich was paid for work on almost six hundred felony cases, including fourteen capital cases, and six felony appeals.[58]

Such poor representation is not limited to Texas. A 2014 study by The Marshall Project found that lawyers have missed the statute of limitations for federal habeas corpus petitions in at least eighty capital cases, including thirty-seven in Florida. Some attorneys did not start working on cases until after the deadline; others were not appointed until after the deadline; several filed petitions in the wrong court; one sent petitions to the courts by regular mail instead of overnight; and judges reneged on extensions when they discovered that they lacked the authority to grant them. In one case, an incorrect date was introduced by the prosecution, incorporated by the Mississippi Supreme Court into an opinion, and then used by an attorney to calculate the filing deadline—which turned out to be incorrect.[59]

Some briefs that are filed on time are useless. Leslie Ribnik, the lawyer assigned to represent Robert Gene Will in the Texas Court of Criminal Appeals, filed a twenty-eight-page brief for Will that included twenty pages that were identical to a brief that he had filed in the case of Angel Maturino Resendiz, who was executed in 2006 after Ribnik missed the deadline for filing an appeal in his case in federal court. The Court rejected Will's appeal. A doctor later testified that Ribnik was so impaired by Parkinson's disease that he was unfit to handle Will's appeal.[60]

Toby C. Wilkinson filed a brief on behalf of Justin Chaz Fuller that was partly copied from an appeal he had filed seven years earlier for Henry Earl Dunn.[61] The brief for Fuller contained complaints about testing done on a gun used by the co-defendant in Dunn's case—which obviously had nothing to do with Fuller. The Texas Court of Criminal Appeals denied Fuller relief and he was executed in 2006. Three years after "representing" Fuller, Wilkinson filed a brief for Daniel Clate Acker that was partly copied from his brief for Fuller and also contained nonsensical passages copied from Acker's letters. Acker was executed in 2018. Despite this performance, Wilkinson was appointed in 2013 to represent Micah Brown in a capital trial. Brown was sentenced to death.[62]

These lawyers represented people whose lives were at stake. Every judge and prosecutor in these cases knew of their incompetence. And yet these lawyers were assigned to cases over and over again, enabling judges and the prosecutors to pretend that the right to counsel had been honored. The right to a lawyer was meaningless for their clients.

Twenty years after *Gideon v. Wainwright*, the American Bar Association warned of a "crisis in indigent defense funding" and exhorted, "We must be willing to put our money where our mouth is; we must be willing to make the constitutional mandate [of counsel for people accused of crimes] a reality." Another ABA report in 1993 found that "long-term neglect and underfunding of indigent defense has created a crisis of extraordinary proportions in many states throughout the country." A 2004 ABA report concluded, "Thousands of persons are processed through America's courts every year either with no lawyer at all or with a lawyer who does not have the time, resources, or in some cases the inclination to provide effective representation." In 2012, yet another ABA report observed that "defense of the indigent accused in the United States still fails to provide the counsel promised by the Supreme Court."[63]

Of course, there are exceptions. There are public defender offices, court-appointed lawyers, attorneys at civil rights and human rights organizations, and lawyers in private practice who take cases pro bono who provide very good representation. But they are the exception, not the rule, and justice should not depend on whether a defendant is lucky enough to be assigned a good lawyer.

The criminal legal system fails poor defendants for several reasons. First, many state and local governments have resisted the right to counsel, failing to establish adequate systems to ensure representation of poor people accused of crimes. What arrangements exist often lack the funding necessary for competent representation. In addition, many programs for providing representation are dependent on judges, county commissions, governors, and others whose primary interest is the fast and inexpensive processing of cases. Finally, for many poor people, the right to counsel is unenforceable, because the Supreme Court has offered little recourse, before or after trial, to those assigned incompetent lawyers.

Haphazard Systems

Poor people accused of crimes in the federal courts are represented by public defender programs in all but two of the ninety-four federal districts; and, in all the districts, by appointed lawyers who are paid by the federal government. The Criminal Justice Act of 1964, later amended in 1970, established this system for appointing and compensating lawyers for indigent defendants, reimbursement of reasonable expenses, and payment for experts and investigators necessary for an adequate defense.[64]

But the federal government—which provides more than $500 million in grants to state and local law enforcement agencies each year—does not contribute anything to the cost of providing lawyers in state, county, and municipal courts, where the overwhelming majority of criminal cases are prosecuted.[65] In those courts, the responsibility for providing and paying for lawyers falls upon state and local governments. Doing it right costs money—although not nearly as much as the amounts spent on law enforcement and prosecution.

The decisions in *Gideon v. Wainwright, In re Gault,* and *Argersinger v. Hamlin* created a new and substantial expense for many governments, which were resistant to new spending mandates. In addition, there was no political reason for states to implement this constitutional right. At the time *Gideon* was decided, the Southern states were engaged in massive resistance to the Supreme Court's decision in *Brown v. Board of Education* that required integration of the public schools. These states also resisted the Court's right-to-counsel cases, although they did not receive as much attention for it. Many states simply passed the mandate down to their counties and localities, resulting in a patchwork of systems with neither the structure nor the funding necessary to realize the constitutional right to counsel.

Even before *Gideon*, some states had provided lawyers for the accused in some criminal cases. In a number of them, lawyers were required to represent poor people pro bono as a matter of professional obligation, or representation was organized as a charitable initiative.[66] The New York Legal Aid Society, the oldest and largest provider of legal services to the poor in the United States, was founded in 1876 and took its first criminal case in 1910.[67] Los Angeles County established a public defender office in 1914.

In May 1963, barely two months after the *Gideon* decision, the Florida legislature adopted a statute creating public defender offices in each of the state's judicial circuits. Twenty-eight states and the District of Columbia now have government-administered public defender programs.[68] Some have statewide public defender systems that employ full-time lawyers, investigators, social workers, and support staff. Many of those programs have lawyers and staff who specialize in certain areas such as the death penalty and other complex crimes, representation of children, and issues of mental illness. These programs recruit law school graduates and have training programs and supervision of attorneys to make maximum use of their limited resources.

In other states, representation is provided primarily at the county level. Counties and municipalities may provide representation in a variety of ways: through public defender offices, by appointing lawyers to cases and paying them by the case or by the hour, or by contracting with one or more lawyers or firms to handle certain types of cases for a flat rate. In these states, there may be wide variation in the quality of representation. Some California counties have outstanding public defender offices, while others rely on low-bid contracts. The public defender offices in New York City have long provided competent representation, but it was not until a 2017 law that many upstate counties began implementing plans to provide counsel when a defendant is first charged in court, reduce caseloads, and improve the quality of representation.[69]

In a system that depends on appointed lawyers from private practice, whether an accused person receives adequate representation depends on who makes the appointment, the qualifications of the lawyers appointed, the fees they are paid, and the availability of experts and investigators. In many places, judges appoint lawyers to represent the poor. Any lawyer may be eligible; some may put their business cards on the judge's bench to show they are available. If there are any qualifications, they may be defined in terms of number of years in practice and number of trials; many of the worst lawyers have a long record of taking criminal appointments and therefore meet the qualifications. There may be no supervision of the lawyers appointed. James Fisher, Robert Wayne Holsey, Judy Haney, Calvin Burdine, and Robert Gene Will were all represented by court-appointed lawyers.

Jurisdictions that contract with law firms or individual lawyers to handle cases often award contracts based on the lowest bid. A lawyer or firm may contract to handle a certain number of cases or all of the criminal cases in a county for a flat annual rate. These programs are known for the exceptionally short shrift that poor clients receive and the lack of money spent on investigative and expert assistance—which in many places comes directly out of the lawyer's bottom line. One contract defender in California repeatedly fought off low bidders by reducing his budget from 41 percent of the prosecutor's budget in 2000 to only 27 percent in 2005. Yet, in 2006, he was undercut by a bid that was almost 50 percent less than his by a firm that would have to spend even less time on each case.[70] Another California lawyer, working with two associates and no investigators, contracted with a rural county to handle more than five thousand cases per year. He managed the volume by convincing 70 percent of his clients to plead guilty at their first court appearance, usually after thirty seconds of discussion.[71]

Underfunding

Whatever system is in place, a national study found that inadequate funding "continues to be the single greatest obstacle to delivering 'competent' and 'diligent' defense representation"—resulting in "attorneys attempting to provide defense services while carrying astonishingly large caseloads."[72] As their budgets have become strained, state legislatures and local governments are increasingly unwilling to adequately fund the defense of poor people accused of crimes.

Lawyers who contract with courts to handle large numbers of cases for a flat fee have an incentive to spend as little time as possible on each case. The same is true of lawyers appointed to individual cases who are paid by the hour or by the case, invariably at below-market rates in state and local courts. In Tennessee, for example, appointed counsel are paid no more than $50 per hour in noncapital cases, with limits ranging from $1,500 to $3,000 for most felonies. Wisconsin did not raise its hourly rate from $40 to $70 until 2020. In South Carolina, appointed lawyers are paid $40 to $60 per hour, with a maximum of $3,500 for any case involving any number of felony charges.[73] In addition, court-appointed attorneys in many states must petition the court for additional funds to pay for investigators and experts.

In civil cases, courts routinely award fees much higher than those paid to lawyers appointed to defend the poor; paralegals and law clerks are compensated at higher rates in bankruptcy, civil rights, employment, Social Security, and other cases than what experienced court-appointed attorneys are paid in criminal cases.[74] As a result, some of the lawyers seeking appointments are those without good alternative options. "You either have very inexperienced attorneys right out of law school for whom any money is better than no money," one Virginia prosecutor said. "Or you have people who are really bad lawyers who can't make a living except off the court appointed list."[75]

Public defender programs are the most cost-effective way of providing quality representation because they are staffed with lawyers, investigators, and social workers who specialize in criminal defense. But they must be adequately funded, or they will face overwhelming workloads and high staff turnover. Some public defender systems were initially established with close-to-adequate funding levels, but their financial support typically has not kept up with increased caseloads.[76]

The public defender office in Wilkes-Barre, Luzerne County, Pennsylvania, was so underfunded that from 2003 to 2009 it sent only one public defender to juvenile court for about four hours per week—leaving children vulnerable to a vast kickback scheme engineered by two judges. First, Judge Michael Conahan arranged to close the county juvenile detention facility and contracted instead with two private juvenile detention centers; then Judge Mark Ciavarella sentenced thousands of children to those detention centers, which received tens of millions of dollars in fees. The two judges received $2.8 million in kickbacks from the owners of the centers. Judge Ciavarella sentenced children to detention at more than twice the rate of other juvenile judges in the state. Over half of the children were sentenced without a lawyer being present. The county's chief public defender, upon being told about the high rate of detention and the absence of lawyers, responded that his office did not "have the time or the manpower to intervene." After a nonprofit organization brought the "kids for cash" scandal to light in 2008, Conahan and Ciavarella were convicted and sentenced to prison.[77]

Yet Luzerne County's board of commissioners still refused to provide the funding necessary for public defenders to represent their clients. Albert J. Flora Jr., appointed chief public defender in 2010, attempted to tackle the many problems stemming from underfunding of the office, but encountered constant opposition from county officials. He submitted reports documenting "rampant deficiencies in representation" owing to the office's dearth of lawyers and support staff. The board of commissioners rejected his requests for additional funds in 2010 and 2011, and, in 2012, reduced funding for the office by 12 percent and implemented a hiring freeze after several lawyers left the office.[78]

With no other option, Flora, joined by three people charged with crimes, filed suit in April 2012 against the county and the county manager. They asked the court to order the county to lift the hiring freeze and to provide adequate funding. The complaint described how overwhelming caseloads made it impossible for public defenders to represent their clients. Public defenders were often unable to interview their clients before preliminary hearings and on occasion could not attend the hearings, at which judges then set unaffordable bail. Public defenders had to postpone other hearings, resulting in delays that left their clients in jail longer. They filed pleadings without full knowledge of their clients' cases. They routinely missed filing deadlines. There were not enough investigators; sometimes secretaries with no training in investigation were sent out to take statements from witnesses. Because of the lack of investigation, public defenders were unable to engage in effective plea negotiations with prosecutors and provide their clients with informed advice. Attorneys with little appellate training or experience were required to handle appeals.[79] In early 2013, Flora brought to the attention of the court and county officials that three thousand delinquency adjudications by Judge Ciavarella had not been expunged as ordered by the Pennsylvania Supreme Court in 2009.[80] The county fired Flora in April 2013.

On appeal of the suit challenging the lack of funding for the public defender office, the Pennsylvania Supreme Court ultimately held that the right to counsel had been violated by the "widespread, systematic and constructive denial of counsel" resulting from inadequate funding. The Court anticipated that there could be other suits, as public defender offices in other counties were "chronically underfunded and understaffed."[81] But that was unlikely because any public defender who brought a suit could be fired as easily as Flora was. A few days after being fired, Flora filed a federal suit against the county claiming that his termination was in retaliation for filing the earlier suit and for reporting the noncompliance with the expungement order. The case was resolved in 2018 with a payment of $250,000 to Flora.[82]

Examples of extreme underfunding can be found all over the country. In one Louisiana judicial district, the public defender office handled 943 cases in 2015 with just one full-time attorney and two part-time contract attorneys and a budget of $230,000. The district attorney's budget was five times as big.[83] In Missouri, the number of cases handled by the statewide public defender program increased by more than twelve thousand in a six-year period ending in 2005, but the program received no additional staff during that time. The director of the state public defender commission informed the state government in 2011 that "triage has replaced justice in Missouri's courts" and that people were languishing in jail "for weeks or even months with no access to counsel." By 2019, 329 public defenders in Missouri had to deal with more than 87,000 cases. As of January 2020, more than 4,600 defendants, several hundred of them in jail, were on wait lists for attorneys. Judges in Missouri have even ordered public defenders to violate their ethical obligations and represent clients when they were too overworked to do so.[84]

In complex cases, an adequate defense requires not only competent attorneys, but also experts to evaluate the prosecution's forensic evidence, assess the defendant's mental illness or intellectual disability, and often analyze the traumatic upbringing the defendant suffered as a child. In many states, a defense lawyer must ask the judge to appoint an expert by showing that, given the prosecution's case and the client's potential defenses, the area of expertise will be a significant factor at trial.[85] Even then, the Supreme Court has held that poor defendants are entitled to only one expert, who may be selected by the judge, while the prosecution can essentially hire any experts it wants. The Arkansas Supreme Court, for example, has repeatedly held that judges may assign doctors from the state mental hospital, who usually have a strong pro-prosecution bias, as experts for the defense.[86] Judges often deny applications for funds for experts, and they are seldom overruled by appellate courts, leaving the accused defenseless.

Federico Martinez–Macias was represented at his capital trial in El Paso, Texas, by a court-appointed attorney who failed to present an alibi witness, relied upon an incorrect assumption about a key evidentiary point, and failed to interview witnesses who could have rebutted the prosecutor's case. Setting aside his conviction, the Fifth Circuit Court of Appeals dryly noted, "The state paid defense counsel $11.84 per hour. Unfortunately, the justice system got only what it paid for." Martinez–Macias was released after nine years on death row.[87] Across the country, too many poor defendants are getting only the minimal defense that state and local governments are paying for.

Lack of Independence

Independence is a crucial requirement of an adversary system. When someone is charged with a crime by the government, with its vast investigatory and prosecutorial machinery, that person must know that his attorney is solely committed to his defense. Unfortunately, this is often not true.

Many chief public defenders are appointed by governors, county commissions, judges, commissions whose members are mostly appointed by governors, or other political entities whose primary goal may be processing a high volume of cases at low cost.[88] Public defenders facing these pressures may be reluctant to stand up for their clients—or, like Albert Flora in Luzerne County, may be fired if they do.

After being hired in January 2022 as director of the Oregon Office of Public Defense Services, Stephen Singer faced a crisis: the agency had only one-third of the attorneys it needed to provide representation for poor people accused of crimes, according to a report by the American Bar Association, and hundreds of people charged with crimes were without lawyers. Singer soon found himself in disagreement with Oregon Supreme Court Chief Justice Martha Walters, who met weekly with him, about how to manage the crisis. Singer asserted that he needed independence from the court system to function properly. On August 10, Walters asked the state's public defense commission to fire Singer. After the commission deadlocked, 4–4 with one absence, Walters fired all nine commissioners. She then reappointed five of them—four of whom had voted to fire Singer— and added four new members. The newly constituted commission fired Singer by a vote of 6–2.[89]

Beginning in 1996, attorneys at the first regional public defender office in Texas started screening recently arrested people at the jail and getting some released on bail and many cases dismissed, saving more than $1 million per year in jail costs. They also won acquittals in about half their trials. The district attorney in Val Verde County responded by closing his files to the public defenders while leaving them open to private attorneys, and judges stopped appointing the public defenders to cases. County commissioners shut down the public defender program, forgoing $68,000 in state funds and the savings in jail costs. Without the public defenders, people remained in jail for months without seeing lawyers. One of them was Diego Morin, who was charged with capital murder but did not see a lawyer until eight months after requesting one. The chair of the Texas Bar's Committee on Indigent Defense observed, "Nobody really wants there to be an effective defense system because if there is, [judges] won't be able to get elected again by shooting fish in a barrel." A survey of Texas public defenders found that interference by county commissioners and interference by the judiciary were their second and third greatest concerns, just under "lack of resources."[90]

Other public defenders have been fired for doing their job. Nicholas White, a well-regarded chief public defender in Georgia, was fired in 2016 by the Houston County Board of Commissioners after he sought funding for one additional lawyer for his office and suggested the county might be sued if it refused the request. Public defenders in the office were handling three hundred cases a year—twice national standards.[91] The chief public defender and chief deputy in Montgomery County, Pennsylvania, filed a friend-of-the-court brief in the Pennsylvania Supreme Court in 2020 in a case regarding bail practices. They described "dysfunctional bail practices that result[ed] in unnecessary and prolonged pretrial detention" in the county.[92] The county's chief operating officer, Lee Soltysiak, demanded that Chief Public Defender Dean Beer withdraw the brief.[93] According to Beer, county chief judge Thomas Del Ricci made the same demand. Beer complied, but he and Deputy Chief Keisha Hudson were still fired.

Lawyers who are directly appointed by judges or contract to handle large volumes of cases may be more loyal to the judges who pay them than to their clients. Defense attorneys who are financially reliant on the judge may be unwilling to ask for continuances when they are unprepared, challenge a prosecutor's strike of a juror that appears to be racially motivated, apply for funds for experts and investigators, or take other actions that may displease the judge.

If they do stand up for their clients, they may soon find themselves out of work. In Henrico County, Virginia, one lawyer challenged the low limit on fees paid to appointed counsel for representing defendants in felony cases; the lawyer was removed from the case, and one judge announced that any lawyer who raised the issue would be removed from the list of appointed counsel.[94] A Utah county terminated the contract of a lawyer to handle appeals of poor people convicted of crimes after the lawyer criticized the county's refusal to provide adequate funding for the case of a man under death sentence. "The state gives enormous resources to the prosecution," attorney Samuel Newton said. "The state must similarly commit to equally and adequately support criminal defense attorneys." A county commissioner said that this criticism was "harmful to the County's reputation."[95]

In many jurisdictions that rely on court-appointed defense counsel, elected state court judges often appoint lawyers known for processing cases quickly. Judges may do this to keep the docket moving, to control the outcome, or even as a form of political patronage. In the early 1990s, a study of homicide cases in Philadelphia found that "Philadelphia's poor defendants often find themselves being represented by ward leaders, ward committeemen, failed politicians, the sons of judges and party leaders, and contributors to the judges' election campaigns."[96] A study of court appointments and campaign contributions in Houston between 2005 and 2018 found that judges assigned cases to their donors at more than double the rate that they assigned cases to nondonors. These lawyers were not being appointed because they were better attorneys; their clients were more likely to be sent to jail or prison and on average received longer sentences. Jerome Godinich, who continued to be assigned cases in Houston after missing the deadline for review by the federal courts in two capital cases, was assigned many cases by one judge, Jim Wallace. Godinich donated $9,000 to Wallace between 2005 and 2014, and Wallace appointed Godinich to 1,974 cases between 2004 and 2018. Between 2014 and 2020, Godinich was paid more than $800,000 for cases before Judge Wallace.[97]

Conversely, trial judges are sometimes unwilling to appoint qualified lawyers who, they fear, will actually defend their clients' rights vigorously. In multiple capital cases in Georgia, experienced attorneys have successfully overturned their clients' convictions or death sentences on appeal—yet judges have refused to appoint them to continue representing those same clients when facing retrial.[98] A judge refused to appoint an expert capital attorney from the NAACP Legal Defense and Educational Fund to continue representation of a poor defendant in a new trial, even though the reason for the new trial was that the defendant's original court-appointed attorney had provided ineffective legal assistance.[99]

Some judges reserve sanctions not for incompetent lawyers but for those who zealously advocate for their clients. The lawyers who represented Frank Martinez Garcia at his capital trial in Texas told courts that Garcia had been tested and was of average intelligence; however, there had been no testing. The lawyer assigned to represent Garcia in state post-conviction proceedings obtained $5,000 for a psychological evaluation but kept the money without investigating Garcia's intellectual functioning. In fact, Garcia had failed three grades, had been diagnosed with a learning disability and placed in special education classes, and had a full-scale IQ of 55. In 2011, two experienced capital lawyers, Richard H. Burr and James Marcus, worked furiously to notify the Texas Court of Criminal Appeals that Garcia's sentence was based on misrepresentations and that he was not eligible for the death penalty because of his intellectual disability. The Court denied their petition and Garcia was executed. The Court held Burr and Marcus—not Garcia's earlier lawyers—in contempt and fined them because they failed to file their petition more than seven days before the execution date.[100] In 2015, David Dow, a law professor and founder of the Texas Innocence Network, arguably missed the seven-day deadline; one judge concluded that his filing was actually on time. The Texas Court of Criminal Appeals suspended Dow from practicing before it for a year.[101]

There are many reasons beyond campaign contributions and a desire to speed through their docket that judges not only allow but perpetrate violations of the right to counsel. A judge may refuse to

appoint qualified lawyers precisely *because* they successfully overturned a judgment made by her court. In addition, most state judges
are elected, and many see a tough-on-crime reputation as necessary
for reelection. Beyond that, judges in America continue to be over-
whelmingly white and generally affluent; some are no doubt biased,
implicitly or otherwise, against the disproportionately nonwhite and
usually poor people charged with crimes in their courtrooms.

Other judges place a higher priority on minimizing costs than on
the right to counsel. When death penalty advocate Edith Jones was
chief judge of the Fifth Circuit Court of Appeals, she sent the chief
judges in all the federal courts of appeals a memorandum about "cost
containment" in complex cases, which recommended limiting the
number of experts allowed to defendants, placing "an outside dollar
limit on all experts," and "establishing guidelines for general costs of
representation."[102]

Finally, some judges simply do not think the right to counsel is
very important. At a state bar meeting, Jean Hoefer Toal, chief justice
of the South Carolina Supreme Court, gave her opinion of *Alabama
v. Shelton*, in which the Supreme Court held that a defendant has the
right to an attorney in a case that may result in a suspended sentence:
"*Alabama v. Shelton* is one of the more misguided decisions of the
United States Supreme Court . . . so I will tell you straight up we
[are] not adhering to *Alabama v. Shelton* in every situation."[103]

The Most Fundamental Right, Unenforceable

Most poor people accused of crimes take whichever lawyer is
assigned to them. But on occasion a defendant realizes that his lawyer
is incompetent. Unfortunately, there is little the defendant can do
about it, either at trial or on appeal.

In 1988, the judge presiding over the capital case of Gregory Wilson in Covington, Kentucky, posted a notice seeking a lawyer under
the heading "PLEASE HELP. DESPERATE." William Hagedorn,
who had been suspended from the practice of law multiple times, vol-

unteered and was appointed. Another lawyer who had never handled a felony case responded to the judge's plea and was appointed to assist Hagedorn. Wilson learned that police had come to Hagedorn's house and retrieved eight bags of stolen property from underneath the living room floor. But what bothered Wilson most was that when he called attorney Hagedorn on the number that he had given him, the person who picked up the phone answered, "Kelly's Keg."[104] Kelly's Keg was a bar across the street from the courthouse.

When he was next brought to court, Wilson complained to the judge that he needed a real lawyer—not one who, in Wilson's words, was "unprepared, ill-trained, ill-equipped, and lacked the necessary competence and experience." The judge said Wilson could retain any lawyer he wanted, but Hagedorn was the lawyer the court was providing. The judge also told Wilson that he could represent himself, but Wilson responded, "I don't know how to defend myself."[105] With no other choice, Wilson went to trial with Hagedorn as his lawyer. Hagedorn missed parts of the trial. He cross-examined only a few witnesses; he had missed the direct testimony of one of them because he had been out of the courtroom. A federal judge later called his performance "one of the worst examples that I have seen of the unfairness and abysmal lawyering that pervade capital trials."[106] Wilson was sentenced to death.

What more could Wilson have done? He objected. He made specific complaints about his appointed lawyers, who were clearly incapable of defending a capital case. The judge gave Wilson the meaningless option to hire a lawyer or represent himself. In upholding his conviction and death sentence, the courts attributed Hagedorn's performance to Wilson's supposed lack of cooperation.[107] Wilson was spared execution only because Kentucky's governor commuted his sentence many years later.

Some people in Wilson's situation make the mistake of representing themselves. Kenneth Dwayne Dunn thought that the lawyers who represented him at his first capital trial in Houston, Bob Hunt and Ruben Guerrero, were so bad that he filed a malpractice suit against them. Before his retrial, Dunn informed the judge that the malpractice suit was pending, that Hunt had complained about having to retain a lawyer to respond to it, and that he did not trust Hunt and Guerrero to act in his best interest. He asked for other lawyers, even providing the names of two. Nevertheless, the judge appointed Hunt and Guerrero to defend Dunn.[108] Instead of going to trial with lawyers whom he was suing for malpractice, Dunn chose to represent himself and was sentenced to death. He was executed in 1999.

Judges have even ignored objections by the appointed lawyers themselves. An Alabama judge refused to replace court-appointed attorneys in a capital case after they requested to be removed because they lacked experience in criminal cases and were not competent to defend such a case. The client received a death sentence, which was upheld by the Alabama Supreme Court, and he was executed in 2010.[109] In all of these cases, judges should have provided other lawyers or at least inquired into the defendants' complaints. Instead, however, many judges accuse defendants of having other motives in complaining about their lawyers.

In theory, the right to counsel can be protected after trial by showing that the lawyer who represented the accused was ineffective. But there are many barriers to prevailing on a claim of ineffective assistance. In *Strickland v. Washington* in 1984, the Supreme Court held that the right to counsel is violated only if a lawyer's representation "fell below an objective standard of reasonableness" *and* there is a reasonable probability that the outcome of the trial would have been different if the lawyer had not been ineffective. In addition, judges must be "highly deferential" in assessing the performance of the lawyer, who is "strongly presumed to have rendered adequate assistance" and to have "made all significant decisions in the exercise of reasonable professional judgment."[110] Employing these presumptions, courts have approved of all sorts of malpractice as "strategy" or "tactics." A federal appeals court said that a lawyer's failure to do *any* investigation in a capital case was "strategic" and that, therefore, "we do not look to see what a further investigation would have produced."[111]

The Supreme Court also abandoned its previous position that "the right to have the assistance of counsel is too fundamental and absolute to allow courts to indulge in nice calculations as to the amount of prejudice arising from its denial."[112] Instead, judges can make crude guesses as to whether, without the lawyer's errors, "the result of the proceeding would have been different."[113] Usually, the judges who rule on whether a lawyer was ineffective did not preside at the trial where that lawyer represented the defendant. They cannot possibly know whether the outcome might have been different because they did not see the witnesses who testified and have no idea how the jury assessed the case. Thurgood Marshall—the only justice then on the Court who had defended people accused of crimes—dissented, arguing that the standard adopted by the majority is "so malleable that, in practice, it will either have no grip at all or will yield excessive variation" in how it "is interpreted and applied." He observed, "It is often very difficult to tell whether a defendant convicted after a trial in which he was ineffectively represented would have fared better if his lawyer had been competent."[114]

Justice Marshall was right. Former federal judge and FBI director William S. Sessions called *Strickland* "unrealistic and damaging."[115] Just how unrealistic and damaging is illustrated by the case of a lawyer who, at the time of the defendant's trial, was being disbarred for, among other things, suing public officials for "being members of a pedophile ring that kidnapped local schoolchildren." As one judge wrote, under the Supreme Court's decision in *Strickland*, the "fully licensed lawyer with her head full of fantasies and 'with complete lack of insight into the wrongfulness of her actions' was counsel enough to satisfy the Sixth Amendment!"[116]

Jeffrey Leonard was tried in Kentucky in 1983 for committing

murder during an armed robbery. His trial lawyer, Ferdinand Radolovich, did essentially no preparation for the penalty phase of the
trial. Indeed, Radolovich could not have investigated Leonard's
background because he did not even know his client's real name.
Leonard was tried under the name "James Earl Slaughter," even
though his real name was in the prosecution's file and in four different places in the trial court record. Because he did no investigation,
Radolovich never learned that his client had a mental disability that
probably resulted from brain damage and that he had suffered a horrific childhood. In a hearing on Leonard's claim of ineffective assistance, Radolovich testified that he had tried six capital cases and had
headed an organized crime unit for a New York prosecutor's office.
Neither statement was true.[117]

A federal district court overturned the death sentence. "The result
of such ineffective assistance," the judge wrote, "is that the jury never
saw [Leonard] for whom he really was . . . an individual who, with
proper treatment, was a good candidate for rehabilitation, who had
loving family members who would stand by him and support him."[118]
The Sixth Circuit Court of Appeals agreed that Radolovich's performance was deficient. Nevertheless, it upheld the death sentence,
concluding that the outcome would not have been different even if
the lawyer had presented evidence of Leonard's likely brain damage,
childhood abuse, and other mitigating factors.[119] A governor of Kentucky later recognized Radolovich's incompetence and commuted
Leonard's sentence to life in prison without parole.[120]

Robert Holsey, whose lawyer drank a quart of vodka each night
during Holsey's trial and was soon to be convicted and disbarred for
stealing his clients' money, had his death sentence overturned by a
Georgia trial judge because "his trial lawyers had rendered ineffective
evidence . . . in regard to mitigating circumstances evidence about
his limited intelligence and his troubled, abusive childhood." However, the Georgia Supreme Court reinstated the death sentence, hold-

ing that Holsey had not shown that the outcome would have been different if he had been competently represented. A federal appellate court upheld the death sentence.[121] Georgia executed Robert Holsey in 2014.

Courts upheld the death sentence imposed on Jesus Romero even though his lawyer introduced no evidence at the penalty phase and argued to the jury: "You are an extremely intelligent jury. You've got that man's life in your hands. You can take it or not. That's all I have to say."[122] Courts also held that Ricky Drayton had not been prejudiced when his lawyer said to the jury, "You want to sentence him to death, O.K."[123] Both Romero and Drayton were executed.

The Sixth Amendment provides for the assistance of counsel *at trial*. A person convicted at a trial because of an incompetent lawyer can seek to vindicate the right to counsel and overturn that conviction only on a direct appeal or in state post-conviction and federal habeas corpus proceedings. But to do that, he needs the assistance of a new lawyer—whom he may be unable to obtain.

The same day it decided that Clarence Earl Gideon had a right to a lawyer at trial, the Supreme Court held that two people convicted in a California trial court had a right to counsel for an initial appeal because it was unfair that "the rich man can require the court to listen to argument of counsel before deciding on the merits, but a poor man cannot."[124] A decade later, however, after President Richard Nixon's four appointments to the Court, the Court decided that providing lawyers for further stages of review would be too much justice. Claude Moffitt was convicted of forgery in North Carolina. He was provided a lawyer at his trial and for an appeal to the North Carolina Court of Appeals. But he was denied a lawyer to petition the North Carolina Supreme Court and the U.S. Supreme Court for review. A federal appellate court agreed that Moffitt had a right to a lawyer, but the Supreme Court held, in an opinion by Justice William Rehnquist in 1974, that the state had no duty "to duplicate the legal arsenal that may be privately retained" by a person of means.[125]

In another opinion by Justice Rehnquist, the Court held in 1987 that there is no right to a lawyer in the state post-conviction process.[126] In 1989, the Court upheld Virginia's refusal to provide lawyers in post-conviction proceedings even for people under death sentence. In his opinion for the majority, Justice Rehnquist said, "Virginia may quite sensibly decide to concentrate the resources it devotes to providing attorneys for capital defendants at the trial and appellate stages of a capital proceeding."[127] He was apparently unaware that Virginia had decided not to concentrate its resources at either end of the criminal legal system. The average payment to court-appointed lawyers in capital cases in Virginia in 1985 was $784.56 per case.[128]

Most states provide lawyers to represent people under death sentence in post-conviction proceedings, and a few states provide lawyers in other kinds of cases as well. But that does not mean these lawyers are competent. Texas nominally requires the appointment of "competent counsel" in death penalty cases, but the Texas Court of Criminal Appeals has ruled this means only that the lawyer must be "'competent' at the time he is appointed," based on his "qualifications, experience, and abilities"; how the lawyer actually represents the client is irrelevant.[129] Federal law provides lawyers for people under death sentence to bring habeas corpus claims in the federal courts,[130] and a few people are represented by public interest organizations and volunteer lawyers—primarily those facing the death sentence or with viable claims of innocence. The vast majority of people in prison, however, have no right to a lawyer for state post-conviction or federal habeas corpus proceedings.

Theoretically, people convicted of crimes can write and file their own petitions for post-conviction review. But most have no legal training; many are barely literate, some have major mental illnesses, and some are intellectually disabled. Exzavious Gibson was a Georgia

death row inmate with an IQ in the 80s. He was taken to court for a
hearing on whether his court-appointed lawyer had represented him
competently at trial. But Gibson had no lawyer at the hearing. This is
what happened when he was given the opportunity to cross-examine
his former lawyer:

> **The Court:** Mr. Gibson, would you like to ask Mr. Mullis
>   any questions?
> **Gibson:** I don't have any counsel.
> **The Court:** I understand that, but I am asking, can you tell
>   me yes or no whether you want to ask him any questions
>   or not?
> **Gibson:** I'm not my own counsel.
> **The Court:** I'm sorry, sir, I didn't understand you.
> **Gibson:** I'm not my own counsel.
> **The Court:** I understand, but do you want, do you, individu-
>   ally, want to ask him anything?
> **Gibson:** I don't know.
> **The Court:** Okay, sir. Okay, thank you, Mr. Mullis, you can
>   go down.[131]

Gibson tendered no evidence, examined no witnesses, and made no
objections. The judge denied Gibson relief and the Georgia Supreme
Court upheld the denial, ruling that Gibson had no right to a lawyer
at the hearing.[132]

"A Procedural Maze of Its Own Creation"

While setting a very low bar for what constitutes "effective representation" by a lawyer, the Supreme Court established very strict technical requirements that lawyers must satisfy in order to raise issues
on appeal or in post-conviction proceedings. At John Sykes's trial
for third-degree murder in Florida, his lawyer did not object when

the prosecution introduced his earlier confession into evidence, and therefore the court did not hold a hearing on whether the admission was made voluntarily and in compliance with the warnings required by *Miranda v. Arizona*. Two federal courts ruled that Sykes was entitled to such a hearing, but, in *Wainwright v. Sykes*, the Supreme Court in an opinion by Justice Rehnquist held that the federal courts could not consider whether the confession was legally obtained because Florida's "contemporaneous objection" rule required the lawyer to object when the statement was introduced.[133]

Failing to object is one of the most common errors made by lawyers in trial courts. Whatever the issue—whether a confession was involuntary, whether a judge correctly instructed the jury, or whether the prosecutor made impermissible arguments—it will never be reviewed if the defense attorney does not object. The objection "preserves" the issue. Cases decided after *Wainwright v. Sykes* established additional, virtually impenetrable barriers to review if a lawyer failed to comply with a technical rule. A lawyer's mistake or negligence does not excuse failure to preserve an issue. A lawyer may choose not to assert a right because it is without merit under existing law at the time; but if that right is later recognized by the courts, the lawyer's failure to preserve the issue still bars the defendant from raising it on appeal.

Michael Smith was sentenced to death in Virginia. On appeal to the Virginia Supreme Court, his lawyers did not argue that the testimony of a psychiatrist at his trial violated his constitutional rights—because the Virginia Supreme Court had rejected the argument in another case. Lawyers are taught not to raise issues that have no merit. Three years after Smith's appeal, however, the U.S. Supreme Court held in a Texas case that the admission of a psychiatrist's testimony could violate the constitutional rights of a defendant. Smith's lawyers petitioned in federal court for relief based on the new decision. The U.S. Supreme Court held, by a vote of 5–4, that because his lawyer had acted reasonably in not presenting the issue to the Virginia Supreme

Court, it could not be considered by the federal courts.[134] In dissent, Justice John Paul Stevens pointed out that "the record . . . unquestionably demonstrates that [Smith's] constitutional claim is meritorious, and that there is significant risk that he will be put to death because his constitutional rights were violated." The Court, Justice Stevens said, "has lost its way in a procedural maze of its own creation."[135] Because he had a lawyer who did exactly what a lawyer is supposed to, Smith was put to death.

Roger Keith Coleman was also sentenced to death in Virginia. His state post-conviction lawyer filed the notice that he would be appealing three days late. The Supreme Court, citing "the respect that federal courts owe the States and the States' procedural rules," held that the federal courts could not consider the issues raised by Coleman because the Virginia Supreme Court had refused to consider them after the notice was filed late.[136] Justice Blackmun, in dissent, called the Court's decision a continuation of its "crusade to erect petty procedural barriers" that were "creating a Byzantine morass of arbitrary, unnecessary, and unjustifiable impediments to the vindication of federal rights."[137] The Supreme Court also held that Coleman could not claim that his lawyers were ineffective in missing the deadline because he had no right to a lawyer at that stage of the process. Instead, the Court held that the lawyers were Coleman's "agents" and he was bound by what they did.[138] Coleman and others like him have no choice but to take whatever lawyer is assigned to them, yet any malpractice by the lawyer is attributed to the client.

The Court has been very strict in penalizing people for mistakes made by their lawyers—even when their lawyers have been misled. A federal judge mistakenly gave Keith Bowles's lawyer seventeen days to file a notice of appeal after denying his petition for habeas corpus; a statute and court rule allowed only fourteen days. The lawyer filed a notice of appeal on the sixteenth day. Attorneys for the state moved to dismiss the appeal because it was beyond the fourteen days allowed. The Supreme Court held that no exceptions were allowed to the fourteen-day limit. Justice David Souter argued in dissent, "It is intolerable for the judicial system to treat people this way, and there is not even a technical justification for condoning this bait and switch."[139]

In *Wainwright v. Sykes*, Justice Rehnquist claimed that a rule requiring defense lawyers to recognize and challenge constitutional errors immediately would result in a trial "as free of error as possible."[140] He ignored the fact that this rule encourages prosecutors to commit errors such as introducing irrelevant or improper evidence, misstating the law, making impermissible arguments to the jury, or standing by silently when a judge makes an error. A prosecutor may plan ahead of time to make an improper argument. If the defense lawyer—caught by surprise—objects in the few seconds she has, the judge may uphold the objection, but if the lawyer fails to object, the prosecutor will get away with it and there will be no appellate review because there was no objection. The California Supreme Court condemned a prosecutor in one case for improperly arguing that a defendant was a "killing machine" and may have killed other people, but allowed the conviction to stand because the defense lawyer did not object.[141]

Although people convicted at trial can lose the ability to contest their convictions if their lawyers fail to object or preserve an issue, those failures themselves—no matter how crucial—are seldom found to constitute ineffective assistance of counsel. The result is that people convicted or even sentenced to death because of their attorneys' mistakes have no recourse. After the Mississippi Supreme Court refused to consider issues of prosecutorial misconduct in the case of Alvin Hill because his lawyer did not object to them, the same court rejected in a single paragraph a claim that counsel was ineffective. The dissent argued, "Where two clear cut reversible errors were not available on direct appeal to a condemned defendant solely because his lawyer goofed, that would seem to make a prima facie case for ineffective assistance of counsel."[142]

Because of these legal rules, a person's life or liberty may depend upon whether he is assigned a good or a bad lawyer. For example, two defendants were sentenced to death for the same crime in separate trials a few weeks apart in the same Georgia county. Lawyers for one challenged the procedure by which the jury pool was constituted, saying that it produced a pool that did not represent a fair cross section of the community; lawyers for the other did not. A federal court later held that the procedure was unconstitutional and granted a new trial to the first defendant, who was resentenced to life imprisonment. The court refused to address the issue in the case of the other defendant because his lawyers did not raise it before trial, and the defendant was executed.[143] Switching the lawyers for the two defendants would have changed the outcome in the two cases—crucially, which person was executed.

The Supreme Court has said that there is "no inequity in requiring [a defendant] to bear the risk of attorney error that results in a procedural default."[144] However, as Justice Hugo Black wrote, dissenting in a case that was dismissed because of a lawyer's error, it is "contrary to the most fundamental ideas of fairness and justice" to punish a client, who "was simply trusting his lawyer to take care of his case as clients generally do," for the errors of the lawyer.[145] Justice would be achieved by placing the responsibility for preventing errors on the party that commits or benefits from them.[146] But while courts punish the clients of incompetent lawyers, the lawyers themselves almost always get away unscathed.[147]

Obtaining a Full Measure of Justice

The Supreme Court left the right to counsel to state and local governments, which generally see little reason to expend resources on behalf of poor people, let alone poor criminal defendants. As Attorney General Robert F. Kennedy said in 1963, "The poor man charged with crime has no lobby."[148] Even in the rare case when a court finds that someone's right to counsel was violated, there are usually no consequences for the governmental entity that failed to provide the funding and public defender programs necessary to ensure proper representation, the judge who appointed an incompetent lawyer, or the appointed lawyer.

As a result, many of the major players in the criminal legal system like things just the way they are. If everyone accused of a crime really had the benefit of legal assistance, the "meet 'em and plead 'em" system would grind to a halt. People accused of crimes would be treated as individuals. There would, on occasion, be hearings on legal issues and trials in more cases. This would take more time and more resources. Fewer people would be convicted.

Prosecutors take advantage of incompetent lawyers foisted upon the poor. They exploit the ineptness of defense counsel to win convictions at trial and prevent courts from addressing constitutional violations, while simultaneously arguing that even the most outrageously incompetent lawyers satisfy the right to counsel. When their convictions have been reversed by courts, prosecutors have argued for stricter enforcement of procedural rules, not better counsel to avoid unconstitutional trials in the first place.

Harold Clarke, chief justice of the Georgia Supreme Court, observed with regard to the right to counsel in 1993, "We set our sights on the embarrassing target of mediocrity. I guess that means about halfway. And that raises a question. Are we willing to put up with halfway justice? To my way of thinking, one-half justice must mean one-half injustice, and one-half injustice is no justice at all."[149]

However, there are examples throughout the country of what is required to ensure competent representation for people accused of crimes. First, there must be a structure in place, centered on public defender offices, to ensure that lawyers, investigators, social workers, and support staff are available and that limited resources are used as effectively as possible. Good public defender programs recruit lawyers dedicated to criminal defense and provide training and supervision to ensure their competence. They have units dedicated to areas of specialization such as capital and other complex cases, appeals, and representation of children and the mentally ill.

A study found that people represented by the Defender Association of Philadelphia had lower conviction rates and a much lower probability of receiving a life sentence than defendants with appointed counsel. The Harris County Public Defender was similarly found to produce better outcomes for clients than private, court-appointed lawyers. A study of felony cases across the United States found that defendants with public defenders and those who hired their own attorneys had similar outcomes, but those with assigned counsel were more likely to be convicted and more likely to be sent to prison.[150] Public defenders have also made a huge difference in death penalty cases. Colorado, Georgia, North Carolina, South Carolina, Virginia, and other states have created capital units within their state public defender systems. These dedicated units have helped bring about a steep decline in the number of death sentences imposed—from around 290 a year in the 1990s to around 35 a year between 2016 and 2020. In 2004, when it created capital defender offices, Virginia was second only to Texas in the number of executions since the 1970s. Between 2011 and 2021, Virginia courts did not impose any death sentences. Virginia repealed its death penalty law in 2021.[151]

Second, public defense programs must be independent of the executive and judicial branches. Public defenders should be accountable to a board of trustees appointed by different officials so that no one person controls the board. For example, the North Carolina Commission on Indigent Defense Services includes one person appointed by the chief justice of the state supreme court, one appointed by the governor, two appointed by the legislature, and one each appointed by the state bar association, the public defender association, the Academy of Trial Lawyers, the Association of Black Lawyers, and the Association of Women Lawyers.[152] The public defenders in Missouri were able to challenge their excessive caseloads in the state courts because they were governed by an independent commission.[153] The Defender Association of Philadelphia, an independent nonprofit organization, was able to bring suits challenging bail practices and the detention of people accused of probation violations.[154] In jurisdictions without public defender offices, lawyers should be appointed not by judges but by an independent entity, such as the Office of Assigned Counsel in San Diego.

Third, lawyers representing the poor, whether they are in public defender offices or in private practice, must be trained and supervised. Public defender offices in Colorado, Kentucky, and elsewhere have developed outstanding programs coordinated by full-time training directors. They have initial and ongoing programs to ensure that public defenders and attorneys in private practice who accept appointments to criminal cases know of developments in the law, science, and other important areas.

Fourth, all of this requires money. Public defender programs must have the resources to hire enough lawyers, investigators, social workers, and other staff so that they have manageable caseloads and can represent all their clients effectively and ethically. Public defenders should be paid salaries corresponding to those of people working for the prosecution. Appointed lawyers must be paid reasonable, per-hour fees for themselves and for their investigators. They must also have resources to retain the experts needed to evaluate the prosecution's forensic experts in areas such as ballistic, hair, fingerprint, and DNA evidence, assess their clients' mental health and level of intellectual ability, and otherwise assist in the preparation and presentation of the defense.

This kind of justice is not beyond the reach of our society. Governments amply fund prosecutors' offices and law enforcement agencies. And some have established and funded very good public defender programs. The Public Defender Service for the District of Columbia has long provided exemplary representation of poor people—in part because of its outstanding training program, reasonable caseloads, supervision of its attorneys, and compensation comparable to that paid to federal prosecutors. The Bronx Defenders and other public defender offices have shown the value of a holistic defense of clients in which public defenders work in interdisciplinary teams to address both the immediate case and the client's underlying life circumstances.[155] There are many other examples.

The people who staff those offices, as well as many others who receive court appointments or work in public interest law offices, are the people who see that the right to counsel is realized in many cases. As a result of their efforts, some people accused of crimes receive professional advice and zealous advocacy through what is to them the strange and foreign land of the criminal courts. Because of them, some innocent people avoid conviction; some troubled youths are diverted to drug, alcohol, mental health, job training, and other programs instead of prisons; some people who were wrongfully convicted obtain their release; and some people live instead of being put to death by the government. Their example should prompt legislatures and courts to take their eyes off the embarrassing target of mediocrity and take aim at a full measure of justice.

4

Judges and the Politics of Crime

Dangerous precedents occur in dangerous times. It then becomes the duty of the judiciary calmly to poise the scales of justice, . . . undisturbed by the clamor of the multitude.

—Judge William Cranch, 1807[1]

One's right to life, liberty, and property, to free speech, a free press, freedom of worship and assembly, and other fundamental rights may not be submitted to vote; they depend on the outcome of no elections.

—United States Supreme Court, West Virginia State Board of Education v. Barnette *(1943)*[2]

After the U.S. Supreme Court overturned the convictions and death sentences of the Scottsboro Boys in *Powell v. Alabama* in 1932—establishing the right to counsel for defendants facing capital charges—the cases returned to a trial court in rural Alabama. Haywood Patterson was the first defendant to be retried. In 1933, an all-white jury found him guilty and sentenced him to death. However, Judge James Edwin Horton overturned the conviction, ruling that it was not supported by the evidence. The next year, Horton—who had won reelection unopposed in 1928—was voted out of office.[3]

Six decades later, in 1993, the Texas Court of Criminal Appeals—

the state's highest court for all criminal cases—reversed the conviction in a particularly notorious capital case, *Rodriguez v. State*.[4] In response, a former chair of the state Republican Party called for Republicans to take over the court. The next year, Stephen W. Mansfield ran against the author of the *Rodriguez* decision, Charles F. Campbell. Mansfield promised to expand use of the death penalty, make it easier to uphold convictions, and sanction attorneys who file "frivolous appeals especially in death penalty cases." During the campaign, it was revealed that Mansfield had been fined for practicing law without a license in Florida, had lied about where he was born and the amount of time he had spent in Texas, and had claimed extensive experience in criminal law though he had very little.[5] Yet Mansfield won. In the same year, Sharon Keller won a seat on the same court promising to apply "the perspective of a prosecutor" as a judge.[6] By 1999, the Court of Criminal Appeals was entirely filled with Republicans—a complete reversal from only six years before.[7] In 2000, Keller was elected presiding judge of the court, boasting that she had written "more capital murder opinions—43—than any judge during [her] tenure."[8]

After the Republican takeover, the Court of Criminal Appeals became renowned for its willingness to overlook violations of defendants' constitutional rights and for its seemingly single-minded dedication to executing people as quickly as possible. A 2004 article in *Texas Monthly* found the Court "disregarded exculpatory DNA evidence, threats of torture, bad lawyering, and in some cases, all common sense to uphold convictions in keeping with its tough-on-crime philosophy."[9]

In 1998, the Court, in an opinion by Keller, refused even to allow a hearing on whether Roy Criner was innocent of aggravated sexual assault after two DNA tests established that semen recovered from the victim did not come from him. Criner had been sentenced to ninety-nine years. Keller wrote, "The DNA evidence shows merely that the victim had sexual relations with someone other than [Criner] at a time relatively near her death," and speculated that Criner could have worn a condom or failed to ejaculate. In a 2000 interview, Keller acknowledged that Criner might be innocent, but argued that he had not proven it and described the victim as "promiscuous." Dissenting judge Tom Price said the case made the court a "national laughingstock."[10] After another DNA test of a cigarette butt found at the scene provided further evidence of Criner's innocence, the trial judge, prosecutor, and sheriff all recommended that Criner be pardoned. The Texas Board of Pardons and Paroles, notoriously reluctant to favor such requests, voted unanimously to recommend a pardon, which was granted by Governor George W. Bush.[11]

The new Republican majority on the Court of Criminal Appeals also assigned incompetent lawyers to represent people sentenced to death, as discussed in the previous chapter, and even insisted that they had received adequate representation. For Ricky Kerr's post-conviction proceedings, the Court gave him a lawyer who filed a perfunctory, six-page document that did not challenge Kerr's conviction and death sentence because, as the lawyer later admitted, he did not realize that such challenges were the purpose of a post-conviction petition. After the Court denied Kerr's request for a new lawyer and the trial judge set an execution date, James Marcus of the nonprofit Texas Defender Service filed a real post-conviction petition and requested a stay of execution. Even though prosecutors did not object, the stay was denied. Judge Morris Overstreet, dissenting, described the majority's review of the case as a "farce" and warned that the Court would have "blood on its hands" if Kerr were executed.[12] Federal Judge Orlando Garcia granted a stay and criticized the Court of Criminal Appeals' "cynical and reprehensible attempt to expedite [the] execution at the expense of all semblance of fairness and integrity."[13] Marcus sought post-conviction relief for Kerr a second time, and the Court of Criminal Appeals allowed it to proceed—over Keller's dissent—claiming that his original lawyer "was competent and qualified" when appointed and had made "an innocent mistake."[14] The case was sent back to the trial court, where the judge determined that Kerr's original trial lawyers completely failed to prepare for the punishment phase of the trial and recommended that his death sentence be set aside. The Court of Criminal Appeals vacated the death sentence; Keller again dissented.[15]

In an adversary system, the judge is supposed to be a neutral arbiter, concerned only with the achievement of justice. However, judges are elected in many states and, in recent decades, elections for judgeships have increasingly become expensive campaigns dominated by claims about who can be toughest on crime. These political pressures undermine the pursuit of justice in multiple ways. Judges who uphold the law, as they are required to do, have been voted out of office. Some judges make rulings with an eye on their upcoming elections and what could be used against them in a campaign. Judicial elections favor former prosecutors, many of whom have what Sharon Keller promised and delivered: "the perspective of a prosecutor." Some judges even outsource the core judicial function of writing opinions and orders to the prosecution, signing documents that were drafted by prosecutors without the slightest change. The result is a playing field that is heavily tilted against people accused of crimes, especially in the most high-profile cases.

How Judges Become Judges

The independence and impartiality of the judiciary have been a central theme in the United States since the founding of the nation. The indictment of King George III in the Declaration of Independence includes the charge, "He has made Judges dependent on his Will alone, for the tenure of their offices, and the amount and payment of their salaries."[16] In *Tumey v. Ohio* in 1927, the U.S. Supreme Court overturned a system in which a mayor sat in judgment of alleged violators of a Prohibition ordinance—but was not paid unless he convicted and fined at least some of the defendants. The Court held, "Every procedure which would offer a possible temptation to the average man as a judge to forget the burden of proof required to convict the defendant, or which might lead him not to hold the balance nice, clear, and true between the state and the accused denies the latter due process of law."[17]

Impartiality requires that judges be insulated from political pressures. As Justice John Paul Stevens said at a convention of the American Bar Association in 1996, quoting Florida Supreme Court Justice Ben Overton, it "was never contemplated that the individual who has to protect our individual rights would have to consider what decision would produce the most votes."[18] Judicial impartiality is also demanded by the American Bar Association's Model Code of Judicial Conduct, which states that "a judge shall not be swayed by public clamor or fear of criticism," and requires that a judge "disqualify himself or herself in any proceeding in which the judge's impartiality might reasonably be questioned"—including situations where one of the parties has made a significant campaign contribution to the judge, or where the judge "has made a public statement . . . that commits or appears to commit the judge to reach a particular result." The code also says that a candidate for judge may not, "in connection with cases, controversies, or issues that are likely to come before the court, make pledges, promises or commitments that are inconsistent with the impartial performance" of a judge's duties.[19]

Judges have not always been subject to the ballot box. After the American Revolutionary War, judges in all thirteen states were selected either by the governor or by the state legislature and held office so long as they maintained "good behavior," typically as determined by the legislature; they could not be removed simply because their rulings were unpopular. Direct election of judges was largely a product of the period of populist Jacksonian democracy and was motivated by the belief that the judiciary was too closely allied with property owners.[20] By the Civil War, two-thirds of the states had established elected judiciaries, a pattern followed by most new states thereafter. Concerns that elections made it possible for political party machines to control judges led to reforms in a few states, such as appointment of judges by the governor from a list recommended by a judicial selection committee, with a retention election held after the judge's initial term. Still, elections remain the most common means of selecting judges. As of 2015, trial judges were elected by popular vote in twenty-nine states and parts of four others; in another six states, they were subject to retention elections at the end of each term in office.[21] Twenty-two states used elections to select judges for their state supreme courts, and another sixteen required retention elections even for their highest courts.

Elections for judgeships had usually remained relatively sleepy affairs until recent decades. Judicial elections received greater attention beginning in the 1980s because of two major forces: the realignment of the American political system and the national obsession with crime that peaked in the 1990s. As the perception of a violent crime wave took hold in the American imagination, politicians found that favoring the death penalty was an easy way to demonstrate their toughness on crime. Florida governor Bob Graham showed that, as one observer noted, "nothing [sells] on the campaign trail like promises to speed up the death penalty." When running for reelection in 1982 and when campaigning for the Senate in 1986, Graham stepped up the number of death warrants he signed as governor, even though federal courts were then granting automatic stays of execution.[22]

In 1988, the George H.W. Bush presidential campaign repeatedly told the story of Willie Horton, a Black convicted murderer who had been allowed out of prison under a furlough program in Massachusetts while Bush's opponent, Michael Dukakis, was governor. After his release, Horton tortured a white man and raped his white fiancée. "By the time we're finished," Bush's campaign manager Lee Atwater said, "they're going to wonder whether Willie Horton is Dukakis's running mate."[23] Four years later, determined to avoid Dukakis's fate, Bill Clinton scheduled the execution of Ricky Ray Rector, a brain-damaged Black man who had been sentenced to death by an all-white jury, shortly before the New Hampshire primary—and then flew back to Arkansas to reject the final clemency petition in person.[24] In 1994, George W. Bush defeated Texas governor Ann Richards (who had overseen forty-five executions in four years), arguing that the state should execute even more people, more quickly. And it did—in his six years as governor, Texas carried out 152 executions. In New York, longtime governor and death penalty opponent Mario Cuomo was defeated by George Pataki, who promised to reinstate capital punishment (which he did once in office).[25]

In this political climate, judicial elections also became contests over who could be the toughest on crime and the most determined to execute people. In 1986, California governor George Deukme-jian announced his opposition to the retention of Rose Bird, chief justice of the California Supreme Court, and two other justices on the Court because of their votes to overturn death sentences. All three were voted off the Court after a campaign dominated by the issue of the death penalty, allowing Deukmejian to appoint their replacements.[26] In the following years, the California Supreme Court affirmed nearly 97 percent of the capital cases it reviewed; its readiness to find that errors at trial in capital cases were harmless reflected what one observer called a "desire to carry out the death penalty."[27]

In Texas, as described earlier, judicial elections in the mid-1990s transformed the Court of Criminal Appeals, turning it into a virtual rubber stamp for convictions and death sentences. In Mississippi, Justice Joel Blass lost his seat on the state's supreme court in 1990 to a challenger who accused him of being soft on crime and promised to be a "tough judge for tough times." Two years later, Justice James Robertson lost his seat on the court to a "law and order candidate" who attacked him for, among other things, stating the simple fact that the U.S. Supreme Court had ruled that the death penalty could not be imposed for rape where there was no loss of life.[28]

Adopting a tough-on-crime image by advocating for the death penalty became a winning strategy in elections for president, governor, and other positions. In judicial elections, where voters are generally less informed about the candidates and may have little idea of the nature of a judge's job, it is comparatively easy to demonize a judge for a small number of decisions—or even a single decision—that can be portrayed as "pro-criminal." Constitutional rights are dismissed as mere "technicalities." Attack advertisements appeal to voters' fear of violent crime by highlighting horrific acts where the perpetrator escaped execution because of some action that could somehow be traced to that judge.

In 1996, opponents of Tennessee Supreme Court Justice Penny White made her election a referendum on whether Richard Odom should be put to death; the Court had vacated his death sentence while upholding his conviction. A mailer from the Tennessee Conservative Union described in detail Odom's crime—a gruesome rape-murder of an elderly woman—and claimed that Justice White was the reason that he would not be executed. A state Republican Party mailer read: "Richard Odom was convicted of repeatedly raping and stabbing to death a 78 year old Memphis woman. However, Penny White felt the crime wasn't heinous enough for the death penalty—so she struck it down." These advertisements neglected to mention that Odom's sentence was vacated because of a constitutional violation in the trial court, that the entire Tennessee Supreme Court had voted to overturn the sentence, and that Odom could be sentenced to death again (as indeed occurred).[29] White was voted off the Court.

In 2008, Michael Gableman launched a television attack ad against Wisconsin Supreme Court Justice Louis Butler, which included side-by-side images of Justice Butler and child molester Reuben Lee

Mitchell. The faces of Butler and Mitchell, both of whom are Black, overlap at the end of the ad. "Butler found a loophole," the advertisement said. "Mitchell went on to molest another child. Can Wisconsin families feel safe with Louis Butler on the Supreme Court?"[30] The advertisement was misleading in multiple ways: Butler had not voted to free Mitchell as a judge; instead, Butler's connection to Mitchell was that he had represented him as his public defender twenty years earlier—which meant he had a responsibility to present on appeal any legal grounds to overturn his conviction. And the Wisconsin Supreme Court ruled that the error raised by Butler was harmless and affirmed Mitchell's conviction, so Mitchell was not released at the time; he served his entire sentence and only then was released and committed another crime. Nevertheless, Butler lost the election.

The politicization of judicial elections reflected a growing perception that rulings by judges were to be decided by popular vote, not the law. Politicians unabashedly attempted to intimidate judges by threatening their reelection prospects. Shortly after Penny White's defeat, Tennessee governor Don Sundquist said, "Should a judge look over his shoulder about whether they're going to be thrown out of office? I hope so."[31]

Given the increasing polarization of American politics, power over the judiciary became a high-priority objective for parties and interest groups. Decades of attacks on judges eroded the once-conventional understanding of the judiciary as a neutral body. As early as 1971, future Supreme Court justice Lewis Powell authored a memo for the U.S. Chamber of Commerce arguing that "the judiciary may be the most important instrument for social, economic and political change," and calling for business groups to compete more actively in the legal realm.[32] Politicians came to see elections for judges as an easy way to harness the power of the judiciary for partisan or ideological purposes. As the president of the Ohio State Bar said after a particularly expensive state supreme court election, "The people with money to spend who are affected by Court decisions have reached the conclusion that it's a lot cheaper to buy a judge than a governor or an entire legislature and he can probably do a lot more for you."[33]

The people with money to spend may not particularly care about the fates of criminal defendants—often they are business owners and corporations more concerned with civil litigation and government regulation. But getting voters to care about, say, the amount of punitive damages imposed in a case is much more difficult than getting them to care about whether or not people charged with gruesome crimes are put to death. So special interests have taken to using crime tactically in judicial elections to achieve other ends. In 2013 and 2014, for example, more than half of all television advertisements in state supreme court races—and more than four-fifths of all negative ads—addressed whether candidates were tough on crime.[34]

In 2004, Justice Warren McGraw, a Democrat, was up for reelection to the West Virginia Supreme Court of Appeals against Republican challenger Brent Benjamin. A well-financed campaign ruthlessly attacked McGraw, accusing him of being soft on crime. One organization ran advertisements criticizing the justice for joining a decision requiring a trial judge to grant probation to a man who had been convicted of molesting, at the age of fourteen, his younger half-brother. Don Blankenship, the CEO of Massey Energy, a coal company, contributed $1.7 million of $2.5 million raised by the organization. Blankenship also spent another $500,000 on independent expenditures to defeat McGraw. Blankenship had a personal interest in the election because his company, Massey Energy, had an appeal pending in the Court of an award by a jury of $50 million in damages against it.[35] Benjamin won by fewer than fifty thousand votes. Once on the Court, Benjamin twice declined to recuse himself from the case and cast a deciding vote to overturn the verdict against Massey. (The U.S.

Supreme Court eventually ruled that Benjamin should have recused himself because of Blankenship's support.)[36]

In 2014, American Freedom Builders—an organization dedicated to "limited government and free market economic solutions"— backed Ohio Supreme Court Justice Judith French, who was running for reelection. The organization ran an ad praising her for upholding convictions or severe sentences for "a murderer who shot his girlfriend in front of her 3-year-old daughter," "a man who repeatedly raped his 8-year-old daughter," and "a psychopath who murdered and burned the bodies of two innocent girls." In October, French introduced Ohio governor John Kasich, who was also running for reelection, at a Republican Party rally. "I am a Republican and you should vote for me," she said. "Whatever the governor does, whatever your state representative, your state senator does, whatever they do, we are the ones that will decide whether it is constitutional, we decide whether it's lawful. . . . So, forget all those other votes if you don't keep the Ohio Supreme Court conservative."[37]

In 2010, business groups including the U.S. Chamber of Commerce, the National Association of Manufacturers, and the American Tort Reform Association targeted Thomas Kilbride, chief justice of the Illinois Supreme Court, because he had been part of a court majority that overturned a law limiting damage awards for medical malpractice. However, the campaign against Kilbride was not about malpractice awards. One television advertisement featured three actors wearing orange jumpsuits and posing as convicted criminals who graphically described the violent crimes they supposedly had committed. Two of the actors said, "Kilbride sided with us over law enforcement or victims." Kilbride raised more than $2.8 million— half from the state Democratic Party, with major contributions from labor groups. His campaign ran advertisements praising him as a "tough" judge and highlighting his support from law enforcement.[38] He was retained in 2010. Ten years later, however, billionaires and dark money groups with Republican, conservative, and corporate ties spent $6.2 million opposing Kilbride's retention. Hedge fund owner Ken Griffin contributed $4.5 million, and a packing materials magnate contributed $1 million. Despite spending $4.6 million and running TV advertisements showing him fist-bumping a group of law enforcement officers and claiming he was "backed by the blue," Kilbride received 56.5 percent of the vote, less than the 60 percent necessary for retention.[39]

Regardless of who wins, these expensive elections damage the credibility of the courts. In 2006, Sue Bell Cobb won an election to become chief justice of the Alabama Supreme Court, boasting that she had "locked up murderers and child abusers." She and her opponent together spent more than $8 million.[40] After she retired, she wrote an article titled "I Was Alabama's Top Judge. I'm Ashamed by What I Had to Do to Get There," criticizing an electoral system that forces candidates to raise money from lawyers who will appear before them and business groups that have stakes in pending cases. "Donors want clarity, certainty even, that the judicial candidates they support view the world as they do and will rule accordingly," she wrote. "They want to know that the investments they make by donating money to a candidate will yield favorable results."[41]

"I never felt so much like a hooker down by the bus station in any race I've ever been in as I did in a judicial race," said Justice Paul E. Pfeifer, a Republican elected to the Ohio Supreme Court in 1992. A study of the court in 2006 found that its justices routinely sat on cases involving insurance companies, corporations, and labor and plaintiffs' lawyers after receiving campaign contributions from them. Justices often received contributions after a case of a contributor was argued before the court but before it was decided. Six of the ten justices in the study sided with their contributors more than 70 percent of the time.[42]

Judges who must stand for election are well aware of how the political landscape has changed in the past forty years. Even judges who want to follow the Constitution know the potential career costs of reversing a conviction or sentence. As Supreme Court Justice Byron White observed, "If a judge's ruling for the defendant . . . may determine his fate at the next election, even though his ruling was affirmed and is unquestionably right, constitutional protections would be subject to serious erosion."[43] This is particularly true in capital cases, given their susceptibility to being transformed into attack ads.

The Influence of Elections on Judicial Behavior

Not only do judicial elections select for judges who promise to be "tough on crime"; they also encourage judges to use criminal trials to their political advantage. As we have seen, some judges use the power of appointing defense lawyers to pay back their campaign contributors at the expense of defendants. Judges tend to use sentencing decisions to bolster their crime-fighting credentials when facing election. A study of more than 22,000 criminal cases in Pennsylvania in the 1990s found that elected judges handed down significantly harsher sentences as their elections drew nearer; on average, a sentence imposed shortly before Election Day was likely to be 24 to 37 percent longer than one near the beginning of a judge's term. Similarly, a study of sentencing decisions for serious crimes in Washington State between 1995 and 2006 found that, on average, a sentence given just before a contested reelection was almost seven months longer than one just after election.[44]

Judges have manipulated judicial proceedings to maximize public attention before an election. In 1993, Peter Bard was arrested and charged with murdering a popular deputy sheriff in Louisville, Kentucky, less than a week before an election. The judge to whom the case had been assigned announced that arraignment would be held immediately after the arrest, instead of the following week in accordance with the usual practice, and pressured Bard's public defender to let a different judge, Jim Shake, preside over the arraignment in a courtroom filled with television cameras—because, the judge said, "Jim's on the ballot Tuesday."[45]

Robert Austin was a lower court judge in Alabama running for a higher court on a law-and-order campaign. He stood to benefit from publicity he would receive from presiding over a capital case in the two weeks before the election. He denied a motion for a continuance by the defense attorney, who was suffering from a serious infection that was a complication of polio. He also denied motions to change venue because of pretrial publicity and to recuse himself because of his pending election. The denials were front-page news. The jury convicted the defendant and recommended the death penalty before Election Day. Austin won the election.[46]

The need to stay in the good graces of powerful allies can undermine elected judges' objectivity. In his 1996 reelection campaign, Nevada Supreme Court Justice Cliff Young "formed a highly-visible political alliance with the State's attorney general, who in numerous campaign advertisements publicly 'urged all Nevadans' to vote for Justice Young," in the words of another justice on the same court. Young "repeatedly published his appreciation for the attorney general's support."[47] The attorney general is not just any politician, but one who is regularly involved in litigation before the state supreme court.

Judges must also contend with the fact that elected district attorneys are often powerful politicians. While this may generally give them an incentive to favor the prosecution, it has a particularly pernicious influence in the context of jury selection. Under the Supreme Court's decision in Batson v. Kentucky, trial judges must decide whether the prosecution's use of peremptory strikes against people of color in jury selection is racially motivated.[48] A judge who rejects a prosecutor's proffered reason for striking a minority juror is essentially accusing her of both racism and lying—striking the juror because of race and then giving a pretextual reason for the strike. A judge who is wary of incurring the wrath of the district attorney will hesitate before rejecting the prosecutor's reasons.

Similarly, judges who are subject to the approval of their constituents may think twice before granting a change of venue when a defendant cannot receive a fair trial because of the sentiments of the local community. As the Mississippi Supreme Court has acknowledged, a judge who grants the change of venue "might be perceived as implying that a fair trial cannot be had among his or her constituents and neighbors"—a perception that could come back to hurt her at election time.[49]

After escaping from prison in Maryland, Wayne Coleman, George Dungee, and Billy and Carl Isaacs were charged with six murders in a small rural community in Georgia. The local media coverage included the local sheriff's public statements that he wanted to "pre-cook them several days, just keep them alive and let them punish," and an editorial that compared the defendants to rattlesnakes and rabid dogs. A local citizen who served as a juror testified that the opinion of "everybody" before the trial was "fry 'em, electrocute 'em."[50] The elected trial judge, faced with a choice between his community's urge for a quick and violent response to the crime and the defendants' constitutional rights, refused to grant a change of venue. The local juries returned guilty verdicts and death sentences for Coleman, Dungee, and Carl Isaacs. (Billy Isaacs testified against them in exchange for being spared the death penalty.) The elected Georgia Supreme Court upheld the convictions and sentences. However, a federal appellate court set aside the convictions because "highly prejudicial publicity had saturated and inflamed the community to the extent that there was overwhelming prejudice" against the defendants.[51]

In recent years, the influence of politics on judges' decisions has only become stronger as more money has paid for more attack ads. A study by the Center for American Progress found that large influxes of spending on judicial elections made judges significantly more likely to rule against criminal defendants. Joanna Shepherd and Michael Kang analyzed state supreme court decisions in criminal appeals and concluded, "The more TV ads aired during state supreme court judicial elections in a state, the less likely justices are to vote in favor of criminal defendants."[52] The evidence is overwhelming. Elections produce a judiciary that is often biased against criminal defendants, particularly in capital and other high-profile cases.

The Prosecutor-to-Judge Pipeline

Judicial elections make it more likely that judges will be former prosecutors who built their public profiles by aggressively prosecuting high-profile cases. Once elected, those judges sometimes maintain close relationships with the prosecutors they used to work with. In Georgia's Chattahoochee Judicial Circuit, three consecutive district attorneys became superior court judges after trying high-profile capital cases. As district attorney, Mullins Whisnant personally tried many of the ten capital cases his office prosecuted in 1976 and 1977, five of which involved Black defendants tried before all-white juries for murders of white victims. In his last capital prosecution—which involved a highly publicized rape, robbery, kidnapping, and murder of a white Methodist church organist by an African American—Whisnant made a highly improper plea to the jurors to join a "war on crime" and "send a message" by sentencing the defendant to death.[53]

After Whisnant became a judge in 1978, his chief assistant, William Smith, took over as district attorney. Smith personally prosecuted several capital cases, including the highly publicized trial of the "Silk Stocking Strangler," a Black man accused of murdering several elderly white women. When a federal court set aside a death sentence in another case because Smith's closing argument was a "dramatic appeal to gut emotion" that "has no place in a courtroom," Smith called a press conference to announce that he would seek death again in the retrial of the case. After a federal court vacated a death sentence in another case, Smith called a press conference to denounce the "sensationalism" and "emotionalism" of the reviewing court.[54]

After Smith became a judge in 1988, his chief assistant, Doug Pullen, succeeded him as district attorney. In 1995, after prosecuting eight capital cases, Pullen announced an interest in the next superior court opening. The same year, it was discovered that the relationship between the court and the district attorney's office was so close that prosecutors, not judges, had decided how new cases would be assigned to judges for the previous six years—funneling the more serious homicide and drug cases to Whisnant and Smith. Nevertheless, the governor appointed Pullen to the bench, where he served until 2011 before resigning while being investigated for judicial misconduct.[55]

Once elected to the judiciary, some former prosecutors continue to prosecute from the bench. At the 1991 capital trial of Carl Wayne Buntion in Houston, Judge William Harmon, a former prosecutor, taped a photograph of the "hanging saloon" of Texas judge Roy Bean on the front of the bench with his name superimposed over Bean's, and said that he was doing "God's work" in seeing that Buntion would be executed. A U.S. district court found that Harmon also bullied the defense lawyers, met privately with prosecutors, pandered to the media, and "well before the presentation of evidence . . . decided that Buntion was guilty and should die." It set aside the conviction, but the Court of Appeals for the Fifth Circuit reversed and reinstated the conviction and death sentence. Texas executed Buntion in 2022.[56] While presiding over the capital case of a person he had previously prosecuted, Harmon responded to a suggestion that some death row inmates be transported to court by saying, "Could we arrange for a van to blow up the bus on the way down here?" In yet another capital case, Harmon allowed the victim's father to yell obscenities at the defendant in the presence of jurors and the press.[57]

Ronald D. Castille was an assistant district attorney in Philadelphia from 1971 to 1985 and district attorney from 1986 to 1991. In 1986, Castille authorized his assistants to seek the death penalty for Terrance Williams, who was accused of a murder in the commission of a robbery. Williams was convicted and sentenced to death.[58] In 1993, Castille won election to the Pennsylvania Supreme Court, boasting that he had sent forty-five people to death row while district attorney.

Almost three decades later, a trial court ordered the release of records that revealed that the assistant district attorney who prosecuted Williams had failed to disclose to his lawyers exculpatory evidence—that the murder was in response to sexual abuse and that a prosecutor had promised to write a letter to the parole board on behalf of the prosecution's key witness. The court ordered a new sentencing hearing. The prosecution appealed to the Pennsylvania Supreme Court. Lawyers for Williams moved that Castille, who was then chief justice, recuse himself because he had "personally authorized his Office to seek the death penalty" in the case. Castille denied the motion and, in 2014, voted with his fellow justices to reverse the trial court's order and reinstate the death sentence. He also issued a concurring opinion denouncing the "obstructionist anti-death penalty agenda" of Williams's attorneys from the Federal Community Defender Office and warned that they could turn court proceedings "into a circus where [they] are the ringmasters." In 2016, the U.S. Supreme Court held that Castille's involvement in the case gave rise to "an unacceptable risk of actual bias" and set aside the decision of the Pennsylvania Supreme Court.[59] The following year, the Pennsylvania Supreme Court, now without Castille (who had retired in 2014), affirmed the decision of the trial court setting aside the death penalty.[60] Williams was sentenced to life in prison.

Ghostwritten Orders

The alliance between elected judges and prosecutors can lead judges to outsource their core responsibilities to the prosecution. Many judges adopt, usually verbatim, judicial orders that were written by prosecutors. These are often long and detailed opinions containing extensive findings of credibility and other facts as well as legal analysis that are binding on later reviewing courts. Such ghostwritten orders are not the fair and objective findings of impartial judges but the arguments of the prosecution, containing one-sided and exaggerated "findings" prepared for strategic advantage. The Supreme Court and just about every other court has disapproved of ghostwritten orders, but they still uphold them as if they had been prepared by judges.[61]

A group of former Alabama judges and past state bar presidents reported that the wholesale adoption of orders written by prosecutors is the "routine practice of Alabama trial court judges" in capital post-conviction cases."[62] Alabama judges have signed ghostwritten orders despite dozens of typographical errors, and, in one case, a judge signed a proposed order over a misspelling of his own name.[63] In another case, an Alabama judge signed an eighty-nine-page "Proposed Memorandum Opinion" prepared by the state attorney general's office the day after receiving it. The judge did not even strike the word "Proposed" or make a single edit to the eighty-nine pages before signing it. A federal appellate judge said during argument in the case, "I don't believe for a second that that judge went through 89 pages in a day and then filed that as his own." Nonetheless, the court deferred to the findings in the ghostwritten opinion, as had the Alabama courts, in upholding the conviction and death sentence. In a footnote, the court merely took the "opportunity to once again strongly criticize the practice of trial courts' uncritical wholesale adoption of the proposed orders or opinions submitted by a prevailing party."[64] It is hard to imagine a more hollow criticism.

Courts in other states engage in the same practice.[65] Texas judge William Harmon resolved a habeas corpus case by signing thirty-five pages of findings of fact and conclusions of law that were "a verbatim adoption of the State's proposed findings," in the words of a federal court. In another case, after a Texas judge adopted the state's response as the court's findings and conclusions, the Court of Criminal Appeals upheld it six days later in a one-page order. A study of 211 Texas capital cases found that trial judges adopted the prosecutor's findings in 189 (90 percent) of the cases. And the Court of Criminal Appeals adopted those findings in 180 of 204 cases in which both the trial court findings and the Court of Criminal Appeals orders were available.[66]

In Georgia, after a hearing in the case of Lawrence Jefferson, the judge's law clerk asked the assistant attorney general for an order upholding Jefferson's conviction and death sentence. The resulting document was "spit out by the word processors at the state attorney general's office without even correcting spelling errors and other mistakes that originally appeared in the state's . . . reply brief" (the prosecutors' written argument). The draft order also discussed an affidavit of a witness that had not been submitted in Jefferson's case, but in another case. The judge signed the order, which was upheld by the Georgia Supreme Court. A federal court eventually set aside Jefferson's death sentence.[67]

The "findings of fact" contained in these ghostwritten orders often make it impossible for a reviewing court to overturn the conviction or sentence. Appellate courts accept and rely upon these findings unless the defendant proves that they are clearly erroneous, which effectively means that an appellate court must accept findings if they are plausible.[68] For example, an order prepared by an Alabama assistant attorney general and adopted by a judge concluded that Eugene Clemons was not intellectually disabled—which would have made him ineligible for the death penalty—by "finding" that he had been faking on every IQ test on which he scored below 70.[69]

Prepared orders consistently find that a lawyer's failure to present certain evidence did not constitute ineffective assistance of counsel because the lawyer made a strategic decision not to present that evidence. They also "find" that evidence that was not presented by the defense attorney would not have made a difference in the outcome of the case. In the case of Arthur Lee Jones, the order prepared by an assistant attorney general denied a claim of ineffective assistance by "finding" that the defense attorney's failure to give an opening statement, to put on any evidence about the defendant's life, or even to give a closing argument on the issue of penalty were all "strategic" decisions.[70] Jones was executed by Alabama in 1986. Even when a court-appointed lawyer admitted that it was "malpractice" for him not to consult with an expert about some of the issues in a case, the ghostwritten order did not mention the testimony or any of the other deficiencies in the lawyer's representation.[71]

A state judge signed four orders written by the prosecution to maintain the death sentence imposed on Cornelius Singleton, an intellectually limited Black man who was sentenced to death by an all-white jury in Mobile, Alabama. One denied Singleton's claim of racial discrimination by the prosecutors, who struck nine Black jurors to obtain an all-white jury, stating that the "Court knows from having presided over dozens of cases tried by the two prosecutors who tried the present case that they did not remove all black veniremen from the juries in all or even a majority of the cases they tried." That statement was simply not true; in the case of another Black man tried by an all-white jury in Mobile, local criminal defense attorneys testified that the district attorney's office had a practice of excluding Blacks from jury service. Singleton was executed in 1992. The same judge signed another forty-seven-page ghostwritten order without modification in 1990. That order rejected a claim of ineffective assistance of counsel; much of the language in the order also appeared in an order denying a similar claim in another case signed by another judge in a different part of the state.[72]

Overriding Life

For many years, judges in some states had an additional lever they could pull to show how tough they were: they could override jury sentences of life imprisonment and impose the death penalty. In the vast majority of states with the death penalty, a death sentence can be imposed only by a jury, which must be unanimous in most states. In the 1970s, however, Alabama, Florida, and Indiana gave the trial judge the power to override a jury's sentencing decision, in either direction: from death to life or from life to death. Delaware judges were granted the same power in 1991.

Judicial override was eliminated in Indiana by the state legislature in 2002 and in Delaware, Florida, and Alabama after its constitutionality was called into question by a 2016 U.S. Supreme Court case.[73] While it was in operation, however, it clearly demonstrated the influence of judicial elections. In Delaware, where judges are not elected, override worked almost exclusively in one direction: from death to life. In seventeen cases, the judge imposed a life sentence despite a jury's vote for death; only once did a judge override a jury's recommendation of life. In the three states with elected judges, however, the inverse happened. Between 1972 and 2011, judges in Florida overrode 166 jury recommendations of life imprisonment but only eighty-eight death recommendations. In one Florida case, the judge told the clerk of court before trial that once the "good, fair minded people" on the jury had "convict[ed] the son-of-a-bitch," he would sentence him to death. After the jury recommended a sentence of life imprisonment, the judge overrode it and imposed the death penalty. The Florida Supreme Court vacated the death sentence after the clerk disclosed the conversation over fifteen years after it occurred.[74] Indiana judges overrode ten recommendations of life imprisonment while overriding nine death recommendations.[75]

Alabama was the most extreme: judges overturned life sentences ninety-eight times and death sentences only nine times between 1976

and 2011. As of 2015, six people had been freed from death row
in Alabama after being exonerated; three were there only because
judges ignored jury recommendations of life and imposed the death
penalty. Not coincidentally, Alabama is a state where capital punishment plays a central role in judicial elections. A television ad for Judge
Ferrill McRae—who overrode jury recommendations of life more
than any other judge in the state—announced that he had "presided
over more than 9,000 cases, including some of the most heinous murder trials in our history," while listing the names of people whom he
had sentenced to death.[76] In 1995, Justice John Paul Stevens observed,
dissenting from a Supreme Court decision upholding judicial override in Alabama,

> The Framers of our Constitution knew from history and
> experience that it was necessary to protect . . . against
> judges too responsive to the voice of higher authority. . . .
> The higher authority to whom present-day capital judges
> may be too responsive is a political climate in which judges
> who covet higher office—or who merely wish to remain
> judges—must constantly profess their fealty to the death
> penalty. Alabama trial judges face partisan election every
> six years. The danger that they will bend to political pres-
> sures when pronouncing sentence in highly publicized cap-
> ital cases is the same danger confronted by judges beholden
> to King George III.[77]

Restricting Review by Federal Courts

Federal judges do not face elections; they have life tenure after being
appointed by the president and confirmed by the Senate. Habeas
corpus proceedings before federal judges have been essential in protecting constitutional rights that were ignored by state courts and
have resulted in many convictions being vacated after they had been

affirmed by state courts. However, federal judges are certainly not immune to politics. Congress has periodically passed laws seeking to curb the independence of federal judges. In addition, nominations to the Supreme Court and lower federal courts have increasingly been politicized, highlighted by public battles over Supreme Court nominations such as the refusal in 2016 of the Republican-controlled Senate to consider President Obama's nominee so that the next president—a Republican, they hoped—could fill the vacancy with a conservative and its rushed confirmation of Amy Coney Barrett near the end of the Trump administration. As the tenuous conservative majority on the Court in the 1990s and early 2000s has evolved into today's radical right-wing 6-3 majority, the ability of federal courts to protect the rights of defendants in criminal courts has been progressively restricted.

As discussed in the previous chapter, the Supreme Court has adopted a number of technical rules that often prevent federal courts from addressing legal issues, no matter how compelling. The ability of the federal courts to protect a defendant's constitutional rights was further restricted by the Antiterrorism and Effective Death Penalty Act, or AEDPA, passed at the height of law-and-order politics in 1996.[78] The act was largely intended to speed up federal habeas corpus proceedings brought by death row inmates. One provision established a one-year statute of limitations for federal habeas corpus petitions. As previously discussed, many lawyers assigned to represent people in capital cases missed the deadline, costing their clients any review by the federal courts.[79] The overwhelming majority of poor people convicted of crimes have no access to a lawyer and no way to file petitions within the deadline—or at all.

AEDPA's most draconian limitation is a requirement that federal courts show great deference to the decisions of state courts. A federal court may not grant habeas relief unless the state court's decision "was contrary to, or involved an unreasonable application of, clearly established Federal law, as determined by the Supreme Court of the United States."[80] The Supreme Court has held that federal courts must accept the legal conclusions of the state courts "so long as 'fair-minded jurists could disagree' on the correctness of the state court's decision."[81] The Court also added that, in cases challenging the effectiveness of counsel, federal courts should be "doubly deferential"—to the presumption that counsel rendered adequate assistance established in the Court's decision on ineffectiveness, *Strickland v. Washington*, and to the decisions of state courts as required by AEDPA.[82]

The Supreme Court and AEDPA have severely restricted when a federal court may hold a hearing to consider evidence of a constitutional violation. The Court reversed decisions by a federal district court judge and court of appeals that Barry Lee Jones was denied his right to counsel because the lawyer who represented him at his death penalty trial in Arizona failed to present medical evidence that the victim had sustained her injuries when she was not with Jones. Justice Clarence Thomas, in the Court's decision, criticized the district court judge for conducting a seven-day hearing—which he described as "sprawling"—and receiving evidence of the lawyer's incompetence. He did not take issue with the conclusion that Jones had been convicted in violation of his right to counsel, but ruled that Jones was not entitled to the hearing where he proved it. Thomas also held in the same opinion that another death-sentenced man was not entitled to a hearing to show that he met a requirement the Court had adopted to present a claim of ineffective assistance of counsel. Justice Sonia Sotomayor, in dissent, said that the Court's holding "reduces to rubble" the right to counsel of many habeas corpus petitioners, and observed, "Two men whose trial attorneys did not provide even the bare minimum level of representation required by the Constitution may be executed because forces outside of their control prevented them from vindicating their constitutional right to counsel."[83] This is the fear of too much justice—the refusal to conduct a hearing because of what might be proven at it.

Even if a federal court concludes that a state court's decision was an unreasonable application of Supreme Court precedent—that is, that a constitutional violation undeniably occurred—it can still deny relief if the error was "harmless." In habeas corpus review, a federal court must assess a state court's finding of harmless error for reasonableness. The Supreme Court even held that federal courts must apply *two* harmless error tests before overturning a state court decision— one under the Court's prior precedents and the other under AEDPA. Ervine Davenport was shackled at the waist, wrist, and ankles at his trial for murder in Michigan. Jurors saw the shackles during the trial. Lawyers for the State conceded that the shackling was unconstitutional, but argued that it was harmless error. A Michigan court accepted that argument and affirmed his conviction. The Supreme Court held that the state court's ruling was not unreasonable and therefore upheld Davenport's conviction—reversing a decision of a federal court of appeals that had concluded that "the shackles branded Davenport as having a violent nature," thereby denying him a fair trial.[84]

The Supreme Court has repeatedly invoked AEDPA to reverse decisions of federal courts of appeals finding constitutional violations and granting habeas corpus relief. For example, the Court summarily reversed a decision of the Ninth Circuit finding ineffective counsel at the penalty phase of George Russell Kayer's capital trial in Arizona. The state court did not set out its reasons for concluding that the outcome would not have been different even if his lawyers had presented certain mitigating evidence. Nevertheless, the majority speculated on "what arguments or theories . . . could have supported the state court's" determination and held that a fair-minded jurist could have concluded that the mitigating evidence was not strong enough when considered with the aggravating circumstances.[85] Three justices dissented.

In the penalty phase of Matthew Reeves's capital trial in Alabama, his lawyers obtained funds for a clinical neuropsychologist to testify that Reeves was intellectually disabled—but never contacted the neuropsychologist. Instead, they called a psychologist who had previously examined Reeves for competency and sanity. The psychologist told the lawyers that she had not evaluated Reeves for intellectual disability and that her prior evaluation would not serve their purposes. Nevertheless, they presented her testimony at a penalty phase that lasted only an hour and a half.[86] Three federal appellate judges agreed that Reeves was denied the effective assistance of counsel. The Supreme Court summarily reversed that decision, finding that the Alabama court's rejection of Reeves's claim was not unreasonable based on its speculation about what strategy the lawyers may have adopted.[87] Justice Sotomayor, dissenting, said the majority, by adopting "an utterly implausible reading of the state court's decision," had turned "'deference' . . . into a rule that federal habeas relief is never available to those facing execution."[88] Alabama executed Reeves in 2022.

James Fisher, as discussed in the previous chapter, was sentenced to death in Oklahoma but spared execution because a federal court of appeals recognized the incompetence of his court-appointed lawyer. Fisher's petition to the federal courts was filed in 1993, before AEDPA became law. Under today's law, it is likely that the decision of the Oklahoma Court of Criminal Appeals rejecting his claim of ineffective assistance of counsel would have survived federal review and Fisher would have been executed.

Expediting Executions

As the composition of the Supreme Court changed with the appointment of three justices by President Donald Trump, it became more hostile to people sentenced to death and criminal defendants in gen-

eral. Justice Neil Gorsuch suggested at the end of an opinion upholding Missouri's method of carrying out executions that federal courts
should be reluctant to grant stays of execution for people under death
sentence.[89] Justice Sotomayor pointed out in dissent that the issue of
stays was "wholly irrelevant" to the case before the Court, which
involved complex issues regarding lethal injection that divided the
lower courts as well as the Supreme Court, and argued that Gorsuch was advocating "a radical reinvention of established law and the
judicial role."[90]

As an example of how the Court should treat stays, Justice Gorsuch
pointed to the Court's decision by a vote of 5–4 to vacate a stay that
had been granted unanimously by three federal appellate judges in a
case involving Alabama's refusal to allow an imam to accompany a
Muslim to the execution chamber, while allowing a Christian chap-
lain to accompany Christian prisoners to their executions. The majority said that a stay was not appropriate because of the "last-minute
nature" of the application. Justice Elena Kagan, in dissent, pointed
out that the challenge had been filed just five days after Domineque
Ray had been told that his imam would not be permitted. She added
that allowing the execution was "profoundly wrong" because of the
Constitution's clear command "that one religious denomination cannot be officially preferred over another."[91] The Court later granted a
stay in the case of a Buddhist death row prisoner in Texas who challenged the state's refusal to allow his Buddhist spiritual adviser in the
execution chamber, but it was too late for Ray, who was executed by
Alabama once the stay was vacated.[92]

The Court vacated stays of execution issued by lower federal
courts—and upheld denials of stays—in order to allow the federal
government to carry out thirteen executions in the last six months of
the Trump administration. After seventeen years in which there had
been no federal executions, the federal government executed more
than three times as many people in six months as it had in the previous six decades. As Justice Sotomayor observed, the Supreme Court

"repeatedly sidestepped its usual deliberative processes . . . allowing it to push forward with an unprecedented, breakneck timetable of executions."[93]

The cases presented a number of important issues—for example, whether Brandon Bernard was entitled to a hearing on his claim that prosecutors withheld exculpatory evidence and elicited false testimony at his trial; whether Wesley Purkey, who suffered from Alzheimer's disease, and Lisa Montgomery, who was experiencing dissociative psychotic episodes while awaiting her execution, could be put to death even though federal judges found it likely that they had no rational understanding of why they were being executed; whether courts should apply contemporary diagnostic standards to determine whether two men were intellectually disabled and thus not subject to execution (instead of relying on earlier findings made under now outdated standards); whether the execution of two men infected with COVID-19 with the drug pentobarbital would cause such lung damage that they would experience "a sensation of drowning akin to waterboarding"; and whether one of the death sentences was subject to a reduction under the First Step Act of 2018, which allowed the reassessment of existing sentences for certain offenses. The Supreme Court vacated a stay in one case even though it was set for argument before the Court of Appeals for the Fourth Circuit. In another, it allowed the government to skip the usual procedure of appealing to the Court of Appeals and vacated a stay issued by the district court. "This expedited spree of executions," Justice Sotomayor wrote, "is not justice." Many important issues presented by the cases "never receive[d] a meaningful airing."[94]

Achieving Fair, Independent, and Impartial Judges

As a member of the Arizona state senate in 1974, future Supreme Court justice Sandra Day O'Connor was part of an effort that won approval of a state constitutional amendment that replaced the election of judges with merit selection for the supreme court, the court of appeals, and the trial courts in Arizona's two most populous counties. The amendment provided for appointment of judges by the governor from a list of three names recommended by a judicial qualifications commission. The nominating commissions include lawyer members nominated by the board of governors of the state bar, appointed by the governor, and confirmed by the senate as well as nonlawyer members appointed by the governor and confirmed by the senate. After a two-year term, judges must stand for retention in an election.[95]

After leaving the Supreme Court in 2006, Justice O'Connor spent over a decade sounding the alarm about the threat to judicial independence posed by "the flood of money coming into our courtrooms by way of increasingly expensive and volatile judicial election campaigns." Describing an Illinois Supreme Court race that cost $9 million, she noted that the winner of the election asked, "How can people have faith in the system when such obscene amounts of money are used to influence the outcome of judicial elections?" and later voted to overturn a $450 million verdict against one of his campaign contributors. Justice O'Connor observed that a person "might have a very good reason to doubt whether it was fair," and asked whether someone "would want to be standing in front of a judge who faced an upcoming election if your cause was legally right but politically unpopular." O'Connor advocated for a merit selection system like the one she helped establish in Arizona.[96] But other states have not followed her recommendations.

While a merit selection system can result in the selection of judges based upon a careful consideration of qualifications, retention elections are susceptible to some of the same problems as traditional contested elections. In retention elections, there is no comparison among candidates, so a judge standing for retention may be a target for various groups dissatisfied with her decisions on issues ranging from crime to abortion, and voters can express their disapproval of the judge with no consideration of whether the replacement judge will be any better. As previously discussed, three justices were voted off the California Supreme Court and Penny White was voted off the Tennessee Supreme Court in retention elections after they were challenged based on their votes in death penalty cases. After the Iowa Supreme Court unanimously legalized same-sex marriage, the three justices on the ballot in 2010 were voted off the court after a campaign that saw large contributions by out-of-state organizations.[97]

In some jurisdictions, judges never face election. Massachusetts judges serve a single lengthy term—until age seventy.[98] Judges in the District of Columbia serve a fifteen-year term upon appointment. A commission receives input from lawyers, court staff, and members of the public and evaluates judges based on their work product, legal scholarship, dedication, efficiency, and demeanor without regard to the outcomes reached in cases. If the commission finds a judge "well qualified," she is appointed to a new fifteen-year term. The commission has the power to remove a judge for willful misconduct, persistent failure to perform judicial duties, conduct that is prejudicial to the administration of justice, or a mental or physical disability that interferes with the proper performance of the judge's duties.[99]

In these systems, governors—and in the District of Columbia, the president—nominate judges from a list proposed by a commission that makes recommendations based on qualifications. The nominations are subject to consent by one branch of the legislature. This results in the selection of many capable and qualified individuals who would otherwise be unwilling to seek a judgeship if they had to endure the fundraising, campaigning, and attack ads required by an election. In addition, people who come before the courts and the public have more confidence in judges who do not have to worry about offending a particular segment of the population in order to raise campaign funds or stay in office. Most importantly, a system in which judges do not stand for election ensures that each judge will be independent—that, in the words of former Supreme Court chief justice Owen Roberts, he is "free to say his say, knowing, as the founding fathers meant he should know, that nothing could reach him and that his conscience was as free as could be."[100]

In states that use elections, Justice O'Connor suggested policies that could "make those elections less nasty, expensive, and destructive," such as requiring longer terms in office, voter guides, civics education, and disqualification from participating in cases where there is reason to doubt a judge's impartiality.[101] In 2009, the U.S. Supreme Court held that Justice Brent Benjamin of the West Virginia Supreme Court should have recused himself in the case involving Massey Energy, whose CEO had spent $3 million to get him elected. The Court reiterated that a defendant's right to due process is violated when his case is not heard by a "neutral and detached judge."[102] But the effort to influence Benjamin was immense and dealt with a case pending before the court when the contributions were made. When campaigns center on candidates for judge promising to be tough on crime, a reasonable person has good reasons for questioning their impartiality in high-profile criminal cases. Nevertheless, judges who run such campaigns seldom disqualify themselves, relying on fictions of impartiality while ignoring political realities.

While Cliff Young was running for reelection to the Nevada Supreme Court in 1996—trumpeting his endorsement by the state's attorney general—Thomas Nevius's death sentence appeal was before the Court. Nevius moved to disqualify Justice Young on two grounds: first, that the justice's political ally, the attorney general, was representing the state in his case; and second, that the justice had boasted about his crime-fighting credentials, specifically that he voted to uphold the death penalty seventy-six times. As a fellow justice on the Court wrote, "If Justice Young enhances his crime-fighting record by raising his seventy-six death judgments to seventy-seven in this case, it seems to me that Nevius may have the right to complain that Justice Young should not have been sitting on his case."[103] Nevertheless, the Court denied the disqualification motion and upheld Nevius's convictions and death sentence.

After Ohio Supreme Court Justice Judith French told the audience at a 2014 Republican Party election rally that they should vote for her because "the Ohio Supreme Court is the backstop for all those other votes you are going to cast," the Ohio Civil Service Employees Association moved for the justice to recuse herself from a pending case. The union had sued Republican governor Kasich and other party officials, arguing that the state budget passed by the GOP-controlled legislature was unconstitutional, and had won an initial victory in a lower appellate court. French's statements at the rally—"Whatever the governor does, whatever your state representative, your state senator does, whatever they do, we are the ones that will decide whether it is constitutional"—seemed to make out as clear a case of bias that one could. Yet French simply decided not to recuse herself, and even wrote the majority opinion overruling the lower court and upholding the earlier budget bill.[104]

Just six days before the 2014 election, the Ohio Supreme Court issued an opinion written by French upholding the death sentence for a Black man convicted for the murder of a white police officer. Three of the Court's seven members dissented on the grounds that the death penalty was not warranted because mitigating circumstances outweighed aggravating circumstances.[105] It is inconceivable that French, who was running advertisements about how tough she was, could have decided the case any other way so close to the election. She won reelection.[106]

Judges who realize that, because of political considerations, they cannot "hold the balance nice, clear, and true," in the words of the Supreme Court in *Tumey v. Ohio*, have a duty to recuse themselves. Defense lawyers have a duty to move to disqualify judges whose campaign platforms make it difficult for them to handle the cases before them fairly. In reviewing disqualification issues, trial and appellate courts should face the reality of the political pressures on judges, but they seldom do.

Another way to mitigate political pressures is to modify the judicial assignment system so that trial judges rotate between different judicial districts. When out of the district where she was elected, a judge is relieved from the pressure of having to portray herself as the protector of her community. And a judge would not have to stand for election in the very place in which she had made controversial rulings.

Regardless of how judges are selected, they should not be responsible for the appointment of lawyers for poor persons accused of crimes. Just as judges must be independent of improper influences, the lawyer for a person accused of a crime must be independent of the judiciary and prosecution and be accountable solely to the person being represented. Judges have assigned cases to lawyers who have contributed to their campaigns and for other improper reasons. And many lawyers appointed by judges do not zealously represent their clients for fear of displeasing the judge and losing future business. For these reasons, counsel for poor people accused of crimes must be selected by a public defender office or a program charged with protecting the best interests of the accused.

Judges must also perform their role of deciding cases impartially and not delegate the writing of orders and opinions to lawyers for one side. Judges are responsible for fairly setting out the facts so that they can be relied upon by appellate courts. Those courts cannot function properly when trial judges sign off on inaccurate and one-sided orders prepared by the prosecution.

The discretion of trial judges on crucial matters should be reviewed on the basis of objective standards that are carefully applied on appeal and in post-conviction proceedings. Reviewing courts should acknowledge the political pressures on trial judges; where judges have given in to such pressures, their rulings should not receive the deference normally accorded to trial judges. Currently, findings of fact by trial judges are reviewed under the abuse-of-discretion and clearly erroneous standards, which overturn trial court decisions only if they were flagrantly wrong. Under the Antiterrorism and Effective Death Penalty Act, federal courts, when reviewing state court judgments in habeas corpus proceedings, must presume the correctness of findings of fact by state courts. This deference is based on the notion that the trial judge is best able to determine the credibility of witnesses and hence the weight of the evidence, but it is unwarranted when a judge abandons the judicial role and adopts the perspective of the prosecutor—or an order written by a prosecutor.

Even when judges do not adopt ghostwritten orders, their rulings may be based on political considerations more than legal ones. The Supreme Court recognized this source of bias in *Sheppard v. Maxwell* in 1966. After extensive pretrial publicity, the murder trial of Dr. Samuel H. Sheppard began just two weeks before a November election in which the trial judge was up for reelection and the chief prosecutor was a candidate for judge. The Supreme Court held that Sheppard was entitled to habeas corpus relief because the trial judge had failed to protect his right to a fair trial by taking measures such as continuing the case until after the election, changing the venue, and controlling the trial participants' release of prejudicial information to the press.[107]

Since *Sheppard*, however, the Supreme Court has not mandated procedures to minimize the risk of prejudice in such volatile situations or established objective standards for the review of similar discretionary rulings by elected trial judges. Most courts have shown little inclination to acknowledge the fact that many of those rulings are likely influenced by political considerations. A reexamination of the deference given to elected judges on discretionary matters is urgently needed. Courts should frankly acknowledge and address the political pressures created by elections. In addition, Congress and the

Supreme Court should restore the ability of the federal courts to fully review criminal convictions in state courts, so that constitutional rights can be enforced by judges who cannot be swept from office for making a controversial decision. That includes allowing federal courts to hold hearings and permit the presentation of evidence of constitutional violations.

Ideological reliability and party loyalty are not what we should want in judges. In 1940, Justice Hugo Black wrote for the Supreme Court (in a decision reversing death sentences imposed on four Black men that had been upheld by the elected judges of the Florida Supreme Court), "Under our constitutional system, courts stand against any winds that blow as havens of refuge for those who might otherwise suffer because they are helpless, weak, outnumbered, or because they are non-conforming victims of prejudice and public excitement."[108] Courts cannot serve that function if the judges presiding over them are constantly forced to choose between the Bill of Rights and their prospects for reelection. If we are to achieve impartial justice, we must ensure that judges need answer only to the Constitution and the laws of the United States, not to the shifting tides of political expediency.

5

The Whitewashed Jury

Providing an accused with the right to be tried by a jury
of his peers gave him an inestimable safeguard against the
corrupt or overzealous prosecutor and against the compli-
ant, biased, or eccentric judge.

—*United States Supreme Court*, Duncan
v. Louisiana, *1968*[1]

In 1987, Timothy Foster, a nineteen-year-old Black youth accused
of the murder of an elderly white woman in Georgia, faced a death
penalty trial. The two prosecutors planned to try the case before an
all-white jury. As is often the case, this was not difficult. Ninety-
eight people were summoned for jury selection; only eleven were
Black. The judge excused some people because of medical conditions
or other reasons that they were unable to serve and struck others "for
cause"—because they knew a witness, had already made up their
minds, or could not be fair for some other reason. That left forty-two
prospective jurors, only four of whom were Black. Georgia law gave
the prosecutors ten peremptory strikes that they could use to remove
prospective jurors. They struck all four of the Blacks to get the all-
white jury they wanted.[2] In his closing argument, District Attorney
Stephen Lanier urged the jury to sentence Foster to death to "deter
other people out there in the projects." At the time, Black families,

including the Fosters, occupied thirty-two of the thirty-four units in the local housing project.[3] The jury sentenced Foster to death.

For most of American history, the use of peremptory strikes to ensure all-white juries was routine. In 1965, the Supreme Court explicitly allowed prosecutors to target "Negro and white, Protestant and Catholic" with peremptory strikes in the case of Swain v. Alabama. Robert Swain, a nineteen-year-old Black man, was accused of raping a seventeen-year-old white girl in Talladega County, Alabama, in 1962. Although 26 percent of the population of Talladega County was Black, no Black person had served on a jury in recent decades, if at all.[4] Only six Blacks were available for jury service in Swain's case; the prosecutor used peremptory strikes to remove all six. The all-white jury found Swain guilty and sentenced him to death. The Supreme Court upheld the jury selection by a 6–3 vote, holding that a peremptory strike could be exercised on the basis of race.[5] Justice Byron White wrote in the majority opinion that a peremptory strike could be based on "real or imagined partiality" and "sudden impressions and unaccountable prejudices" based upon the appearance, gestures, "race, religion, nationality, occupation or affiliations of people summoned for jury duty." A defendant challenging a prosecutor's use of peremptory strikes had to prove that the prosecutor struck Blacks "in case after case, whatever the circumstances, whatever the crime and whoever the defendant or the victim may be" so that no Black person ever served on a jury.[6]

The decision in Swain allowed prosecutors to continue to strike people of color with impunity. A manual for prosecutors in Dallas County, Texas, instructed them to "not take Jews, Negroes, Dagos, Mexicans, or a member of any minority race on a jury, no matter how rich or how well educated." Dallas County prosecutors struck 405 of 467 eligible Black jurors in one hundred felony trials between 1983 and 1984.[7] The longtime district attorney in Jackson, Mississippi, Ed

Peters, stated in 1983 that his "philosophy" was to "get rid of as many" Blacks as possible with peremptory strikes. Peters struck seven Black prospective jurors in the case of Leo Edwards, a Black man who was sentenced to death by an all-white jury in a community that was over 40 percent African American. A federal court rejected a claim of discrimination despite finding that the strikes were based on "a sincerely held belief that a Black juror was ordinarily less sympathetic to the prosecutor and to law enforcement officials than a white one."[8] Mississippi executed Edwards in 1989. A prosecutor in Chambers County, Alabama, used twenty-four strikes against twenty-four African Americans to get three all-white juries (for a mental competency trial, a trial on the charges, and a resentencing) in the case of Albert Jefferson, a Black man. He was sentenced to death. It was later discovered that the prosecutor had divided prospective jurors into four lists—"strong," "medium," "weak," and "Black"—and prioritized striking every single Black before any "weak" white.[9]

In 1983 and 1984, Supreme Court Justice Thurgood Marshall pointed out that the practice of prosecutors striking Blacks to get all-white or predominantly white juries had reached "epidemic proportions."[10] The decision in *Swain* had received "universal and often scathing criticism," he wrote, because its burden of showing prosecution strikes against Blacks in case after case was "nearly insurmountable." Requiring that many suffer discrimination before any defendant can object, he wrote, was inconsistent with the right to equal protection of the law.[11]

In 1984, James Batson, a Black man, was tried for burglary and the receipt of stolen goods in Louisville, Kentucky. During jury selection, the prosecutor used his peremptory strikes to remove all four Black people from the jury panel. The all-white jury convicted Batson. The Supreme Court granted review in the case and finally acknowledged that peremptory challenges had been "used to discriminate against black jurors" and that the "crippling burden of proof" adopted in

Swain had rendered a prosecutor's peremptory challenges "largely immune from constitutional scrutiny."[12] The Court decided, by a vote of 7–2, in the case of *Batson v. Kentucky* that a defendant could raise a claim of discrimination based on a pattern of striking Blacks in his case alone. If the defense lawyer objected to such a pattern, the prosecutor was required to give reasons for the strikes. The trial judge was then to determine whether the prosecutor struck the prospective jurors for the reasons given or because of their race.[13] So a judge may disallow a peremptory strike only upon finding that the prosecutor intentionally discriminated on the basis of race and lied about it by giving a false reason.

Justice Marshall wrote a concurring opinion commending the decision as a historic step forward, but, he warned, it would not end the racially discriminatory use of peremptory strikes. In many communities where only one or two Black citizens would be subject to strikes, a prosecutor could strike them because of their race without establishing the pattern required by the Court. And even where there was a pattern, "any prosecutor can easily assert facially neutral reasons for striking a juror, and trial courts are ill equipped to second-guess those reasons." In addition to simple dishonesty, he continued,

> a prosecutor's own conscious or unconscious racism may lead him easily to the conclusion that a prospective black juror is "sullen," or "distant," a characterization that would not have come to his mind if a white juror had acted identically. A judge's own conscious or unconscious racism may lead him to accept such an explanation as well supported. . . . Even if all parties approach the Court's mandate with the best of conscious intentions, that mandate requires them to confront and overcome their own racism on all levels—a challenge I doubt all of them can meet.[14]

The only way to prevent discrimination, Marshall concluded, was to eliminate peremptory challenges altogether.

Batson v. Kentucky was decided the year before Timothy Foster stood trial in Georgia. His lawyers pointed out in a motion filed before trial that local prosecutors had "over a long period of time excluded members of the black race from being allowed to serve on juries with a black Defendant and white victim."[15] In addition, District Attorney Lanier was assisted in Foster's case by Douglas Pullen, who was then an assistant district attorney in a judicial district based in Columbus. That district had sent eight Black people to death row in the previous ten years; six of them were sentenced to death by all-white juries. In five cases against Black defendants, Pullen had used twenty-seven peremptory strikes to remove twenty-seven Black prospective jurors to get all-white juries.[16]

After the prosecutors used their strikes against the four Blacks to get an all-white jury, Foster's lawyers challenged the strikes. In response, District Attorney Lanier claimed that his approach to jury selection was to discriminate against women, not Black people. He pointed out that "eighty percent" of his strikes were against women and that "three of the four blacks were women."[17] Lanier then gave a number of reasons for striking Black prospective juror Eddie Hood: Lanier said his *only concern* was that Hood had an eighteen-year-old son, who was about the same age as Foster, but then gave eight more reasons for striking Hood. Among them were that he had a son who had received a suspended sentence for theft, he did not maintain eye contact while being questioned, his wife worked in a mental hospital, he was asked few questions by the defense lawyers, his brother had counseled drug offenders, and he had asked to be excused from jury service. Even though Hood had stated four times that he could impose the death penalty if the evidence warranted it, Lanier and Pullen told the judge that they thought he could not because his church, the Church of Christ, "definitely takes a stand against the death penalty."[18] Lanier had not asked Hood about any of these reasons when he questioned him during the jury selection process.

Lanier gave twelve reasons for striking one Black woman and nine for striking another. He then said that he would have accepted another Black juror, Marilyn Garrett, except that she was a teacher's aide in Head Start. He then cited "her age being so close to the defendant." Garrett was thirty-four; Foster was nineteen. Lanier added seven other reasons for striking Garrett, including that she was a woman, she was divorced, she appeared nervous, she looked at the floor when questioned, and she was asked few questions by the defense lawyers. Lanier, who said one reason for striking Hood was that he asked to be excused, said a reason for striking Garrett was that she *did not ask to be excused* from jury service.[19] As with Hood, Lanier had not asked Garrett about any of these reasons. Judge John Frazier said that he "was satisfied that *Batson* ha[d] been satisfied."[20]

At least two of the jurors struck by Lanier understood what had happened. "When I came home," Eddie Hood said later, "I told my wife . . . 'More than likely, they're not going to want too many of "us" on the jury.'" Marilyn Garrett thought that prosecutors treated her "like I was a criminal." She recalled,

> They just kept asking me over and over why I had two jobs. I was a single parent trying to take care of my children. It irritated me. They really got me in a defensive mode, and then they said I was indignant. They had me in tears when I went out of there.[21]

Foster's lawyers challenged the jury strikes again in a motion for a new trial and moved for disclosure of the prosecution's notes regarding jury selection because they "should be available to this Court and other Courts which examines the intent of the State."[22] Judge Frazier denied the motion for disclosure. At the hearing on the motion for a new trial, Lanier stated that he would only testify about his reasons for the strikes if Foster's attorneys would not have access to his notes. After Judge Frazier assured him that his notes would remain private, Lanier gave even more reasons for his strikes. Lanier changed his main reason for striking Eddie Hood, testifying that "the bottom line" was Hood's affiliation with the Church of Christ.[23] He gave two new reasons for striking Marilyn Garrett: she was a social worker (she wasn't), and her cousin had been arrested on drug charges (which the prosecution had learned only after jury selection). Judge Frazier again ruled that there had been no discrimination. On appeal, the Georgia Supreme Court affirmed the conviction and death sentence, holding that the reasons for the strikes were "clear and reasonably specific."[24]

Foster was on the way to execution. But in 2006, different lawyers representing him obtained the prosecution's file—which the prosecutors had been so adamant about keeping secret—under Georgia's Open Records Act. The file contained four different copies of the list of ninety-eight people summoned for jury service, with the names of the Black citizens highlighted in green and marked with a "B." Each list included a key noting that the green highlighting indicated Blacks. The lists had been circulated in the district attorney's office. The file also contained questionnaires that had been completed by the prospective jurors, with the juror's race circled on the questionnaires of the Black respondents. The file contained handwritten notes on some of the Black prospective jurors, identifying them as B#1, B#2, and B#3. It also contained a draft memorandum by an investigator in the prosecutor's office evaluating the Blacks and concluding, "If it comes down to having to pick one of the black jurors, [Marilyn] Garrett, might be okay." It also had a list of six names titled "Definite NO's." The first five names were African Americans. (One of them was disqualified before the jury strikes were exercised.) Another handwritten document was titled "Church of Christ" and contained the notations: "doesn't take a stand on Death Penalty," "left for each individual member," and "*NO. NO Black* Church."[25]

Despite this compelling evidence of discrimination, Judge Richard M. Cowart denied Foster's state habeas corpus petition, holding that the lists with the green highlighting had been circulated "to help pick a fair jury." He did not address anything else in the file before concluding that the prosecution had put forward "multiple race-neutral reasons for striking each juror."[26] The Georgia Supreme Court declined without comment to review the evidence.

The U.S. Supreme Court reversed the Georgia courts in an opinion by Chief Justice John Roberts. The Court found that many of Lanier's reasons had "no grounding in fact" or were misrepresentations and that reasons he gave for striking Black people also applied to white people whom he accepted. Chief Justice Roberts noted that the prosecutors' reasons for striking Hood shifted over time and were riddled with inconsistencies and falsehoods. Lanier accepted two white jurors who had sons about the same age as Foster and Hood's son. Chief Justice Roberts dismissed as "nonsense" Lanier's claim that Hood's son had a conviction for "basically the same thing that this defendant is charged with"; Hood's son received a suspended sentence for stealing hubcaps, while Foster was charged with capital murder. Lanier misrepresented the position of the Church of Christ when he said it was strongly against the death penalty. While Lanier said that he had struck Hood because his wife worked at a mental hospital, he had accepted a white person who worked at the same hospital. Another reason Lanier gave for striking Hood—that the defense lawyers had not asked Hood about Foster's age, the insanity defense, and publicity—was simply not true.[27]

Lanier told Judge Frazier that he decided to strike Marilyn Garrett at the last minute. But she was on the list of "Definite NO's" that the prosecutors created before jury selection. Lanier said that he struck Garrett because she was thirty-four and he was "looking for older jurors." But he did not strike eight whites under the age of thirty-six. Lanier said he struck Garrett because she was divorced, but he did not strike three whites who were divorced. Lanier said that he struck Garrett because the defense lawyers had not asked her about insanity, alcohol, or publicity. But, as with Hood, this was not true.[28] Chief Justice Roberts concluded, "The focus on race in the prosecution's file plainly demonstrates a concerted effort to keep black prospective jurors off the jury."[29]

The discrimination in Foster's case was finally recognized, but only because the prosecutors did not destroy their notes from jury selection. When Foster's attorneys obtained records in another capital case prosecuted by the same district attorney's office, the file did not contain any notes regarding jury selection. But Timothy Foster's case is not unique. In 2007, Noel Chua was convicted of murder, in another Georgia county, for illegally prescribing drugs that led to an overdose. Six years later, his lawyer found, in District Attorney Stephen Kelley's records, a memorandum written by Camden County commissioner Steve Berry that said, "I would avoid blacks on this jury. I understand you have some constitutional concerns there that have to be kept in mind, but try to avoid them." Jackie Johnson, who had prosecuted Chua with Kelley and became district attorney when Kelley became a judge, fought for three years to keep the memorandum secret. Once the courts ruled that it had to be released, she conceded that Dr. Chua's conviction was invalid and agreed to a sentence of time served for involuntary manslaughter.[30]

The Whites-Only Jury Box

Racial discrimination in selecting jurors has a long history, interrupted only briefly in a few places during Reconstruction, when African Americans served on juries in some parts of the South.[31] In 1879, the Supreme Court declared a West Virginia statute that limited jury service to "white males" unconstitutional, but on the same day it rejected a challenge to the exclusion of Blacks from juries in a Virginia county in which no Black person had ever served on a jury, on the grounds that there was no state law prohibiting Blacks from serving.[32] Over the next half century, the Court upheld practices that completely excluded Blacks from the jury box, as states developed pervasive regimes of racial subordination that prevented Blacks from voting and from serving on juries. The result was all-white juries that convicted Black defendants and punished them harshly while refusing to punish violence by whites against Blacks.[33]

Mississippi led the way. After white supremacists obtained power over the state's majority-Black population through unrelenting violence, they convened a constitutional convention in 1890 to bring about "a white man's government based upon white man's rule." The new constitution prevented Blacks from voting by adopting literacy tests and poll taxes and prohibiting those with certain criminal convictions from voting. By 1892, 68,000 of the 110,100 white adult males were registered voters, but only 8,615 of the 147,205 Black adult males were registered. Mississippi's approach was "so effective that it was widely copied by other southern states."[34] In 1892, to ensure that no Black served on a jury, Mississippi passed a law requiring each county board of supervisors to create a list of registered voters who could serve as jurors based on their "good intelligence, sound judgment and fair character." The U.S. Supreme Court unanimously upheld the law in the case of a Black man sentenced to death by an all-white jury, holding that discrimination, to be illegal, "must be the result of the constitution or laws of the state, not of the administration of them."[35]

Blacks "virtually disappeared from the southern jury box by 1900, even in counties where they constituted an overwhelming majority of the local population," according to law professor Douglas Colbert.[36] In 1910, the Supreme Court upheld South Carolina's law requiring jury commissioners to select men of "good moral character" and "sound judgment" as prospective jurors, saying that the law "simply provides for an exercise of judgment in attempting to secure competent jurors of proper qualifications."[37] Many states and the federal government adopted the "key man" system of jury selection, under which a jury commission, usually appointed by the local judge, compiled a master list of prospective jurors on the recommendation of civic and political leaders—"key men"—based on vague qualifications. An Alabama law required jury commissioners to select people "generally reputed to be honest and intelligent" and "esteemed in the community for their integrity, good character and sound judgment." Several northern cities required "intelligence, experience and integrity." This system was used by most courts for most of the twentieth century.[38]

Judges usually appointed white jury commissioners who knew few, if any, people of color during a period of widespread segregation. They easily concluded that there were no Black people qualified for jury service. Discrimination was not limited to the South. The California Supreme Court found in 1939 that no African American "had ever been placed on the venires [prospective juror pools] or called for jury service in criminal cases in Merced County."[39]

In 1935, in *Norris v. Alabama*, the U.S. Supreme Court considered the retrials of the "Scottsboro Boys," the nine Black youths accused of raping two white women, discussed earlier. There were no Blacks on the jury rolls in Jackson County, where the defendants were indicted, or in Morgan County, where the cases were eventually tried. Officials in both counties testified that not a single Black person was qualified for jury service. Samuel Leibowitz, the defense lawyer, presented testimony that many African Americans in each county were qualified. As the Supreme Court summarized with regard to Morgan County, "Men of intelligence, some of whom were college graduates, testified to long lists (said to contain nearly 200 names) of such qualified negroes, including many businessmen, owners of real property and householders." The Court held that the "long-continued, unvarying, and wholesale exclusion" of Blacks from the jury lists denied equal protection.[40]

Many jury commissions responded to Norris by including only a few token people of color on the jury lists—with the Supreme Court's approval. In 1945, the Court rejected a challenge to the practice by Dallas jury commissioners of putting only one Black person on each grand jury list. Even though a commissioner admitted, "We had no intention of placing more than one negro on the panel," the Court maintained that it was "unconvinced that the commissioners deliberately and intentionally limited the number of Negroes on the grand jury list."[41]

Even when people of color were included in the master juror list, officials found ways to keep them off juries. Atlanta officials chose prospective jurors in the 1950s by drawing cards containing the names of people in the jury pool from a box. The names of white people were on white cards and those of Blacks on yellow cards. The practice continued until James Avery, a Black man, challenged it after being sentenced to death by an all-white jury. All sixty people selected for his case by drawing cards were white.[42] The Supreme Court put an end to the practice and reversed Avery's conviction.

The Supreme Court eventually abandoned its requirement of total exclusion and held that discrimination could be established by proof of substantial underrepresentation.[43] The Court did not hold that women should be fairly represented on juries until 1975.[44] In assessing the degree of underrepresentation of a race or gender, however, the Court considered only "absolute disparities": the difference between the percentage of a group in the jury pool and its percentage in the jury-eligible population. For example, the Court found a constitutional violation where Mexican Americans made up 79 percent of a county's population but only 39 percent of those summoned to grand jury service, an absolute disparity of forty percentage points.[45]

The Supreme Court has not said how great such an absolute disparity must be to be illegal, but courts have found constitutional violations where the disparity was greater than ten percentage points.[46] If Blacks make up less than 10 percent of a county's population, however, it is impossible to show an absolute disparity of ten percentage points. This makes it impossible for African Americans to challenge underrepresentation in 75 percent of the counties in the United States—including, as the Iowa Supreme Court has observed, every county in Iowa. For Latinos and Asian Americans, challenges are effectively barred in 90 percent of counties.[47]

At some point before 1977, one Georgia prosecutor, Joseph Briley, instructed the jury commission of Putnam County to underrepresent Blacks and women by about ten percentage points in order to avoid a finding of discrimination. The U.S. Supreme Court reversed a conviction and death sentence because of this jury rigging, but no action was taken against Briley. He tried thirty-three death penalty cases between 1974 and 1981. In the twenty-four cases in which the defendants were Black and the victims were white, Briley used 96 out of his 103 strikes against Blacks.[48]

Discrimination in Jury Selection Today

Criticism of the "key man" system led to the Federal Jury Selection and Service Act of 1968, which mandated the random selection of a fair cross section of citizens for juries in federal courts.[49] Most states also abandoned the "key man" system for a random selection process from lists such as the list of registered voters and that of licensed drivers. One might think that random selection of the jury pool, coupled with *Batson v. Kentucky*, would prevent racial discrimination in jury selection. But there are still many ways to exclude people of color from a jury. It is easy for prosecutors to obtain all-white juries in largely white communities where few members of racial minorities will be summoned for jury service. But even where people of color are a much larger part of the community, each step of the jury selection process can be used to winnow them out.[50]

The first step is identifying prospective jurors and getting them to court. People of color are often underrepresented on the lists of registered voters and licensed drivers.[51] Many do not appear on voter registration lists because they are disenfranchised owing to felony convictions. Over half of the states prohibit jury participation by people with felony convictions, and most of the others limit their jury participation in some way. Thirty percent of Black men are banned from jury service because of convictions.[52]

When Diapolis Smith, a Black man, was tried for murder in Kent County, Michigan, African Americans constituted 7.28 percent of the county's jury-eligible population, but only 6 percent of those who appeared in the pool of prospective jurors. African Americans were less likely than whites to receive or return the questionnaires notifying them that they had been selected for jury service. Of the people who returned questionnaires, officials excused those who said they would have difficulty serving because of a hardship such as childcare obligations, transportation problems, or the inability to take time away from work. An expert testified that excusing people because of childcare obligations and transportation problems had a disproportionate impact on Blacks. One reason was that in Kent County 64 percent of African American households with children were headed by single parents, as opposed to only 19 percent of white households with children.[53] As a result, there were only three Blacks in the jury panel for Smith's trial and none on the jury that found him guilty. Both the Michigan Supreme Court and the U.S. Supreme Court rejected Smith's challenge to this underrepresentation.[54]

Juries may be less representative based on their size. Arizona and Utah have eight-person juries in some noncapital felony cases, and Florida, Connecticut, Indiana, and Massachusetts have six-person juries in some noncapital felony cases. Many more states provide for six- or eight-person juries for misdemeanor cases. Smaller juries are less racially representative than twelve-person juries. They have a reduced likelihood of any minority representation and even less chance of having two or more people of color.[55]

The number of people of color is reduced even further at the next stage of the process—when prospective jurors may be struck "for cause" if a judge decides that they cannot fairly and impartially decide the case. Jurors may be asked about anything that would reveal bias, such as whether they know or are related to the defendant or a witness and whether they have made up their minds about the defendant's guilt or innocence based on the pretrial publicity. They may also be asked whether they have negative views of law enforcement and whether they believe that the criminal legal system is unfair to people of color. People of color are more likely to express these views because of their experiences or the experiences of their families and communities. For instance, a Black prospective juror at a capital trial in Shreveport, Louisiana, said that he could not serve as a juror because he found the massive memorial to the Confederacy in front of the courthouse offensive.[56] Prosecutors will usually be successful in persuading the judge to remove people with those views for cause. A study of 316 trials in Louisiana between 2009 and 2017 found that Blacks were 33 percent of the prospective jurors but were the targets of 59 percent of successful challenges for cause by prosecutors. A study of more than 1,300 felony trials in North Carolina found that Black prospective jurors were removed for cause more frequently than white jurors. One scholar concluded that prosecutors' challenges for cause "systemically reduce the representation of nonwhite jurors . . . to an even greater extent than peremptory strikes."[57]

In capital cases, potential jurors are also asked if they would have any difficulty voting to impose the death penalty. Those who indicate that they cannot fairly consider it will be struck for cause. This process produces juries that one law professor describes as "uncommonly conviction- and death-prone, as well as disproportionately punitive and inclined toward believing the prosecution."[58] Nevertheless, the Supreme Court has upheld this process of "death qualification."[59] It often results in the removal of more people of color, who may have reservations about the death penalty because of the history of discrimination in its infliction. An analysis of seven capital trials in Louisiana found that 36 percent of Black prospective jurors were excluded on the basis of their opposition to the death penalty, but only 20 percent of white prospective jurors were excluded for that reason.[60]

For all these reasons, prosecutors can shape the composition of the jury pool even before they need to use their most potent weapon: the peremptory strike. Often the prosecutor can exclude enough people of color for cause that the rest can be removed with peremptory strikes. Earl McGahee faced a capital trial in Dallas County, Alabama, where 55 percent of the population was Black. After questioning the prospective jurors, the prosecution moved to dismiss nine jurors for cause. All nine were Black. The judge dismissed eight of them because they had said they could not consider the death penalty. After removals for cause, there were sixty-six remaining prospective jurors, of whom only sixteen were Black. The prosecution used sixteen of its twenty-two peremptory strikes against the Blacks to get an all-white jury. The jury recommended the death penalty and the judge imposed it. In twelve cases, the Dallas County prosecutor "used 79 percent of his peremptory strikes to exclude African Americans from jury service, resulting in many all-white or nearly all-white juries in a majority black county."[61]

Prosecutors in most states have around ten peremptory strikes in felony cases, fewer strikes in misdemeanor cases, and more in death penalty cases. In Alabama, however, after removals for cause, the prosecution and defense take turns exercising peremptory strikes until they are left with twelve jurors and, usually, two alternates, which often allows prosecutors to exercise twenty or more peremptory strikes. This is how a prosecutor was able to use twenty-two strikes in the case of Earl McGahee. In the case of Jeffrey Lee, the prosecutor exercised twenty-one peremptory strikes—all against Blacks—after the judge granted seventeen of the prosecution's eighteen removals for cause against Blacks.[62] While McGahee's conviction was overturned by the Eleventh Circuit Court of Appeals because of racial discrimination, the same court upheld Lee's conviction and death sentence, saying there was no discrimination.

Batson v. Kentucky was supposed to prevent prosecutors from using peremptory strikes on the basis of race. However, the Supreme Court began weakening its core holding almost immediately. Two months after *Batson* was decided, the Court held that the decision did not apply retroactively to earlier cases. It issued the ruling in the case of Earl Allen, a Black man convicted of murder in Illinois by an all-white jury after the prosecutor struck seven Blacks and two Latinos. The Court, without briefing or argument, expressed confidence that the jurors who decided the case were free from bias. Justice Marshall argued in dissent that the prosecution's strikes resulted in a "significant and unacceptable" threat to the accuracy of the trial.[63]

In 1991, the Court upheld a New York prosecutor's reason for striking two Latino prospective jurors—that because they spoke Spanish they might not accept an interpreter's English translation of witness testimony given in Spanish. Justice Sandra Day O'Connor wrote in a concurring opinion, "No matter how closely tied or significantly correlated to race the explanation for a peremptory strike may be, the strike does not implicate the Equal Protection Clause unless it is based on race."[64]

In 1995, the Court abandoned *Batson*'s requirement that a prosecutor's justification for a strike be related to the case being tried and allowed prosecutors to offer trivial reasons instead. In *Purkett v. Elem,* a Missouri prosecutor said that he struck one Black man because he had "long hair hanging down shoulder length, curly, unkempt hair" as well as a "mustache and goatee type beard," and a second because he also had "a mustache and goatee type beard." He said he did not "like the way they looked," and "the mustaches and the beards look suspicious to me." The Eighth Circuit Court of Appeals held that the prosecutor discriminated in exercising the two strikes.[65] The Supreme Court, however, found that the prosecutor's reasons were race-neutral and sufficient to overcome any inference of discrimination because a beard, a mustache, and long, unkempt hair were not characteristics "peculiar to any race." The Court said that a prosecutor's reason may be "implausible or fantastic" or even "silly or superstitious" and does not have to be "a reason that makes sense." "The Court's unnecessary tolerance of silly, fantastic, and implausible explanations," Justice John Paul Stevens wrote in dissent, "demeans the importance of the values vindicated by our decision in *Batson*."[66]

Prosecutors may employ many strategies to prevent people of color from serving on juries. Sometimes they may find reasons to remove all or most of them for cause. If there are just one or two people of color left in the jury panel and the prosecutor strikes them, judges often rule that prosecutors are not required to give reasons because there is no pattern of strikes. The Louisiana Supreme Court twice held that no pattern was established when a prosecutor struck five of eight Black prospective jurors.[67] Many courts have also ruled that allowing one or two people of color on a jury is evidence that the strikes of others were not racially motivated. The Arkansas Supreme Court has repeatedly said, "The best answer the State can have to a charge of discrimination is to point to a jury which has black members."[68]

When a prosecutor strikes a potential juror out of racial bias, nothing will happen unless the defendant's lawyer objects. But an objection to a peremptory strike is a uniquely personal one; the defense lawyer is asserting that the prosecutor intentionally discriminated on the basis of race and lied about it by giving pretextual reasons for the strike. Judges, prosecutors, and defense lawyers often know each other and encounter each other frequently; judges are often former prosecutors who previously worked with the prosecutors before them. A defense lawyer may be hesitant to accuse a prosecutor of discriminating and lying, and a judge may be reluctant to rule against the prosecutor. As one lawyer described it:

> I've raised Batson challenges in several cases. Uniformly, the prosecutors challenged express something akin to outrage. How dare I suggest that they might be engaged in racial gerrymandering?
>
> The reaction of most judges is not much better. There is a resigned reluctance to hold a Batson hearing. . . . As though the task of scrutinizing a prosecutor was somehow beyond their ken.
>
> I have difficulty recalling a case in which a judge found the reasons offered by a prosecutor for striking a juror on account of race or gender . . . to be pretextual. Batson challenges are empty challenges.[69]

In addition, as discussed earlier, many elected judges may find it politically impossible to rule that a prosecutor intentionally discriminated and then asserted a false reason for the strike. As Washington Supreme Court Justice Tom Chambers observed, "*Batson* was doomed from the beginning because it requires one elected person to find that another elected person (or one representing an elected person) acted with a discriminatory purpose. This has proved to be an impossible barrier."[70]

Just in case they are challenged, prosecutors invariably have race-neutral reasons for their strikes at the ready. Juror questioning is a fruitful source of reasons. Some people of color say that, although they have reservations about law enforcement, the criminal legal system, or the death penalty, they can decide the case fairly based on the evidence presented at trial. Some courts will not remove those jurors for cause because, as the District of Columbia Court of Appeals observed, the belief that the criminal courts are unfair to Blacks "is neither uncommon nor irrational."[71] Prosecutors will remove them with a peremptory strike and use their reservations as the race-neutral reason for striking them.[72] After observing that prosecutors frequently give "negative experience with law enforcement" or "skepticism about the fairness of the criminal justice system" as reasons for strikes, Justice Jim Humes of the California Court of Appeal wrote that "in light of the undeniable evidence" of racial bias by law enforcement and in the criminal legal system, "reflexively allowing these strikes compounds institutional discrimination by excluding more minorities than nonminorities from juries."[73]

In 1987, the year that Timothy Foster was tried, Jack McMahon, a senior lawyer in the district attorney's office in Philadelphia, told fellow prosecutors during a videotaped training session, "When you do have a black juror, you question them at length. And on this little sheet that you have, mark something down that you can articulate later." This makes it possible, McMahon explained, to say the strike was not for race, but because "the woman had a kid about the same age as the defendant and I thought she'd be sympathetic to him," or "she's unemployed and I just don't like unemployed people."[74]

No one outside of the district attorney's office was aware of the training session, but ten years later, when McMahon challenged Philadelphia district attorney Lynne Abraham for her position, she released a videotape of it. Attorneys for Harold Wilson, who had been prosecuted by McMahon and sentenced to death in 1989, presented to a court the videotape and a study of peremptory strikes by the Philadelphia district attorney's office over twenty years. The study established that Philadelphia prosecutors struck Black jurors at twice the rate of other jurors, and that a Black person called for jury duty in a homicide case prosecuted by McMahon was nearly 4.25 times more likely to be peremptorily struck than a person who was not Black. The court found that McMahon had discriminated and granted Wilson a new trial. Wilson was eventually acquitted after DNA testing of blood from the crime scene disclosed a source that was neither Wilson nor one of the victims.[75] Courts found discrimination based on the videotaped training session in the cases of three other people prosecuted by McMahon and sentenced to death.[76] However, the Pennsylvania Supreme Court rejected a challenge in another capital case in which McMahon used fourteen of nineteen strikes against Black prospective jurors. The same court rejected claims of discrimination in cases prosecuted by other Philadelphia prosecutors, holding that the recording did not prove a policy of discrimination by the office.[77]

An Illinois appellate court speculated, "Surely, new prosecutors are given a manual, probably entitled, 'Handy Race-Neutral Explanations' or '20 Time-Tested Race-Neutral Explanations.'" Citing reasons for strikes that had been upheld, the court suggested that the list included "too old, too young, divorced, 'long, unkempt hair,' free-lance writer, religion, social worker, renter, lack of family contact, attempting to make eye-contact with defendant, 'lived in an area consisting predominantly of apartment complexes,' single," and "over-educated."[78]

Indeed, many prosecutors have such lists. The Texas District and County Attorneys Association distributed a list called "*Batson* Basics" at its Prosecutor Trial Skills Course in 2004. Among the ready-to-use race-neutral reasons were

- Single; unmarried with children
- Body language; poor facial expression
- Long hair and a goatee
- Earrings (male) or a nose ring
- Wore sunglasses; T-shirt

- Chewing gum
- Didn't speak
- Very vocal
- Angry
- Expressionless
- Inattentive
- Worked for a labor union
- Teachers; postal workers; courthouse employees
- Psychologists; consumer advocates
- No religious preference.[79]

The North Carolina Conference of District Attorneys distributed a one-page "cheat sheet" titled "*Batson* Justifications: Articulating Juror Negatives" at a statewide trial advocacy course called "Top Gun II." Besides many of the reasons given at the Texas conference, the North Carolina list included others such as

- Age . . .
- Attitude—air of defiance, lack of eye contact with Prosecutor, eye contact with defendant or defense attorney
- Body Language—arms folded, leaning away from questioner, obvious boredom . . .[80]

Manuals used by California prosecutors provide "encyclopedias of stock, court-approved 'race neutral' reasons." One, *The Inquisitive Prosecutor's Guide*, lists seventy-seven race-neutral reasons for striking jurors.[81]

These lists are filled with subjective descriptions of appearance and demeanor that may apply to just about anyone. It is often impossible for a judge to know whether they are true. As the Texas Supreme Court observed, "*Batson's* promise cannot be fulfilled if its requirements may be satisfied merely by ticking off a race-neutral explanation from a checklist."[82] A North Carolina judge found that, in 173 capital cases, "prosecutors statewide struck 52.8 percent of eligible black venire members, compared to only 25.7 percent of all other eligible venire members." The probability of such a disparity occurring in a process where race is irrelevant is less than one in ten trillion.[83] Every study of peremptory strikes by prosecutors—including studies of strikes in Alabama, Illinois, Louisiana, Mississippi, Pennsylvania, and Texas—has revealed stark disparities between strikes of people of color and strikes of whites.[84]

These studies show that the rule declared in *Batson* simply does not work. The North Carolina Supreme Court acknowledged in 2020 that until that time it had never held that a prosecutor intentionally discriminated in striking a Black prospective juror. In 2019, Justice Goodwin Liu of the California Supreme Court observed that it had been "more than 30 years since" the California Supreme Court had "found *Batson* error involving the peremptory strike of a black juror." Judge Gregg Costa of the federal appellate court that covers Louisiana, Mississippi, and Texas noted in 2018 that the court had found a violation of *Batson* in only two of the hundreds of cases that had come before it.[85] As one study concluded, "There is perhaps no arena of public life or governmental administration where racial discrimination is more widespread, apparent, and seemingly tolerated than in the selection of juries."[86]

A growing number of judges agree. In 2013, the Washington Supreme Court observed that "a growing body of evidence shows that racial discrimination remains rampant in jury selection. In part, this is because *Batson* recognizes only 'purposeful discrimination,' whereas racism is often unintentional, institutional, or unconscious." In 2018, Judge Elsa Alcala of the Texas Court of Criminal Appeals pointed out that the willingness of courts to accept "any implausible or outlandish reason" for a strike rendered *Batson* "meaningless."[87]

Even the most conscientious prosecutors and judges may be unable to determine whether a strike is based to some extent on race. "No one, not even the lawyer herself, can be certain whether a decision to exercise a peremptory challenge rests upon an impermissible racial, religious, gender-based, or ethnic stereotype," Supreme Court Justice Stephen Breyer wrote. "How can trial judges second-guess an instinctive judgment the underlying basis for which may be a form of stereotyping invisible even to the prosecutor?" A member of the Texas Supreme Court made a similar observation: "It is now clear we cannot always detect how many of those strikes are racially motivated, no matter how hard we try."[88]

Bias After the Jury Has Been Selected

However the jury is selected, there remains the danger that individual members will bring their own racial biases into the jury room. In 1974, William Andrews and Pierre Dale Selby, two Black men, were tried for murder by an all-white jury in Utah. At a lunch recess during the trial, the jurors discovered a note with the words "Hang the N——" and a drawing of a figure hanging on a gallows. The trial judge only told the jurors to "ignore communications from foolish people." Both defendants were convicted and sentenced to death. The U.S. Supreme Court refused to hear the case, even though, as Justice Marshall pointed out, no court had held a hearing on what he called this "vulgar incident of lynch-mob racism" or attempted to determine who wrote the note and what influence it had on the jurors.[89]

In theory, a conviction or death sentence can be reversed if the defendant can show evidence of racial bias among the jurors. Miguel Angel Peña-Rodriguez was convicted of unlawful sexual contact and harassment in Colorado. Afterward, two jurors disclosed that, during deliberations, one of the other jurors said that he knew, based on his experience in law enforcement, that Mexican men had a sense of entitlement and were physically controlling of women. He also said during deliberations that "nine times out of ten Mexican men were guilty of being aggressive toward women and young girls." He said that Peña-Rodriguez's alibi witness was not credible because, among other things, the witness was "an illegal." (In fact, the witness had testified that he was a legal resident.) The Colorado courts refused to consider the issue of the juror's bias because of a rule that prohibited inquiry into jury deliberations. The U.S. Supreme Court, in a 5–3 decision, decided that the Constitution requires a hearing when statements of racial bias by jurors cast doubt on the fairness of the verdict.[90]

Johnny Bennett, an African American, was sentenced to death by an all-white jury in South Carolina in 2000. One of the jurors explained that he voted for the death penalty because Bennett "was just a dumb n———." The South Carolina courts upheld the verdict on the grounds that the juror was not racially biased at the time of the sentencing. A federal court set aside Bennett's death sentence because of the racism of the juror and racial appeals made by the prosecutor to the jury.[91]

Unfortunately, the courts often do nothing even in cases of blatant racism. Keith Tharpe, a Black man, was sentenced to death in Georgia by a jury that included one person who said, "After studying the Bible, I have wondered if black people even have souls," and "In my experience, there are two types of black people: 1. Black folks and 2. (n-word)." He said he felt that Tharpe "wasn't in the 'good' black folks category" and therefore "should get the electric chair."[92] The Georgia courts and the federal courts refused to consider the issue on procedural grounds, even though Supreme Court Justice Sonia Sotomayor warned of "an appalling risk that racial bias swayed Tharpe's sentencing." Tharpe died of natural causes before Georgia could execute him.[93] A juror at the Oklahoma capital trial of Julius Jones, a Black man, remarked to another juror that the proceedings were a waste of time and they should "just take the n——— out and shoot him

behind the jail." The jury sentenced Jones to death. The Oklahoma
Court of Criminal Appeals said that Jones could not raise the issue
because he had previously raised an issue of juror misconduct, even
though he was not aware of the racial slur at that time.[94]

Even if they are not overtly racist, jurors often bring to the jury
box, either consciously or subconsciously, stereotypes and assump-
tions that, in the words of one scholar, lead them to see "black culpability and white victimization, . . . black immorality and white
virtue, . . . blacks as social problems and whites as valued citizens."
These attitudes affect the jury's core functions of determining the
credibility of witnesses and assessing facts.[95] Whether because of conscious or unconscious racism, all-white juries often treat Black defendants significantly more harshly than white defendants.

In 1986, the Supreme Court recognized that a juror's decision may
be influenced by a belief "that blacks are violence prone or morally
inferior," as well as "subtle, less consciously held racial attitudes" such
as a fear of Blacks. The Court reversed the death sentence imposed on
Willie Lloyd Turner in Virginia because his lawyer was not allowed
to ask prospective jurors about their racial attitudes during jury selection. But it upheld his conviction, holding that jurors' predispositions
were only likely to influence the sentencing decision, not the verdict
of guilty or not guilty. Of course, as Justice William Brennan pointed
out in dissent, a juror who would vote for the death penalty because
of racial prejudices could be influenced by those same prejudices in
deciding between guilt and innocence. The Court majority also held
that questioning of prospective jurors about their racial attitudes was
required only in death penalty cases involving interracial crimes,
and that trial judges had discretion to limit the form and number of
questions.[96]

Juries are supposed to protect ordinary citizens from the overwhelming prosecutorial power of the state. Too often, however—and
especially if they are entirely white—they become a forum in which

popular racial stereotypes or prejudices end up deciding a minority defendant's fate. And, too often, courts find ways to ignore racial bias, holding that defense lawyers failed to raise the issue properly or simply ignoring evidence of racism among jurors.

Replacing Discrimination with Justice

A diverse jury can reduce the influence of conscious and unconscious racism and increase the likelihood of a just outcome. The Washington Supreme Court has observed that studies show that all-white juries "tend to spend less time deliberating, make more errors, and consider fewer perspectives," while "diverse juries were significantly more able to assess reliability and credibility, avoid presumptions of guilt, and fairly judge a criminally accused [individual]." Diverse juries have a broader perspective gained through varied life experiences. A study found that diverse juries discuss more of the evidence presented at trial, make fewer inaccurate statements about that evidence, and are more willing to discuss racism. As Justice O'Connor has written, "The outcome of a minority defendant's trial may turn on the misconceptions or biases of white jurors," and "there is substantial reason to believe that the distorting influence of race is minimized on a racially mixed jury."[97] Decisions of representative juries are also seen as more legitimate and are accorded greater respect by all segments of the community. As the Washington Supreme Court observed,

> If we allow the systematic removal of minority jurors, we create a badge of inferiority, cheapening the value of the jury verdict. And it is also fundamental that the defendant who looks at the jurors sitting in the box have good reason to believe that the jurors will judge as impartially and fairly as possible.[98]

The Washington Supreme Court has attempted to minimize racism in jury selection. It first adopted a rule requiring that, "when the sole member of a racially cognizable group has been struck from the jury," the party exercising the strike must give reasons for the strike and the judge must make a determination of discrimination.[99] The court also replaced *Batson's* requirement of intentional discrimination with an "objective observer" standard: "If the court determines that an objective observer could view race or ethnicity as a factor in the use of the peremptory challenge, then the peremptory challenge shall be denied." An objective observer is one who takes into account "implicit, institutional, and unconscious biases, in addition to purposeful discrimination." The trial judge must consider how peremptory strikes were used in the current case or past cases, how the prospective jurors were questioned, and whether a reason given might be associated with a race or ethnicity. Reasons that historically have been used to discriminate, such as a prospective juror's distrust of law enforcement or belief in racial profiling, are presumptively invalid. And vague reasons based on demeanor—such as appearing "inattentive" or "confused"—may be asserted only after providing notice to the judge so that the behavior can be verified.[100]

Because this is an objective inquiry, an appellate court reviewing a trial judge's ruling allowing a peremptory strike makes its own determination of whether the strike was permissible and does not employ the deferential standard that the U.S. Supreme Court adopted, under which a judge's decisions are upheld unless they are "clearly erroneous." Applying the two standards, the Washington State Supreme Court concluded in one case that a trial court had properly rejected a challenge to a prosecutor's strike under the *Batson* standard, but that, under the new, objective standard, race appeared to be a factor behind the strike and therefore reversal was required.[101]

In addition, court officials should be required to keep records of how each party used its peremptory strikes in every case. Discrimination may not be apparent when the prosecution strikes a few people of color in one case, but it becomes undeniable when prosecutors strike people of color at several times the rate they strike other potential jurors over many cases. Prosecutors are less likely to engage in such extensive discrimination if records of their strikes are compiled and made available to the public.

A more effective way to prevent discrimination is to eliminate peremptory strikes altogether, as Justice Marshall proposed. Justice Breyer, various state and federal judges, and a number of academics have also called for the elimination of peremptory strikes.[102] Justice Steven González of the Washington Supreme Court said that the peremptory strike "propagates racial discrimination, contributes to the historical and ongoing underrepresentation of minority groups on juries, imposes needless administrative and litigation costs, results in less effective juries, amplifies resource disparity in jury selection, and mars the appearance of fairness" without any "material benefits."[103]

However, in the years since it has been proposed, only Arizona has eliminated peremptory strikes, doing so starting in 2022. Another possible solution is reduction of the number of peremptory strikes. A study of jury selection in the federal Southern District of New York found that "there is more opportunity for mischief than benefit in the present numbers of allowed peremptory challenges." Another analysis concluded, "If peremptories are critical to protect each side against truly oddball jurors, then fewer than five strikes should be enough." According to an analysis done for the California courts, "Reducing peremptory challenges would reduce direct and administrative costs for the courts, reduce disruptions to the lives of people reporting for jury service, enhance public confidence in the jury system, and have only a modest effect on lawyers' practices."[104]

There is no good excuse for the continued use of peremptory strikes to keep people of color from serving on juries. This problem can be solved. Adoption of the Washington rule, limiting each side to three peremptory strikes, and keeping statistics on the exercise of those strikes would make a significant difference. And more could be done, such as requiring that a certain percentage of the jury be of the same race as the person accused of a crime or completely eliminating peremptory strikes.

In addition, the courts must be more attentive to actual racism among jurors. They should hold hearings to examine the evidence of racial bias and, on finding that it was present, they should not hesitate to vacate the defendant's conviction or death sentence. Racism will continue to infect trials as long as judges continue to pretend that it does not exist, among prosecutors or among jurors.

6

Courts of Profit

You can pay what you have, you can call whoever you
need to call, go to an A.T.M. if you need to, do what you
need to do. Call friends, call family, call your employer.
But until you get $300 here tonight, you won't be able
to leave.

—*Judge Richard A. Diment, Municipal Court,*
Bowdon, Georgia, 2014[1]

On September 23, 2014, Vera Cheeks, a Black woman in her fif-
ties, received a citation for failing to come to a complete stop
at a stop sign. The next month she entered a guilty plea in municipal court in Bainbridge, Georgia. The judge imposed a $135 fine,
which came with a $27 fee for the Georgia Crime Victims Emer-
gency Fund. Cheeks, who was unemployed and caring for her ter-
minally ill father, did not have the money, so the judge sentenced her
to three months' probation and ordered her to meet with a probation
officer. The officer—an employee of the private company Red Hills
Community Probation, LLC—told Cheeks that she now owed $267,
including $35 per month in probation fees, and demanded that she
pay $50 before leaving the courthouse. Cheeks did not have $50 in
cash, so she could not leave the building until her fiancé pawned her
engagement ring and some lawn equipment to raise the money. She
had to report weekly to her probation officer, who threatened her

with arrest if she failed to make any required payments. "It was like they were thugs and gangsters taxing poor people that don't have income and keeping them in the system, and when they can't pay, throwing them in jail," Cheeks later said.[2]

In May 2016, Ronald Egana was arrested and charged with illegal possession of marijuana, stolen property, and a gun in St. Bernard Parish, Louisiana. His bail was set at $50,000. His friend Tiffany Brown contacted Blair's Bail Bonds in New Orleans to get Egana released from jail. According to a later lawsuit, she was originally informed that this would cost her $865, but upon arrival she was told that she would have to pay more or wait to see if Egana's bail would be reduced. Even after it was lowered to $26,000, Blair's charged Brown and Egana's mother a nonrefundable bail fee of $3,275: 12 percent of the bail amount, plus $155 in administrative fees and undisclosed charges. Because they could pay only $1,615, Blair's lent them the remaining $1,660. As a condition of the loan, Blair's required that Egana wear an ankle monitor—for which it charged him an additional $10 per day. In September, after Egana failed to make his required payments, he was arrested at work by two armed bounty hunters and brought not to court or the jail, but back to Blair's Bail Bonds, which demanded $2,300 from Egana's mother. Egana lost his job because he had been arrested at work. At this point, Blair's had been paid more than $3,800, but Egana was still required to wear an ankle monitor. In March the next year, one of the same bounty hunters seized Egana—while he was attempting to attend a court hearing—and released him only after his mother was able to borrow $1,500 to pay Blair's. Finally, in May 2017, two bounty hunters arrested Egana and turned him over to the jail—even though his family had at that point paid more than $6,000.[3]

The stories of Vera Cheeks and Ronald Egana illustrate one of the most astonishing failings of our criminal legal system: once Cheeks and Egana came into contact with that system, they became easy targets for courts and private companies more interested in making money than in pursuing justice. For the Bainbridge, Georgia, municipal court and for Red Hills Community Probation, Cheeks was not just someone who had run a stop sign, but a source of revenue. For Blair's Bail Bonds, Egana was not a customer, but a product—someone whose liberty they could repeatedly hold ransom for cash.

What made Cheeks and Egana attractive to private companies was that they were poor. Well-off people can pay a $135 traffic fine and walk out of court free. They can raise $26,000 or put up collateral to post bond with the court—money they will get back if they appear in court. Alternatively, if they have to use a bondsman, they can pay the $3,275 fee up front and avoid add-on fees for "services" such as ankle monitoring. By contrast, poor people can be sucked into a cycle of debt and fees that forces them to pay far more than any fine the court imposed. What makes this business model especially pernicious is that the prospect of imprisonment—a power that belongs to the government—is leveraged to coerce poor people into paying whatever they can. If they fail to make their required payments, they can be sent to jail.

This is not the way the system is supposed to work. Most people believe there are no debtors' prisons in the United States. In 1970, the Supreme Court held that extending a defendant's prison time beyond the statutory maximum because he could not pay a fine was an illegal violation of the Equal Protection Clause of the Fourteenth Amendment.[4] The following year, the Court specified that a defendant cannot be "subjected to imprisonment solely because of his indigency."[5] In 1983, the Court held that someone cannot be sent to jail because of an inability to pay a fine.[6] In short, no one should go to jail because he is unable to pay a fine or fees. In addition, as discussed previously, any person facing a potential loss of liberty because of inability to pay is entitled to a lawyer at any court proceeding where liberty may be denied.[7]

Unfortunately, courts all over the country routinely disregard these requirements. The threat of jail is the linchpin of a widespread system of extracting money from those who have the least of it. State, county, and local governments, unwilling to increase taxes, raise money by levying fees on poor people found guilty of minor infractions. Those same governments have also privatized numerous functions within the criminal legal system, from bail enforcement and probation supervision to completely private prisons. Privatization can result from a lack of government resources, lobbying by for-profit companies, or simply the belief that the private sector is more efficient than the state. (One Georgia judge said, arguing for private probation, "I don't think the government should be in competition with private business.")[8] People charged with crimes become exposed to companies motivated solely by profits—not by deterrence, rehabilitation, or public safety, let alone justice.

This system harnesses the unique power of governments to make money for themselves and private companies. It coerces people into pleading guilty so they can get out of jail and take care of their families. The ultimate effect is not to achieve justice but to maintain class divisions and aggravate inequality.

Money-Hungry Courts

Ferguson, Missouri, is famous because it is where Darren Wilson, a white police officer, shot and killed Michael Brown, an eighteen-year-old unarmed Black man, in 2014. The city also relies heavily on its court and police as sources of revenue. Ferguson is one of ninety municipalities in St. Louis County ranging in population from twelve residents to over fifty thousand; each is responsible for arranging its own police services, and eighty-one have their own courts.[9]

The U.S. Department of Justice found that "the City [of Ferguson] considers revenue generation to be the municipal court's primary purpose" and that the city's finance director had commended the court's judge for his success in "significantly increasing court collections over the years."[10] In Ferguson and many other towns and small cities, policing, prosecution, and the resolution of cases are motivated not by public safety but by collecting fines and fees to provide revenue.

Most people come into contact with the judicial system through municipal courts, not the state and federal courts that are often depicted in the media. People are summoned to municipal courts for traffic violations or for petty crimes such as disturbing the peace. Most cases are settled quickly with the imposition of a fine and related fees. Poverty is an enormous disadvantage. A person who cannot afford to pay fines and fees on the day they are imposed may be required to pay more through installments accompanied by monthly fees and may even be jailed for failure to pay, while those who can pay resolve their cases immediately and never risk being sent to jail.

Municipal courts vary greatly, even within a single county. One municipality in St. Louis County—Pine Lawn, population 3,275, 96 percent Black, with a per capita income of $13,000—collected more than $1.7 million in fines and fees in 2013. The more affluent city of Chesterfield, with fourteen times the population, collected just $1.2 million.[11] That year, court fines and fees were the largest single source of revenue for at least fourteen municipalities in the county, including Pine Lawn.[12] Across the country, anti-tax sentiment, stagnant property values in rural areas, and increasingly stingy state budgets have combined to reduce traditional sources of municipal revenue. Richer, whiter towns can support themselves with property taxes. Poorer towns with more minorities and less valuable real estate rely on their municipal courts—placing a financial burden on those people least able to bear it.[13]

Each municipality can have its own municipal code, police force, and court. In small towns, the judge may work part-time and hold court for a few hours once or a few times a week. In some courts, there are no prosecutors or defense lawyers; a police officer presents the prosecution's case. The police departments are under pressure to issue citations and arrest people, and the judges are under pressure to impose and collect fines and fees.[14]

Towns that treat their courts as cash cows are found all over the country. Georgetown, a village in central Louisiana with fewer than five hundred people, collected almost $500,000 in fines in 2018—92 percent of its general revenues. Seven other Louisiana towns brought in more than 80 percent of their money from fines and fees.[15] New York has 1,250 town and village courts in which fewer than one-quarter of the judges are lawyers. Judges in these courts, which many towns depend on for revenues, have summarily jailed people over personal disputes, sent people to jail for failure to pay fines, and levied hundreds of thousands of dollars of excessive fines.[16] An investigation by the New Jersey Supreme Court found that many municipal courts in that state were raising money through procedures, such as fining people for contempt, that "at times have more to do with generating revenue than the fair administration of justice." One particularly inventive judge secretly reclassified traffic fines as fines for contempt citations—thereby diverting money from the county to the local municipality—in order "to curry favor with the municipalities that continued to employ him as a judge."[17]

In Ohio, mayors can preside over almost three hundred "mayor's courts" even if they are not attorneys. According to longtime Ohio Supreme Court justice Paul E. Pfeifer, the courts' principal concern is "what's in the cash register at the end of the evening." The American Civil Liberties Union of Ohio found that the state's mayor's courts and municipal courts routinely imprisoned people who were unable to pay fines and court costs.[18] In response, the Ohio Supreme Court issued a memorandum informing judges that they must determine ability to pay before jailing people (and reminding them that "the purpose of [fines and costs] is *not* to generate revenue for the local municipality, county, or the State of Ohio").[19]

A court can bring in revenue only if the police generate large volumes of citations, which requires aggressive policing. Many departments have been found to be imposing quotas to boost enforcement activities. In 2010, the New York City Police Department was embarrassed by recordings of supervisors insisting that officers meet quotas for tickets, stop-and-frisks, and arrests. The City of Los Angeles paid $7.9 million in judgments and settlements to officers who accused their department of maintaining a secret quota system for traffic tickets. In Douglasville, Georgia, a police lieutenant offered a steak dinner to his officers if they averaged more than five tickets per shift, and the court clerk generated a report listing, for each officer, the number of tickets written and the revenue they could be worth.[20]

Ferguson's police force made arrests based on the municipal code with the explicit aim of generating revenue. The Department of Justice found that "officers routinely conduct stops that have little relation to public safety and a questionable basis in law" and "routinely issue multiple citations during a single stop, often for the same violation."[21] When the police are white and the population is largely non-white, the consequences are predictable. In Ferguson, which had a primarily white police force, African Americans constituted 67 percent of the city's population yet were the subject of 85 percent of traffic stops, 90 percent of citations, and 93 percent of arrests from 2012 to 2014. These disparities were only exacerbated in municipal court. Compared with other defendants, Black people were 68 percent less likely to have their charges dismissed and were more likely to have their cases persist for longer durations, to face a higher number of mandatory court appearances, and to have warrants issued against them.[22]

Small police forces under pressure to issue citations often have thin budgets because of the funding constraints faced by small towns and cannot take advantage of the economies of scale from which larger departments benefit. For example, St. Louis City and St. Louis County together contain sixty different police departments; only a quarter are accredited or certified, and many lack standards in areas such as hiring, training, pay, disciplinary procedures, and use of force.[23] Municipal police forces often hire officers on a part-time basis for little more than minimum wage, forcing them to rely on inexperienced officers who may not be suited for the job. As one police chief said, "Unfortunately, sometimes there's not a lot of money to hire what you need, you just have to make do with what you have."[24] An investigation revealed that many departments in the Chicago suburbs have "lax and often unenforced policies regarding the use of deadly force." Between 2005 and 2018, police officers in those suburbs shot people 113 times, and yet none faced any kind of disciplinary action.[25]

Fragmented, underpaid, and poorly trained police forces, under constant pressure to generate citations and arrests to help fill municipal coffers, are a threat to public safety. According to one study, police tend to do a worse job of solving violent and property crimes in towns and cities that depend more heavily on fines and fees, especially those with small police departments.[26] A patchwork of municipalities targeting the same sources of revenue can also lead to confusion and harassment. For example, one ten-mile stretch of road in St. Louis County crosses through sixteen different municipalities—each of which could cite a motorist for a single violation such as an expired license plate, and each of which has its own code, enforcement policy, and court system.[27] One obvious solution is to merge police forces and court systems on the county level, or to merge surrounding towns into a larger city. This would enable economies of scale and greater professionalism of the police and the courts and would prevent small towns from using the criminal legal system as a major source of revenue. Unfortunately, such mergers are rare because those who benefit from the system are resistant to change.

The point of all this policing is to get people into court, where they can be subject to two types of monetary penalties. First, fines can be imposed as punishment for offenses committed. Second, almost every court assesses various fees that significantly increase the costs for the people coming before them. One person who pled guilty to retail theft in Allegheny County, Pennsylvania, was ordered to pay $121 in restitution and twenty-seven fees that added up to $1,500.75.[28] Most of these fees are allocated to different agencies by legislatures, county commissions, and city councils that would rather collect a few dollars at a time from people found guilty of minor offenses than raise sales, property, or income taxes that are paid by constituencies with the political power to resist such tax increases.

Some fees pay for the criminal legal system: there may be a fee for "court costs," a fee to support prison construction, a fee for a crime victims fund, a fee to fund DNA testing, a fee for the public defender, and even a fee for the prosecution.[29] In North Carolina, courts collect fifty-two distinct fees that support everything from courts and jails to schools. The Georgia legislature decided to fund the state's public defender system with surcharges to criminal and traffic fines, bond and bail fees, and civil filing fees, in addition to a $50 fee to apply for a public defender. Washington State charges defendants a fee for a jury—$250 for a twelve-person jury and $125 for a six-person jury. In at least forty-one states, people can be charged room and board for the time they are kept in jail and prison. People who avoid incarceration can still be charged probation fees. In Massachusetts, people on probation are charged at least $50 per month; although the fee can be waived, judges often fail to determine whether someone sentenced to probation has the ability to pay the fee.[30]

Fees on criminal defendants may be directed to the most tangentially related purposes. In California, for example, fees are used to fund the Fish and Game Preservation Fund and the Traumatic Brain Injury Fund; in Georgia, fees go to the Brain and Spinal Injury Trust Fund, the Peace Officers' Annuity and Benefit Fund, and the Sheriff's

Retirement Fund; in Pennsylvania, fees are directed to emergency medical services, the Firearm Education and Training Fund, and services for victims of domestic violence. In Florida, Kentucky, and Oklahoma, some court fees flow directly into general revenues.[31] As one Oklahoma lawmaker said, "You see a legislative leadership and a governor willing to use criminals as an ATM to fund other parts of government."[32]

Some courts charge more esoteric fees as well. In 2016, Cleopatra Harrison was charged a $150 "victim's fee" in Columbus, Georgia, after she declined to testify against her boyfriend in a domestic abuse case. When Harrison couldn't produce the money, she was told she had to pay within one week or a warrant would be issued for her arrest. In addition, while still in the courthouse, she was handcuffed, jailed, and charged with providing "false information." Her boyfriend paid $212.50 to get her out of jail.[33] Judges even impose made-up fees with no basis whatsoever. In New York, multiple localities charge probation fees with no basis in state law.[34] In Grady County, Georgia, Judge J. William Bass Sr. routinely charged defendants "administrative costs" of up to $800—and then requested that his salary be increased by 50 percent because, he claimed, he had brought in more than $350,000 for the county per year.[35]

What happens once fines and fees have been imposed depends on how much money a person has. Often, even if they can come up with a few hundred dollars, this represents a major financial shock that can compromise their ability to pay for food, rent, or utilities. If they do not have enough cash or credit, judges threaten jail to try to force them to come up with money any way they can. Unrepresented poor people are routinely sent to jail simply because they cannot pay their fines, despite clear holdings of the U.S. Supreme Court to the contrary.

In Eastpointe, Michigan, one judge repeatedly sentenced people to pay in full or go to jail immediately. When one defendant asked,

"Is it pay or stay?" the judge responded, "Yes, sir." In Grand Rapids, Michigan, a homeless man was charged $2,600 in fines and fees for destroying property and resisting arrest. The judge demanded a $50 down payment; when the defendant could only come up with $25, he was jailed for twenty-two days. In Perry County, Alabama, Judge Marvin Wiggins told a group of defendants that they could raise cash by donating blood across the street: "If you do not have any money and you don't want to go to jail, consider giving blood today and [bring] your receipt back, or the sheriff has enough handcuffs for those who do not have money."[36]

More often, defendants are allowed to leave the courtroom but required to pay on a schedule, sometimes at high interest rates. If they fail to pay, judges in many jurisdictions will issue warrants for their arrest, which can lead to jail time. Edward Brown was cited for not mowing the lawn around his small house in Ferguson, Missouri. The city condemned the house and then gave him citations for trespassing and for having a dog without a rabies vaccination. Unable to pay $464 in fines and fees, Brown was jailed multiple times, eventually becoming homeless.[37] Judges rarely grant hearings to evaluate whether a defendant can actually pay his fines and fees, even though such a determination is required by Supreme Court precedent. In Ohio, an ACLU investigation found that defendants were routinely jailed for ten days—without being offered a lawyer, without a determination of their ability to pay, and without the ability to post bond—for failing to stay current with their payment plans. In some counties, the cost of being transported to jail is added to their court-related debt.[38]

The architects of the Constitution, in response to the historical legacy of the British king "assessing unpayable fines to keep his enemies in debtor's prison," drafted the Eighth Amendment, which bars both "excessive bail" and "excessive fines," according to Supreme Court Justice Anthony Kennedy.[39] Yet state and local governments routinely deprive thousands of poor people of their liberty because of their inability to pay excessive fines and fees. The Obama administration's Council of Economic Advisers found that "in some jurisdictions, approximately 20 percent of all jail inmates were incarcerated for failure to pay criminal justice debts."[40] In general, spending time behind bars does not eliminate debt stemming from fines and fees (although some jurisdictions accept jail time in lieu of cash), and many inmates are even charged a daily fee while in jail. One study estimates that four in five people leave prison owing money to the court system.[41]

In some jurisdictions, courts have yet another way to collect their money. People who cannot pay their fines and fees can be sentenced to "restitution centers" run by the state prison systems, where they must stay—paying daily fees for room and board—until they have worked enough to pay off their court debt. Most of the money earned by inmates of these facilities goes not to pay restitution to crime victims but to pay for room and board and to pay off fines and fees incurred for offenses that, in most cases, did not require prison time. These centers not only help the state collect money from poor people, they also provide cheap labor to local businesses. "If it weren't for the restitution center, I would seriously have trouble running my business," admitted the owner of a fast-food restaurant in Mississippi.[42] In Georgia, Ora Lee Hurley was sentenced to a $705 fine and 120 days in the Gateway Diversion Center in 2006. She remained locked in the facility after her sentence expired because she was unable to pay her fine. According to Hurley, she could leave only to work at a restaurant, where she made $700 per month after taxes—$600 of which was withheld for room and board. Eight months after her original sentence expired, she was released after a legal organization intervened on her behalf.[43]

Diversion programs are alternatives to jail that enable people charged with minor crimes to live in their community while performing community service or getting services such as counseling or drug treatment. These programs reduce jail populations while helping people deal with the issues that brought them into the system. But some diversion programs charge fees that many cannot afford. In Alabama, the median cost is $1,600 per year (on top of any other fines and fees)—an unmanageable expense for many poor people.[44] Those who cannot pay are denied the benefits of diversion—which may include avoiding a conviction and jail—because of their poverty.

In some jurisdictions, diversion programs seem to be a mechanism to extract money from people who commit minor offenses. In Maricopa County, Arizona, for example, where possession of any amount of marijuana is a felony, people who can pay $1,000 for a ninety-day diversion program can have the charges dismissed. Those who cannot pay the fee must remain in the program longer—paying for periodic drug tests—or face prosecution. Of the $1,000 fee, $650 goes directly to the county prosecutor's office.[45] Diversion programs are also a way for private companies to make money from the criminal legal system. A ProPublica investigation found that many people who bounce small checks in Illinois are referred by prosecutors to private "diversion programs" that charge them hundreds of dollars to attend classes in order to avoid criminal charges.[46]

Unpaid court debt can entail a wide range of negative consequences. People convicted of some crimes can lose the right to vote or the right to carry a weapon and can be barred from jury service; in some jurisdictions, they cannot regain those rights so long as they have outstanding court debt. Unpaid fines and fees can prevent people from getting a certificate of discharge to get out of bankruptcy or having their criminal record sealed, and can make it harder for them to borrow money, find employment, or rent housing.[47] The city of LaGrange, Georgia, began attaching unpaid court debt to residents' utility bills; April Walton had her utilities shut off because of a seven-year-old fine for a misdemeanor drug offense.[48]

In addition, many states allow courts to suspend or revoke the driver's licenses of people who fail to pay traffic-related fines and fees, typically without any consideration of their ability to pay; in some states, defendants can also lose their license for failure to pay any criminal debt, even if it is completely unrelated to driving. According to a 2019 estimate, at least eleven million licenses were suspended because of failure to pay court debt.[49] Taking away people's driver's licenses often prevents them from being able to work, making it impossible for them to pay their debts and plunging them even further into poverty.

In recent years, legal organizations have challenged court fees and practices that punish poor people solely for their inability to pay those fees. As part of a settlement in a class action lawsuit, officials in Bainbridge, Georgia—where Vera Cheeks was detained in the courthouse—agreed to stop jailing people or holding them in the courthouse until they can come up with cash. After another class action lawsuit, officials in Columbus, Georgia, agreed to abolish the victim's fees that landed Cleopatra Harrison in jail.[50] In California, San Francisco, Alameda, Contra Costa, and Los Angeles Counties stopped charging court fees under their discretion, and the state legislature abolished twenty-three administrative fees in 2020. In 2018, the California legislature ended the practice of charging children in juvenile courts fees for representation by a lawyer, electronic monitoring, drug testing, probation supervision, and detention.[51] Similar bills repealing juvenile fees have been passed in Colorado, Maryland, New Jersey, New Mexico, and Oregon.

There has also been a backlash against the practice of revoking driver's licenses over unpaid fines and fees. Federal district courts in multiple states have prohibited the automatic revocation of a driver's license for failure to pay court debt.[52] The chief prosecutors in some jurisdictions no longer prosecute people for driving without a license if their licenses were revoked or suspended for financial reasons.[53] Most significantly, at least thirteen states have passed legislation since 2017 ending the suspension of licenses solely because of court debt.[54]

Some jurisdictions have also emphasized that people cannot be jailed solely for failure to pay court debt. In 2016, the Michigan Supreme Court imposed rules requiring judges to assess whether people have the ability to pay fines and fees before sending them to jail. In 2018, Mississippi adopted a law saying the same thing. And in 2021, the Idaho Supreme Court barred the practice of issuing an arrest warrant for a person's unpaid court debt without assessing his ability to pay.[55] Of course, this principle was established by the U.S. Supreme Court decades ago, so there is no assurance that new rules will put an end to this practice. The example of Colorado is instructive. In 2014, the state enacted a law to eliminate jail time for persons who are unable to pay monetary penalties. However, some municipal judges set court dates for each required payment and then jailed people for failing to appear in court. The legislature passed another law in 2016 to close the loophole. Nevertheless, some judges continued to flout the law; one repeatedly jailed and threatened poor defendants unable to pay their fines and fees, telling one, "Make sure you have those payments made, or make sure you bring your toothbrush, because you'll have to go over to the jail."[56] As long as governments and judges continue to put revenue generation over their constitutional responsibilities, people will still go to jail or prison because of their poverty.

Profiting from Probation

Probation was traditionally a program of supervised release in which a person who has been found guilty of an offense complies with conditions imposed by a judge and is supervised by public employees in order to avoid criminal behavior and become a useful and productive member of society. The purpose was rehabilitation and it did not cost people on probation anything. Today, however, probation has become a way of collecting fines and fees for governments and a source of additional monthly income for private companies. In many jurisdictions, people who cannot pay fines and fees when they are imposed are sentenced to probation to pay the amount owed in installments; people who can pay up front are not sentenced to probation. The purpose of this type of probation is the collection of fines and fees.

Courts could simply ask probationers to send checks or money orders to the courthouse. Many jurisdictions, however, have outsourced the debt collection function to private probation companies. This is possible because forty-four states allow people to be charged for probation services—typically around $40 per month—even if the only service is debt collection. Private companies are happy to provide collection services—"pay-only probation"—at no cost to the government, pocketing the monthly fee, especially since they can use the courts to punish people who do not pay on time.[57] Many companies pay bonuses to their employees based on the amount of money they collect, giving them an incentive to squeeze whatever they can out of people who are on probation. Because of flat monthly probation fees, the poorest people, who need the most time to pay off their debts, end up paying the most in probation fees. If they fall behind, private probation officers threaten them with jail. Some courts delegate to the probation company both the determination of whether a probationer has the ability to pay the amount owed and even the function of preparing arrest warrants.[58]

Adel Edwards, a fifty-four-year-old intellectually disabled Black man who lives on food stamps, was fined $500 for burning leaves in his backyard without a permit. Because he did not have the money, a municipal court in rural Georgia placed him on probation for a year and ordered him to pay $44 per month in "supervision" fees to Red Hills Community Probation. When Edwards could not make an immediate payment to Red Hills, he was jailed until a friend paid $250 to get him out. After his release, Edwards was unable to make his payments because he had no cash income. After his period of probation expired, he owed more than $600 on his $500 fine. His probation officer instructed him to report for another eleven months and threatened to take out a warrant for his arrest if he did not continue to pay.[59]

The threat of jail exists to induce people to pay whatever they can. Some probation officers employ the strategy of issuing an arrest warrant for nonpayment so that the person is arrested and jailed pending a probation revocation hearing. The officer then negotiates with the probationer or his family, collects a partial payment, and asks the judge to release the probationer from jail. As one officer said, "I always try and negotiate with the families. . . . They have to see that this person is not getting out unless they pay something."[60] Often the period of probation is extended to give the person more time to pay his debt—and to give the probation company more revenue in monthly fees.

A person placed on traditional probation as a sentence for a crime may be required to meet regularly with a probation officer, perform community service, or complete a drug treatment program, anger management class, or some other program. Supervising people convicted of crimes in order to reduce the likelihood of recidivism is a quintessential state function. However, the companies that have taken over probation also make money providing the "services" that courts often mandate as conditions of probation. The probation companies bill the services to the people on probation—increasing their indebtedness and often keeping them on probation even longer.

In addition to their initial fines and fees and monthly probation fees, people may be required to pay fees for electronic monitoring, drug testing, continuous alcohol monitoring, ignition interlock devices, background checks, and classes in domestic violence, anger management, or other subjects.[61] Private probation companies often offer these services and classes as another source of revenue. A Human Rights Watch report found that many classes were of questionable value; for some, participants only had to buy workbooks from the probation company and take a short test at the end of the book. One Alabama court official said of the classes, "They tend to be expensive and from what I can tell they tend to be bullshit."[62] The combination of monthly "supervision" fees and add-on fees, collected from a captive customer base, can be extremely lucrative. At their peak, private probation companies in Georgia supervised 80 percent of people on misdemeanor probation and brought in $40 million in fees each year—on top of any fines and fees paid to the state.[63]

Some companies even bill probationers for services that are not ordered by courts. Rita Luse and Marianne Ligocki were both put on probation in Georgia because they could not pay fines incurred for traffic offenses. According to a lawsuit, in addition to charging $44 per month for probation supervision, Sentinel Offender Services ordered them—and at least a hundred other people—to take drug tests, which cost $15 each, even though the judges in their cases had not required the tests.[64] Thomas Barrett was required to pay $360 per month for an alcohol monitoring bracelet—even though abstaining from drinking alcohol was not a condition of his probation.[65]

Probation companies have strong incentives to encourage judges to find violations in order to get probationers' sentences extended—so they can collect more in monthly fees. In Missouri, Aimey Stude had her probation extended by a year for failing to return a form in the mail and was eventually jailed for missing check-ins with her probation officer.[66] Jason DeFriese was put on probation for a traffic violation in Missouri. He had to pay $50 per month to Private Correction Services, get drug testing, and pay other fees. When PCS found that DeFriese failed a drug test—even though an independent lab found conflicting results—he was sentenced to a new, two-year period of probation and required to wear a continuous alcohol monitoring bracelet (costing him $91 per week) and install an alcohol ignition interlock device on his car (costing him more than $200 per month). After ninety days without any positive results from the alcohol monitor, DeFriese asked a judge to release him from it, but his probation officer successfully opposed his request; DeFriese had to wear (and pay for) the bracelet for another five months.[67] When Steven Gibbs told his probation officer at Providence Community Corrections in Tennessee that he could not afford to make a payment, the officer told him that he had failed a drug test—even though an independent lab found that Gibbs was clean. According to Gibbs, the probation officer then threatened to "write [him] up" unless he made his payments.[68] Private probation companies sometimes even misdirected payments made by probationers, crediting them to the company's account rather than to the court.[69]

Private probation companies participate heavily in local and state politics—through lobbying and campaign contributions—to protect their ability to make money off the poor. In Georgia, the private probation industry was made possible in the first place by a 2000 bill championed by Bobby Whitworth, chair of the state's Board of Pardons and Paroles. He was paid $75,000 by an owner of a private probation company. The bill became law—and Whitworth was convicted of influencing legislative action for pay while serving as a state official, and served six months in prison.[70] Most states have only minimal oversight regimes, which allows abuses to continue unchecked. Private probation companies have even resorted to illegal payments to judges in exchange for referring defendants to them.[71] The end result is that many people end up paying far more to private companies than they initially owed in fines and fees—or they end up in jail because of their inability to pay their debts to those companies.

This use of courts, police, and probation to generate public funds and private profit does not serve any semblance of justice. The purpose of the legal system is to hold people accountable for unlawful behavior, impose just and reasonable punishment, and help people avoid unlawful behavior in the future without regard to how much money it brings in. Private probation companies have no incentive to provide meaningful rehabilitative services, but every incentive to extend the period of probation and add money-generating requirements such as drug testing. Probation supervision should be carried out by probation officers who are on the public payroll and whose objective is to help probationers deal with the issues that resulted in their criminal behavior so that they become useful and productive citizens.

The Inequality of Money Bail

Maurice Walker, a mentally ill man whose only income was $530 per month in Social Security disability payments, was arrested in September 2015 in Calhoun, Georgia, for being a "pedestrian under the influence"—walking while intoxicated. He was jailed because he could not come up with $160 in cash to make bail, even though the charge was not punishable with jail time. He could not seek a reduction of bail until his first court hearing eleven days later. While in jail, Walker could not take the medication he needed for his mental illness.[72]

For many minor violations, a person is issued a citation and told to report to court on a particular date. However, people arrested and taken into custody even for minor offenses may be held in jail unless they can "post bail"—put up a certain amount of money or property that will be returned only if they appear at all their court dates as scheduled. The purpose of bail is to ensure that a person who is released returns to court.

In 1983, the Supreme Court held that depriving an individual of "conditional freedom simply because, through no fault of his own, he cannot pay" violates the Fourteenth Amendment.[73] As New York's highest court explained, "The policy of our law favors bail because of the presumption that the prisoner is innocent. . . . The amount must be no more than is necessary to guarantee his presence at the trial."[74] And yet, on any given day, almost half a million people in jail—more than 70 percent of the jail population—have not been convicted of anything but cannot afford to post bail.[75] At the Rikers Island jail in New York, the median bail for detainees awaiting trial in 2017 was $5,000; according to one defense attorney, judges routinely used unaffordable bail to "lock people up before trial if they had a hunch that they might re-offend." In Pennsylvania in 2016 and 2017, the average bail was more than $38,000 (although some counties allowed defendants to post 10 percent of the bail amount), and more than half of defendants were unable to post bail.[76]

People without the cash to make bail have one other option: the bail bond industry. A bail bond company or bail bondsman "posts bond" for the defendant; without putting up any cash, the bondsman agrees to pay the defendant's full bail amount to the court if the defendant does not appear when required. The bondsman carries insurance that covers the cost if the defendant does not appear. Defendants pay bail bondsmen a nonrefundable fee—usually 10 percent of the bail amount—for this guarantee. If a defendant cannot pay the fee up front, a bondsman may allow him to pay in installments, but failing to make a payment exposes a person to late fees and high interest rates. Bail bond companies also impose additional fees, such as a fee for electronic monitoring. For instance, one person in California who had a chronic medical condition was charged $300 for each hospital visit because he had to have his ankle monitor removed and reattached each time.[77] In addition, these companies often require that the defendant's family members or friends put up collateral worth the cost of the bond or to agree to pay the full amount if the defendant fails to appear. Bail bonds were used to secure 49 percent of pretrial releases of felony defendants in large urban counties in 2009, and annual industry revenues are approximately $2 billion.[78] The only other country that allows bail bond companies is the Philippines.[79]

Failing to appear in court when required is a violation of the law, and ordinarily, courts rely on the police and prosecutors to enforce the law. For unique historical and political reasons, however, most states have authorized bail bond companies to ensure that people for whom they have posted bail appear in court. If defendants fail to appear, bail bond companies have the power to seize them—virtually anywhere, by any means, and with no judicial oversight—and bring them to court. They may use that power to obtain additional funds from defendants and their families.

In Nevada, hundreds of pages of complaints with the state Division of Insurance document industry tactics for squeezing money out of defendants and their families. Bail bond agents came to the house of a defendant's family—with a Taser—and threatened to kick down the door, break their windows, and take their cars if they did not con-vince the defendant to turn himself in. A bail bond company offered another defendant $4,000 for her car, but, after she turned it over, said it was worth only $1,100 and demanded more money; when she came up with cash to pay off the company, they refused to return the car and threatened her with jail. In a third case, a bail bond company seized a car that had not been pledged as collateral and refused to return it.[80] In California, the Department of Insurance reported that bail bond companies forged property liens, kidnapped defendants to extort money from their families, and stole collateral posted by their customers.[81]

The New York Times found, simply by calling bondsmen and asking about prices, that some were charging prices exceeding those allowed by state law, citing "lock-up fees" that do not exist. In California, Jake's Bail Bonds charged a defendant's father $39,755 for a $5,000 bond, claiming the remainder was for "actual, reasonable and neces-sary" expenses—including a $19,500 "recovery cost percentage" and $4,425 for "equipment"—and threatened to foreclose on his house. Six years after the father paid, a bondsman at Jake's sent a second notice of foreclosure, now claiming that he owed $117,500. In a rare response to unscrupulous industry practices, California prosecutors charged the bondsman with attempted extortion. A judge later dismissed the charges, but the bondsman surrendered his bail license in a confidential settlement. In North Carolina, in order to collect an outstanding fee, a bail bondsman tried to jail a person whose charges has already been resolved with a guilty plea.[82] The result of these practices in different states is a massive transfer of wealth from poor people to the bail industry.

People without the money to pay a bondsman must wait in jail until their first court appearance, which may not be for weeks, while wealthier people walk free. People in jail have a strong incentive to plead guilty, particularly if they will be released in exchange for their plea. Jail itself is notoriously unpleasant, and remaining in jail can result in a loss of employment, eviction for failure to pay rent, and inability to take care of family members.[83] Some courts have "jail clearing days" in which those people who plead guilty are released; the others go back to jail and wait an indeterminate amount of time for trial.

Many people who cannot make bail plead guilty—even if they are innocent—in order to get on with their lives. Those with money, and therefore their liberty, have a better chance of avoiding conviction, and, if convicted, have a better chance of getting probation instead of a jail or prison sentence. An empirical analysis found that defendants who are released shortly after arrest—those who make bail or are released on their promise to return to court—are 14 percentage points less likely to be convicted than those who are not, primarily because they are less likely to plead guilty, and are 25 percent more likely to be employed three to four years later.[84] A comparison of nonfelony cases in New York City found that only 53 percent of those released at some point before their cases closed were convicted; for those held in jail the entire time, the conviction rate was 92 percent. And a study of felony cases in urban counties found that people detained before trial plead guilty almost three times as fast as those not detained, suggesting that they plead largely to get out of jail.[85] In effect, the money bail system severely punishes people simply because they cannot come up with the money to secure their release.

In addition, the bail system disfavors people of color, who are more likely to remain in jail pending trial. Separate analyses of data from Kentucky and Pennsylvania found that Blacks are significantly less likely than whites to be released on their own recognizance (simply on their promise to return to court in the future), even after accounting for legally relevant factors such as the charged offense and criminal history. Another study of Miami and Philadelphia concluded that judges are more lenient toward whites, most likely because of both explicit and unconscious biases. In cases from three federal districts in the Midwest, the odds of a Black defendant being detained before trial were 77 percent higher than those for whites; in New York City, the odds were 48 percent higher for Blacks and 14 percent higher for Latinos.[86]

Not only do cash bail systems send people to jail because of their lack of income, but they also provide no apparent public safety benefits. In 2018, the Philadelphia District Attorney's office established a presumption against cash bail for twenty-five different charges, accounting for more than half of all cases; in the following year, it found no increase in the proportion of people rearrested prior to trial or in the proportion that failed to appear in court.[87] Washington, DC, virtually eliminated money bail in the early 1990s. In 2017, 94 percent of those arrested in the nation's capital were released before trial. Eighty-eight percent of them made all scheduled court appearances.[88] New Jersey largely eliminated cash bail in 2017, with no significant impact on reappearance or rearrest rates.

Other jurisdictions have taken similar steps. A 2016 constitutional amendment in New Mexico prohibited jailing people because they could not make bail, although it gave judges increased discretion to detain people if they were dangerous or posed a flight risk.

In 2019, the New York legislature voted to abolish money bail for most nonviolent offenses, although it later modified the law. In 2021, the Illinois legislature and governor completely eliminated cash bail (effective in 2023).[89]

Even where cash bail remains, there is no need for bail bond companies. Kentucky, Oregon, and Wisconsin all banned for-profit bail bond companies decades ago.[90] In those states, defendants typically pay 10 percent of their bail amount to the court and get it back if they do not miss any court appearances.

Courts have become more willing to take action against bail policies. In 2017, a federal district court found that bail procedures in Harris County, Texas—where court officials required secured bonds from people they knew to be indigent, and arrestees were pressured to plead guilty in exchange for time served—were unconstitutional and that their purpose was "to achieve pretrial detention of misdemeanor defendants who are too poor to pay, when those defendants would promptly be released if they could."[91] The county agreed not to require cash bail for most people charged with misdemeanors. Since then, according to the court-appointed monitor, the proportion of misdemeanor defendants who were rearrested within one year has remained the same, while the people charged saved tens of millions of dollars per year.[92] Several other courts have ruled that judges must consider a defendant's ability to pay when setting bail, including the Supreme Judicial Court of Massachusetts and the California Supreme Court.[93]

However, progress on bail reform has been vulnerable to shifts in the political wind. The bail bond industry, with its national organization, the American Bail Coalition, has long been a major force in statehouses across the country. The bail industry intervenes to block bail reform initiatives and back key county supervisors, elected judges, and influential state legislators. As of 2019, a CNN study found that "the powerful bail industry has derailed, stalled or killed reform efforts in at least nine states." In Iowa, a pilot bail reform program was blocked in the state legislature after the owner of a bail bond company stepped up contributions to lawmakers and hired a lobbying firm in the state capital.[94] In Alaska, a 2016 bill severely limiting the use of cash bail was gutted in 2019 under new Governor Mike Dunleavy, who had actively campaigned against reform. In New York, police organizations and prosecutors—backed by President Trump—bitterly opposed bail reform both before and after it went into effect on January 1, 2020. In April 2020, their allies in the state legislature passed a bill that expanded the number of cases where bail could be imposed. In California, after the legislature passed a bill in 2018 to eliminate cash bail, industry groups successfully campaigned to repeal the bill in a 2020 referendum. As one lobbyist said, "You don't eliminate an industry and expect those people to go down quietly."[95]

Running Prisons for Profit

Finally, for-profit companies make money by incarcerating people convicted of crimes. Locking people up seems like a quintessentially public function. Traditionally, jails and prisons were run by local, state, or federal governments and staffed by government employees. That began to change in the 1980s, as the prison population began to soar. In 1980, just under 200 of every 100,000 adult residents were in prison; by 1995, that number had almost tripled to around 550.[96] At the same time, America's political landscape was changing. The 1980 election of Ronald Reagan signaled the rise of a conservative ideology that assumed that the private sector could do anything better than the government. Private prison companies were willing to build or renovate prisons to house the burgeoning prison population in exchange for long-term contracts to operate them, at the same time that legislators were looking for ways to shrink the size of government.[97]

Private companies already operated—and continue to operate—within government-run facilities, running commissaries that overcharge inmates for basic items like soap and medical supplies, expensive telephone and video visitation services, financial services that charge exorbitant fees, low-quality food services, and medical facilities that often provide poor patient care.[98] In the 1980s, governments began to outsource the construction and operation of prisons to private companies. From 1990 to 2009, the number of people in private prisons grew by a factor of 17.[99] Private companies run not only jails, prisons, and detention centers but also halfway houses, day reporting centers, and reentry services.[100] In 2021, the two largest private prison operators, CoreCivic and the GEO Group, owned and operated more than two hundred facilities and brought in more than $4 billion in revenues.[101] In one common type of contract, a private company takes over day-to-day management of a facility and is paid a fixed rate per inmate per day; the rate is set by a bidding process, in which firms compete by offering low bids. The physical facility may be one owned by the government, or it may be constructed by the prison company. Many contracts include guaranteed minimum occupancy rates, meaning that the government has to continue paying even if crime rates fall. Because the prison operator is paid a set fee, its goal is to operate the facility at as low a cost as possible.[102]

Private prisons were supposed to save taxpayer money, but they do not even achieve that goal. Comparing private and public prisons is difficult because private prisons tend to have a higher proportion of minimum-security inmates and because of accounting differences. Studies that correct for these issues have found no clear cost advantage for private prisons. A recent audit in Georgia found that it costs the state $44.56 per day to house inmates in state-run prisons, as compared with $49.07 in private prisons for similar offenders. The Arizona Department of Corrections found it costs virtually the same amount to house minimum-security inmates in private and public prisons, while private prisons cost almost 10 percent more for medium-security inmates.[103] Two academic reviews of multiple studies found no significant difference in costs between the two types of prisons.[104]

In response to the Georgia audit, the GEO Group claimed that it spends more money than state-run facilities to "improve offender rehabilitation services and outcomes." Recidivism rates for private prisons, however, are no better than those of state-run prisons, after accounting for differences in the prison populations. A study of Florida prisons found no significant difference in recidivism rates; in another analysis of Oklahoma prisons, inmates of private facilities were more likely to be rearrested than those in state prisons. A 2013 study of Minnesota prisoners found that being incarcerated in a private rather than a government prison increased an individual's chance of being rearrested by 13 percent and his chance of being reconvicted by 22 percent.[105] More generally, the Department of Justice found that the frequency of safety and security incidents is higher in federal private prisons than in those run directly by the government. Multiple studies of state prisons have found that violence is more common in private than in public prisons.[106]

Some private prison companies may even be keeping people behind bars longer, which has the effect of increasing their revenues and the costs to governments. A study in Mississippi found that private facilities held people for an average of ninety days longer for similar offenses than did state-run prisons—which, at a typical rate of $50 per prisoner-day, translates into $4,500 more revenue for the prison company.[107] Inmates stayed in private prisons longer because they received more citations for conduct violations, either because the prisons were run less well or because the prison companies issued citations more aggressively for the purpose of getting more revenue. Moreover, a lawsuit against Management & Training Corporation documented abysmal conditions at its East Mississippi Correctional

Facility. One inmate was beaten by other prisoners while shackled, another was beaten for fourteen minutes before anyone intervened, guards frequently failed to respond to requests for medical assistance, and the prison had no psychiatrist on staff to oversee its many inmates with mental illnesses.[108]

These poor outcomes should not be a surprise. Prison administrators control the circumstances in which inmates live. They determine when and how an inmate will be disciplined. Because private prisons are motivated to minimize costs, they typically maintain minimal staffing levels and pay corrections officers less than their government counterparts. The average salary for corrections officers and jailers in the private sector is more than $6,000 less than for those working for state or local governments; at the East Mississippi Correctional Facility, they make less than $12 per hour.[109] Also, the proportion of officers to inmates is about 30 percent lower in private than in public prisons.[110] Investigations found not only that private prisons in Tennessee and Mississippi are understaffed, but also that their employees receive insufficient or in some cases no job training. A newspaper investigation found that private prisons in Florida were routinely understaffed, often with inexperienced guards, and frequently violated security requirements. One private prison in Idaho was nicknamed "gladiator school" because its correctional officers, unable to impose order owing to understaffing—a fact hidden by falsified records—allowed prison gang leaders to maintain order.[111]

Private prison companies want enough people in prisons, jails, immigration detention centers, juvenile facilities, and other programs they run to produce greater profit margins, so they engage in political activity to ensure a steady stream of inmates. According to one report, "private prison companies have had either influence over or helped to draft model legislation such as 'three-strikes' and 'truth-in-sentencing' laws, both of which have driven up incarceration rates and ultimately created more opportunities for private prison companies to bid on contracts to increase revenues."[112]

The industry spends $5 million per year lobbying statehouses across the country, and it spends millions of dollars in campaign contributions.[113] Prison companies also build connections by hiring former government officials, including former directors of the Federal Bureau of Prisons. Before a 2012 vote in the Florida legislature that would have privatized much of the state's prison system, the GEO Group donated more than $1 million to state politicians and parties. GEO donated $225,000 to a super PAC supporting Donald Trump's 2016 presidential campaign and $250,000 to his inaugural committee, hired as lobbyists one of the president's fundraisers and two former aides to Attorney General Jeff Sessions, and held a major conference at the Trump National Doral—and won a contract to run an immigration detention center.[114]

Some states have backed away from private prisons, either because of reduced need or because of the industry's problems, and, as of 2017, twenty-two states had none at all. The total private prison population was still 39 percent higher in 2017 than in 2000. Five states—Hawaii, Montana, New Mexico, Oklahoma, and Tennessee—housed more than one-quarter of their inmates in private facilities.[115]

As state prison populations have plateaued, private prison companies have increasingly focused on the growing market for immigration-related detention. More than 70 percent of people detained by Immigration and Customs Enforcement (ICE) were housed in private facilities in 2017.[116] Upon taking office, President Joseph Biden directed the Department of Justice to end the use of private prisons for federal inmates. The private prison companies responded by turning some of their prisons into immigration detention centers, which were not covered by Biden's directive. As of November 2021, CoreCivic, the GEO Group, and their subsidiaries had received about $3 million per day from the federal government during the Biden administration—more than during the Trump or Obama administrations—mostly from ICE. The private companies also entered into agreements with some local governments, which accept federal funds to hold federal inmates, to house those inmates in private facilities.[117]

The criminal legal system is supposed to serve the ends of justice, not profit. However, too many people and institutions see courts, probation, and prison as places to make money. Government reliance on court fees for revenue, part-time courts with part-time judges, probation companies that multiply the fees they can extract from people, bail bondsmen who combine the worst characteristics of loan sharks and vigilantes, and prison companies that profit by keeping people behind bars longer—none of this has anything to do with justice. It also results in a colossal waste of society's resources. Communities would be far better served by city or county governments with full-time courts, professional police departments dedicated to public safety, public probation officers who help people become useful and productive citizens, and public prisons and jails dedicated to rehabilitation, not just punishment. In order to realize this future, however, the criminal legal system must be dedicated to justice and human welfare, not the pursuit of profit.

7

The Madness of Measuring
Mental Disorders

We must at least acknowledge in ourselves the inability to understand in full the workings of the human mind. Where we must pretend to such capacity, however, we should grant ourselves and those who suffer most from our mistakes the benefit of an admittedly grave doubt.

—*Judge Irving Goldberg*[1]

Incarceration in America routinely makes mentally ill people worse. And just as routinely it renders stable people psychiatrically unwell. Our system is quite literally maddening.

—*Psychiatrist and author Christine Montross*[2]

In elementary school, Andre Lee Thomas began to hear voices—auditory hallucinations. His grandmother and mother heard messages from God, but it is still extremely unusual to hear voices at such a young age. He tried to kill himself several times as a teenager. In early 2004, his behavior "became increasingly 'bizarre,'" as a judge of the Texas Court of Criminal Appeals later put it: "He put duct tape over his mouth and refused to speak; he talked about how the dollar bill contains the meaning of life; he stated that he was experiencing déjà vu and reliving events time and again; he had a religious fixation and heard the voice of God."[3] In March 2004, he tried to kill himself twice; an emergency room doctor wrote, "Thomas is psychotic. He thinks something like Holodeck on Star Trek [simulated reality] is happening to him."[4]

Later that month, Thomas killed his wife (from whom he was separated), their four-year-old son, and her thirteen-month-old daughter. He stabbed each victim with a different knife, cut out the children's hearts and a part of his wife's lung (thinking it was her heart), and stabbed himself in the heart. He later explained to the police that his wife was Jezebel, their son was the Antichrist, and her daughter was also evil. He used different knives so he would not "cross contaminate" their blood and "allow the demons inside them to live," and stabbed himself in the heart to make sure those demons died. In jail, Thomas said that his wife and the children were still alive and cutting out their hearts had freed them from evil. While reading the Bible five days after the murders, he came across Matthew 5:29: "If your right eye causes you to sin, gouge it out and throw it away." He then gouged out his right eye.[5]

Thomas was tried in Grayson County, Texas, after doctors at a state hospital claimed that he "has clearly exaggerated symptoms that he might be experiencing, and may have even fabricated some symptoms of psychosis."[6] Thomas, who is Black, was convicted and sentenced to death by an all-white jury including four members who said that they objected to mixed-race marriage. (Thomas's wife was white.) In prison, Thomas tried to kill himself by slashing his throat. Afterward, he said, "The government is conspiring to read my mind. That's why I ripped out my right eye. That's the righteous side. They can't hear my thoughts no more. I cut my throat. Got to shed a little blood to save the world." He later tore out his remaining eye—and ate it, so the government couldn't put it back in his head to read his thoughts.[7]

The Texas Court of Criminal Appeals and the Fifth Circuit Court of Appeals rejected appeals based on Thomas's mental disorders and the jurors opposed to interracial marriage.

The Promise of Fair and Just Treatment

The idea that people with serious mental illnesses should not be held fully responsible for their actions has a long history. In his eighteenth-century *Commentaries on the Laws of England*, William Blackstone wrote:

> Idiots and lunatics are not chargeable for their own acts, if committed when under these incapacities: no, not even for treason itself. Also, if a man in his sound memory commits a capital offence, and before arraignment for it, he becomes mad, he ought not to be arraigned for it: because he is not able to plead to it with that advice and caution that he ought. And if, after he has pleaded, the prisoner becomes mad, he shall not be tried: for how can he make his defence? . . . If, after judgment, he becomes of nonsane memory, execution shall be stayed: for peradventure, . . . had the prisoner been of sound memory, he might have alleged something in stay of judgment or execution.[8]

These principles are rooted in common sense. No one chooses to have a mental disorder. And those who suffer from them may be completely out of touch with reality and lack any ability to reason and make judgments. Large majorities of the population oppose executing the mentally ill and think that people with mental disorders, even if they have committed violent crimes, should be treated in mental health programs.[9] And yet, across the United States, the largest concentrations of mentally ill people are found in jails and prisons. Depending on the jurisdiction, people with mental illness make up anywhere from one-quarter to more than one-half of all people behind bars. About 10 percent to 25 percent of prisoners suffer from serious mental illnesses, such as major affective disorders or schizophrenia. One nationwide survey found that more than a quarter of people in jail suffered "severe psychological distress" in the preceding month, and more than two in five had been diagnosed with a mental disorder.[10] Many people with mental disorders are sentenced to long prison terms. Dozens of mentally ill people have been executed or are currently waiting on death row.[11]

American law maintains some of the protections listed by Blackstone. A person's mental functioning is relevant at four potential points in a criminal case. First, in most states, someone accused of a crime can claim insanity as a defense—that, at the time he committed the offense, he did not understand that it was wrong. However, it is almost never successful. Second, in all courts, a person accused of a crime must be able to understand the proceedings and relate to his attorney. The Supreme Court has held that a defendant who "lacks the capacity to understand the nature and object of the proceedings against him, to consult with counsel, and to assist in preparing his defense may not be subjected to a trial."[12] But courts often decide that a defendant is "competent" to stand trial without sufficient understanding of the complex issues involved. Third, in a capital case, mental illness can be raised as a mitigating circumstance that weighs against imposition of the death penalty. Fourth, the Supreme Court confirmed in 1986 that the Eighth Amendment protection against cruel and unusual punishment forbids execution of the "insane."[13] However, the definition of insanity adopted by the Court is so narrow that many people who have no understanding of what is happening to them or why can still be put to death. In summary, the criminal legal system does not deal with the widespread problem of mental illness with the care one would hope for in the twenty-first century.

A Parallel Universe of Punishment

In her 2018 book *Insane: America's Criminal Treatment of Mental Illness*, journalist Alisa Roth writes, "Today, the country's largest providers of psychiatric care are . . . the jails in Chicago, Los Angeles, and New York City."[14] The reality for people with mental disorders is that there is simply not enough care to go around, with shortages of psychiatrists, psychologists, social workers, outpatient treatment centers, crisis centers, and hospital beds. After the United States embraced the policy of deinstitutionalization—releasing people from mental hospitals into the community—the number of people confined in mental hospitals fell from more than 558,000 in 1955 to about 35,000 in 2015. Unfortunately, the needed community-based mental health programs, treatment centers, and housing and job opportunities that were a critical component of the policy never materialized.[15] Few treatment options are left for those unable to rely on their families for support. Many people with serious mental illnesses or disorders— such as schizophrenia, bipolar disorder, major depression, traumatic brain damage, and post-traumatic stress disorder—function well in society, but some end up on the streets, in shelters, and in jails and prisons. They may experience on occasion illogical thinking, delusions, hallucinations, or mood swings that affect their perceptions of reality, judgment, impulse control, and ability to process information.

Some people with mental disorders have difficulty maintaining stable jobs and family relationships, making them more likely to be poor or homeless. They are at greater risk of developing substance abuse problems. For these reasons, some of them are frequently arrested for drug possession or for "quality of life" offenses such as panhandling, littering, public urination, or sleeping in public places. Once caught up in the criminal legal system, they are less likely to make bail than other defendants; even when they do make bail, they spend more time in jail before being released.[16]

The lack of care in the civilian community has driven tens of thousands of people with serious mental health problems into a parallel universe devoted not to treatment but to identifying and punishing the guilty—a universe largely populated by police, lawyers, judges, and correctional officers who often have little to no training in the complexities of mental illness. Legal principles often require very precise determinations of a person's mental functioning that lawyers, judges, and jurors are ill equipped to make. No one understands exactly how the mind works. A person's mental condition can change radically from one day to the next. Yet the law assumes that questions of mental functioning have definite answers: a defendant can understand what is going on at trial or he cannot; someone condemned to die understands why he will be put to death or he does not. And so the police, courts, jails, and prisons take action based on the faulty premise that a person's mental state can be accurately and definitively assessed.

The tragic consequences begin when people with mental disorders come in contact with the police. In April 2015, Daniel Covarrubias, a thirty-seven-year-old Native American and Latino in the grip of hallucinations, went to a hospital in Tacoma, Washington, "to get the cameras out of his eyes," according to a lawyer. Walking home that day, he heard sirens behind him, ran into a lumberyard for no known reason, and climbed a pile of wood. Lumberyard employees called the police, who arrived and ordered him to "show [his] hands." Covarrubias was killed by five gunshots, holding a mobile phone.[17]

Every year, police in America shoot and kill about one thousand people—about one-quarter of them actively "in the throes of mental or emotional crisis." Almost half of the people killed by police in Massachusetts over a decade were "suicidal, mentally ill or showed clear signs of crisis."[18] In most of these incidents, the police are called not because of a crime, but because someone is worried about the unusual behavior of the person who ends up dead.

Some of these people are killed by the police because they have no place to turn. After months or years seeking treatment, when someone goes into crisis, a friend or family member calls 911; when emergency dispatchers are notified about erratic behavior, they often send the police. Many police officers have little training in de-escalating confrontations with people in mental health crises. Instead, their instincts are to act forcefully, take control of the situation, and be alert to possible threats to themselves or bystanders. Keith Vidal's stepfather called the police to try to get Keith hospitalized; Keith, who had been diagnosed with schizophrenia, was behaving abnormally. When the police arrived, he was holding a screwdriver and refused to put it down. The officers called for backup. According to eyewitnesses, the next policeman to arrive, Bryon Vassey, announced, "I'm here to kick ass and take names." He told one of the other officers to use a Taser on Keith and the officer Tased him. During a struggle that ensued over the screwdriver, Vassey shot Keith in the chest, killing him.[19]

More often, people with mental illnesses arrested for minor offenses go through a familiar pattern: psychological screening and perhaps minimal treatment during a short jail stay, release into the community, and then another arrest. People who are arrested multiple times in a given year are three times as likely to suffer from serious or moderate mental illness as the overall population.[20] Those facing more serious charges encounter a different set of hurdles.

According to popular mythology, people who commit crimes can easily escape responsibility by claiming insanity. In practice, the insanity defense is rarely claimed and virtually never successful. In most states, the defendant must prove that he did not understand the action he was performing at the time of the crime or did not know that the action was wrong. Therefore, a paranoid schizophrenic person who kills someone who he thinks is an evil spirit will probably be found guilty because he knows he is killing someone and he knows that murder is a crime. Poor people accused of serious crimes are unlikely to be able to hire the experts necessary to mount an insanity defense, and juries are rarely sympathetic to it. In practice, fewer than 1 percent of felony defendants raise the insanity defense, and it is usually rejected.[21]

A much more fundamental issue is that of competency for trial. In the 1960 case *Dusky v. United States*, the Supreme Court held that a defendant can be tried only if he "has sufficient present ability to consult with his lawyer with a reasonable degree of rational understanding" and "has a rational as well as factual understanding of the proceedings against him."[22] Later, in *Drope v. Missouri*, the Court specified that the defendant must have "the capacity to understand the nature and object of the proceedings against him, to consult with counsel, and to assist in preparing his defense."[23]

This makes sense. If a person's thought process is so disordered that he cannot understand the charges against him or the legal procedures or relate to his attorney, he cannot have a fair trial. In practice, however, people with serious mental illnesses who have difficulty interacting with their lawyers are routinely subject to proceedings that they do not understand. The prosecution almost always claims that the defendant is faking his symptoms, even when the crime in question was long preceded by bizarre behavior, paranoia, delusions, self-mutilation, suicide attempts, and mental health treatment.

State psychiatrists and judges often focus narrowly on whether the defendant knows why he is in court, what he is charged with, what penalty he might suffer, and the rudiments of the trial process. Someone who suffers from paranoid schizophrenia may be able to pass this test, yet still suffer from severe delusions that impair his ability to understand the proceedings and work with a lawyer to protect his interests. According to one well-regarded trial manual, only "floridly psychotic" defendants will be found incompetent.[24] Establishing that someone is not competent to stand trial may require expensive expert testimony. While prosecutors usually have access to as many experts of their choosing as they want, indigent defendants are generally limited to a single expert, whom they are not entitled to select.[25] Faced with competing experts, whose opinions have been described by the Supreme Court as "at best a hazardous guess," even a well-meaning judge can only speculate about what the defendant's mental state truly is.[26] In particularly notorious cases, pressure from the community to bring the defendant to trial swiftly may also weigh on the scales, especially for elected trial judges.

If a defendant is found not competent to stand trial, he is typically committed to a state mental hospital and placed in a program intended to "restore" him to competency—to stand trial. He may be drilled in the basics of courtroom functioning and given medication to control his symptoms.[27] This continues until mental health experts at the hospital report that the defendant is competent to stand trial and the judge agrees. After Andre Lee Thomas gouged out his right eye, he was found incompetent to stand trial. But after forty-seven days in a state hospital, the doctors and the judge decided that he could be tried.

The application of the competency standard can result in ludicrous outcomes. Scott Panetti first displayed signs of mental illness, including "early schizophrenia," in 1978. He was diagnosed with schizophrenia in 1986; that year, his wife reported that he had buried some furniture outside because of "a belief the devil was in the furniture." He was hospitalized at least fourteen times, both voluntarily and involuntarily. On September 8, 1992, Panetti shaved his head, sawed off the end of a shotgun, dressed in camouflage "jungle" gear, drove to the home of his estranged wife's parents, and shot and killed them in front of his wife and three-year-old daughter.[28]

Panetti surrendered to the police the same day. Over the next several months, he underwent several mental evaluations. One jury could not decide whether he was competent to stand trial, but in September 1994 a second jury determined that he was. (In most states, competency is decided by a judge, but in Texas and some other states either party can request a jury determination.) The next year, the judge granted Panetti's request to waive his right to counsel and represent himself, despite his history of mental illness. At his trial, Panetti—who had stopped taking his antipsychotic medication—wore a purple cowboy suit and attempted to call hundreds of witnesses, including the Messiah, John F. Kennedy, and the Pope. His standby counsel (assigned by the judge to provide advice to Panetti) described the trial as "a judicial farce, and a mockery of self-representation."[29] The jury convicted Panetti and sentenced him to death. Less than two months later, the court found him *not* competent to waive the appointment of counsel for state post-conviction proceedings. In his appeals, his lawyers argued that Panetti had not been competent to stand trial or to represent himself, but these claims were all rejected.[30]

Panetti was allowed to represent himself in his 1994 trial because of a recent Supreme Court case. In 1984, Richard Allen Moran shot and killed three people, including his wife, and unsuccessfully tried to kill himself. Two psychiatrists concluded that, although he was severely depressed, he was competent to stand trial, and the prosecution sought the death penalty. After initially pleading not guilty, Moran asked to discharge his attorneys, represent himself, and plead guilty. Asked why, "Moran responded that . . . he opposed all efforts to mount a defense. His purpose, specifically, was to prevent the presentation of any mitigating evidence on his behalf at the sentencing phase of the proceeding."[31] The trial judge approved the request. (The Supreme Court previously held in 1975 that a person accused of a crime can give up the right to a lawyer and represent himself so long as he is advised of the "dangers and disadvantages of self-representation.")[32] Moran pleaded guilty and was sentenced to death. In 1993, the Supreme Court affirmed the conviction and death sentence, holding that the standard for competency for trial—whether a defendant can understand the proceedings, consult with counsel, and assist in his defense—is the *same* as the standard to represent oneself at trial.[33] Moran was executed in 1996.

Unlike what happened in the cases of Panetti and Moran, an Indiana trial judge denied a request by Ahmad Edwards, who had a history of schizophrenia and delusions, to represent himself at his trial for attempted murder and other crimes. The judge may have been influenced by a document Edwards filed that included nonsensical passages such as the following:

> The appointed motion of permissive intervention filed therein the court superior on, 6–26–01 caused a stay of action and apon it's expiration or thereafter three years the plan to establish a youth program to and for the coordination of aspects of law enforcement to prevent and reduce crime amoung young people in Indiana became a diplomatic act as under the Safe Streets Act of 1967, "A omnibuc considerate agent . . .[34]

The judge, however, ruled that Edwards was competent to stand trial, and, represented by appointed counsel, he was convicted. The Supreme Court affirmed his conviction. It distinguished Edwards's case from *Moran*, in which a defendant was allowed to waive his right to a lawyer, because that case involved a guilty plea, while Edwards sought to represent himself at a trial. The Court held that *the state has a right to require a defendant to stand trial with an appointed attorney.*[35]

Once people with serious mental illness are caught up in the criminal legal system, they are likely to spend time in confinement—awaiting a court date, being "restored to competency," or serving out a sentence—where they face an additional set of challenges. Jails and prisons were not designed to address the needs of mentally ill people, nor are the vast majority of their staff trained to work with them. Inmates must consistently follow rules, and corrections officers often intimidate them with force or the threat of force. Summary penalties can be meted out for minor infractions. People with some mental illnesses can have difficulty comprehending and following rules and may respond combatively to threats from officers, leading to repeated punishments. As a result, they are more likely to be placed in solitary confinement and tend to remain in solitary confinement longer, causing further psychological deterioration.[36] Repeated infractions also make it harder for people with mental illness to be released before the end of their maximum sentences.[37] Even if they manage to avoid disciplinary action, people in prison are separated from their families and communities, subject to long periods of monotony, and often witness or fear violent acts, all of which can harm their mental health.

Jails and prisons often fall far short of providing mental health care that is adequate by any standard. Chronic shortages of psychologists and psychiatrists mean that people may have to wait months before receiving any treatment. This problem is exacerbated by private companies that contract to provide health care services within jails or prisons for a low flat rate. Therapy can consist of brief discussions shouted through a cell door—or even, in one federal prison, "passing out coloring books and puzzles."[38] In these circumstances, mental health care primarily consists of medication designed to suppress the symptoms of illness.

Some correctional officers and some entire institutions treat people with mental illness with unbridled cruelty. In 2012, Darren Rainey, who was schizophrenic, was scalded to death in a 160-degree shower by officers in a Florida prison.[39] According to an investigation, multiple inmates diagnosed with schizophrenia at Augusta State Medical Prison in Georgia were assaulted by officers—beaten with batons, kicked in the face, choked, or rammed headfirst into a wall. At the South Fulton Municipal Regional Jail in Georgia, women with mental illnesses—many simply unable to make bail or incompetent to stand trial—were kept in solitary confinement. A visit by investigators found cells soiled by overflowing toilet water, smeared feces, pools of urine, metal beds without bedding, and many women who were completely unresponsive. A federal judge called these conditions "repulsive" and added that the people responsible "really ought to have a hard time sleeping at night."[40]

Conditions in jails and prisons punish people for being mentally ill on top of the statutory punishment for the crimes of which they are convicted. This system results, for many people, in a cycle of rearrest, reconviction, and reincarceration. Some others experience prolonged imprisonment without treatment for their mental disorders. And some are put to death.

Executing the Mentally Ill

The stakes are highest when people with mental illness are charged with capital crimes. The Supreme Court, in *Ford v. Wainwright*, held that people who are "insane" cannot be executed. Justice Thurgood Marshall wrote, "We may seriously question the retributive value of executing a person who has no comprehension of why he has been singled out and stripped of his fundamental right to life."[41] However, the definition of "insane," set out in Justice Lewis Powell's concurring opinion, is extremely narrow: "The Eighth Amendment forbids the execution only of those who are unaware of the punishment they are about to suffer and why they are to suffer it."[42]

Prosecutors are free to seek the death penalty against anyone who is found competent to stand trial; the standard established in *Ford* applies only at the time of execution. Because capital cases often involve particularly horrific crimes, public pressure to ensure that someone is convicted can lead prosecutors and judges to be less careful in evaluating competency than they should be.

Under current death penalty statutes, a death sentence is available only for certain types of murder. If the prosecution seeks the death penalty and the defendant is convicted, the trial continues to a sentencing phase, where the issue of the defendant's mental illness often becomes particularly important. In most states, when deciding on the sentence, a jury must determine whether an aggravating factor exists (for example, that the murder was committed in the course of a felony such as robbery) and then weigh it against any mitigating factors. Both the prosecution and the defense may put on a wide range of evidence to support aggravating or mitigating factors.

Severe mental illness could serve as a powerful mitigating factor because of, in the words of Supreme Court Justice Sandra Day O'Connor, "the belief, long held by this society, that defendants who commit criminal acts that are attributable . . . to emotional and mental problems may be less culpable than defendants who have no such excuse."[43] However, mental disorders that frighten jurors can have the opposite effect. James Eugene Bigby suffered from paranoid schizophrenia. At trial, a psychiatrist testified that Bigby had killed his friend Mike Trekell because of a delusion that Trekell was involved in a massive conspiracy stemming from an employer's refusal to pay Bigby money that he believed he was owed. Bigby then killed Trekell's infant son as an "irrational act" explained only by his mental illness. The jury also learned that Bigby's mental illness could not be controlled or treated—and saw that he had to be restrained during trial.[44] This took place in Texas, where the jury must consider a defendant's "future dangerousness" when deciding on the death penalty. A jury may very well conclude that someone who kills people because of an uncontrollable mental illness is a continuing danger to society and therefore should be executed. The Fifth Circuit Court of Appeals, in overturning Bigby's death sentence, referred to his mental illness as a "double-edged sword" because it made him seem more dangerous to the jury.[45] Another jury sentenced Bigby to death, and he was executed in 2017.

Once on death row, some people with severe mental illness have been allowed to waive their appeals, effectively seeking out death at the hands of the state. Charles Rumbaugh, who was sentenced to death in Texas, attempted to prevent any appeals on his behalf. At a hearing in federal court to determine whether he was competent to waive his appeals, Rumbaugh attacked a deputy U.S. marshal, shouting "Shoot!" and successfully induced the marshal to shoot him in the courtroom, although not fatally. Nevertheless, the judge held that Rumbaugh was competent to waive his appeals. The Fifth Circuit Court of Appeals agreed, holding that because Rumbaugh "is mentally ill . . . with no hope of successful treatment which would reduce his current mental discomfort to a tolerable level," his decision to give up his appeals was the result of a "rational decision-making process."[46] As a result, Rumbaugh's parents were blocked from intervening, allowing him to be executed. In dissent, Judge Irving Goldberg criticized this emphasis on Rumbaugh's apparent rationality, pointing out that "Rumbaugh's logic almost certainly operates in service of his mental disorder." The problem, Goldberg wrote, is that "we are not told whose definition of rationality applies to this mind, but we are told nonetheless to invoke some nebulous normative concept imbued with an aura of systemic legal perfection."[47] It is possible that a person may be so devoid of hope that he thinks it preferable to die rather than continue living. But the machinery of the criminal legal system should not simply acquiesce in his suicide by execution.

Once a date is set for a person's execution, there may be an issue of whether he is competent to be executed under the standard set in *Ford v. Wainwright*. Many people have been executed who not only suffered from severe mental impairments but also did not appreciate why the state was putting them to death—or even that they were about to die. In the days before his 1992 execution in Arkansas, Ricky Ray Rector not only was observed howling and barking like a dog, but also said that he planned to vote for Bill Clinton, the governor who set his execution date; Rector set aside his dessert from his last meal to enjoy later—after his execution, presumably.[48] Johnny Frank Garrett was executed by Texas in 1992 believing that he was immune to lethal injection and would be saved by supernatural forces. Monty Allen Delk's last words before being executed by Texas in 2002 included, "I am the warden. Get your warden off this gurney and shut up. . . . You are not in America. This is the island of Barbados, people will see you doing this."[49] John Ferguson, a Black man who suffered from paranoid schizophrenia, told three psychiatrists "that he had been anointed the Prince of God, that he would be resurrected at some point after his execution to sit at 'the right hand of God,' and that he would eventually return to Earth." The Florida trial court held that Ferguson was competent for execution even though he genuinely believed that he was the Prince of God. The Eleventh Circuit of Appeals agreed, treating Ferguson's delusions as a religious belief and warning against treating unusual religious beliefs as proof of mental illness.[50] Florida executed Ferguson in 2013.

At a hearing in federal district court to determine whether Scott Panetti—who had attempted to call the Messiah, John F. Kennedy, and the Pope as witnesses at his trial—was competent for execution, experts testified that Panetti believed his execution was part of "spiritual warfare" between good and evil. As the Supreme Court later summarized, "Although [Panetti] claims to understand 'that the state is saying that [it wishes] to execute him for [his] murder[s],' he believes in earnest that the stated reason is a 'sham' and the State in truth wants to execute him 'to stop him from preaching.'"[51] The Court ruled that a prisoner could only be put to death if he had a "rational understanding of the reason for the execution."[52] On remand, the district court found that Panetti *did* have a "rational understanding of his crime, his impending death, and the causal connection between the two," and upheld his death sentence.[53] As of 2017, Panetti believed that "Texas has implanted a listening device in his tooth that sends command messages to his brain," that "CNN anchor Wolf Blitzer displayed [his] stolen [prison] ID card during a report," and that he was "the father of actress and singer Selena Gomez."[54] His competency to be executed is still being litigated.

In its 2007 *Panetti* decision, the Supreme Court admitted that "a concept like rational understanding is difficult to define."[55] A half century earlier, Justice Felix Frankfurter wrote that the execution of a person with severe mental illness "turns on the ascertainment of what is called a fact, but which in the present state of the mental sciences is at best a hazardous guess."[56] We have severe qualms about executing people whose mental state precludes an understanding of why they are being killed. But we are no closer than ever to being able to ascertain what goes on inside someone's mind. This question is becoming more prevalent today, as an increasing number of people on death row are elderly and suffering from dementia. After several strokes and a diagnosis of vascular dementia, Vernon Madison could no longer remember the crime for which he received the death sentence. In 2019, the Supreme Court stayed his execution, ruling that dementia could make a prisoner incompetent to be executed if it prevented him from having a rational understanding of why the state wants to execute him.[57] Now, by asking judges or juries to determine the "rational understanding" of a person whose mind has been ravaged by dementia, the law is plumbing the depths of the unknowable—with people's lives on the line.

Justice for People with Mental Illness

Since 2000, many people with mental disorders arrested for misdemeanors and some less serious felonies in Miami-Dade County have been diverted from the criminal courts and into comprehensive community-based treatment and support services. Judge Steven Leifman launched the Criminal Mental Health Project in Miami-Dade County after seeing that people with mental disorders were cycling through the court repeatedly. The project operates a crisis intervention program that has provided training to more than seven thousand law enforcement officers from all of the local municipalities, the public schools, and the corrections system. The officers receive "40 hours of specialized training in psychiatric diagnoses, suicide intervention, substance abuse issues, behavioral de-escalation techniques . . . and local resources for those in crisis."[58] The training prepares officers to recognize the symptoms of mental illnesses, de-escalate confrontations, and take the mentally ill to crisis stabilization centers instead of jail.

In the nine years ending in 2018, crisis intervention officers responded to over 90,000 mental health crisis calls. They diverted over 17,000 people from jail, assisted over 55,000 in accessing community-based treatment, and arrested only 152. The number of people being booked into jail each year dropped from about 118,000 to 53,000. "The average daily population in the county jail system . . . dropped from 7,200 to 4,200 . . . and the county has closed one entire jail facility at a cost-savings to taxpayers of $12 million per year." Treatment in the community costs money, too, but it is less expensive than holding people in jail, which exacerbates mental disorders and increases the likelihood of people being rearrested. Just 97 individuals accounted for 2,200 arrests over a five-year period in Miami-Dade County; they spent 27,000 days in jail and 13,000 days in acute care mental health crisis units at a cost of $16 million.[59]

In addition to crisis intervention, the Criminal Mental Health Project (CMHP) screens all people booked into jail; for those identified with mental illnesses or substance abuse disorders, it develops individualized transition plans intended to improve mental health, support community living, and decrease behavior that could result in rearrest. Charges may be dismissed or modified as part of the program. CMHP staff monitor participants for up to a year following reentry into the community to ensure they receive necessary support and services. Although three-fourths of the participants are homeless at the time of arrest and severely psychiatrically impaired, recidivism rates have decreased from about 75 percent to 20 percent annually.[60]

The Criminal Mental Health Project has also established a new Center for Mental Health and Recovery to provide comprehensive treatment for individuals with serious mental illnesses. The facility, in a building of 181,000 square feet with capacity for 208 beds, includes a crisis stabilization unit, various levels of mental health treatment, dental and primary health care, job training programs, and housing for the homeless.[61] Judge Leifman and Miami-Dade County have shown how comprehensive community mental health programs can help people with mental disorders avoid behavior that harms them and the community and that results in them being sent to jails and prisons.

Much of the country lacks adequate preventive mental health resources, but some other communities are finding ways to respond to issues of mental health and prevent harm. From 2011 to 2022, Houston moved more than 25,000 homeless people into housing, reducing homelessness by 63 percent; the city saved millions of dollars that had been spent on jailing 20,000 homeless people a year for public intoxication and using ambulances to get them to medical care.[62] Several cities, including Denver, Colorado, and Eugene, Oregon, are using behavioral health specialists trained in crisis response instead of police to respond to mental health crises.[63] Many states have created mental health courts that provide people with mental disorders who have been arrested with an alternative to navigating the criminal legal system. Studies have found that people in those courts are more likely to utilize treatment and less likely to be rearrested than those in traditional courts.[64] However, the courts are not a substitute for comprehensive community mental health services.

Nineteen states and the District of Columbia have adopted extreme risk protection acts—often called "red flag" laws—that authorize courts to prohibit persons who may be a danger to themselves or others from possessing guns.[65] Florida adopted its law in 2018 in response to a teenage gunman killing fourteen students and three staff members at Marjory Stoneman Douglas High School. The shooter had been the subject of dozens of 911 calls before he carried out the attack.[66] In the four years after the law was passed, Florida courts issued more than eight thousand risk protection orders. Studies have found that perpetrators in other mass shootings exhibited troubling behavior that warned of what was to come. The laws have also prevented some people from having easy access to guns when they were most at risk of suicide.[67]

While people with mental disorders accused of minor offenses can be diverted from the legal system, more careful attention must be given to those accused of serious crimes. Governments must provide the resources needed for informed and reliable evaluations. Some public defender offices have units that specialize in the representation of people with mental disorders as well as resources that social workers and mental health experts need to evaluate their clients. Public defenders in Colorado represented James Holmes, who fired into the audience of a movie theater, killing twelve and wounding seventy. After conducting a comprehensive investigation of his life, the public defenders presented two psychiatrists and other witnesses who testified at his capital trial in 2015 that Holmes was "genetically loaded" to develop a psychotic disorder as a result of mental illness on both sides of his family, and that at the time of the crimes he experienced delusions, paranoid thinking, and other symptoms of schizophrenia.[68] The jury spared Holmes from the death penalty. That kind of justice is not available in states that limit court-appointed lawyers to a single, modestly paid expert.

Courts must more realistically apply the competency standard adopted by the Supreme Court to ensure that people are tried only if they understand the proceedings and are capable of working with their lawyers. Scott Panetti was found to be competent for trial and competent for execution, but he was neither. A finding that a person is competent when he is not means that his lawyer must represent him even though the person may not be able to relate basic information and make important decisions, such as whether to testify or plead guilty. As we have seen, courts have on occasion even allowed people like Panetti to discharge their lawyers and represent themselves. Some, like Richard Allen Moran, have in a moment of depression decided to plead guilty, even when it means they will be sentenced to death, only to find that they cannot take it back when they realize the mistake they have made. People who are not competent to stand trial and who pose a serious risk of danger to themselves or to other people are confined in a psychiatric hospital until they become competent. Sherman Noble, who was diagnosed as paranoid schizophrenic, was held for eighteen years in a jail or mental hospital because he was not competent for trial. He was then found competent and sentenced to death.[69]

Ohio and Kentucky have passed laws that prohibit the death penalty for people who commit crimes while suffering from severe mental illness.[70] Other states should follow their example. Mental illness must be taken into account in all types of sentencing. Again, no one chooses to have a mental disorder. People who cannot understand the legal system and work with their lawyers should not be processed through the courts. No one—including those who judge the mentally ill—fully understands complex brain disorders and the extent to which actions are the manifestation of mental disorders. Justice requires dealing with these issues with humility, compassion, humanity, and recognition of the lack of control that some people have over their thoughts and actions.

8

An Excess of Punishment

> He asked himself whether human society had the right to
> impose upon its members, on the one hand its mindless
> improvidence and, on the other hand, its merciless provi-
> dence; to grind a poor man between the millstones of need
> and excess—need of work and excess of punishment.
>
> —*Victor Hugo,* Les Misérables[1]

Six people on death row escaped from the Mecklenburg Correctional Center in Virginia on May 31, 1984. As Supreme Court
Justice Thurgood Marshall recounted in a later opinion, "Armed
with makeshift knives, these inmates took hostage 12 prison guards
and 2 female nurses. The guards were stripped of their clothes and
weapons, bound, and blindfolded. The nurses also were stripped of
their clothes, and one was bound to an inmate's bed." Wilbert Lee
Evans, a death row inmate who did not attempt to escape, stepped in
to protect the hostages. "Don't hurt anybody and everything will be
allright," he said to the escapees. He also intervened to prevent one
of the nurses from being raped. One of the officers later said, "It is
my belief that had it not been for Evans, I might not be here today."[2]

Evans himself had shot and killed a deputy sheriff in 1981.[3] He
had been sentenced to death based on a finding that he was a future
danger to society. After the escape, Evans's lawyers argued that his
intervention to save the lives of the guards and nurses showed that

the jury's prediction of future dangerousness was inaccurate and there was no basis for his death sentence. For six years, state officials refused to release reports from the internal investigation of the escape. Evans's lawyers obtained them the day before his scheduled execution in 1990. The next day, the U.S. Supreme Court denied Evans's request for a stay of execution, over Justice Marshall's dissent. After observing that the state conceded "that the sole basis for Evans' death sentence—future dangerousness—in fact *does not exist*," Justice Marshall wrote, "A system of capital punishment that would permit Wilbert Evans' execution notwithstanding as-to-now unrefuted evidence showing that death is an improper sentence is a system that cannot stand."[4] On a copy of Marshall's dissent, Evans wrote, "Please bury this with me." Evans was executed that evening.

The example of Wilbert Lee Evans—who was sentenced to death only because of an erroneous prediction that he was a danger to society—shows the impossibility of predicting at the time of sentencing what someone will be like years later. There are many people who were convicted of murder and sentenced to death but had their death sentences reversed, were resentenced to imprisonment, were eventually paroled, and lived productive, law-abiding lives. One was James Woodson, who in 1974 joined three other men in a convenience store robbery because one of them threatened to kill him if he did not participate. He waited in the car while two men entered a store and one of them killed the cashier. Woodson maintained his innocence, but was found guilty of first-degree murder, which required the death penalty under North Carolina law. However, the U.S. Supreme Court held in 1976 in Woodson's case that a mandatory death penalty was unconstitutional because it did not permit consideration of "compassionate or mitigating factors stemming from the diverse frailties of humankind" in deciding whether death should be imposed. Woodson was sentenced to life in prison.[5] He was paroled after serving seventeen years. For the next twenty-eight years until his death in 2018, he worked as the kitchen manager of the Raleigh Rescue Mission, was active in Trinity United Faith Church in Raleigh, and was a lay minister who returned to prison to preach to inmates.[6]

Tony Amadeo was sentenced to death at age eighteen in Georgia in 1977 for his involvement with two other men in a robbery and murder. The U.S. Supreme Court reversed his conviction because the prosecutor had directed the jury commissioners in the county where Amadeo was tried to underrepresent Blacks and women on the master jury lists, from which citizens were chosen for jury duty.[7] After the reversal, Amadeo pleaded guilty in exchange for a sentence of life imprisonment. In prison, he was a model inmate. He completed vocational training programs in woodworking and worked in prison woodshops for over twenty years. He took college classes in prison and graduated summa cum laude and valedictorian of his class of prisoners from Mercer University in 1995. He provided hospice care to fellow prisoners. After thirty-eight years in prison, Amadeo was released on parole. A few years later, he was operations manager of a Texas ranch of over eight hundred acres, responsible for hundreds of cattle, a hundred white-tail deer, and other animals, and part of an effort to grow "the best flavored meat possible."[8]

Jimmy Lee Horton and Pless Brown Jr. were burglarizing an apartment in Macon, Georgia, in 1980 when they were interrupted by the woman who lived in the apartment and a man accompanying her, who was the district attorney of the county. The man borrowed a gun from a neighbor and tried to stop the burglars but was fatally wounded in the ensuing gunfire. Horton was sentenced to death by an all-white jury, while Brown was sentenced to life imprisonment by a jury that included five Blacks. A federal court reversed Horton's conviction upon finding that the prosecutor had discriminated in using his peremptory strikes to obtain the all-white jury.[9] Horton was sentenced to life in prison in 1993. He was also a model inmate.

After he had served thirty years in prison, wardens, counselors, and other prison officials recommended him for parole based on his work as a supervisor of paint crews in prison, his stabilizing presence for younger inmates, and the remorse he had shown for the crime. He was paroled in 2011. Ten years later, he had spent time working on construction projects, was happily married to a woman he met while in prison, and was a law-abiding citizen.

Woodson, Amadeo, and Horton are proof that judges and juries can be mistaken about whether someone is a danger to society or incapable of redemption. They and many others show that, in many cases, neither execution nor life in prison without any possibility of release is necessary to punish crime and protect society.

Centuries of Inhumanity

Punishments for people convicted of crimes in the United States are often excessively, unreasonably harsh. Many people have been sentenced to spend long periods of time in crowded prisons where they have been subject to inhumane conditions and practices.

Punishments have long been imposed more heavily on Black people and members of other minority groups. Prior to the Civil War, laws and courts recognized slavery in many states. The Fugitive Slave Clause of the U.S. Constitution even specified that slaves who escaped into another state should be returned to their masters. The criminal law in many states expressly differentiated between crimes committed by and against Blacks and whites. For example, Georgia law provided that the rape of a white female by a Black man "shall be" punishable by death, while the rape of a white female by anyone else was punishable by a prison term from two to twenty years. The rape of a Black woman was punishable "by fine and imprisonment, at the discretion of the court."[10]

These disparate punishments continued long after the abolition of slavery. The legal system failed to protect freed Black people from

lynch mobs, which killed well over 6,500 people.[11] Officials failed
to prosecute people who carried out lynchings and other acts of ter-
rorism against Blacks. The threat that Congress might pass an anti-
lynching statute in the early 1920s led Southern states to switch to a
slightly more subtle form of racial control: death sentences imposed
by all-white juries. The practice of "legal lynchings" was so successful that the number of executions increased to an average of 165
a year in the 1930s, while the number of lynchings declined from
230 in 1892 to less than 30 a year in the 1930s. Executions reached
an all-time high of 199 in 1935.[12]

During the one hundred years of Jim Crow—endorsed by the
Supreme Court's 1896 decision in *Plessy v. Ferguson*, which approved
racial segregation under the doctrine of "separate but equal"—racial
discrimination was not only allowed but required by law in many
states. The state courts in the South also played a central role in per-
petuating slavery through the convict leasing system, under which
African Americans were arrested—often on vague charges such as
vagrancy—and then leased to plantations, railroads, turpentine
camps, coal mines, and other businesses that needed cheap labor.
Many convicts were literally worked to death.[13]

Prisons, which replaced convict leasing, often featured barbaric
conditions and brutal practices. At the Mississippi State Penitentiary,
better known as Parchman Farm, "shootings and beatings were common; murders went unreported; the maximum security unit was a
torture chamber. Trusties [inmates given responsibilities for guarding
other inmates] brutalized inmates, who, in turn, brutalized each other."[14] In Arkansas, prisoners were lashed with a leather strap for minor
infractions, given electrical shocks to their bodies' sensitive parts, and
crowded into barracks where "homosexual rape was so common and
uncontrolled that some potential victims dared not sleep; instead they
would leave their beds and spend the night clinging to the bars near-
est the guards' station."[15] A federal judge found that prisoners at the

California State Prison at San Quentin were "regarded and treated as caged animals, not human beings."[16] A federal court ended the practice in an Indiana prison of shackling prisoners to bed frames for up to two and a half days without use of the toilet so that they "had to lie in their own filth."[17]

Beginning in the 1960s, some reformers sought to end the barbaric treatment of prisoners and focus on rehabilitation. Donald Cabana, who started as a guard in the Massachusetts prisons and was later warden at Parchman Farm in Mississippi, later wrote: "A growing chorus increasingly called for sweeping change, demanding . . . a penal system that put rehabilitation on an equal footing with punishment, and a judicial system that was truly blind when dispensing justice."[18] Many states offered vocational and educational programs, counseling, and even college classes to people in prison. But the prison population exploded and the efforts for reforms were largely abandoned in favor of a steady march to mass incarceration.

In 1972, fewer than 200,000 people were held in state and federal prisons with maximum sentences of one year or more. The number climbed to 320,000 in 1980 before shooting up to 740,000 in 1990 and reaching 1.5 million in 2005.[19] Between 1985 and 2000, a new state or federal prison opened every week.[20] This increase in the prison population resulted from the so-called wars on crime and drugs waged by politicians. In 1994, for example, Congress passed the Violent Crime Control and Law Enforcement Act, which gave states financial incentives to pass "truth-in-sentencing" laws requiring people convicted of certain violent crimes to spend at least 85 percent of their maximum sentence in prison. From 1980 to 2013, state and local spending on prisons and jails increased three times as fast as spending on K–12 schools.[21]

In this increasingly punitive climate, the purpose of sentencing shifted decisively from rehabilitation to punishment. Educational and vocational opportunities available in prison were cut back or eliminated. The 1994 crime bill made people in prison ineligible for Pell Grants, making it impossible for many to participate in college programs. Idealistic wardens and commissioners of corrections were replaced by people promising to be harsh and unforgiving. Many commissioners built "supermax" prisons to show how tough they were. But there were not enough prisoners requiring the highest level of security to fill the supermax prisons, so other prisoners were housed in them.[22] Congress passed the Prison Litigation Reform Act of 1995, which stripped the federal courts of much of their power to remedy unconstitutional conditions or practices. Conditions in prisons and jails deteriorated across the country.[23]

Today, almost 2 million people are incarcerated in prisons, jails, and other types of detention facilities. The United States has the highest incarceration rate in the world, more than four times the global average and more than eight times the median rate in all of Europe.[24] Mass incarceration has been accompanied by mass probation and parole: almost 4 million people are subject to supervision within the community.[25] The demographic profile of people in prison and under court supervision reflects the continuation of historical practices that mete out punishment based on the race of the accused and the race of the victim. In 2010, almost one in every ten African American men between the ages of twenty-five and twenty-nine was behind bars. One study estimates that one in every three Black men has been convicted of a felony, which in many states entails a lifetime of disadvantages in gaining employment, finding housing, and participating in politics and other spheres.[26]

The problem of police violence against Black people has received widespread attention, particularly after the killings of Michael Brown, Philando Castile, Breonna Taylor, George Floyd, and many others. Police are far more likely to stop, search, arrest, assault, and kill Black people than white people, to a degree that cannot be explained by crime rates or poverty. The same disparities exist further downstream in the criminal legal system, from charging to pretrial release to conviction to sentencing to execution.

Discrimination and Death

Many states, the federal government, and the military have laws authorizing the death penalty. Since 2007, the number of states allowing death as a punishment has declined from thirty-eight to twenty-seven, as legislatures have repealed statues and state courts have prohibited it. At the end of 2021, ten states that have the death penalty had not carried out an execution in ten years. The overwhelming majority of death sentences are imposed by states in the South. Texas has carried out over 570 executions since 1976, followed by Oklahoma, which has executed 118. Virginia, which has the third highest total, 113, repealed its death penalty statute in 2021.[27]

The death penalty has been mostly abandoned by modern democracies. It is forbidden in Canada, Mexico, and the European Union. In 2019, the only countries that executed more people than the United States were China, Iran, Saudi Arabia, Iraq, and Egypt.[28] In the United States, people have been executed despite gross prosecutorial misconduct, incompetent defense lawyers, or judges intent on winning their next election. Some did not kill anyone and had no intention to kill anyone—typically participants in robberies when someone else fired a gun. Some were innocent of the crimes for which they were convicted. Some were mentally ill or intellectually disabled.

After declaring the death penalty unconstitutional in 1972 because it was being inflicted in an arbitrary and discriminatory manner, the Supreme Court upheld a new generation of death penalty statutes in 1976.[29] However, the Court struck down laws that made death mandatory for certain crimes and held that juries must decide whether to sentence someone to death based on consideration of factors for and against the sentence. And the Court ruled that death may no longer be imposed for rape, robbery, kidnapping, or other crimes in which the victim was not killed.[30] This leaves murder as the only crime for which people are sentenced to death.

The Court also decided that certain people were not subject to the death penalty. In 2002, in *Atkins v. Virginia*, the Court held that death is an excessive and disproportionate penalty for intellectually disabled people (then called "mentally retarded"). Three years later, the Court ruled in *Roper v. Simmons* that it is also excessive and disproportionate for someone who committed a crime while under the age of eighteen.[31]

The prohibitions against capital punishment for juvenile offenders and people not convicted of murder are straightforward to apply. Protecting intellectually disabled people from being executed, however, has proven more complicated because prosecutors may contest whether some people are in fact intellectually disabled. In *Atkins*, the Supreme Court endorsed the definition of intellectual disability offered by the experts in the field: "significantly subaverage intellectual functioning" and limitations in at least two skill areas, with an initial onset before age eighteen.[32] The Court, however, gave the states latitude to determine how to apply these definitions.

Some states established standards that made it difficult for people facing the death penalty to prove intellectual disability. The Florida Supreme Court interpreted a state statute to create a bright-line rule: only people with an IQ of 70 or lower could qualify as intellectually disabled.[33] In other words, a score of 71 on an IQ test qualified someone for execution, even though IQ test scores have a margin of error of several points. From 2002 through 2013, all twenty-four people claiming intellectual disability in capital cases in Florida were found not to be intellectually disabled. In 2014, the U.S. Supreme Court ruled that Florida's absolute cutoff was unconstitutional because it ignored the imprecision of IQ tests.[34]

The Texas Court of Criminal Appeals invented its own test for intellectual disability in 2004 in *Ex parte Briseño*. After observing that Texas case law already contained a definition of intellectual disability (the one cited in *Atkins*), the Court nevertheless added seven other factors to consider, including: "Can the person hide facts or lie effectively in his own or others' interests?" and "Did the commission of [the capital] offense require forethought, planning, and complex execution of purpose?"[35] These factors, the American Association on Intellectual and Developmental Disabilities later stated in a brief, "are based on false stereotypes about mental retardation that effectively exclude all but the most severely incapacitated."[36]

From 2002 through 2013, only eight out of forty-five defendants in Texas succeeded on their claims of intellectual disability. One who lost and was executed was Marvin Wilson, "a man who could not handle money or navigate a phone book, a man who sucked his thumb and could not always tell the difference between left and right, a man who, as a child, could not match his socks, tie his shoes or button his clothes," and who scored a 61 on an IQ test as an adult.[37] In 2017, the U.S. Supreme Court prohibited the use of the *Briseño* factors, calling them "an invention of the [Court of Criminal Appeals] untied to any acknowledged source," in its decision to overturn the death sentence of Bobby Moore. On remand, the Court of Criminal Appeals still found that Moore was not intellectually disabled—and was again overruled by the Supreme Court. Finally, the Court of Criminal Appeals accepted the Supreme Court's determination that Moore was intellectually disabled and he was resentenced to life in prison. Moore was paroled in 2020.[38] Since the Supreme Court's decision, the Texas court has found seven other death-sentenced inmates intellectually disabled and ineligible for the death penalty.[39]

Georgia has outdone Florida and Texas. Federal appellate judge Adalberto Jordan observed in 2013, "In the last 30 years not a single capital defendant in Georgia has been able to establish intellectual disability when the matter has been disputed." A state statute

imposes on the defendant the burden of proving that he is intellectually disabled *beyond a reasonable doubt*. While the prosecution must
prove guilt beyond a reasonable doubt at a criminal trial, most other
issues in most courtroom settings require only a preponderance of
the evidence—more likely than not. As Judge Jordan pointed out,
"Georgia's beyond-a-reasonable-doubt standard requires a level of
certainty that mental health experts simply cannot provide."[40]

Warren Hill consistently tested in the 2nd to 3rd percentile in academic achievement and intelligence as a child. His IQ was approximately 70, as evidenced by tests beginning at the age of seven.[41] At
a hearing in 2000, four experts testified that Hill was intellectually disabled; three experts for the state testified that he was not.
In 2002, a state court judge ruled that Hill had demonstrated his
intellectual disability by a preponderance of the evidence—and that,
under *Atkins*, Georgia's reasonable doubt standard was unconstitu-
tionally severe. The next year, however, the Georgia Supreme Court
reversed and upheld the reasonable doubt standard and Hill's death
sentence.[42] In 2010, a three-judge panel of the Eleventh Circuit
Court of Appeals hearing Hill's case rejected the reasonable doubt
standard, concluding that it "will necessarily result in the deaths of
mentally retarded offenders by incorrect identification." However,
the panel was overruled by the full twelve-judge Eleventh Circuit,
over the dissents of three judges, on the grounds that the Georgia
Supreme Court's decision, while perhaps incorrect, was not unreasonable enough to warrant reversal under the highly deferential
standard established by the Antiterrorism and Effective Death Penalty Act.[43] In a final plot twist, in 2013, all three state experts who
had testified that Hill was not intellectually disabled changed their
earlier opinions based upon the review of additional information.
Despite the agreement of *all seven* experts that Hill was intellectually
disabled, the state and federal courts found procedural barriers to

considering his claim that he was not eligible for the death penalty.[44] Georgia executed Hill in 2015.

The case of Warren Hill demonstrates that Georgia's standard ensures that any person whose intellectual disability is not absolutely certain can be executed—virtually the opposite of the Supreme Court's holding in *Atkins*. Yet the Georgia Supreme Court continues to uphold the "beyond a reasonable doubt" standard; it rejected a challenge to that standard as recently as 2021.[45]

The execution of intellectually disabled people is one of the most glaring examples of the injustice of the death penalty. Another is the execution of people because of their race. Throughout its history, the death penalty has been disproportionately imposed on Black men. In the 1972 case *Furman v. Georgia*, when the Supreme Court overturned existing death penalty statutes, Justices William Douglas and Thurgood Marshall cited studies finding discrimination in the infliction of the death penalty, which they attributed to the "untrammeled discretion" of courts in deciding whether to impose death. Justice Potter Stewart wrote, "If any basis can be discerned for the selection of these few to be sentenced to die, it is the constitutionally impermissible basis of race."[46]

Despite the racial disparities in the application of the death penalty, the states that adopted new death penalty statutes made only small tweaks to the previous statutes and retained the discretion that made discrimination possible. The new statutes allowed the death penalty if certain "aggravating factors" were found, such as murder in the commission of certain crimes such as robbery, or murder of a police officer or firefighter.[47] Most states added a catchall aggravator covering any murder that is "heinous, atrocious or cruel," "cold, calculated and premeditated," or "outrageously vile, horrible and inhuman"—that is, almost all murders.[48] The death sentence is supposed to be imposed only if the aggravating factors outweigh any "mitigating factors," which can include anything about the life and background of the person facing the death penalty.[49] Under these statutes, almost all murders qualify for death, providing ample room for racial prejudice to influence the fateful decisions made by prosecutors and juries.

As discussed earlier, prosecutors decide whether to seek the death penalty and whether to offer a lesser sentence in exchange for a guilty plea. In most jurisdictions, these critical decisions are made by one person, the elected district attorney, who is usually a white man. Some prosecutors seek the death penalty frequently. Many never do so. The elected head prosecutors of five separate jurisdictions—four white men and one white woman—alone oversaw a total of 440 death sentences in forty years.[50] Many cases in which the death penalty is imposed are indistinguishable from hundreds of other murder cases in which it is not. For example, many murders occur in the commission of robberies, but only a handful are prosecuted as death cases. This enormous discretion makes it possible for racial prejudice to infect prosecutors' decisions.

Race can also influence the prosecution in more subtle ways. Prosecutors make charging decisions based in part on the strength of the evidence that law enforcement has brought to them. Often, the amount of available evidence differs depending on the victim's race, because local law enforcement officers investigate crime in white communities much more aggressively than crime in Black communities. This results in the prosecutor having stronger evidence with which to seek harsher sentences in white-victim cases than in cases where the victim is a minority.

An investigation into why some cases are singled out for capital prosecution will often reveal the influence of race, class, and politics. Community outrage—in particular over interracial crimes—the prominence of the victim, the insistence of the victim's family on a death sentence, the social and political clout of the family, and the amount of publicity regarding the crime are often important factors in determining the severity of the punishment sought. For example, over a seventeen-year period in Georgia's Chattahoochee Judicial Circuit, prosecutors often met with the families of white victims, discussed the death penalty with them, and issued press releases announcing that they would seek the death penalty. However, the same prosecutors failed to meet with the families of Black victims and often did not even notify them when a case had been resolved. Over that period, African Americans were the victims in 65 percent of homicides in the circuit, but 85 percent of the capital cases involved white victims.[51] In the United States as a whole, African Americans make up about 13 percent of the population but are the victims in about half of all murders. In some of the Southern states that most often impose the death penalty, African Americans are the victims of over 60 percent of the murders. Yet 76 percent of the cases in which the death penalty has been carried out since 1976 have involved white victims.[52]

The Eighth Amendment prohibits "cruel and unusual punishment," which includes the arbitrary imposition of the death penalty, as the Supreme Court held in 1972. The Fourteenth Amendment guarantees all people the "equal protection of the laws." The Supreme Court, however, has turned a blind eye to the arbitrary and racially discriminatory way that the death penalty is applied.

Warren McCleskey, as discussed earlier, was a Black man who challenged his death sentence for the 1978 murder of a white police officer in Georgia. His evidence included two statistical studies of over two thousand cases resulting from homicides committed in Georgia from 1973 to 1979—"far and away the most refined data ever assembled on any system of punishment," according to Supreme Court Justice William Brennan.[53] The studies demonstrated that McCleskey and other Black people had in all likelihood been sentenced to death because their victims were white, and would not have been sentenced to death if their victims had been Black. The death penalty was imposed in

22 percent of cases involving Blacks convicted of murders of whites, but only 1 percent of cases involving Blacks convicted of murders of Blacks. A later analysis of the same cases found that defendants who killed white victims were more than seventeen times as likely to be executed as those who killed Black victims.[54] Justice Brennan summarized what the statistics meant to McCleskey and others facing the death penalty:

> At some point in this case, Warren McCleskey doubtless asked his lawyer whether a jury was likely to sentence him to die. A candid reply to this question would have been disturbing. First, counsel would have to tell McCleskey that few of the details of the crime or of McCleskey's past criminal conduct were more important than the fact that his victim was white. Furthermore, counsel would feel bound to tell McCleskey that defendants charged with killing white victims in Georgia are 4.3 times as likely to be sentenced to death as defendants charged with killing blacks. In addition, . . . 6 of every 11 defendants convicted of killing a white person would not have received the death penalty if their victims had been black, while, among defendants with aggravating and mitigating factors comparable to McCleskey's, 20 of every 34 would not have been sentenced to die if their victims had been black. . . . The story could be told in a variety of ways, but McCleskey could not fail to grasp its essential narrative line: there was a significant chance that race would play a prominent role in determining if he lived or died.[55]

The Supreme Court, by a vote of 5–4, affirmed McCleskey's death sentence, rejecting his claim that he had been denied equal protection of the law. In other areas of the law, the Supreme Court had accept-

ed statistical disparities as compelling evidence of racial discrimination. Justice Lewis Powell's majority opinion, however, argued that
McCleskey's challenge was different. Because "discretion is essential to the criminal justice process," Justice Powell said, McCleskey
was required to present "exceptionally clear proof" that "the deci-
sionmakers in McCleskey's case acted with discriminatory purpose."
Furthermore, he said, the public policy considerations behind prosecutorial discretion "suggest the impropriety of our requiring prosecutors to defend their decisions to seek death penalties"[56]—even
though the same Supreme Court had just the year before required
prosecutors to explain why they had struck a disparate number of
Blacks during jury selection.[57] Ultimately, the majority ignored the
evidence of racial discrimination because "McCleskey committed an
act for which the United States Constitution and Georgia laws permit
imposition of the death penalty."[58] This simply sidestepped the argument that of the many people potentially subject to the death penalty
under Georgia law, race was determining which ones were actually
sentenced to death.

The Court also rejected McCleskey's claim that, because of the
influence of race, the death penalty in Georgia was imposed in an arbitrary and capricious manner in violation of the Eighth Amendment.
While recognizing "some risk of racial prejudice influencing a jury's
decision," Justice Powell credited the Court's own "unceasing efforts
to eradicate racial prejudice from our criminal justice system" with
creating safeguards that limited that risk. But, as part of these "unceasing efforts," Justice Powell cited two cases not decided until after
McCleskey's trial—*Batson v. Kentucky* and *Turner v. Murray*—which,
in retrospect, have failed to prevent the discrimination they were
supposed to stop. As Justice Brennan noted in his dissent, the Court's
supposed "unceasing efforts" showed "not the elimination of the
problem but its persistence."[59] Ultimately, the Court held that racial
disparities "are an inevitable part of our criminal justice system"

and declined "to assume that what is unexplained is invidious." The acceptance of racial disparities as "inevitable" is a disturbing abdication of the Court's responsibility to end racial discrimination. Justice Brennan, in dissent, pointed out that the disparities established by the studies were consistent with Georgia's history of different punishments for "crimes committed by and against blacks and whites, distinctions whose lineage traced back to the time of slavery."[60]

The Supreme Court's decision in *McCleskey* has been roundly criticized. As one law professor wrote, referring to *McCleskey* has become shorthand for "cases in which the Supreme Court failed the Constitution's most basic values."[61] After his retirement, when asked if he could change any vote from his time on the Court, Justice Powell replied, "*McCleskey v. Kemp.*" By then, he had concluded that the death penalty should be abolished because it "brings discredit on the whole legal system."[62]

Since the Court's decision in *McCleskey,* one study after another has further documented racial discrimination in the imposition of the death penalty. The United States General Accounting Office reported in 1990 that its analysis of twenty-eight studies found such disparities. In twenty-three of the studies, "race of victim was found to influence the likelihood of being charged with capital murder or receiving the death penalty." A 2014 review of thirty-six studies in twenty-four jurisdictions found race-of-victim disparities in a majority of jurisdictions and race-of-defendant disparities in a minority of them.[63]

The evidence of racial discrimination in the application of the death penalty has failed to sway the Supreme Court, but it has contributed to the slow decline of capital punishment. In 2015, the Connecticut Supreme Court, in holding that a legislative repeal of the death penalty applied to people already on death row, noted that all capital punishment sentencing systems "inevitably open the door to impermissible racial and ethnic biases."[64] The Washington Supreme Court unanimously held in 2018 that the death penalty was being imposed in an "arbitrary and racially biased manner" and violated the state constitution. The Court based its decision on a statistical study showing that Blacks were between 3.5 and 4.6 times as likely to be sentenced to death as non-Blacks.[65] Unlike the U.S. Supreme Court in *McCleskey*, the Washington Supreme Court concluded that racial discrimination could be addressed only by examining—and rejecting—the system as a whole.

Greater awareness of racial discrimination is one reason that the number of death sentences and the number of executions have been declining since the late 1990s. Other factors include a significant decline in violent crime, over 185 exonerations of people formerly on death row, increasing consciousness of the high costs of prosecuting a capital case, the availability of life imprisonment without parole as an alternative to the death penalty, and, most importantly, improvements in the quality of representation for people facing the death penalty.[66] In 1999, 279 people were sentenced to death and 98 were executed; in 2019, only 34 people were sentenced to death and only 22 were executed. In a country with sixteen thousand homicides and only a handful of executions every year, who is selected to die is fundamentally, inescapably arbitrary.[67] Thirty years ago, Mississippi Supreme Court Justice James Robertson said to the Senate Judiciary Committee,

> I could take every death sentence case that we have had where we have affirmed, give you the facts and not tell you the outcome, and then pull an equal number of murder cases that have been in our system, give you the facts and not tell you the outcome, and challenge you to pick which ones got the death sentence and which ones did not, and you couldn't do it.[68]

That is as true today as it was then. In 2015, Supreme Court Justice Stephen Breyer, "after considering thousands of death penalty cases and last-minute petitions over the course of more than 20 years," concluded, "I see discrepancies for which I can find no rational explanations. . . . The imposition and implementation of the death penalty seems capricious, random, indeed, arbitrary. From a defendant's perspective, to receive that sentence, and certainly to find it implemented, is the equivalent of being struck by lightning."[69]

Life Without Hope

The recent decline in death sentences has been more than compensated for by a rise in extremely harsh prison sentences. From 2000 to 2020, the number of people on death row fell for twenty consecutive years from 3,593 to 2,469; over the same period, the number of people serving sentences of life imprisonment grew from 127,677 to over 160,000. More than 55,000 of them were serving sentences of life without the possibility of parole. Another 42,000 were serving "virtual life" sentences, with a minimum of fifty years in prison before the possibility of parole.[70]

In general, parole refers to the conditional release of a prisoner before the end of his sentence. He then spends the rest of his original term "on parole," living in the community but under the supervision of a parole officer. Someone in prison may become eligible for parole after a certain amount of time stipulated by his sentence (for example, a sentence of "25 years to life" means that the defendant will become eligible after twenty-five years), but whether he is actually released is decided by a parole board or similar entity.

Although life imprisonment without the possibility of parole is often considered an alternative to the death penalty, the widespread desire to "throw away the key" has led to its frequent use to punish people who were not the most incorrigible and did not commit the most heinous crimes. In a large majority of states, people can be sentenced to life without parole for non-homicide crimes, and often for crimes that do not involve violence against people, such as burglary or selling drugs. In more than half of all states, life without parole is mandated for some crimes or by "habitual offender" statutes such as three-strikes laws.[71]

Aron Tuff was arrested in Moultrie, Georgia, in 1995 for possession of 0.3 grams of crack cocaine. Because he had two prior felony convictions—for drug possession and burglary—he was sentenced to life without parole, even though none of his offenses involved violence. In Alabama, Roberto Cruz was convicted of transporting marijuana in 2003. He had previously been convicted of conspiracy to distribute drugs and cocaine possession, and—because marijuana trafficking is defined as a violent crime in Alabama—he was sentenced to life without parole. Both Tuff and Cruz were released many years later after nonprofit legal organizations intervened on their behalf.[72] There are hundreds more people like them still behind bars for life who were not so fortunate. They have no right to a lawyer to seek a reduction of their sentences.

In 2016, more than twelve thousand people were serving life without parole for crimes in which no one was killed—often something as simple as serial sale and possession of drugs.[73] But even people convicted of violent crimes are incarcerated long past the age when they are likely to commit such offenses. Only 4 percent of homicides are committed by people above the age of sixty (who make up 23 percent of the overall population); a study of federal offenders found that of those released at age sixty-five or older, only 4 percent were rearrested, convicted, and reincarcerated in the next eight years, compared with 35 percent of people released in their twenties. Yet because so many defendants receive sentences of life without parole, there are many people still in prison who are in their sixties or seventies.[74] This imposes considerable costs on the prison system, especially given the increasingly poor health of inmates as they become older.

Despite the obvious cruelty of locking someone up with no hope of release, especially when this punishment is vastly disproportionate to the crimes he committed, the Supreme Court has held that sentences of life without parole "may be cruel, but they are not unusual" and thus not prohibited by the Eighth Amendment.[75] The one exception has been sentences of life without parole imposed on people for crimes they committed under the age of eighteen. Terrance Jamar Graham was sentenced to life in prison in Florida—a state that had previously eliminated parole across the board—for armed burglary, attempted robbery, and multiple probation violations. In 2010, however, the United States Supreme Court overturned Graham's sentence, holding that life without parole cannot be imposed for non-homicide crimes committed by children. The Court reasoned that children, compared with adults, have a "'lack of maturity and an underdeveloped sense of responsibility'; they 'are more vulnerable or susceptible to negative influences and outside pressures, including peer pressure'; and their characters are 'not as well formed.'" As a result, the sentence of life without parole is disproportionate for them.[76]

Children can still be sentenced to life imprisonment without parole for murder. In 2012, however, in *Miller v. Alabama*, the Supreme Court held that states cannot automatically impose that sentence for a murder committed before the age of eighteen. "By making youth (and all that accompanies it) irrelevant to imposition of that harshest prison sentence," Justice Elena Kagan wrote for the majority, a mandatory sentence of life without parole "poses too great a risk of disproportionate punishment."[77] In 2016, the Supreme Court held in *Montgomery v. Louisiana* that the rule of *Miller* was retroactive, meaning that everyone who had been sentenced to life without parole for murders committed as juveniles had to be made eligible for parole, or they had to be resentenced taking into account their individual characteristics. The Court said that "sentencing a child to life without parole is excessive for all but 'the rare juvenile offender whose crime reflects irreparable corruption,'" but left it to prosecutors, judges, and juries to identify those children who are irreparably corrupt.[78]

Twenty-five states and the District of Columbia have abolished life imprisonment without parole for children.[79] However, the Supreme Court still allows the remaining states to sentence people to life without parole for murders committed before age eighteen if a sentencing judge concludes that the child exhibits "such irretrievable depravity that rehabilitation is impossible and life without parole is justified."[80] Some states have taken up the challenge of making that showing in earnest. In Louisiana, 258 people became eligible for resentencing because of *Montgomery*, but prosecutors sought new sentences of life without parole for more than 30 percent of them.[81] There are still more than a thousand people serving sentences of life without parole for crimes committed when they were children. Given the highly subjective standards used in these cases, it is not surprising that Black children are much more likely to be sentenced to life without parole for killing white victims than white children are for killing Black victims.[82]

In 2021, in *Jones v. Mississippi*, the Supreme Court made it easier to sentence children to life in prison without parole by holding that a judge does not have to specifically determine that a child is "permanently incorrigible" in order to impose that sentence. Just days later, Evan Miller—of *Miller v. Alabama*—was resentenced to life in prison without parole for a murder he committed when he was fourteen.[83]

Severe and Disproportionate Sentences

Many people serving life or virtual life sentences in prison were sentenced under the habitual-offender statutes that were the fashion in the 1980s and 1990s among state politicians eager to show that they were tough on crime. The best known were three-strikes laws that imposed harsh sentences on defendants convicted of felonies whose prior records included serious or violent felony convictions. The Supreme Court upheld such laws in 1980 in the case of William Rummel, who was convicted in Texas for accepting $120.75 to repair an air conditioner and then failing to repair it. He had previously been convicted of credit card fraud and using a forged check, from which he had netted a total of approximately $108. Because all three of these offenses were felonies, he was given a mandatory sentence of life imprisonment. By a 5–4 vote, the Supreme Court upheld Texas's three-strikes law on the grounds that states have a significant interest "in dealing in a harsher manner with those who by repeated criminal acts have shown that they are simply incapable of conforming to the norms of society."[84]

Under California's three-strikes law passed in 1994, people convicted of a felony with prior convictions for two serious or violent felonies were sentenced to life in prison, with the possibility of parole typically after twenty-five years, even if the third conviction was for a nonviolent offense. In 2020, California prisons held more than forty thousand people serving life or virtual life sentences—33 percent of the entire prison population. Across the country, the number of people serving life sentences doubled from 1984 to 1992 and then doubled again by 2008.[85]

The vast majority of the people affected by California's three-strikes law received their increased sentences for nonviolent offenses.[86] Gary Ewing was sentenced to twenty-five years to life for stealing three golf clubs—a felony that could have been prosecuted as a misdemeanor. (His prior "strikes" were for three burglaries and one robbery.) Ewing appealed to the U.S. Supreme Court, arguing that his sentence was so grossly disproportionate to his crime that it violated the Eighth Amendment's ban on cruel and unusual punishment. Justice Breyer pointed out that in California, without considering prior convictions, the maximum sentence for grand theft was four years, only first-degree murder could qualify for a sentence of twenty-five years to life, and most people whose first conviction was for first-degree murder had actually served only ten to fifteen years. But, in a 5–4 decision, the Court upheld Ewing's sentence, holding that the three-strikes law "reflects a rational legislative judgment, entitled to deference."[87] The same day, the Court upheld the sentence of Leandro Andrade, who received two consecutive terms of twenty-five years to life under California's three-strikes law—meaning he was not eligible for parole until he had served fifty years—for stealing $150 worth of videotapes from two stores.[88]

Today, more than half of all states and the federal government have some type of three-strikes law, many of which mandate a life sentence for the third qualifying felony.[89] Under Alabama's habitual-offender law, almost any felony counts as a strike; if a person's fourth strike is a "Class A" felony, he receives a life sentence or even an automatic sentence of life without parole, depending on what the prior felonies were. Alvin Kennard was convicted of robbing a bakery in Alabama in 1983 at age twenty-two. Four years before, he had pleaded guilty to three counts of second-degree burglary for a single incident in which he broke into an unoccupied gas station. Because those three counts qualified as three separate strikes, he was sentenced to life without parole. Kennard spent thirty-six years in prison before being released when a nonprofit organization took up his case and a judge agreed to change his sentence.[90]

The widespread adoption of habitual-offender statutes, as well as other laws that increase sentences (such as those requiring stiffer penalties for committing certain crimes in the vicinity of a school or with a weapon), is a major reason why so many people spend so much time in prison. As Louisiana Supreme Court Chief Justice Bernette Johnson wrote, dissenting in one case, "This man's life sentence for a failed attempt to steal a set of hedge clippers is grossly out of proportion to the crime and serves no legitimate penal purpose."[91] Although the failure and enormous costs of the "wars" on crime and drugs have been widely recognized, the harsh sentencing laws that they produced are still with us, with minor modifications in some states.

Severe sentencing laws also had the predictable effect of ratcheting up prison terms for the populations that were most heavily targeted by law enforcement. By the early 2000s, African Americans were four times as likely as whites to be arrested for felonies in California, but were ten times as likely to be serving a "second strike" sentence and thirteen times as likely to be serving a "third strike" sentence in that state.[92]

Prosecutors make greater use of habitual-offender sentencing enhancements with minority defendants than with whites.[93] In 1995 in Georgia, 375 people were serving sentences of life imprisonment for a second drug trafficking conviction; 369 of them—more than 98 percent—were Black. Even in a state where Blacks are arrested and imprisoned for drug offenses at higher rates than whites, this figure seems impossible. What made it possible was a statute that purported to require a life sentence but effectively gave prosecutors discretion over whether or not to request that sentence. From 1990 to 1994, Georgia prosecutors chose to invoke the "mandatory" life sentence for 202 out of 1,107 African Americans who were eligible for it, but only *one* out of 167 eligible whites.[94]

When Freddie Stephens challenged these gross disparities in court, the Georgia Supreme Court initially held by a 4–3 vote that the evidence had established a prima facie case of racial discrimination. Ten days later, the state attorney general and all forty-six district attorneys—all white—filed a petition for rehearing with the court, claiming that the ruling would "paralyze the criminal justice system" and threaten the state's death penalty law.[95] Three days after the petition was filed, one justice bowed to political pressure and changed his vote, and the court upheld the sentencing scheme, holding that prosecutors must be allowed to "exercise their discretion in determining who to prosecute, what charges to bring, which sentence to seek, and when to appeal."[96]

Sadly, Georgia is not an isolated case. As of 2016, more than 10,400 people in the United States were serving sentences of life imprisonment for nonviolent offenses, more than half of them for drug crimes. An earlier study of nine states and the federal prison system estimated that 65 percent of the people sentenced to life imprisonment without the possibility of parole for nonviolent offenses were Black, and another 16 percent were Latino. In Louisiana, more than 91 percent were Black; the figure was 79 percent in Mississippi.[97]

African Americans have also been disproportionately targeted by other severe sentencing laws passed during the war on drugs of the 1980s and 1990s. Although these laws did not single out racial minorities by name, some were written to virtually guarantee a discriminatory impact—most famously those applying to possession of powder cocaine versus crack cocaine. (The two forms of cocaine are chemically almost identical.) In 1986, Congress passed a law that established a 100-to-1 sentencing disparity between crack and powder cocaine. For example, while a drug trafficking offense involving 500 grams of powder cocaine would result in a mandatory minimum sentence of five years, the same mandatory minimum would apply for trafficking involving only 5 grams of crack cocaine. In 1988, Congress added a mandatory minimum sentence of five years for simple possession of 5 grams of crack cocaine; possession of a small amount of powder cocaine by a first-time offender remained a misdemeanor with a maximum sentence of one year.[98]

As federal legislators must have known, African Americans were less likely than whites to use powder cocaine but more likely to use crack cocaine. Even so, because there are far more white people than Black people in the U.S., there were more white than Black users of either type of cocaine.[99] However, because of law enforcement priorities—such as more intensive policing in poor neighborhoods and racial profiling in traffic and pedestrian stops—people who use crack cocaine are more likely to be arrested than people who use powder cocaine, and Blacks who use crack cocaine are the most likely to be arrested of all. In 2006, for example, 82 percent of the people convicted of federal crack cocaine offenses were Black, 8 percent were Hispanic, and 9 percent were white; among those convicted of powder cocaine offenses, 27 percent were Black, 58 percent were Hispanic, and 14 percent were white.[100] Laws targeting crack cocaine combined with racially discriminatory policing to impose much harsher penalties on minority drug users than on whites.

Edward Clary was arrested for possession with intent to distribute 66.76 grams (about two ounces) of crack cocaine, for which the minimum sentence was ten years. A person would have to have 5,000 grams (about 11 pounds) of powder cocaine to qualify for the same minimum sentence. Clary challenged the 100-to-1 disparity. A federal judge found that, in fifty-seven crack cocaine cases in the same federal district, the total amount of drugs in all the cases weighed less than 4,000 grams—not reaching the 5,000-gram threshold for powder cocaine—and that fifty-five of the defendants were Black. "The logical inference to be drawn," he wrote, "is that the prosecutors in the federal courts are selectively prosecuting black defendants who were involved with crack, no matter how trivial the amount, and ignoring or diverting whites when they do the same thing." The judge concluded that the 100-to-1 sentencing disparity constituted unconstitutional racial discrimination.[101] However, his ruling was reversed by the Eighth Circuit Court of Appeals, which denied that Congress had a racially discriminatory purpose in enacting the 100-to-1 ratio and therefore held that the unequal impact on African Americans essentially did not matter.[102] Eventually, the Fair Sentencing Act of 2010 changed the 100-to-1 ratio to an 18-to-1 ratio, so now possession of 28 grams of crack cocaine carries the same penalty as possession of 500 grams of powder cocaine.[103]

The unequal impact of severe sentencing laws—often resulting from legislative targeting or unbridled prosecutorial discretion—is one reason why our country's prisons are so full of people of color. But minorities are disadvantaged at every stage of the criminal legal process. It is not only that Black people are more likely than whites to be stopped—or shot—by the police. Once arrested, for whatever conduct, people of color suffer significantly worse outcomes than whites at every stage from setting bail through sentencing.

As discussed earlier, members of racial minorities are less likely to be released before their trial; as a result, they are more likely to be convicted because they have a strong incentive to plead guilty to a minor charge in order to get out of jail, and they are less able to assist in preparing their defense. In addition, people of color tend to be charged with more serious offenses than whites when prosecutors decide what charges to bring. One study of federal prosecutions showed that, all other things being equal, Black defendants are 65 percent more likely than whites to face charges that carry mandatory minimum sentences.[104]

Some studies show that prosecutors present harsher plea offers to minority defendants than to whites. In Wisconsin, among defendants charged with misdemeanors, prosecutors were willing to drop all charges that could entail incarceration for 37 percent of whites but only 21 percent of Blacks. In New York City, African Americans were 70 percent more likely than whites to receive plea offers that required incarceration (as opposed to deals that allowed the defendant to walk free immediately), even after controlling for legally relevant factors.[105]

As a result of all these factors, people of color—particularly young Black men—are more likely to be convicted and face harsher sentences than whites. Florida established a point system (taking into account the offense, the defendant's prior record, and other factors) that is supposed to ensure consistent sentencing. Nevertheless, Blacks convicted of the most serious felonies still received sentences 68 percent longer than those handed out to whites with the same number of points. Chase Legleitner and Lamar Lloyd both pleaded no contest to two counts of armed robbery before the same Florida judge; each had one prior misdemeanor and scored the same number of points. Legleitner, who is white, was sentenced to time served (less than two years); Lloyd, who is Black, to twenty-six years.[106]

This pattern is repeated across the country and for many different categories of crimes. The U.S. Sentencing Commission found that African American men in federal courts receive sentences that are 19 percent longer on average than similarly situated white men, largely because whites are more likely to benefit from the judge's discretion to reduce a sentence below the guidelines. In Wisconsin, the average sentence for Black defendants was 33 percent longer than the overall average. In New York City, the odds of being sentenced to incarceration were 30 percent higher for Blacks than for whites. There is even evidence that African Americans with darker skin receive longer sentences than those with lighter skin, who in turn are sentenced to more time than whites. (All of these analyses accounted for factors such as the offense involved and the defendant's criminal history.)[107]

As a result of these disparities in pretrial release, charging, and sentencing—on top of discriminatory policing—African Americans are held in prison at a rate five times that of whites, and in jail at a rate three times that of whites. Latinos are held in prison at a rate 50 percent higher than that of whites.[108] These striking figures result in part from the fact that Latinos and African Americans are disproportionately poor, and the types of crime targeted most heavily by the criminal legal system tend to correlate with poverty. But they also result from unequal treatment of people of different races at every step from arrest through bail hearings, charging decisions, and plea bargains to sentencing.

Mass Probation

The scale of incarceration in the United States is staggering: almost 2 million people in prison or jail at any one time. But the American criminal legal system manifests itself in another way: mass probation. As of 2020, 3.9 million people—more than one out of every sixty-six adults—were subject to some form of community supervision by the criminal legal system: 3 million on probation (up from only 816,000 in 1977) and 862,000 on parole.[109] Probation is imposed by a judge as part of a sentence, either instead of a term of incarceration or following a term of incarceration. The person under supervision is not incarcerated but must comply with various conditions set by statute or by the judge; failure to do so can be cause for incarceration. As discussed earlier, people who are assessed fines and fees but are too poor to pay them are often sentenced to probation and required to pay a monthly probation fee in addition to paying their fines and fees in installments.

Probation was originally conceived of as an appropriate sentence for people who could be punished without resort to prison or jail. A person convicted for the first time might be sentenced to probation and required to perform community service or demonstrate the ability to live a law-abiding life. However, it was influenced by the same political currents that transformed the rest of the criminal legal system beginning in the 1970s and 1980s. Judges began imposing more conditions and lengthier terms on probationers, and probation officers began enforcing them more strictly. Politicians and government officials also sought to make people pay for the costs of their own probation, which was completely unrealistic. The typical state now imposes between ten and twenty standard conditions on many probationers. Common conditions include not "indulging in any unlawful, disrespectful or disorderly conduct or habits"; obtaining full-time employment or attending school; performing a certain number of hours of community service; and paying fines, supervision fees, court costs, restitution, and charges for electronic monitoring, drug tests, and classes about driving under the influence and anger management. In Georgia and much of Texas, someone on probation must "avoid persons or places of disreputable or harmful character." In addition, many jurisdictions add what law professor Fiona Doherty calls "be good" provisions. People on probation in Georgia must "be of general good behavior"; those in Rhode Island must "keep the peace and remain on good behavior"; and those in California must not "become abandoned to a vicious life."[110] With so many conditions, many people placed on probation are set up to fail.

People who do not have an alcohol problem and whose crimes did not involve the abuse of alcohol are routinely required not to consume alcohol and, in some states, not to live in a place where alcoholic beverages are present or regularly consumed. This may severely limit someone's chances of finding housing if he cannot afford his own home.[111] Similarly, those who do not have a drug problem and whose crimes did not involve drugs are often nevertheless required to undergo regular drug testing, which can be onerous and expensive. A requirement that probationers not associate with a person with a criminal record seems reasonable, but the requirement may make it impossible for probationers to live with family members who were convicted of minor offenses years ago. Courts often impose curfews as conditions of probation. A person who is dependent on public transportation to get to work and is delayed in getting home by circumstances beyond his control may have his probation revoked for violating curfew.

As probation has changed, the role of the probation officer has changed from bringing about rehabilitation to strict enforcement of the rules and collection of fines and fees. And, as discussed earlier, officers often work for private companies that profit by squeezing money out of the people they supervise. Probation officers in many places have extraordinary powers to set conditions and determine who will be sent back to jail or prison. They commonly require people under their supervision to "report" at a time and place of the officer's choosing; visit them, unannounced, at home or at work; and subject them to warrantless searches that would otherwise violate the Fourth Amendment's prohibition of unreasonable searches. Probation officers in some places may act as prosecutor, witness, judge, and jury in deciding whether probationers have violated the conditions of probation. Upon finding a violation, some probation officers have the power to impose a wide range of sanctions, including increased reporting, curfews, limits on travel, community service, work requirements, participation in a treatment program, and electronic monitoring. They may also ask a court to revoke probation. Some states even allow probation officers to send people directly to jail or prison for short periods of time.[112]

Having to comply continuously with so many rules, enforced unevenly by often unsympathetic probation officers, may be difficult or impossible for people who lack stable family, housing, or employment—those most likely to end up under correctional supervision in the first place. Sociologist Victor Rios, after studying the experiences of thirty boys on probation in Oakland, California, concludes: "No matter how crafty a young person was at attempting to stay away from trouble, his probation officer found a way to 'violate' him, arrest him again for the smallest of infractions."[113] One in every four admissions to state prison is the result of a technical violation of probation or parole; in Kansas, Kentucky, Missouri, South Dakota, and Utah, technical violations are responsible for more than half of prison admissions.[114] The discretion afforded to probation officers is also one reason why African Americans are more likely than whites to have their probation revoked. In one study, Blacks were 50 percent more likely than whites to be jailed for a technical violation such as missing an appointment with a parole officer, after controlling for legal factors.[115]

If an officer decides to revoke someone's probation, that person is entitled to minimal procedural protections. In 1973, the Supreme Court held that someone facing probation revocation is entitled to a hearing, but not necessarily one before a judge, and without the right to the assistance of a lawyer.[116] In addition, a violation does not have to be proven beyond a reasonable doubt to revoke someone's probation; in most states, it only needs to be proven by a preponderance of the evidence. Finally, several states allow probation revocation not only for violations of specific conditions but also for unspecified bad conduct; in Idaho, for example, revocation is allowed for violations and "for any other cause satisfactory to the court."[117] In the face of these odds, it is often difficult to mount a defense against revocation of probation.

There is another well-trodden pathway from probation to jail. Many of the people held in jail are also there at least in part because of violations of probation or parole. Ordinarily, someone arrested for a minor offense is released on his own recognizance or required to post a bond to go free pending trial. If a person on probation is arrested, however, his supervising officer can issue a detainer requiring him to stay in jail pending resolution of the charges.[118] A judge may also set bail or detain a person because he is on probation. In Philadelphia, half of all people in jail are being held on probation or parole detainers; in San Antonio and the surrounding county, the figure is 32 percent.[119] If the person is found guilty of the charge for which he was arrested, that also counts as a violation of probation.

One reason there are 3 million people on probation is that probation sentences are often unnecessarily long. A study by the Pew Charitable Trusts found that states could significantly reduce probation terms without increasing the risk of recidivism.[120] There is simply no need to subject so many people, the vast majority of whom were not convicted of violent offenses, to such punitive supervision, hampering their efforts to build better lives for themselves and their families and placing them constantly at risk of incarceration. Probation can play a positive role in the criminal legal system, allowing people to stay out of jail or prison while performing community service, participating in diversion or restorative justice programs, or dealing with addiction issues in order to build a successful life in the community. But in too many instances, the conditions of probation may be so onerous that they do more harm than good.

The Uncertainty of Parole

In many states, how long a person stays in prison after being convicted of a crime depends on whether he is released on parole. One consequence of our country's increasingly punitive attitude toward criminal penalties has been severe restrictions on parole. As of 2020, more than 105,000 people were serving sentences of life imprisonment but could hope to be paroled before their deaths.[121] Yet many of those people have little realistic chance of ever leaving prison.

In 1977, Reynaldo Rodriguez pleaded guilty to second-degree murder in Michigan. Judge Gary McDonald gave him a sentence of life imprisonment because it would make him eligible for parole in ten years, sooner than if he received a sentence of fifteen to thirty years. Seventeen years later, Rodriguez came up for parole. On the basis of his initial crime and his lack of a criminal history, the parole board's scoring chart indicated that he should be released after fourteen years; in addition, he had become head mechanic in the prison shop and received recommendations from Judge McDonald, his supervisors, and a prison psychologist. Yet the board denied him parole because the "nature of crime as described in public hearing causes further concern."[122] Thirty-nine years after he was sentenced, Rodriguez was still in prison.

Parole is at the discretion of a parole board. "There is no constitutional or inherent right of a convicted person to be conditionally released before the expiration of a valid sentence," the Supreme Court held in in 1979.[123] As a result, states can establish whatever systems they like for granting or denying parole, and parole boards can make their decisions based on a broad range of criteria and following

widely varying procedures. Nineteen states have no minimum qualifications for board membership, and another eleven require only a
college degree. In some states, parole applicants have no right to
appear before the board. Virtually all states allow input from victims
and prosecutors. The majority of states do not provide attorneys to
applicants who cannot afford a lawyer, and most others do so only in
rare circumstances. Some parole boards do not have to give a written
reason for denying parole. And, in some states, the parole board can
even decide never to reconsider the applicant.[124]

The Supreme Court has observed that a parole decision can depend
on "purely subjective appraisals by the Board members." Some states
allow boards to deny parole because of highly subjective factors such
as "adverse public concern or notoriety," the risk that the inmate
might end up on welfare, or the applicant's "culture, language, values, mores, judgments, communicative ability and other unique
qualities."[125] In practice, however, the most important determinant
of whether someone is released is usually the crime that landed him in
prison in the first place. In a nationwide survey, board chairs ranked
"nature of the present offense" and "severity of current offense" as
the two most important factors they consider, by a wide margin.[126]
Parole boards also make decisions based on unproven allegations. At
Roosevelt Price's 2013 parole hearing in Missouri, one board member said, "I think you've been involved in other murders that you
haven't been caught for," even though he had never been charged
with any homicides other than the one he was in prison for. The
"facts" that parole boards consider do not have to be consistent with
those established at conviction or sentencing, there are no limitations
on hearsay, and the applicant has no right to confront opposing witnesses.[127] And although parole decisions often have the same practical effect that sentencing decisions have, applicants have no right to
appeal to the courts, except to argue that the statute governing parole
itself is illegal or that the parole board violated the law in some way.

States have recently begun trying to reduce their prison populations, but most reforms have focused on nonviolent offenders. As a result, the prospects of parole have become much more remote for people serving life sentences, especially those who committed violent crimes. In 1980, only 14 percent of people leaving prison had served their maximum terms; by 2012, that figure was 22 percent. Not surprisingly, Black inmates are less likely to be paroled than whites.[128]

There is never any real political downside to denying parole, but releasing someone from prison—especially someone who committed a particularly violent or notorious crime—can provoke intense popular backlash. One nationwide survey found that, in the eight jurisdictions that provided data for the entire period, the average time served by people with life sentences for murder convictions doubled from 11.6 years in the 1980s to 23.2 years in 2000–2013 (and those figures exclude people who died in prison).[129]

A sentence of twenty-five years to life is supposed to give a person a real chance of leaving prison in his lifetime. Yet, in many parts of the country, such a sentence gives a group of people appointed by the governor the power to keep someone in jail indefinitely to punish him for his original crime. Parole is a unique aspect of sentencing law, where boards can impose punishment for virtually any reason, with the most minimal of procedures and no effective oversight. Yet for more than 100,000 people, it is their only real chance to avoid dying in prison.

Clemency—The Last Resort

There is one other way to escape from the burden of an excessive and harsh sentence: executive clemency. The Supreme Court has called clemency "the historic remedy for preventing miscarriages of justice where judicial process has been exhausted."[130] As is well known, the president of the United States has the power to pardon people for federal crimes or to commute (reduce) their sentences. In every state, either the governor or a board can grant pardons or commute sentences imposed in state courts; in some states, the governor can act only on a recommendation by a board. This power is essentially absolute; courts cannot reverse a pardon or an act of clemency or insist that a governor should have issued a pardon or granted clemency when he did not.

Executive clemency can play an important role in cases where there are questions of innocence or there are other reasons for compassion or mercy, such as when someone condemned to death is intellectually disabled or suffers from serious mental disorders. Between 1976 and the end of 2022, 312 death sentences were commuted—most of them in Illinois, as discussed below—while over 1,500 executions were carried out.[131] Virginia governor Douglas Wilder commuted the death sentence of Earl Washington Jr., an intellectually disabled man, in 1994 because of doubts about his guilt. After more sophisticated DNA testing established Washington's innocence, Governor James S. Gilmore III pardoned Washington in 2000. He was released but subject to parole supervision. After the person who had committed the murder for which Washington had been sentenced to death was identified and pleaded guilty, Governor Timothy M. Kaine issued an absolute pardon in 2007. Washington was awarded almost $2 million in damages.[132]

Clemency can also be used to address systemic failings of the criminal legal system. Illinois governor George Ryan, who had supported the death penalty as a state legislator, declared a moratorium on the death penalty in 2000 because he recognized that innocent people were being sentenced to death—including Anthony Porter, who came within two days of execution before a group of journalism students found evidence of his innocence. In testimony to Congress, Ryan said, "I cannot support a system which, in its administration, has proven to be so fraught with error and has come so close to the ultimate nightmare, the taking of an innocent life." Before he left office in 2003, Ryan pardoned four people who had been sentenced to death and commuted the sentences of the remaining 167 people on death row.[133]

However, because governors (and presidents) are highly visible elected officials, clemency decisions tend to be constrained by popular political pressures. For most governors, commutation of a death sentence is typically reserved for rare cases where the defendant is sympathetic for some reason. From 1977 to 2020, Texas executed 570 people, while only three people with death sentences were granted clemency.[134] Wilbert Evans, who protected the lives of prison guards and nurses during an escape, was denied clemency by the governor of Virginia. People serving long prison sentences for nonviolent drug crimes are more sympathetic candidates for clemency. President Barack Obama commuted the sentences of 1,715 people while in office, primarily benefiting people sentenced for nonviolent drug offenses.[135] No president or governor has shown any inclination to use the clemency power to significantly reduce the vast numbers of people in prison for violent crimes or property crimes.

Those seeking a pardon or clemency have only the most minimal procedural rights, if any. "Pardon and commutation decisions have not traditionally been the business of courts," the Supreme Court observed in 1981. "As such, they are rarely, if ever, appropriate subjects for judicial review."[136] In some states, clemency procedures are both shoddy and opaque. In 1999, a federal district judge described Texas's procedures—in which the board members review cases separately, do not always read the entire applications, do not meet, operate without guidelines, and do not explain their decisions—as "extremely poor and certainly minimal." The apparent goal, he continued, was "to protect the secrecy and autonomy of the system rather than carrying out an efficient, legally sound system." Even this, however, was enough to "meet minimal procedural safeguards."[137] In 2014, the Fifth Circuit Court of Appeals upheld Texas's clemency procedures.[138]

Justice in Sentencing

The policies that have sent so many people to death row and prison are the result not of a carefully considered approach to sentencing, but of political posturing and racial animus as politicians waged "wars" on crime and drugs. They were adopted with little understanding of human behavior, with indifference to their financial and human costs, and without regard for the benefits of returning people to their families and their communities. Many people have become aware of the injustice and cruelty of our contemporary age of mass incarceration and mass probation. Despite modest reforms to pare back sentences for nonviolent offenses, however, there are still far too many people in jail or prison. Legislators, prosecutors, and judges need to move on from the past decades' obsession with being "tough on crime" for the sake of appearing tough. Sentences should serve the ends of justice: they should fairly reflect the moral culpability of people who commit crimes, while giving them a real chance of building productive lives in their communities. And extreme penalties, such as the death penalty and life imprisonment without the possibility of parole, must be abandoned altogether.

9

More Justice, Less Crime

> We must learn to regard human beings less in terms of what they do and neglect to do and more in terms of what they suffer.
>
> —*Dietrich Bonhoeffer, 1942*[1]

Excessive punishment is one of the most important problems facing our country today, causing misery for people subject to it and their families, wasting vast resources, and making it harder for millions of people to contribute to society. Some state and local governments are trying different ways to reduce the burden of mass incarceration: eliminating cash bail; declining to arrest or prosecute people where it would serve no purpose; decriminalizing minor offenses such as loitering, disorderly conduct, and marijuana possession; offering treatment for addiction in place of imprisonment for some offenses; providing informed and constructive responses to incidents of domestic violence and mental health crises; ending the imposition of fines and fees on people who cannot afford to pay them and the suspension of driver's licenses for unpaid court debt; and choosing not to charge people under recidivist statutes that produce unconscionably long sentences or to seek sentences of death or life imprisonment without parole. But there is a limit to what can be achieved through these reforms, which focus on specific types of people and offenses or depend on the use of prosecutorial discretion.

Although the rate of violent crime has fallen to half the level of the 1990s, about 800,000 people—40 percent of the total prison and jail population—are incarcerated for crimes classified as "violent," primarily because of the long and inflexible sentences imposed for those offenses. (Some crimes classified as "violent" do not involve any physical harm; they may include burglary and manufacturing and selling drugs.)[2] There is considerable evidence that locking more people up for longer does not reduce violent crime rates. Excessive use of incarceration can result in more crime because of the stress produced by prison conditions and exposure to violence, the negative influences people in prison may have on each other, the harm prolonged incarceration causes to family and social bonds, and the difficulty that people have in finding stable jobs and homes after being released. From the early 1990s to 2020, crime rates fell virtually everywhere, regardless of whether incarceration rates went up or down.[3] A recent review of 116 studies found that prison, compared to other sanctions, either has no effect on reoffending or slightly increases it.[4]

The assumption behind punitive sentencing is that crime is the result of the autonomous, free choices of individuals. It follows that harsh sentences are a morally appropriate response to criminal behavior and will deter such behavior in the future. But, as social psychologist Craig Haney has shown over decades of work, "criminal behavior is often an adaptive response to otherwise pathological, destructive past histories and present environments." Many of those who commit crimes are the "poorest, most traumatized, badly abused and, in that sense, least autonomous citizens."[5] Some spent their childhoods in poverty and in crisis—dealing with life-threatening situations in dangerous neighborhoods and in homes where chaos, violence, and drug and alcohol abuse were common. Some experienced parental neglect; others suffered psychological, physical, and sexual abuse. Some people of color are subject to an "accumulation of race-based social and economic obstacles, indignities and disadvantages, experienced across an entire lifetime." Efforts to correct behavior by placing people in juvenile institutions or adult prisons often result in institutional trauma.[6] As Haney has found, "Most people engage in troubled, problematic behavior because bad things have happened *to* them and too little has been in their lives to turn the resulting troubled trajectories in a different direction." Thus, "no effective strategy of crime control can continue to overlook the situational and social structural roots of criminality."[7]

To achieve a significant, lasting reduction in crime, we must address poverty and racial discrimination, which greatly increase the probability of criminal behavior. Much of the resources devoted to prisons—over $80 billion a year—must be reallocated to high-quality early childhood education programs, community initiatives addressing the traumatic experiences of marginalized children, therapy and drug treatment, educational and vocational opportunities, job placement services, and similar programs. Communities must also fund crisis intervention programs, rapid response teams staffed by mental health specialists, and community mental health centers that, as seen in Miami-Dade County, can help people with mental health issues without involving the criminal legal system.[8]

Communities must also better respond to the problems of drug addiction and over-prosecution of drug offenses. There are more than 1 million arrests for drug possession or distribution each year; more than 400,000 people are in prison or jail for drug offenses, including almost half of the federal prison population. Many other crimes, such as burglary, robbery, and murder, are often committed by people under the influence of drugs or desperate for money to buy drugs. Almost 108,000 people died because of overdoses in 2021, an increase of 15 percent from the year before. Drug addiction is particularly challenging because changes in brain function from drug use can be long-lasting. Even the most conscientious participant in an effective treatment program may relapse—after years of abstinence.[9]

A special session of the United Nations recognized in 2016 that drug addiction is "a complex multifactorial health disorder character-ized by a chronic and relapsing nature" that is treatable and not the result of moral failure. Instead of prosecution, it recommended a pub-lic health approach, treating drug addiction like other chronic con-ditions such as cardiovascular disease and diabetes, with the highest priority given to interventions targeting children and youth.[10] There is a growing recognition that prevention and treatment are superior to prosecution, but there is still a very long way to go. As with mental health, comprehensive community programs that provide treatment before any contact with the criminal legal system would better utilize resources, make communities safer, and help many people live use-ful and productive lives. Unfortunately, in many places, treatment is nonexistent, of poor quality, or too expensive. Fewer than 20 percent of those who need treatment receive it.

We can also decrease the amount of harm caused by crimes. The harm inflicted during a crime is often increased because a firearm is involved. Overall crime rates in the U.S. are not significantly higher than in other high-income countries; the problem is that the crimes that do occur, even if they begin as simple arguments or incidents of road rage, are more likely to end up with someone being shot and killed or severely injured.[11] Over nineteen thousand victims of homicide—79 percent of the total—were killed by guns in 2020; hundreds of thousands more were traumatized because they were shot and wounded, lost a family member or friend to gun violence, or observed others being shot.[12] It is estimated that people purchased 22 million guns in 2020, a 64 percent increase over 2019. There were over six hundred mass shootings—those in which a minimum of four victims were shot—in 2020. That year, guns were also used in 24,000 suicides and at least 368 unintentional shootings by children that resulted in 141 deaths and 242 injuries. Gun violence is the lead-ing cause of death among children, teens, and young adults under the age of twenty-five.[13] Yet, despite all the carnage, some states have passed laws allowing people to carry handguns without a permit or training.[14]

Homicides involving guns have their greatest impact on poor communities and people of color. African Americans were more than twelve times more likely to be a victim of gun homicide than white people in 2020. Although young Black men between the ages of fifteen and thirty-four represent only 2 percent of the total population, they accounted for 38 percent of all gun homicide fatalities in 2020—a rate almost twenty-one times higher than white males of the same age group. Latinos were twice as likely to die by gun homicide as white people.[15]

The states with the highest gun death rates are primarily rural states in the South and West. The five states with the lowest rates of gun deaths have laws requiring licensing of purchasers or a waiting period for purchases with background checks, and laws allowing courts to remove guns temporarily from people who are at extreme risk of harming themselves or others.[16] Other ways to limit gun violence include education efforts regarding firearm safety and storage, policies that enhance economic stability and reduce poverty by increasing employment opportunities and wages, programs that identify people at highest risk for violence and teach them coping and problem-solving skills and provide them with mental health and social support, and laws removing firearms from those under domestic violence restraining orders. Even cleaning up overgrown vacant lots can result in a decrease in gun violence as well as other crimes, with the greatest impact in poor neighborhoods.[17]

When people are convicted of crimes, the entire social context in which they acted must be taken into account, as shown by Haney's work. This occurs at death penalty trials when mitigating circumstances are considered in deciding punishment, but almost all other sentencing decisions are based on the crime committed and the person's criminal record, without regard for the other factors that contribute to criminal behavior. Instead, sentencing decisions must be informed by a full understanding of what led a person to crime and what can be done to prevent violations of the law in the future. This means that defense lawyers must have the time and resources to investigate the life histories of their clients and propose sentences that respond to their particular needs. That cannot happen when people are processed through courts in "meet 'em and plead 'em" sessions, or when prosecutors offer plea bargains that must be accepted or rejected quickly while refusing to disclose any information about the case. Judges must have more flexibility to craft sentences that respond to the factors that contributed to commission of the crimes. That requires abandoning determinate sentencing and mandatory minimums.

Courts must also address the racial disparities that pervade the criminal legal system. They must overcome the fear of too much justice that the Supreme Court used as an excuse to avoid dealing with racial disparities in the infliction of the death penalty, and they must recognize and combat the implicit and explicit racism that produces higher conviction rates and harsher sentences for Blacks and other people of color.

There is a fear that embracing the principles of fairness—full disclosure of information, not relying on jailhouse snitches, competent counsel for the accused, grappling with issues of racial discrimination and unequal treatment—will risk the loss of convictions. But there is far more to be gained by having a system in which all of the participants are fully informed and decisions are made based on a thorough exploration of all of the facts of the crime and the circumstances of the person accused of committing it.

State legislatures and Congress must continue and expand recent efforts to moderate sentencing statutes. Georgia, under the leadership of Republican governor Nathan Deal, changed some nonviolent felonies to misdemeanors and provided for less severe penalties for people convicted of possessing small quantities of drugs. By reducing the sentences that could be imposed, these measures diverted thousands of people from prison, resulting in a decline of almost 19 percent in prison admissions in Georgia over a ten-year period. The number of African Americans being sent to prison dropped by 30 percent to the lowest level in more than three decades.[18] Similar reductions could be brought about in other states and the federal prisons by reclassifying some drug offenses that are now designated "violent" and reducing the sentences that can be imposed for drug and other offenses. These and similar laws contributed to a halt in the growth of the prison population around 2009 and its gradual decline since then. At the federal level, the First Step Act of 2018, passed with bipartisan support, reduced mandatory minimum prison sentences for some drug offenses and allowed courts to sentence low-level, nonviolent drug offenders with minor criminal histories to less than the required mandatory minimum for an offense. The act also expanded early-release programs and required job training and other efforts aimed at facilitating reentry into communities and reducing recidivism.[19]

As discussed earlier, predictions of a person's future dangerousness or prospects for rehabilitation are often inaccurate and contribute to excessive sentences. Realizing this, many jurisdictions have created avenues for people to be released from prison if they can demonstrate that they have overcome the problems that led them to crime. This is essentially what parole is supposed to do, but minimum sentencing requirements and parole boards reluctant to release prisoners have undermined that function. In Ohio, law professor David Singleton started the Beyond Guilt program, which has convinced judges to reduce the sentences of people who accept their guilt, have served a long time in prison, and have shown strong evidence of rehabilitation. This is possible because of a rule in Ohio that allows judges to reduce sentences when it is in the interests of justice.[20]

Other states and the District of Columbia have passed "second look" laws that provide avenues to resentencing for people in prison. In California, a bill passed in 2018 enables district attorneys to petition courts for resentencing. Los Angeles district attorney George Gascón created a unit in 2020 to reassess the sentences of all people who had served more than fifteen years in prison, and other district attorneys have identified people whose sentences should be revisited. The state of Washington passed a similar law in 2020. The same year, Washington, DC, passed a "second look" act that allows people to petition the court directly for resentencing if they have served fifteen years in prison for a crime committed before the age of twenty-five. The American Law Institute recommends that legislatures authorize judicial review of sentences after fifteen years of imprisonment for adult crimes, and after ten years for youth crimes. Other legislative initiatives have been aimed at elderly people who have been in prison for many years and are highly unlikely to commit violent crimes.[21]

The First Step Act of 2018 made certain federal sentencing laws retroactive so that people could seek reduction of long sentences for crack cocaine possession if they would have received shorter sentences for possession of the same amount of powder cocaine. These laws help to mitigate the harshness of sentencing policies and free some people for whom incarceration no longer serves any meaningful purpose. But many states have not adopted such laws, and some that have been adopted do not go far enough. The federal First Step Act, unlike the laws passed in some states and Washington, DC, does not address resentencing for violent crimes.

Restorative justice programs—in which the victims of crimes and community members ask the people who committed the crimes to take responsibility for their actions and make amends to those they have hurt—offer perhaps the most transformative possibilities. They provide an alternative to incarceration, even for people who commit violent crimes. Survivors of crimes often want the opportunity to confront the responsible party, to hold him accountable, to describe the suffering they experienced, and to participate in a process that will right the wrong as much as possible. Restorative justice responds to two failures of the typical response to violent crime: first, the reliance on prisons that not only do not rehabilitate, but contribute to recidivism by, among other things, severing ties to families and communities; and, second, the failure of the current system to address victims' real needs. Many victims understand that simply locking up the people who harmed them will do little to help them or anyone else. In one nationwide poll, 69 percent of crime victims thought that community-based programs were preferable to incarceration as a way to hold offenders accountable.[22]

In Brooklyn, New York, the organization Common Justice, founded by Danielle Sered, diverts people who committed violent crimes into restorative justice circles, with the consent of their victims. Responsible parties come to grips with the harm they caused, survivors get answers to questions that have been haunting them, and they together agree on what restitution the perpetrator can offer. They also develop a plan to reduce the chances that the responsible party will commit a similar crime in the future. If the responsible party successfully completes the plan, which can include a violence intervention program, he does not have to face incarceration.[23] Similar programs have been launched in cities around the United States.

There is accumulating evidence that they work. In New York City, 90 percent of crime survivors given the option choose restorative justice programs over the traditional prosecutorial system, and only 7 percent of responsible parties who have participated in Common Justice's restorative justice process have failed to complete the program because of a crime.[24] A 2017 analysis of sixty separate research projects found that, compared to traditional prosecution, restorative justice programs for children offenders resulted in significantly lower rates of criminal behavior and higher rates of victim satisfaction. In particular, victims were much more likely to feel like their views were considered and that the perpetrator was held accountable. Similarly, a 2013 analysis of ten different restorative justice studies found that face-to-face restorative justice meetings both reduce future arrests and convictions and increase victim satisfaction.[25]

Restorative justice approaches have even been used in a few murder cases. The defendant and the survivors of the victim confront the harm and loss and try to reach an understanding and arrive at a just sentence. In some cases, the process has helped victims' families come to terms with the loss they suffered.[26] Restorative justice may not be appropriate for all people who commit crimes or all people who survive those crimes. In many cases, however, it can do a better job of keeping communities safe than simply locking people up, without the immense harm caused by prison, while respecting and responding to the needs of victims.

America's responses to crime have been based on overconfidence in the value of punishment and a lack of confidence in the ability of people to overcome poverty, racism, trauma, and other life experiences that can lead to street crime. Too often, there has also been an absence of compassion for those with mental disorders, intellectual limitations, and other severe disabilities who are dumped into the criminal legal system because society has not taken responsibility for them in other ways. There has been little appreciation of the extent to which crime is related to the number of children who grow up without a decent education, economic opportunity, or hope for a better future, and of the harm that excessive sentences inflict on individuals, families, and communities. Because of the fear of too much justice, we have been willing to accept too little. As a result, the criminal legal system lacks credibility and legitimacy in the communities that it most deeply affects.

A just criminal legal system is one that considers people charged with crimes as "uniquely individual human beings" subject to "the diverse frailties of humankind," as demanded by Justice Potter Stewart in the 1976 Supreme Court ruling that rejected laws making the death penalty mandatory.[27] It takes into account the many factors that may make a person more likely to commit a crime—poverty, racism, neglect, abuse, witnessing violence, post-traumatic stress disorder, serious mental disorders, and so on—and the inability of prosecutors, judges, or juries to predict who that person will be in the future. A just system responds to a crime both with sanctions that fairly reflect the moral culpability of the person who committed it and with measures that help him become a positive contributor to his community. In an adversary system, justice demands that people accused of crimes be represented by skilled, zealous lawyers with the time, resources, and information necessary to fairly defend their clients, and that cases be heard by judges motivated solely by upholding the law and achieving a just outcome. And justice demands that both courts and governments actively work to redress the systemic racial discrimination that plagues the criminal legal system.

This kind of justice can be realized, as we have described throughout this book. Where it has not been, those responsible must embrace the principles of fairness and equality and overcome the fear that they require too much justice.

Acknowledgments

More people than we can remember have contributed to the ideas in this book. We first met in 2009 at Yale Law School, but the list of people who influenced the book begins much earlier.

Steve was given his first job as a lawyer and has been inspired throughout his life by John Rosenberg, a Holocaust survivor who, after working in the Civil Rights Division of the Justice Department, spent over fifty years working on behalf of poor people in Appalachia. Steve began working on capital cases because of Patsy Morris, a volunteer at the ACLU in Georgia who dedicated much of her life to recruiting lawyers from around the country to represent people under death sentence. In 1979, she asked Steve, George Kendall, and Russell Canan to represent Donald Wayne Thomas, who had been sentenced to death in Georgia. Why them? Because, Patsy told them, she would take anyone she could get. They agreed to take his case and ultimately obtained a decision setting aside his death sentence. They took more cases and, in the early 1980s, moved from Washington, DC, to Atlanta. Steve, Russell, and Robert Morin joined Christine Freeman at what became the Southern Center for Human Rights, where Steve became director. George joined Patsy at the ACLU, where he developed projects that provided representation in capital cases across the South. Steve has relied heavily on George in his litigation, teaching, and writing from the day they agreed to represent Donald Wayne Thomas.

At first, Steve and his colleagues at the Southern Center for Human

Rights responded to the need for lawyers in capital cases like medics on a battlefield: running from one case to another, obtaining last-minute stays of execution, challenging death sentences in the state and federal appellate courts—and, on occasion, in the United States Supreme Court—and representing their clients before juries at trials. A few of the scores of people who joined their efforts were Bryan Stevenson, who later established the Equal Justice Initiative in Alabama; Sarah Geraghty, who spent almost twenty years at the Southern Center litigating issues of prison conditions, debtor prisons, and other injustices before being appointed a United States District Judge by President Joe Biden; paralegals Mary and Lewis Sinclair, who assisted with every trial and hearing that Steve had over three decades; Clive Stafford Smith, who after ten years at the Southern Center established the Louisiana Capital Assistance Center and then went on to international human rights organizations; Ruth Friedman, who challenged death sentences in Alabama and Georgia before going on to lead efforts against federal executions; Robert McGlasson, who helped establish an organization representing death-sentenced people in Texas when that state was carrying out executions at a pace never equaled by any other state; Sara Totonchi, who provided outstanding leadership as public policy director and later executive director of the Center; attorneys Palmer Singleton and Patrick Mulvaney, who co-counseled cases with Steve in the U.S. Supreme Court; Mary Sidney Kelly Harbert, whose examination of legal representation for the poor contributed to establishment of a public defender system in Georgia; Terrica Redfield Ganzy, who joined the Center as an attorney and became its executive director; office manager Julia Robinson Hicks and administrative assistant Patricia Hale, whose years of dedication and hard work facilitated the work of Steve and the Southern Center; Crystal Redd, Sarah Forte, and Tamara Theiss, incomparable investigators; and Atteeyah Hollie, who joined the Southern Center as an intern from Dartmouth, returned first as an investigator and then as a lawyer, and now serves as its deputy director. Charles Ogletree, Steve's colleague at the Public Defender Service in Washington, DC, and later a professor at Harvard Law School, served as chair of the board of directors of the Southern Center for many years, cocounseled cases with the Center's attorneys, and supported its work in every way. There are far too many others to name here.

James joined the board of directors of the Southern Center at the invitation of Maureen Del Duca and Sara Totonchi. While on the board, he has been constantly inspired by the dedication and excellence of the Center's staff members and the leadership of its executive directors, first Sara Totonchi and now Terrica Ganzy. There is no better education in the importance of justice.

Steve was asked to teach at Yale Law School in the spring of 1993. The law school invited him back every year for the next thirty years. During much of that time, he supervised a capital punishment clinic with Miriam Gohara, Ann Parrent, Sia M. Sanneh, Anna VanCleave, and the exceptional lawyers with the capital unit of the Connecticut public defender office. They grappled with the issues addressed in this book, as did the students in the classes he taught at Yale and other law schools. He also benefited enormously from his interactions with members of the faculties at the law schools. He addressed some of the issues discussed in this book in collaboration with co-authors of articles, including Patrick J. Keenan, Sia M. Sanneh, and Katherine Chamblee-Ryan. Steve is particularly grateful to Robert Lawson at the University of Kentucky for his inspiring teaching and example as a public interest lawyer.

James was a student in Steve's class on capital punishment and in the capital punishment clinic. While in law school, he also worked with John Donohue on an empirical study of the arbitrary and discriminatory application of the death penalty in Connecticut. James worked on this book while a professor at the University of Connecticut School of Law, where he benefited greatly from conversations with students and fellow faculty members—particularly Peter Siegelman, with whom he shared many car rides to and from campus.

Many of our students served as research assistants. Those whose research and fact-checking contributed to this book include Ryanne Bamieh, Asli Bashir, Darcy Covert, Lauren Graham, Kim Kawaratani, Jaewon Kim, Amber Koonce, Kate Mollison, Nathan Robinson, Katherine Oberembt, Isadora Ruyter-Harcourt, Joanna Schwartz, and Akanksha Shah.

Our editor, Diane Wachtell, shepherded this project from idea to its final form. Many other people helped produce this book, including Emily Albarillo, Brian Baughan, Andrés Orrego, and Rachel Vega-DeCesario.

There are many others who aided and inspired Steve's work—far too many to mention. Among them are Betsy Biben, Dorothy Ehrlich, Barry Fisher, Jerry Fisher, Bernard Harcourt, Mary Kennedy, Ellen Kreitzberg, Susan Ten Kwan, Gary Parker, Mia Ruyter, Elisabeth Semel, and Gary Sowards. Steve is grateful for having had an ideal childhood growing up on a small family farm in Kentucky, and for his family, particularly his parents, who recognized that segregation was wrong and worked to end it when most people in their community accepted it or remained silent. And he is thankful for Charlotta Norby for her love, encouragement, and inspiration.

James's parents raised him to care about injustice and gave him the education to do something about it. As always, he thanks his wife, Sylvia Brandt, for her love and support, and his children, Willow and Henry, for the joy and wonder they provide every day.

Notes

1. The Myth of the Adversary System

1. Edward Johnes, "The Pardoning Power from a Philosophical Standpoint," *Albany Law Journal* (May 20, 1893): 385–86, 385.

2. Jennifer Hill, "The History and Enduring Legacy of Bloody Caddo," *Bayou Brief*, Dec. 13, 2017.

3. On Glenn Ford, see Andrew Cohen, "Freedom After 30 Years on Death Row," *Atlantic*, Mar. 11, 2014; Andrew Cohen, "The Meaning of the Exoneration of Glenn Ford," Brennan Center for Justice, Mar. 13, 2014; Andrew Cohen, "Glenn Ford's First Days of Freedom After 30 Years on Death Row," *Atlantic*, Mar. 14, 2014; Alexandria Burris, "Glenn Ford, Exonerated Death Row Inmate, Dies," *USA Today*, June 29, 2015.

4. A.M. "Marty" Stroud III, "Lead Prosecutor Apologizes for Role in Sending a Man to Death Row," *Shreveport Times*, Mar. 20, 2015.

5. Kenneth J. Rose, "I Just Freed an Innocent Man from Death Row. And I'm Still Furious," *Washington Post*, Sept. 4, 2014.

6. "Kennedy Brewer: Time Served: 15 Years," Innocence Project; Maurice Possley, "Eddie Lee Howard, Jr.," National Registry of Exonerations, Feb. 25, 2021; Marco Poggio, "Fish & Richardson Helps Free Mississippi Man on Death Row," *Law 360*, Sept. 26, 2021; Radley Balko and Tucker Carrington, *The Cadaver King and the Country Dentist: A True Story of Injustice in the American South* (New York: PublicAffairs, 2018).

7. Browning v. Baker, 875 F.3d 444, 450 (9th Cir. 2017).

8. *DPIC Special Report: The Innocence Epidemic*, Death Penalty Information Center (Feb. 18, 2021).

9. United States v. Garsson, 291 F. 646, 649 (S.D.N.Y. 1923).

10. *25,000 Years Lost to Wrongful Convictions*, National Registry of Exonerations (June 14, 2021).

11. "Death Row Information: County of Conviction for Executed Offenders,"

Texas Department of Criminal Justice, updated Apr. 22, 2022, https://www .tdcj.texas.gov/death_row/dr_county_conviction_executed.html; *Facts About the Death Penalty*, Death Penalty Information Center (Oct. 22, 2022); "Death Row Information: County of Conviction for Offenders on Death Row," Texas Department of Criminal Justice, updated Apr. 22, 2022, https://www.tdcj. texas.gov/death_row/dr_county_conviction_offenders.html.

12. Allan Turner, "Former DA Ran Powerful Death-Penalty Machine," *Houston Chronicle*, July 25, 2007; John Holmes Jr., "Dealing Out Death," *Texas Monthly*, July 2002.

13. Keri Blakinger, "Controversial Death Penalty Lawyer Ron Mock Dead at 72," *Houston Chronicle*, Jan. 9, 2019; Sara Rimer and Raymond Bonner, "Texas Lawyer's Death Row Record a Concern," *New York Times*, June 11, 2000.

14. Paul M. Barrett, "Lawyer's Fast Work on Death Cases Raises Doubts About System," *Wall Street Journal*, Sept. 7, 1994; Burdine v. Johnson, 262 F.3d 336 (5th Cir. 2001) (en banc).

15. Lise Olsen, "Slow Paperwork in Death Row Cases Ends Final Appeals for 9," *Houston Chronicle*, Mar. 21, 2009.

16. Scott Phillips, "Racial Disparities in the Capital of Capital Punishment," *Houston Law Review* 45, no. 3 (Summer 2008): 807–40, 812.

17. See James S. Liebman and Peter Clarke, "Minority Practice, Majority's Burden: The Death Penalty Today," *Ohio State Journal of Criminal Law* 9, no. 1 (Fall 2011): 255–351; Richard C. Dieter, *The 2% Death Penalty: How a Minority of Counties Produce Most Death Cases at Enormous Costs to All*, Death Penalty Information Center (Oct. 2013).

18. *Gideon's Broken Promise: America's Continuing Quest for Equal Justice*, ABA Standing Committee on Legal Aid and Indigent Defendants (Dec. 2004), iv; *Defend Children: A Blueprint for Effective Juvenile Defender Services*, National Juvenile Defender Center (Nov. 2016), 10.

19. Eli Hager, "Louisiana Public Defenders: A Lawyer with a Pulse Will Do," *Guardian*, Sept. 8, 2016.

20. Jeffrey L. Kirchmeier, "Drink, Drugs, and Drowsiness: The Constitutional Right to Effective Assistance of Counsel and the *Strickland* Prejudice Requirement," *Nebraska Law Review* 75, no. 3 (1996): 425–75, 455–60.

21. Richard A. Oppel Jr. and Jugal K. Patel, "One Lawyer, 194 Felony Cases, and No Time," *New York Times*, Jan. 31, 2019; Radley Balko, "How Two Overworked Public Defenders and Six Judges Left a New Orleans Man with a Life Sentence," *Washington Post*, Aug. 28, 2019; *Justice Denied: America's Continuing Neglect of Our Constitutional Right to Counsel*, National Right to

Counsel Committee (Apr. 2009), 85–87; Robert C. Boruchowitz, Malia N. Brink, and Maureen Dimino, *Minor Crimes, Massive Waste: The Terrible Toll of America's Broken Misdemeanor Courts*, National Association of Criminal Defense Lawyers (Apr. 2009), 18–19.

22. Missouri v. Frye, 566 U.S. 134, 143 (2012).

23. Eli Hager, "For Louisiana's Defenseless Poor, It's One for All," *Guardian*, Sept. 9, 2016.

24. Trisha Renaud and Ann Woolner, "Meet Em and Plead Em: Slaughterhouse Justice in Fulton's Decaying Indigent Defense System," *Fulton County Daily Report*, Oct. 8, 1990, 1.

25. Petition for Writ of Habeas Corpus, McGee v. Companaro, No. 2018-RCHM-1 (S.D. Ga. filed Jan. 22, 2010).

26. Stephen B. Bright, "Discrimination, Death and Denial: The Tolerance of Racial Discrimination in the Infliction of the Death Penalty," *Santa Clara Law Review* 35, no. 2 (1995): 433–83, 447 n.87.

27. Daniel S. Harawa, "The False Promise of *Peña-Rodriguez*," *California Law Review* 109, no. 6 (Dec. 2021): 2121–72, 2143–51; Tharpe v. Warden, 898 F.3d 1342, 1345–46 (11th Cir. 2018), *cert. denied*, 139 S. Ct. 911 (2019), ibid. at 913 (Statement of Sotomayor, J., regarding the denial of certiorari) (decrying "truly striking evidence of juror bias" and "an appalling risk that racial bias swayed Tharpe's sentencing"); United States v. Robinson, 872 F.3d 760, 770–71 (6th Cir. 2017).

28. Batson v. Kentucky, 476 U.S. 79 (1986).

29. State v. Saintcalle, 309 P.3d 326, 329 (Wash. 2013); Thomas Ward Frampton, "The Jim Crow Jury," *Vanderbilt Law Review* 71, no. 5 (Oct. 2018): 1593–654, 1624–26; Steve Bogira, *Courtroom 302: A Year Behind the Scenes in an American Criminal Court House* (2005), 260–62; Jeffrey Bellin and Junichi P. Semitsu, "Widening *Batson*'s Net to Ensnare More Than the Unapologetically Bigoted or Painfully Unimaginative Attorney," *Cornell Law Review* 96, no. 5 (July 2011): 1075–130, 1079.

30. McCleskey v. Kemp, 481 U.S. 279, 286–87 (1987); David C. Baldus, George Woodworth, and Charles A. Pulaski Jr., *Equal Justice and the Death Penalty: A Legal and Empirical Analysis* (Boston: Northeastern University Press, 1990).

31. McCleskey v. Kemp, 481 U.S. at 312, 315, 315 n.38, 317.

32. Ibid., 339 (Brennan, J., dissenting).

33. Furman v. Georgia, 408 U.S. 238, 447 (1972) (Powell, J., dissenting).

34. Ristaino v. Ross, 424 U.S. 589, 590 n.1, 596 n.8 (1976).

35. Aldridge v. United States, 283 U.S. 308, 314–15 (1931).

36. Ristaino v. Ross, 424 U.S. at 598 n.10.

37. Rosales-Lopez v. United States, 451 U.S. 182 (1981).

38. Griffin v. Illinois, 351 U.S. 12, 19 (1956).

39. Gideon v. Wainwright, 372 U.S. 335 (1963); Douglas v. California, 372 U.S. 353 (1963).

40. Strickland v. Washington, 466 U.S. 668, 689–90, 694–95 (1984).

41. Riles v. McCotter, 799 F.2d 947, 955 (5th Cir. 1986) (Rubin, J., concurring) (emphasis in original).

2. The All-Powerful Prosecutor

1. Robert H. Jackson, "The Federal Prosecutor," *Journal of the American Judicature Society* 24, no. 1 (June 1940): 18–20, 18.

2. Jed S. Rakoff, *Why the Innocent Plead Guilty and the Guilty Go Free: And Other Paradoxes of Our Broken Legal System* (2021), 25.

3. Bordenkircher v. Hayes, 434 U.S. 357, 358 n.1 (1978); ibid., 370 (Powell, J., dissenting).

4. Ibid., 359 n.2.

5. Ibid., 367 (Blackmun, J., dissenting).

6. Gissendaner v. Seaboldt, 735 F.3d 1311 (11th Cir. 2013); Gissendaner v. State, 532 S.E.2d 677 (Ga. 2000); Gissendaner v. State, 500 S.E.2d 577 (Ga. 1998); Holly Yan, Catherine E. Shoichet, and Moni Basu, "Georgia Inmate Kelly Gissendaner Executed After Failed Appeals," CNN, Sept. 30, 2015.

7. Isabel Hughes, "Court Reaches Required Number of Qualified Jurors in Tiffany Moss Death Penalty Case," *Gwinnett Daily Post*, Apr. 22, 2019; Bill Rankin, "Jury at Impasse over Death Sentence for Gwinnett Woman in Starving Death," *Atlanta Journal-Constitution*, Apr. 29, 2019.

8. *Tipping the Scales: Challengers Take on the Old Boys' Club of Elected Prosecutors*, Reflective Democracy Campaign (Oct. 2019), 2, 6.

9. Penson v. Ohio, 488 U.S. 75, 84 (1988) (quoting Irving R. Kaufman, "Does the Judge Have a Right to Qualified Counsel?," *American Bar Association Journal* 61, no. 5 (May 1975): 569–73, 569) (internal quotation marks omitted).

10. Missouri v. Frye, 566 U.S. 134, 143 (2012) (quoting Lafler v. Cooper, 566 U.S. 156, 170 (2012)).

11. Missouri v. Frye, 566 U.S. at 144 (quoting Robert E. Scott and William J. Stuntz, "Plea Bargaining as Contract," *Yale Law Journal* 101, no. 8 (June 1992): 1909–68, 1912 (emphasis in original)).

12. United States v. Cronic, 466 U.S. 648, 663, 665 (1984).

13. United States v. Cronic, 900 F.2d 1511 (10th Cir. 1990).

14. John F. Pfaff, *Locked In: The True Causes of Mass Incarceration and How to Achieve Real Reform* (New York: Basic Books, 2017), 6.

15. *The Federal Death Penalty System: Supplementary Data, Analysis and Revised Protocols for Capital Case Review*, U.S. Department of Justice (2001), part I.B.

16. *Facts About the Death Penalty*, Death Penalty Information Center (May 20, 2021).

17. James S. Liebman and Peter Clarke, "Minority Practice, Majority's Burden: The Death Penalty Today," *Ohio State Journal of Criminal Law* 9, no. 1 (Fall 2011): 255–351, 265–66.

18. "Pledging No Death Penalty, Larry Krasner Sworn In as Philadelphia's District Attorney," Death Penalty Information Center, Jan. 4, 2018; "DPIC Analysis: The Decline of the Death Penalty in Philadelphia," Death Penalty Information Center, Nov. 16, 2018.

19. Lockyer v. Andrade, 538 U.S. 63 (2003); Ewing v. California, 538 U.S. 11 (2003).

20. Andrew Chongseh Kim, "Underestimating the Trial Penalty: An Empirical Analysis of the Federal Trial Penalty and Critique of the Abrams Study," *Mississippi Law Journal* 84, no. 5 (2015): 1195–256, 1247; 18 U.S.C. § 3553(e); 28 U.S.C. § 994(n); *Guidelines Manual*, U.S. Sentencing Commission (Nov. 2021) § 5K1.1.

21. Rakoff, *Why the Innocent Plead Guilty*, 23.

22. United States v. Ruiz, 536 U.S. 622, 625 (2002).

23. Missouri v. Frye, 566 U.S. at 144 (quoting Rachel E. Barkow, "Separation of Powers and the Criminal Law," *Stanford Law Review* 58, no. 4 (Feb. 2006): 989–1054, 1034).

24. Rakoff, *Why the Innocent Plead Guilty*, 25.

25. Ibid.

26. Kim, "Underestimating the Trial Penalty," 1202.

27. Rakoff, *Why the Innocent Plead Guilty*, 26.

28. Gerard E. Lynch, "Our Administrative System of Criminal Justice," *Fordham Law Review* 66, no. 6 (May 1998): 2117–51, 2135.

29. North Carolina v. Alford, 400 U.S. 25 (1970).

30. *Innocents Who Plead Guilty*, National Registry of Exonerations (2015), 1.

31. Marc Bookman, *A Descending Spiral: Exposing the Death Penalty in 12 Essays* (New York: The New Press, 2021), 113–33.

32. Maurice Possley, "Johnny Lee Wilson," National Registry of Exonerations, updated Aug. 22, 2014.

33. Lafler v. Cooper, 566 U.S. at 186 (Scalia, J., dissenting).

34. United States v. Cervantes-Pacheco, 826 F.2d 310, 315 (5th Cir. 1987).

35. Russell D. Covey, "Abolishing Jailhouse Snitch Testimony," *Wake Forest Law Review* 49, no. 5 (2014): 1375–429, 1375.

36. Alexandra Natapoff, *Snitching: Criminal Informants and the Erosion of American Justice* (New York: New York University Press, 2009), 28; Stephen S. Trott, "Words of Warning for Prosecutors Using Criminals as Witnesses," *Hastings Law Journal* 47, nos. 5–6 (July–Aug. 1996): 1381–432, 1393; United States v. Boyd, 55 F.3d 239, 244 (7th Cir. 1995) (describing drugs and sex); United States v. Burnside, 824 F. Supp. 1215, 1225–45 (N.D. Ill. 1993) (drugs).

37. See State v. Leniart, 215 A.3d 1104, 1149 (Conn. 2019) (Palmer, J., concurring and dissenting); Marquez v. Commissioner, 198 A.3d 562 (Conn. 2019); *Report of the 1989–90 Los Angeles County Grand Jury: Investigation of the Involvement of Jail House Informants in the Criminal Justice System in Los Angeles County*, 74–84 (hereafter *Los Angeles Grand Jury Report*).

38. Alene Tchekmedyian, "A Jailhouse Informant's Lies Put Him in Prison for 37 Years. Now He's Free," *Los Angeles Times*, Aug. 23, 2019; see also Maurice Possley, "Samuel Bonner," National Registry of Exonerations, updated June 19, 2020.

39. Natapoff, *Snitching*; 71–72; State v. Leniart, 215 A.3d at 1136.

40. Natapoff, *Snitching*, 71; Robert Reinhold, "California Shaken over an Informer," *New York Times*, Feb. 17, 1989; Robert W. Stewart, "Jailhouse Snitches: Trading Lies for Freedom," *Los Angeles Times*, Apr. 16, 1989.

41. *Los Angeles Grand Jury Report*, 18.

42. Ibid., 4, 9.

43. Ibid., 16, 17, 76–84, 87–90, 102–5, 108, 110–11.

44. People v. Dekraai, 5 Cal. App. 5th 1110, 1137 (Cal. Ct. App. 2016); Jordan Smith, "Anatomy of a Snitch Scandal: How Orange County Prosecutors Covered Up Rampant Misuse of Jailhouse Informants," *The Intercept*, May 14, 2016; Jordan Smith, "New Evidence Deputies Committed Perjury in Orange County Snitch Scandal," *The Intercept*, Dec. 8, 2016.

45. Pamela Colloff, "How This Con Man's Wild Testimony Sent Dozens to Jail, and 4 to Death Row," *New York Times Magazine*, Dec. 4, 2019.

46. Colloff, "How This Con Man's Wild Testimony Sent Dozens to Jail."

47. Dailey v. State, 965 So.2d 38, 45 (Fla. 2007).

48. Colloff, "How This Con Man's Wild Testimony Sent Dozens to Jail."

49. "The Life and Crimes of Odell Hallmon: 'They Created a Monster,'" *In the Dark*, season 2, episode 5, American Public Media, May 22, 2018 (including a timeline with links to records and transcripts of testimony).

50. Ibid.

51. Ibid.

52. Ibid.

53. "Punishment," *In the Dark*, season 2, episode 6, American Public Media, May 29, 2018 (audio at 10:00 to 15:15).

54. Flowers v. Mississippi, 139 S. Ct. 2228 (2019).

55. Parker Yesko, "Mississippi to Pay Curtis Flowers $500,000 for His Decades Behind Bars," *In the Dark*, American Public Media, Mar. 2, 2021.

56. "The Life and Crimes of Odell Hallmon," American Public Media

57. John Grisham, *The Innocent Man: Murder and Injustice in a Small Town* (New York: Doubleday, 2006); *Final Report*, California Commission on the Fair Administration of Justice (2008), 45–46.

58. Samuel Gross and Kaitlin Jackson, "Snitch Watch," National Registry of Exonerations, May 13, 2015 (showing 102 murder cases and 26 capital cases as of May 13, 2015; the site shows additional cases since 2015 on its "Detailed View" page under the tag for "jailhouse informant," https://www.law.umich.edu/special/exoneration/Pages/detaillist.aspx?View={FAF6EDDB-5A68-4F8F-8A52-2C61F5BF9EA7}&FilterField1=Group&FilterValue1=JI).

59. Robert M. Bloom, "What Jurors Should Know About Informants: The Need for Expert Testimony," *Michigan State Law Review* no. 2 (2019): 345–73, 365–71; State v. Leniart, 215 A.3d at 1139–43.

60. Dodd v. State, 993 P.2d 778, 782–83 (Okla. Crim. App. 2000).

61. Ibid., 782–84.

62. Radley Balko, "Breaking News in the Ryan Frederick Trial," *Reason*, Jan. 29, 2009.

63. *Final Report*, California Commission on the Fair Administration of Justice, 46.

64. Dave Collins, "Lying Prisoners: New Laws Crack Down on Jailhouse Informants," Associated Press, Sept. 14, 2019; Brandi Grissom, "Snitch Testimony Sent Innocent Man to Prison for 18 Years. Texas Lawmakers Hope He's the Last," *Dallas Morning News*, Sept. 20, 2017.

65. Bloom, "What Jurors Should Know About Informants," 363–64.

66. *Final Report*, California Commission on the Fair Administration of Justice, 46.

67. Ibid.

68. Conn. Gen. Stat. §§ 54-86o, 54-86p; Collins, "Lying Prisoners"; State v. Leniart, 215 A.3d at 1150–51 (Palmer, J., concurring and dissenting); Natapoff, *Snitching*, 194–95.

69. Trott, "Words of Warning," 1394.

70. Bennett L. Gershman, "The New Prosecutors," *University of Pittsburgh Law Review* 53, no. 2 (Winter 1992): 393–458, 449.

71. See, e.g., Federal Rule of Criminal Procedure 16. Many states have similar rules. In federal capital cases, the prosecution must provide the defense with a witness list at least three days before trial. 18 U.S.C. § 3432.

72. H. Lee Sarokin and William E. Zuckerman, "Presumed Innocent? Restrictions on Criminal Discovery in Federal Court Belie This Presumption," *Rutgers Law Review* 43, no. 4 (Winter 1991): 1089–111, 1089.

73. Richard A. Rosen, "Reflections on Innocence," *Wisconsin Law Review*, no. 2 (2006): 237–90, 271–72.

74. Brady v. Maryland, 373 U.S. 83 (1963).

75. Miller v. Pate, 386 U.S. 1, 6 (1967).

76. United States v. Bagley, 473 U.S. 667, 670–71 (1985).

77. Ibid., 682.

78. Ibid., 693–707 (Marshall, J., dissenting).

79. Bennett L. Gershman, "Reflections on *Brady v. Maryland*," *South Texas Law Review* 47, no. 4 (Summer 2006): 685–728, 689, 715.

80. Ibid., 688, 691, 722. See also Rosen, "Reflections on Innocence," 272; Bruce Green and Ellen Yaroshefsky, "Prosecutorial Accountability 2.0," *Notre Dame Law Review* 92, no. 1 (Nov. 2016): 51–116, 65.

81. McDowell v. Dixon, 858 F.2d 945 (4th Cir. 1988).

82. N.C. Gen. Stat. § 15A-1415(f).

83. Robert P. Mosteller, "Exculpatory Evidence, Ethics, and the Road to the Disbarment of Mike Nifong: The Critical Importance of Full Open-File Discovery," *George Mason Law Review* 15, no. 2 (Winter 2008): 257–318, 263–65.

84. Ibid., 309–10.

85. N.C. Gen. Stat. § 15A-903(a).

86. John Rubin, "2004 Legislation Affecting Criminal Law and Proce-

dure," *Administration of Justice Bulletin*, no. 2004/06, School of Government, University of North Carolina at Chapel Hill (Oct. 2004), 7–8.

87. Pamela Colloff, "The Innocent Man, Part One," *Texas Monthly*, Nov. 2012; Pamela Colloff, "The Innocent Man, Part Two," *Texas Monthly*, Dec. 2012; "Michael Morton," Innocence Project.

88. Pamela Colloff, "Mark Alan Norwood Found Guilty of Christine Morton's Murder," *Texas Monthly*, Mar. 27, 2013; "Michael Morton," Innocence Project.

89. Brandi Grissom, "Perry Signs Michael Morton Act," *Texas Tribune*, May 16, 2013.

90. Samuel R. Gross et al., *Government Misconduct and Convicting the Innocent: The Role of Prosecutors, Police and Other Law Enforcement*, National Registry of Exonerations (Sept. 1, 2020), 75.

91. Milton C. Lee Jr., "Criminal Discovery: What Truth Do We Seek?," *District of Columbia Law Review* 4, no. 1 (Spring 1998): 7–29, 22–23; *Standards for Criminal Justice: Discovery and Procedure Before Trial*, American Bar Association (ABA) (1st ed. 1970); *Standards for Criminal Justice: Discovery*, ABA (2d ed. 1980), Standard 11-2.1; *Standards for Criminal Justice: Discovery*, ABA (3d ed. 1996), Standard 11-2.1; *Standards for Criminal Justice: Discovery*, ABA (4d ed. 2020), Standard 11-2.1.

92. Florida Rule of Criminal Procedure 3.220(b); *In re* Amendment to Florida Rule of Criminal Procedure 3.220 (Discovery), 550 So.2d 1097 (Fla. 1989).

93. *In re* Amendment to Florida Rule of Criminal Procedure 3.220 (Discovery), 550 So.2d at 1098.

94. N.J. Court Rule 3:13-3(b)(1)(F).

95. Wayne R. LaFave et al., *Criminal Procedure* § 20.2(b) & nn.35 & 36 (4th ed.) (Nov. 2021 update); N.Y. Crim. Proc. Law § 245.20.

96. LaFave et al., *Criminal Procedure*, § 20.2(b) & n.33.

97. Ibid., § 20.2(e) & n.105.

98. "DNA Exonerations in the United States," Innocence Project.

99. Arizona v. Youngblood, 488 U.S. 51 (1988); Marc Bookman, "Does an Innocent Man Have the Right to Be Exonerated?," *Atlantic*, Dec. 6, 2014.

100. "How Eyewitness Misidentification Can Send Innocent People to Prison," Innocence Project, Apr. 15, 2020.

101. State v. Youngblood, 734 P.2d 592 (Ariz. Ct. App. 1986); Bookman, "Does an Innocent Man Have the Right to Be Exonerated?"

102. Arizona v. Youngblood, 488 U.S. at 57–58.

103. Ibid., 61–67 (Blackmun, J., dissenting).

104. Bookman, "Does an Innocent Man Have the Right to Be Exonerated?"

105. Barbara Whitaker, "DNA Frees Inmate Years After Justices Rejected Plea," *New York Times*, Aug. 11, 2000.

106. District Attorney's Office for the Third Judicial District v. Osborne, 557 U.S. 52 (2009).

107. Ibid., 74.

108. Cynthia E. Jones, "Evidence Destroyed, Innocence Lost: The Preservation of Biological Evidence Under Innocence Protection Statutes," *American Criminal Law Review* 42, no. 4 (Fall 2005): 1239–70, 1239–40.

109. Bookman, "Does an Innocent Man Have the Right to Be Exonerated?"

110. Jones, "Evidence Destroyed, Innocence Lost," 1241.

111. Turner v. United States, 137 S. Ct. 1885, 1897 (2017) (Kagan, J., dissenting).

112. Catlett v. United States, 2012 WL 3635827 (D.C. Super. Ct. 2012).

113. Turner v. United States, 137 S. Ct. at 1897 (Kagan, J., dissenting).

114. Ibid., 1898–99 (Kagan, J., dissenting).

115. Ibid., 1893 (internal quotations omitted).

116. Donnelly v. DeChristoforo, 416 U.S. 637, 645 (1974).

117. Darden v. Wainwright, 477 U.S. 168, 179 (1986).

118. Ibid., 198 (Blackmun, J., dissenting).

119. Ibid., 190–92 (Blackmun, J., dissenting) (citing *Model Rules of Professional Conduct* Rule 3.4(e) (1984) and *Standards for Criminal Justice: Discovery*, ABA (2d ed. 1980), Standards 3–5.8(b) and (c), 3–6.1(c)).

120. Darden v. Wainwright, 477 U.S. at 191 (Blackmun, J., dissenting).

121. Ibid., 180 n.12.

122. Ibid., 191 (Blackmun, J., dissenting).

123. Ibid., 180, 182.

124. Ibid., 189, 200 (Blackmun, J., dissenting).

125. Ibid., 205–6 (Blackmun, J., dissenting).

126. United States v. Antonelli Fireworks Co., 155 F.2d 631, 661 (2d Cir. 1946) (Frank, J., dissenting).

127. Kathleen M. Ridolfi and Maurice Possley, *Preventable Error: A Report*

on Prosecutorial Misconduct in California 1997–2009, Veritas Initiative (Oct. 2010), 3.

128. Gross et al., *Government Misconduct and Convicting the Innocent,* 120.

129. State v. Arias, 462 P.3d 1051, 1069 (Ariz. Ct. App. 2020).

130. Ibid., 1061–69.

131. Ibid., 1072 (Jones, J., concurring).

132. Ibid., 1065–66, 1069.

133. Ibid., 1070.

134. State v. Hulsey, 408 P.3d 408, 435 (Ariz. 2018); State v. Arias, 462 P.3d at 1070 (quoting State v. Hulsey, 408 P.3d at 435).

135. State v. Arias, 462 P.3d at 1071.

136. *In re* Martinez, 462 P.3d 36, 49 (Ariz. 2020).

137. Jim Small, "State Bar: Top MariCo Prosecutor Leaked Secret Information, Lied, Sexually Harassed Underlings," *AZ Mirror,* Mar. 5, 2019; Lauren Castle, Robert Anglen, and Anne Ryman, "Juan Martinez's Appeal of His Firing Denied by Maricopa County Panel," *Arizona Republic,* Oct. 6, 2020; Lauren Castle, "Former Maricopa County Prosecutor Juan Martinez Disbarred," *Arizona Republic,* July 17, 2020.

138. State v. Monday, 257 P.3d 551, 555, 557 (Wash. 2011).

139. State v. Walker, 341 P.3d 976 (Wash. 2015).

140. Nick Tabor, "What If Prosecutors Wanted to Keep People *Out* of Prison?," *New York Intelligencer,* Mar. 27, 2018.

141. Matt Daniels, "The Kim Foxx Effect: How Prosecutions Have Changed in Cook County," The Marshall Project, Oct. 24, 2019.

142. Megan Crepeau, "Man in Prison for 29 Years Freed After Cook County Prosecutors Drop Charges," *Chicago Tribune,* Nov. 15, 2017.

143. Richard A. Oppel Jr., "The St. Louis Prosecutor Went After the Establishment. Now the Tables Are Turned," *New York Times,* June 14, 2019; Tony Messenger, "Legal Scholars to Missouri Court of Appeals: Give Lamar Johnson His Day in Court," *St. Louis Post-Dispatch,* Oct. 29, 2019.

144. State v. Johnson, 617 S.W.3d 439 (Mo. 2021).

145. Frances Robles and Alan Blinder, "Florida Prosecutor Takes a Bold Stand Against Death Penalty," *New York Times,* Mar. 16, 2017.

146. Ayala v. Scott, 224 So.3d 755 (Fla. 2017).

147. Julie Shaw, "DA Krasner Wants Pa. Supreme Court to Strike Down State's Death Penalty and Declare It Unconstitutional," *Philadelphia Inquirer,* July 16, 2019; Julie Shaw, "DA Larry Krasner Gives Up Fight in More

Death-Row Appeals, Stirring Concern from Courts, Families," *Philadelphia Inquirer*, May 23, 2019; Joshua Vaughn, "The Successes and Shortcomings of Larry Krasner's Trailblazing First Term," *Appeal*, Mar. 22, 2021.

148. Samantha Melamed, "The Battle in Philly DA's Office: Conviction Integrity Unit Report Shows Rocky Path to Reform," *Philadelphia Inquirer*, June 15, 2021.

149. Moore v. Texas, 139 S. Ct. 666, 670 (2019); Mike Tolson, "A New Era of the Death Penalty in Houston," *Houston Chronicle*, Dec. 20, 2017; Ciara Rouege, "DA Kim Ogg: Texas' Longest-Serving Death Row Inmate Should Get a New Punishment Hearing," KHOU-11, Feb. 2, 2021.

150. Special Directive 20-11, Los Angeles County District Attorney, Dec. 7, 2020, https://www.georgegascon.org//wp-content/uploads/2020/12/SPECIAL-DIRECTIVE-20-11-.docx.pdf.

151. Matt Reynolds, "LA District Attorney's Past Drives His Push Forward for Reform," *American Bar Association Journal*, July 28, 2021; "George Gascón Takes Oath of Office and Institutes Sweeping Reforms to Transform the Largest Criminal Justice Jurisdiction in America," George Gascón, Los Angeles District Attorney (press release), Dec. 8, 2020.

152. "Attorney General William P. Barr Delivers Remarks at the Grand Lodge Fraternal Order of Police's 64th National Biennial Conference," U.S. Department of Justice, Aug. 12, 2019.

153. Parisa Dehghani-Tafti, Mark Gonzalez, and Wesley Bell, "Reform Prosecutors Are Committed to Making Society Fairer—and Safer," *Washington Post*, Aug. 16, 2019.

3. A Poor Person's Justice

1. U.S. 12, 19 (1956).

2. U.S. 648, 654 (1984), quoting Walter V. Schaefer, "Federalism and State Criminal Procedure," *Harvard Law Review* 70 (1956): 1–26, 8.

3. On James T. Fisher Jr., see Fisher v. State, 736 P.2d 1003 (Okla. Crim. App. 1987), *affirmed on rehearing*, 739 P.2d 523 (Okla. Crim. App. 1987) (direct appeal); Fisher v. State, 845 P.2d 1272 (Okla. Crim. App. 1992) (post-conviction review of first trial); Fisher v. Gibson, 282 F.3d 1283 (10th Cir. 2002); Fisher v. State, 206 P.3d 607 (Okla. Crim. App. 2009) (direct appeal of second trial); Scott Cooper, "How Many Lawyers Does It Take to Get a Fair Trial?," *Oklahoma Gazette*, June 19, 2008; Dan Barry, "In the Rearview Mirror, Oklahoma and Death Row," *New York Times*, Aug. 10, 2010.

4. Fisher v. Gibson, 282 F.3d at 1303 n.11; Fisher v. State, 206 P.3d at 611.

5. Fisher v. Gibson, 282 F.3d at 1293; Cooper, "How Many Lawyers Does It Take to Get a Fair Trial?"

6. Fisher v. Gibson, 282 F.3d at 1298.

7. Ibid., 1294, 1300–1301.

8. Ibid., 1289.

9. Fisher v. State, 739 P.2d at 525. Fisher's conviction and death sentence were also upheld on state post-conviction review. Fisher v. State, 845 P.2d 1272.

10. Fisher v. Gibson, 282 F.3d at 1298 ("grossly inept," "sympathy and agreement with the prosecution"), 1300 ("actual doubt and hostility"), 1308 ("sabotaged his client's defense").

11. Fisher v. State, 206 P.3d at 610.

12. "Lawyer's Absences Lead to His Arrest," Daily Oklahoman, Mar. 10, 2006; Wood v. Carpenter, 907 F.3d 1279, 1299 (10th Cir. 2018); State ex rel. Oklahoma Bar Ass'n v. Albert, 163 P.3d 527, 529 (Okla. 2007); Danielle Haynes, "Oklahoma Death Row Prisoner Says Trial Lawyer Was Addicted to Cocaine," UPI, June 17, 2022 (Albert represented Tremane Wood and Keary Littlejohn); "Oklahoma Denies Clemency to Death-Row Prisoner Richard Fairchild Who Suffers from Brain Damage, Hallucinations, and Delusions," Death Penalty Information Center, Oct. 17, 2022 (Albert represented Richard Fairchild).

13. Cooper, "How Many Lawyers Does It Take to Get a Fair Trial?"

14. Fisher v. State, 206 P.3d at 611–12.

15. Barry, "In the Rearview Mirror, Oklahoma and Death Row."

16. United States v. Cronic, 466 U.S. 648, 654 (1984).

17. Powell v. Alabama, 287 U.S. 45 (1932). On the "Scottsboro Boys," see Dan T. Carter, Scottsboro: A Tragedy of the American South, rev. ed. (Baton Rouge: Louisiana State University Press, 2007).

18. Carter, Scottsboro, 18–23.

19. Powell v. Alabama, 287 U.S. at 71.

20. Johnson v. Zerbst, 304 U.S. 458 (1938).

21. Betts v. Brady, 316 U.S. 455, 472 (1942).

22. Gideon v. Wainwright, 372 U.S. 335, 337 (1963).

23. Brief for Petitioner at 14–16, Gideon v. Wainwright, 372 U.S. 335 (1963) (No. 155), 1962 WL 115120.

24. Gideon v. Wainwright, 372 U.S. 335; Anthony Lewis, "High Court Ruling Helps Poor Man to Freedom," New York Times, Aug. 6, 1963.

25. *In re* Gault, 387 U.S. 1, 20 n.26, 73–74 (1967).

26. Argersinger v. Hamlin, 407 U.S. 25, 37 (1972).

27. Ibid., 34 n.4.

28. Scott v. Illinois, 440 U.S. 367 (1979) (holding that a lawyer is not required if the defendant does not face a loss of liberty).

29. Jill Lepore, *These Truths: A History of the United States* (New York: W.W. Norton, 2018), 622–23.

30. Wendy Sawyer and Peter Wagner, *Mass Incarceration: The Whole Pie 2022*, Prison Policy Initiative (Mar. 14, 2022).

31. Anthony Lewis, *Gideon's Trumpet* (New York: Random House, 1964), 205.

32. Bill Rankin, "'I Felt like I Was Just Nothing': Suspect Held Months After Charges Dropped," *Atlanta Journal-Constitution*, Dec. 20, 2003, A1.

33. Dylan Jackson, "Crisis in Georgia's Public Defender System Fuels Case Backlog, Jail Overcrowding," *Atlanta Journal-Constitution*, Nov. 10, 2022; Bill Rankin, "In Georgia, Hundreds of People Charged with Crimes Have No Legal Representation," *Atlanta Journal-Constitution*, Sept. 16, 2022.

34. Robert C. Boruchowitz, Malia N. Brink, and Maureen Dimino, *Minor Crimes, Massive Waste: The Terrible Toll of America's Broken Misdemeanor Courts*, National Association of Criminal Defense Lawyers (2009), 14–17.

35. Texas: Boruchowitz et al., *Minor Crimes, Massive Waste*, 15. Florida: Alisa Smith and Sean Maddan, *Three-Minute Justice: Haste and Waste in Florida's Misdemeanor Courts*, National Association of Criminal Defense Lawyers (2011), 23, tables 9, 15, 23. Kentucky: David Carroll, "NLADA Gideon Alert—Underrepresentation in Kentucky Misdemeanor Courts," *Advocate*, Kentucky Department of Public Advocacy, Nov. 17, 2011; Dave Malaska, "Trampling over the Sixth Amendment: NKY Courts Play Fast and Loose with Rules," *CityBeat* (Cincinnati), Nov. 9, 2011. Michigan: Maura Ewing, "When Does the Right to an Attorney Kick In?," *Atlantic*, Sept. 15, 2017.

36. *Defend Children: A Blueprint for Effective Juvenile Defender Services*, National Juvenile Defender Center (Nov. 2016), 10.

37. Boruchowitz et al., *Minor Crimes, Massive Waste*, 19; "State-By-State Court Fees," NPR, May 19, 2014.

38. Florida: Smith and Maddan, *Three-Minute Justice*, 18. Louisiana: David Jacobs, "'Public Defenders Are Paid to Lose': Louisiana Looking at Reforms to Legal Defense System," *New Orleans CityBusiness*, Nov. 15, 2019.

39. Powell v. Alabama, 287 U.S. at 57.

40. Rothgery v. Gillespie Cnty., 554 U.S. 191, 212 (2008) (quoting Michigan v. Jackson, 475 U.S. 625, 630 n.3 (1986)).

41. Hurrell-Harring v. State, 883 N.Y.S.2d 349, 360 n.3 (N.Y. App. Div. 2009) (Peters, J., dissenting), aff'd as modified, 930 N.E.2d 217 (N.Y. 2010).

42. Brian Chasnoff, "Indigent Often Are Left in a Legal Limbo," San Antonio Express-News, Oct. 10, 2010.

43. Marc Bookman, "This Man Sat in Jail for 110 Days—After He Already Did His Time," Mother Jones, Aug. 6, 2015.

44. Justice Denied: America's Continuing Neglect of Our Constitutional Right to Counsel, National Right to Counsel Commission and Constitution Project (2009), 85–87; Boruchowitz et al., Minor Crimes, Massive Waste, 18–19.

45. John H. Blume and Rebecca K. Helm, "The Unexonerated: Factually Innocent Defendants Who Plead Guilty," Cornell Law Review 100 (2014): 157–91.

46. Memorandum from Abigail Leinsdorf & Atteeyah Hollie Regarding Proceedings in Cordele Superior Court (Mar. 13, 2012) (on file with authors).

47. Pub. Def., Eleventh Cir. of Fla. v. State, 115 So.3d 261, 278 (Fl. 2013).

48. Wilbur v. City of Mt. Vernon, 989 F. Supp. 2d 1122, 1124 (W.D. Wash. 2013).

49. Holsey v. Warden, 694 F.3d 1230, 1275 (11th Cir. 2012) (Barkett, J., dissenting).

50. Marc Bookman, "This Man's Alcoholic Lawyer Botched His Case. Georgia Executed Him Anyway," Mother Jones, Apr. 22, 2014.

51. Haney v. State, 603 So.2d 368, 377–78 (Ala. Crim. App. 1991).

52. Adam Liptak, "A Lawyer Known Best for Losing Capital Cases," New York Times, May 17, 2010; Michael Graczyk, "Texas Lawyer Who Lost All Death Penalty Cases Says He's Done," Associated Press, Aug. 13, 2016.

53. Sara Rimer and Raymond Bonner, "Texas Lawyer's Death Row Record a Concern," New York Times, June 11, 2000; Andrew Tilghman, "State Bar Suspends Troubled Local Lawyer," Houston Chronicle, Feb. 12, 2005.

54. On Joe Frank Cannon, Carl Johnson, and Calvin Burdine: Paul M. Barrett, "Lawyer's Fast Work on Death Cases Raises Doubts About System," Wall Street Journal, Sept. 7, 1994; David R. Dow, "The State, the Death Penalty and Carl Johnson," Boston College Law Review 37, no. 4 (1996): 691–711; Burdine v. Johnson, 262 F.3d 336 (5th Cir. 2001).

55. McFarland v. Lumpkin, 2022 WL 443611 (5th Cir. Feb. 14, 2022).

56. Ruth Bader Ginsburg, "In Pursuit of the Public Good: Lawyers Who Care," lecture at the District of Columbia School of Law, Apr. 9, 2001.

57. Lise Olsen, "Lawyers' Late Filings Can Be Deadly for Inmates," *Houston Chronicle*, Mar. 22, 2009; Lise Olsen, "Death Row Lawyers Get Paid While Messing Up," *Houston Chronicle*, Apr. 20, 2009.

58. "Indigent Defense Data, Harris County Attorney Caseloads Report," Texas Indigent Defense Commission, https://tidc.tamu.edu/public.net /Reports/AttorneyCaseLoad.aspx.

59. Ken Armstrong, "Lethal Mix: Lawyers' Mistakes, Unforgiving Law," *Washington Post*, Nov. 15, 2014; Ken Armstrong, "When Lawyers Stumble, Only Their Clients Fall," *Washington Post*, Nov. 16, 2014.

60. Chuck Lindell, "Lawyer Makes 1 Case for 2 Killers," *Austin American-Statesman*, Feb. 26, 2006; Rosanna Ruiz, "Rail Killer Running Out of Options as Execution Nears," *Houston Chronicle*, Mar. 8, 2006; Mike Tolson, "Death Row Inmate's Effort to Spare Life Gains Momentum," *Houston Chronicle*, Apr. 2, 2012; Will v. Lumpkin, 978 F.3d 933, 936 n.4 (5th Cir. 2020).

61. Maro Robbins, "Convict's Odds Today May Rest on Gibberish," *San Antonio Express-News*, Aug. 24, 2006.

62. Marc Bookman, "10 Ways to Blow a Death Penalty Case," *Mother Jones*, Apr. 22, 2014.

63. *Gideon Undone! The Crisis of Indigent Defense Funding*, American Bar Association and National Legal Aid and Defender Association (1982), 3; Richard Klein and Robert Spangenberg, *The Indigent Defense Crisis*, ABA Criminal Justice Section Ad Hoc Committee on the Indigent Defense Crisis (1993), 25; *Gideon's Broken Promise: America's Continuing Quest for Equal Justice*, ABA Standing Committee on Legal Aid and Indigent Defendants (2004), iv; Joel M. Schumm, *National Indigent Defense Reform: The Solution Is Multifaceted*, ABA Standing Committee on Legal Aid and Indigent Defendants and National Association of Criminal Defense Lawyers (2012), 5.

64. Pub. L. No. 88-455, 78 Stat. 552 (1964) (codified as amended at 18 U.S.C. § 3006A); Pub. L. No. 91-447, 84 Stat. 916 (1970) (codified as amended at 18 U.S.C. § 3006A); see Edward C. Prado, "Process and Progress: Reviewing the Criminal Justice Act," *Law and Contemporary Problems* 58, no. 1 (1995): 51–63.

65. Brian Naylor, "How Federal Dollars Fund Local Police," NPR, June 9, 2020.

66. Sara Mayeux, "What *Gideon* Did," *Columbia Law Review* 116 (2016): 15–103, 21, 27–47.

67. "First Lawyer Assigned to Criminal Cases," Legal Aid Society.

68. Suzanne M. Strong, *State-Administered Indigent Defense Systems, 2013*, U.S. Department of Justice (2016), 1 (listing twenty-eight states but omitting

Georgia, which has a public defender system, and including Maine, which does not).

69. Laurence A. Benner, "The Presumption of Guilt: Systemic Factors That Contribute to Ineffective Assistance of Counsel in California," *California Western Law Review* 45, no. 2 (2009): 263–355, 300–305; William J. Leahy, "The Right to Counsel in the State of New York," *Indiana Law Review* 51 (2018): 145–65, 161–63.

70. *Report and Recommendations on Funding of Defense Services in California*, California Commission on the Fair Administration of Justice (Apr. 14, 2008), 10–12.

71. Laurence A. Benner, "The Presumption of Guilt: Systemic Factors That Contribute to Ineffective Assistance of Counsel in California," *California Western Law Review* 45, no. 2 (2009): 263–355, 304–5.

72. *Justice Denied*, National Right to Counsel Commission and Constitution Project, 7.

73. TN R S CT Rule 13 § 2 (d) (2)-(6); Wis. Stat. Ann. § 977.08(4m); S.C. Code Ann. § 17-3-50(A).

74. See, for example, Caplan v. All American Auto Collision, 36 F.4th 1083, 1089 (11th Cir. 2022) (awarding $350 per hour for attorneys' work on a case brought under the Americans with Disabilities Act); Johnson v. Borders, 2019 WL 8105907, *5, *6 (M.D. Fla. 2019) (awarding an hourly rate of $325 based on experience for one lawyer, $250 for another, $135 for one paralegal, and $110 for another paralegal in a case brought under 42 U.S.C. § 1983), *report and recommendation adopted and confirmed in part*, 2019 WL 8105896, *aff'd in part, vacated in part*, 36 F.4th 1254 (11th Cir. 2022).

75. Laura LaFay, "Virginia's Poor Receive Justice on the Cheap," *Virginian-Pilot*, Feb. 15, 1998.

76. *Justice Denied*, National Right to Counsel Commission and Constitution Project, 65–70.

77. Ian Urbina, "Despite Red Flags About Judges, a Kickback Scheme Flourished," *New York Times*, Mar. 27, 2009; *Report*, Pennsylvania Interbranch Commission on Juvenile Justice (May 2010), 11–12, 17–18, 34, 38–40; Torsten Ove, "Ex-Luzerne County Judge at Center of 'Kids for Cash' Jail Scandal Loses Bid for Lighter Prison Sentence," *Pittsburgh Post-Gazette*, Aug. 26, 2020.

78. Kuren v. Luzerne County, 146 A.3d 715, 718–19 (Pa. 2016).

79. Ibid., 725, 747–48; John Rudolf, "Pennsylvania Public Defenders Rebel Against Crushing Caseloads," *HuffPost*, Oct. 23, 2012.

80. Flora v. County of Luzerne, 776 F.3d 169, 173 (3d Cir. 2015).

81. Kuren v. Luzerne County, 146 A.3d at 717, 725, 743.

82. Flora v. County of Luzerne, 776 F.3d 169; Eric Mark, "Flora Suit Settled by Luzerne Co. for \$250K," *Standard-Speaker* (Hazleton, PA), Aug. 29, 2018, A2.

83. Eli Hager, "When There's Only One Public Defender in Town," The Marshall Project, Sept. 9, 2016.

84. State *ex rel.* Mo. Pub. Def. Comm'n v. Pratte, 298 S.W.3d 870, 877 (Mo. 2009); Memorandum from Cathy R. Kelly, Director, State Public Defender Commission, to Governor Nixon, Members of the Supreme Court, Members of the General Assembly, and Presiding Judges (Oct. 1, 2011) (on file with authors), 2; Katie Moore, "Public Defenders Ordered to Violate Ethics to Keep Defendants Moving Through Court," *Kansas City Star*, Sept. 21, 2021; Crystal Thomas, "Judge Vetoes Plan to Decrease Workloads for Missouri's 'Inundated' Public Defender System," *Kansas City Star*, Jan. 28, 2020; Katie Moore, "Missouri's Public Defender System Is Sued Again, Faces 'Urgent Constitutional Crisis,'" *Kansas City Star*, Feb. 27, 2020.

85. See, e.g., Ake v. Oklahoma, 470 U.S. 68 (1985); McWilliams v. Dunn, 137 S. Ct. 1790 (2017), Little v. Armontrout, 835 F.2d 1240, 1244 (8th Cir. 1987) (en banc) (defendant must show "a reasonable probability that an expert would aid in his defense, and that denial of expert assistance would result in an unfair trial").

86. Ward v. State, 539 S.W.3d 546, 561 (Ark. 2018) (Kemp, C.J., dissenting); Ward v. State, 455 S.W.3d 818, 822–23 (Ark. 2015).

87. Martinez-Macias v. Collins, 810 F. Supp. 782, 786–87, 796–813 (W.D. Tex. 1991); Martinez-Macias v. Collins, 979 F.2d 1067, 1067 (5th Cir. 1992); Gordon Dickinson, "Man Freed in Machete Murder Case," *El Paso Times*, June 24, 1993, 1.

88. Strong, *State-Administered Indigent Defense Systems*, 14–15; Stephen B. Bright and Sia M. Sanneh, "Fifty Years of Defiance and Resistance After *Gideon v. Wainwright*," *Yale Law Journal* 122, no. 8 (2013): 2150–74, 2167–68.

89. Julia Shumway "Board Fires Head of Oregon's Public Defense Agency," *Oregon Capital Chronicle*, Aug. 18, 2022; "After Firing Public Defense Commissioners, New Members Named," Associated Press, Aug. 16, 2022; Andrew Selsky, "Oregon Justice Fires Panel Due to Lack of Public Defenders," Associated Press, Aug. 15, 2022; Conrad Wilson, "Former Oregon Public Defense Leader Files Lawsuit over Firing," Oregon Public Broadcasting, Oct. 11, 2022.

90. Chasnoff, "Indigent Often Are Left in a Legal Limbo."

91. Wayne Crenshaw, "Fired Public Defender Says He Plans to Chal-

lenge Ouster," *Macon Telegraph*, Aug. 3, 2016; Jacob Reynolds, "Staff of Former Houston County Public Defender Respond to Firing," WMAZ, Aug. 5, 2016.

92. *Amicus Curiae* Brief of the Montgomery County Office of the Public Defender, *Philadelphia Cmty. Bail Fund v. Arraignment Court Magistrates*, No. 21 EM 2019 (Pa. Feb. 3, 2020).

93. Samantha Melamed and Vinny Vella, "Montgomery County Has Fired Its Top Two Public Defenders," *Philadelphia Inquirer*, Feb. 26, 2020; Radley Balko, "A Pennsylvania County Fired Its Two Top Public Defenders for Doing Their Jobs," *Washington Post*, Mar. 2, 2020.

94. LaFay, "Virginia's Poor Receive Justice on the Cheap"; "Felony Murder: Soup to Nuts—$575," *Criminal Practice Reporter*, Jan. 28, 1998, 25, 27.

95. Law Office of Samuel P. Newton v. Weber County, 491 F. Supp. 3d 1047, 1053–59 (D. Utah 2020).

96. Frederic N. Tulsky, "Big-Time Trials, Small Time Defenses," *Philadelphia Inquirer*, Sept. 14, 1992, A1, A8.

97. Neel U. Sukhatme and Jay Jenkins, "Pay to Play? Campaign Finance and the Incentive Gap in the Sixth Amendment's Right to Counsel," *Duke Law Journal* 70 (2020): 775–845, 781, 827–30.

98. Grant v. State, 607 S.E.2d 586 (2005); Davis v. State, 403 S.E.2d 800 (Ga. 1991); Birt v. State, 387 S.E.2d 879 (Ga. 1990); Amadeo v. State, 384 S.E.2d 181 (Ga. 1989).

99. Roberts v. State, 438 S.E.2d 905 (Ga. 1994).

100. *Ex parte* Garcia, 2007 WL 1783194 (Tex. Crim. App. June 20, 2007); Statement Concerning Untimely Filing, *Ex parte* Garcia, No. WR 66,977, at 2–3 (Tex. Crim. App. Dec. 20, 2011) (on file with authors); *Ex parte* Garcia, 2011 WL 5189081, at *2 (Tex. Crim. App. Oct. 27, 2011) (Price, J., dissenting); Miriam Rosen, "Delayed Requests for Execution Stays + CCA = Contempt Citations," *Texas Lawyer*, Apr. 13, 2015.

101. Allan Turner, "UH Law Professor, Noted Death Penalty Lawyer, Sanctioned by Texas Court of Criminal Appeals," *Houston Chronicle*, Jan. 20, 2015; Dahlia Lithwick, "Revenge, Not Justice," *Slate*, Mar. 12, 2015.

102. Memorandum from Edith H. Jones to All Chief Circuit Judges, All Circuit Execs., & Gary Bowden (Mar. 11, 2011), 2–4.

103. 535 U.S. 654 (2002); Boruchowitz et al., *Minor Crimes, Massive Waste*, 17 (quoting Chief Justice Jean Hoefer Toal of the Supreme Court of South Carolina, speaking at the South Carolina Bar Association, 22nd Annual Criminal Law Update (Jan. 26, 2007)).

104. Wilson v. Rees, 624 F.3d 737, 739 (6th Cir. 2010) (Martin, J., dissenting).

105. Wilson v. Commonwealth, 836 S.W.2d 872, 878, 882 (Ky. 1992). See also Wilson v. Commonwealth, 975 S.W.2d 901, 902–4 (Ky. 1998); Wilson v. Rees, 624 F.3d 737 (6th Cir. 2010).

106. Wilson v. Rees, 624 F.3d at 741 (Martin, J., dissenting).

107. Wilson v. Commonwealth, 836 S.W.2d at 879.

108. Dunn v. State, 819 S.W.2d 510, 515–18 (Tex. Crim. App. 1991); Dunn v. Johnson, 162 F.3d 302 (5th Cir. 1998).

109. Parker v. State, 587 So.2d 1072, 1100–11003 (Ala. Crim. App. 1991); Ex parte Parker, 610 So.2d 1181 (Ala. 1992) (direct appeal); Parker v. Allen, 565 F.3d 1258 (11th Cir. 2009); Bob Johnson, "Alabama Man Executed in 1988 Colbert County Killing," Associated Press, June 11, 2010.

110. Strickland v. Washington, 466 U.S. 668, 688–90, 694 (1984).

111. Rogers v. Zant, 13 F.3d 384, 386–88 (11th Cir. 1994).

112. Glasser v. United States, 315 U.S. 60, 76 (1942).

113. Strickland v. Washington, 466 U.S. at 694.

114. Strickland v. Washington, 466 U.S. at 707–8, 710, 713 (Marshall, J., dissenting).

115. William S. Sessions, foreword to Norman Lefstein, Securing Reasonable Caseloads: Ethics and Law in Public Defense (Chicago: American Bar Association, 2012), vii.

116. Young v. Runnels, 435 F.3d 1038, 1041 (9th Cir. 2006); ibid. at 1045 (Noonan, J., concurring).

117. Slaughter v. Parker, 187 F. Supp. 2d 755, 827–28 (W.D. Ky 2001).

118. Ibid., 841.

119. Slaughter v. Parker, 450 F.3d 224, 234 (6th Cir. 2006); Slaughter v. Parker, 467 F.3d 511, 512 (6th Cir. 2006) (Cole, J., dissenting from denial of rehearing en banc).

120. Adam M. Gershowitz, "Rethinking the Timing of Capital Clemency," Michigan Law Review 113, no. 1 (Oct. 2014): 1–55, 37.

121. Holsey v. Warden, 694 F.3d 1230, 1231 (11th Cir. 2012).

122. Romero v. Lynaugh, 884 F.2d 871, 875, 877 (5th Cir. 1989).

123. Sheri Lynn Johnson, "Racial Antagonism, Sexual Betrayal, Graft, and More: Rethinking and Remedying the Universe of Defense Counsel Failings," Washington University Law Review 97, no. 1 (2019): 58–112, 85–86; Drayton v. Moore, No. 98-18, 1999 WL 10073 (4th Cir. 1999).

124. Douglas v. California, 372 U.S. 353, 357–58 (1963).

125. Moffitt v. Ross, 483 F.2d 650 (4th Cir. 1973); Ross v. Moffitt, 417 U.S. 600, 616 (1974).

126. Pennsylvania v. Finley, 481 U.S. 551 (1987).

127. Murray v. Giarratano, 492 U.S. 1, 11 (1989).

128. *Projecting Costs for Various Indigent Defense Systems in Virginia for FY 1986*, The Spangenberg Group (1985), 78.

129. *Ex parte* Graves, 70 S.W.3d 103, 114 (Tex. Crim. App. 2002).

130. 21 U.S.C. § 848(e); McFarland v. Scott, 512 U.S. 849 (1994).

131. Petition for a Writ of Certiorari, 1999 WL 33639842 at *5 (quoting transcript), Gibson v. Head, 120 S. Ct. 363 (1999) (denying certiorari); Bill Rankin, "When Death Row Inmates Go to Court Without Lawyers," *Atlanta Journal-Constitution*, Dec. 29, 1996, D5.

132. Gibson v. Turpin, 513 S.E.2d 186 (Ga. 1999).

133. Wainwright v. Sykes, 433 U.S. 72 (1977).

134. Smith v. Murray, 477 U.S. 527 (1986).

135. Ibid., 539, 541 (Stevens, J., dissenting) (emphasis omitted).

136. Coleman v. Thompson, 501 U.S. 722, 726 (1991).

137. Ibid., 758–59 (Blackmun, J., dissenting).

138. Ibid., 753–54 (majority opinion).

139. Bowles v. Russell, 551 U.S. 205, 215 (2007) (Souter, J. dissenting).

140. Wainwright v. Sykes, 433 U.S. at 90.

141. People v. Fuiava, 269 P.3d 568, 625–26, 649 (Cal. 2012).

142. Hill v. State, 432 So.2d 427, 438–40 (Miss. 1983); In re Hill, 460 So.2d 792, 811 (Robertson, J., concurring in part and dissenting in part).

143. Machetti v. Linahan, 679 F.2d 236, 241 (11th Cir. 1982); Smith v. Kemp, 715 F.2d 1459, 1476 (11th Cir. 1983) (Hatchett, J., concurring in part and dissenting in part).

144. Murray v. Carrier, 477 U.S. 478, 488 (1986).

145. Link v. Wabash Railroad Co., 370 U.S. 626, 643 (1962) (Black, J., dissenting).

146. See Darryl K. Brown, "Does It Matter Who Objects? Rethinking the Burden to Prevent Errors in Criminal Process," *Texas Law Review* 98 (2019): 101–53.

147. Lise Olsen, "Slow Paperwork in Death Row Cases Ends Final Appeals for 9," *Houston Chronicle*, Mar. 21, 2009.

148. Statement by Robert F. Kennedy Before the Senate Committee on the Judiciary Regarding S. 1057, the Proposed Criminal Justice Act, 88th Cong. 1 (1963).

149. Chief Justice Harold G. Clarke, "Annual State of the Judiciary Address," reprinted in *Fulton County Daily Report*, Jan. 14, 1993.

150. James M. Anderson and Paul Heaton, "How Much Difference Does the Lawyer Make? The Effect of Defense Counsel on Murder Case Outcomes," *Yale Law Journal* 122 (2012): 154–217; Harris County Public Defender, *Harris County Public Defender: Tenth Year Report* (May 1, 2020); Thomas H. Cohen, "Who Is Better at Defending Criminals? Does Type of Defense Attorney Matter in Terms of Producing Favorable Case Outcomes," *Criminal Justice Policy Review* 25, no. 1 (2014): 29–58, 44.

151. Ankur Desai and Brandon L. Garrett, "The State of the Death Penalty," *Notre Dame Law Review* 94, no. 3 (2019): 1255–312, 1258, 1307; Corinna Lain and Doug Ramseur, "Disrupting Death: How Dedicated Capital Defenders Broke Virginia's Machinery of Death," *University of Richmond Law Review* 56 (2021): 183–306.

152. N.C.G.S. § 7A-498.4.

153. See State *ex rel.* Mo. Pub. Def. Comm'n v. Pratte, 298 S.W.3d 870; State *ex rel.* Mo. Pub. Def. Comm'n v. Waters, 370 S.W.3d 592 (Mo. 2012). See also Pub. Def., Eleventh Cir. of Fla. v. State, 115 So. 3d at 264–65 (challenge to excessive caseloads brought by the elected public defender in Miami-Dade County, Florida).

154. Melamed and Vella, "Montgomery County Has Fired Its Top Two Public Defenders."

155. James M. Anderson, Maya Buenaventura, and Paul Heaton, "The Effects of Holistic Defense on Criminal Justice Outcomes," *Harvard Law Review* 132 (2019): 819–93, 833–50.

4. Judges and the Politics of Crime

1. U.S. v. Bollman, 24 F. Cas. 1189, 1192 (C.C.D.C. 1807) (No. 14,622) (Cranch, J., dissenting).

2. West Virginia State Bd. of Educ. v. Barnette, 319 U.S. 624, 638 (1943).

3. Dan T. Carter, *Scottsboro: A Tragedy of the American South*, rev. ed. (Baton Rouge: Louisiana State University Press, 1992), 265–69, 273.

4. Rodriguez v. State, 848 S.W.2d 141 (Tex. Crim. App. 1993).

5. Janet Elliott and Richard Connelly, "Mansfield: The Stealth Candidate—His Past Isn't What It Seems," *Texas Lawyer*, Oct. 3, 1994; "Do It Now," *Fort*

Worth Star-Telegram, Nov. 12, 1994; "Q & A with Stephen Mansfield: 'The Greatest Challenge of My Life,'" *Texas Lawyer*, Nov. 21, 1994; Janet Elliott, "Unqualified Success: Mansfield's Mandate—Vote Makes a Case for Merit Selection," *Texas Lawyer*, Nov. 14, 1994; John Williams, "Election '94: GOP Gains Majority in State Supreme Court," *Houston Chronicle*, Nov. 10, 1994.

6. Michael Hall, "And Justice for Some," *Texas Monthly*, Nov. 2004.

7. Bruce Nichols, "GOP Candidates Sweep 3 Seats: Appeals Court Will Be All Republican for the First Time," *Dallas Morning News*, Nov. 4, 1998.

8. "Tarrant County League of Women Voters' Guide," *Fort Worth Star-Telegram*, Feb. 28, 2000.

9. Hall, "And Justice for Some."

10. *Ex parte* Criner, No. 36,856-01, slip op. at 4 (Tex. Crim. App. July 8, 1998); *Frontline: The Case for Innocence* (PBS, Jan. 11, 2000); Hall, "And Justice for Some."

11. Bob Burtman, "Innocent at Last," *Houston Press*, Aug. 3, 2000; *Frontline: The Case for Innocence*; Hall, "And Justice for Some."

12. *Ex parte* Kerr, 977 S.W.2d 585, 585 (Tex. Crim. App. 1998) (Overstreet, J., dissenting).

13. Kerr v. Johnson, No. SA-98-CA-151-OG (W.D. Tex. Feb. 24, 1999).

14. *Ex parte* Kerr, 64 S.W.3d 414, 418–20 (Tex. Crim. App. 2002).

15. *Ex parte* Kerr, 2009 WL 874005, at *2 (Tex. Crim. App. 2009).

16. The Declaration of Independence para. 11 (U.S. 1776).

17. Tumey v. Ohio, 273 U.S. 510, 532 (1927).

18. Richard Carelli, "Justice Attacks Judicial Elections: Stevens Says Judges Shouldn't Be Permitted to Raise Campaign Funds to 'Curry the Favor of Voters,'" Associated Press, Aug. 4, 1996.

19. *Model Code of Judicial Conduct*, American Bar Association (2020).

20. Joseph H. Smith, "An Independent Judiciary: The Colonial Background," *University of Pennsylvania Law Review* 124, no. 5 (1976): 1104–56, 1151–53; Larry Berkson et al., *Judicial Selection in the United States: A Compendium of Provisions* (Chicago: American Judicature Society, 1980), 3–6.

21. *Selection & Retention of State Judges: Methods from Across the Country*, Institute for the Advancement of the American Legal System (Sept. 18, 2015).

22. David Von Drehle, *Among the Lowest of the Dead: The Culture of Death Row* (Ann Arbor: University of Michigan Press, 1995), 200–201, 293, 325.

23. Roger Simon, "How a Murderer and Rapist Became the Bush Campaign's Most Valuable Player," *Baltimore Sun*, Nov. 11, 1990.

24. Marshall Frady, "Death in Arkansas," *New Yorker*, Feb. 22, 1993.

25. "For Bush Offspring, Political Foes Can't Kill Criminals Fast Enough," *Chicago Tribune*, Oct. 30, 1994; Erika Casriel, "Bush and the Texas Death Machine," *Rolling Stone*, Aug. 3, 2000; Alan Berlow, "The Texas Clemency Memos," *Atlantic*, July/Aug. 2003; James Dao, "Death Penalty in New York Reinstated After 18 Years: Pataki Sees Justice Served," *New York Times*, Mar. 8, 1995.

26. Leo C. Wolinsky, "Governor's Support for 2 Justices Tied to Death Penalty Votes," *Los Angeles Times*, Mar. 14, 1986; Steve Wiegand, "Governor's Warning to 2 Justices," *San Francisco Chronicle*, Mar. 14, 1986; Henry Unger, "Will Vote Against Grodin, Reynoso, Deukmejian Says," *Los Angeles Daily Journal*, Aug. 26, 1986; Frank Clifford, "Voters Repudiate 3 of Court's Liberal Justices," *Los Angeles Times*, Nov. 5, 1986.

27. Maura Dolan, "State High Court Is Strong Enforcer of Death Penalty," *Los Angeles Times*, Apr. 9, 1995; Maura Dolan, "State High Court Steering a Pragmatic Legal Course," *Los Angeles Times*, Sept. 8, 1993; C. Elliot Kessler, "Death and Harmlessness: Application of the Harmless Error Rule by the Bird and Lucas Courts in Death Penalty Cases—a Comparison and Critique," *University of San Francisco Law Review* 26 (1991): 41–91, 89.

28. Tammie Cessna Langford, "Two Vying for State's High Court," *Sun Herald* (Biloxi, Miss.), June 3, 1990; "On March 10, Vote for Judge James L. Roberts, Jr. for the Mississippi Supreme Court," *Northeast Mississippi Daily Journal*, Mar. 7, 1992, campaign supplement.

29. State v. Odom, 928 S.W.2d 18 (Tenn. 1996); Letter from John M. Davies, President of the Tennessee Conservative Union (June 1996), and "Just Say No!," Tennessee Republican Party campaign brochure (1996), reprinted in Stephen B. Bright, "Political Attacks on the Judiciary: Can Justice Be Done amid Efforts to Intimidate and Remove Judges from Office for Unpopular Decisions?," *New York University Law Review* 72 (May 1997): 308–36, Appendix A; State v. Odom, 137 S.W.3d 572 (Tenn. 2004).

30. Adam Liptak, "Rendering Justice, with One Eye on Re-election," *New York Times*, May 25, 2008; "Racist, Misleading Wisconsin Supreme Court Election Ad: 'Prosecutor'" (TV advertisement), https://www.youtube.com/watch?v=1haqLYB1cw0.

31. Paula Wade, "White's Defeat Poses Legal Dilemma: How Is a Replacement Justice Picked?," *Commercial Appeal* (Memphis), Aug. 3, 1996.

32. Lewis F. Powell Jr., "Confidential Memorandum: Attack on American Free Enterprise System" (Aug. 23, 1971), Powell Papers, Washington and Lee University School of Law.

33. Robert Kaplan, "Justice for Sale," *Common Cause* (May–June 1987), 29–30.

34. Scott Greytak et al., *Bankrolling the Bench: The New Politics of Judicial Elections 2013–14*, Brennan Center for Justice, National Institute on Money in State Politics, and Justice at Stake (Oct. 2015), 48, 51.

35. Laurence Leamer, *The Price of Justice: A True Story of Greed and Corruption* (New York: Times Books, 2013), 200–208, 212–20; State v. Arbaugh, 595 S.E.2d 289, 292–94 (W. Va. 2004), ibid. at 296–301 (Davis. J., dissenting), ibid. at 301–5 (Albright, J., concurring), ibid. at 306–7 (Starcher, J., concurring in part and dissenting in part); Adam Liptak, "Judicial Races in Several States Become Partisan Battlegrounds," *New York Times*, Oct. 24, 2004; Carol Morello, "W. Va. Supreme Court Justice Defeated in Rancorous Contest," *Washington Post*, Nov. 4, 2004; Caperton v. A.T. Massey Coal Co., Inc., 556 U.S. 868, 872–73 (2009).

36. Caperton v. A.T. Massey Coal Co., Inc., 556 U.S. at 884.

37. Christie Thompson, "Trial by Cash," The Marshall Project, Dec. 11, 2014; "Ohio Judicial Election—2014 Campaign Ad," The Marshall Project, YouTube, Nov. 24, 2014, https://www.youtube.com/watch?v=U55Ruh-r20E; "Justice French: Court the 'Backstop' for GOP Legislation," *Columbus Dispatch*, Oct. 26, 2014.

38. Whitney Woodward, "2010 Justice Kilbride Retention in Illinois," *Drake Law Review* 60, no. 3 (2012): 843–86, 860–61, 863, 865; Adam Skaggs et al., "The New Politics of Judicial Elections 2009–10," Brennan Center for Justice (Oct. 2011), 20; "Kilbride Sides with Criminals" (TV advertisement), https://www.youtube.com/watch?v=1o307JqaOEs.

39. Dan Petrella, "Illinois Moves to Prohibit 'Dark Money' in Judicial Races, but It's Unclear What Effect That Will Have on State's Free-Spending Campaigns," *Chicago Tribune*, Dec. 9, 2021; Christie Thompson, "'Law and Order' Still Reigns in State Supreme Court Elections," The Marshall Project, Nov. 6, 2020; "Backed by the Blue" (TV advertisement), https://mycmag.kantarmediana.com/KMIcmagvidbin2/STSUPCT_IL_KILBRIDE_BACKED_BY_THE_BLUE.html; Ray Long, "Speaker Madigan Dealt Blow as Democratic Illinois Supreme Court Justice Concedes Defeat in Retention Bid," *Chicago Tribune*, Nov. 3, 2020; Ray Long, "Madigan, Billionaires Clash in Record-Shattering $10.7 Million Illinois Supreme Court Contest That Threatens Court's Democratic Majority," *Chicago Tribune*, Oct. 23, 2020.

40. "Sue Bell Cobb for Chief Justice—Only," Dems for the People, YouTube, Sept. 27, 2006, https://www.youtube.com/watch?v=y2guyWS57OA;

Eric Velasco, "Sue Bell Cobb, Former Alabama Chief Justice, to Address Downtown Democratic Club Today," *Birmingham News*, Nov. 4, 2011.

41. Sue Bell Cobb, "I Was Alabama's Top Judge. I'm Ashamed by What I Had to Do to Get There," *Politico Magazine*, Mar.–Apr. 2015.

42. Adam Liptak and Janet Roberts, "Campaign Cash Mirrors a High Court's Rulings," *New York Times*, Oct. 1, 2006.

43. Ruth Marcus, "Justice White Criticizes Judicial Elections," *Washington Post*, Aug. 11, 1987.

44. Gregory A. Huber and Sanford C. Gordon, "Accountability and Coercion: Is Justice Blind When It Runs for Office?," *American Journal of Political Science* 48, no. 2 (Apr. 2004): 247–63, 255; Carlos Berdejó and Noam Yuchtman, "Crime, Punishment, and Politics: An Analysis of Political Cycles in Criminal Sentencing," *Review of Economics and Statistics* 95, no. 3 (July 2013): 741–56, 748, 752.

45. Motion to Disqualify Present and Former Members of Jefferson Circuit Court and Jefferson District Court and to Obtain Appointment of a Special Judge from Outside Jefferson County, Commonwealth v. Bard (Ky. Cir. Ct. Jefferson Cty., Nov. 9, 1993) (No. 93CR2373).

46. Adkins v. State, 600 So.2d 1054 (Ala. Crim. App. 1990); Carol Pappas, "Ricky Adkins to Go On Trial Monday; Continuance Denied," *Daily Home* (Talladega, AL) (Oct. 22, 1988); Carol Pappas, "Jury Selection to Begin Today in Adkins Capital Murder Trial," *Daily Home* (Talladega, AL) (Oct. 25, 1988).

47. Nevius v. Warden, 944 P.2d 858, 860 (Nev. 1997) (Springer, J., dissenting).

48. Batson v. Kentucky, 476 U.S. 79 (1986).

49. Johnson v. State, 476 So.2d 1195, 1209 (Miss. 1985).

50. Coleman v. Kemp, 778 F.2d 1487, 1491–1537 (11th Cir. 1985).

51. Dungee v. State, 227 S.E.2d 746 (Ga.) (per curiam); Isaacs v. State, 226 S.E.2d 922 (Ga.) (per curiam); Coleman v. State, 226 S.E.2d 911 (Ga. 1976); Isaacs v. Kemp, 778 F.2d 1482, 1484 (11th Cir. 1985). See also Coleman v. Kemp, 778 F.2d 1487 at 1491–1537.

52. Billy Corriher, *Criminals and Campaign Cash: The Impact of Judicial Campaign Spending on Criminal Defendants*, Center for American Progress (Oct. 2013), 1–2; Joanna Shepherd and Michael S. Kang, *Skewed Justice: Citizens United, Television Advertising and State Supreme Court Justices' Decisions in Criminal Cases*, American Constitution Society (Oct. 2014), 3. See also Paul Brace and Brent D. Boyea, "State Public Opinion, the Death Penalty, and the Practice of Electing Judges," *American Journal of Political Science* 52, no. 2 (Apr. 2008):

360–72; Brandice Canes-Wrone, Tom S. Clark, and Jason P. Kelly, "Judicial Selection and Death Penalty Decisions," *American Political Science Review* 108, no. 1 (Feb. 2014): 23–39; Dan Levine and Kristina Cooke, "In States with Elected High Court Judges, a Harder Line on Capital Punishment," Reuters, Sept. 22, 2015.

53. Defense Exhibits 1A, 2A (admitted at Hearing of Sept. 11–14, 1990), Brooks v. State, 415 S.E.2d 903 (Ga. 1992); the closing argument is set out in full in the appendix to the opinion of Judge Clark, Brooks v. Kemp, 762 F.2d 1383, 1443–48 (11th Cir. 1985) (Clark, J., concurring in part and dissenting in part) (quoting trial transcript at 859–73). *Chattahoochee Judicial District: Buckle of the Death Belt: The Death Penalty in Microcosm*, Death Penalty Information Center (Jan. 1, 1991).

54. Transcript of Hearing of Sept. 11–14, 1990, at 137–48, Brooks v. State, 415 S.E.2d 903 (No. S92A0062); Hance v. Zant, 696 F.2d 940, 952–53 (11th Cir. 1983); Brooks v. Francis, 716 F.2d 780 (11th Cir. 1983); Phil Gast, "District Attorney Criticizes Court for Rejecting Sentence," *Columbus Enquirer* (GA), Sept. 17, 1983.

55. Jim Houston, "Ruling on Judgeship Opens the Door for New Faces," *Columbus Ledger-Enquirer* (GA), Feb. 7, 1995; Trisha Renaud, "DA's Office Assigned Cases to Judges," *Fulton County Report* (GA), Apr. 26, 1995; Chuck Williams and Jim Mustian, "Judge Doug Pullen Announces Retirement After Meeting with JQC Director, Investigator," *Ledger-Enquirer* (Columbus, GA), Aug. 22, 2011; Bill Rankin, "Columbus Judge Pullen Steps Down amid Probe," *Atlanta Journal-Constitution*, Aug. 23, 2011.

56. Buntion v. Dretke, 2006 WL 8453025, **19–22 (S.D. Tex. 2006), *rev'd*, Buntion v. Quarterman, 524 F.3d 664, 674–76 (5th Cir. 2008); Jolie McCullough, "Texas Executes Carl Buntion, the State's Oldest Death Row Prisoner, for Houston Police Officer's Murder," *Texas Tribune*, Apr. 21, 2022.

57. Nichols v. Collins, 802 F. Supp. 66, 79 (S.D. Tex. 1992), *rev'd*., 69 F.3d 1255 (5th Cir. 1995); Brent E. Newton, "A Case Study in Systematic Unfairness: The Texas Death Penalty, 1973–1994," *Texas Forum on Civil Liberties and Civil Rights* 1 (Spring 1994): 1–37, 26.

58. Williams v. Pennsylvania, 579 U.S. 1, 5–7 (2016); Marc Bookman, "When a Kid Kills His Longtime Abuser, Who's the Victim?," *Mother Jones*, Nov. 30, 2015.

59. Williams v. Pennsylvania, 579 U.S. at 6–7, 14.

60. Commonwealth v. Williams, 168 A.3d 97 (Pa. 2017) (affirmed by an evenly divided court).

61. See, for example, Anderson v. Bessemer City, 470 U.S. 564, 572

(1985); In re Colony Square Co., 819 F.2d 272, 275 (11th Cir. 1987); Cuthbertson v. Bigger Brothers, 702 F.2d 454, 458 (4th Cir. 1983).

62. Brief of Amicus Curiae Alabama Appellate Court Justices and Bar Presidents Supporting Petitioner at 15, Hamm v. Allen, 137 S. Ct. 39 (2016) (No. 15-8753), 2016 WL 2605545.

63. Brief for the National Association of Criminal Defense Lawyers as Amicus Curiae Supporting Petitioner at 10–11, Wood v. Allen, 558 U.S. 290 (2010) (No. 08-9156), 2009 WL 2445749.

64. Hamm v. State, 913 So.2d 460, 474 (Ala. Cr. App. 2002); Petition for Certiorari at 12, Hamm v. Allen, 137 S. Ct. 39 (2016) (quoting Oral Argument at 24:50–25:28, Hamm v. Commissioner, 620 F. App'x 752 (11th Cir. 2015)); Hamm v. Commissioner, 620 F. App'x at 756 n.3, 778–82.

65. Stephen B. Bright and Patrick J. Keenan, "Judges and the Politics of Death: Deciding Between the Bill of Rights and the Next Election in Capital Cases," *Boston University Law Review* 75 (1994): 759–835, 803–11; Andrew Cohen, "Letting Prosecutors Write the Law," The Marshall Project, July 18, 2016.

66. Nichols v. Collins, 802 F. Supp. 66, 79 (S.D. Tex. 1992), *rev'd.*, 69 F.3d 1255 (5th Cir. 1995); Order, Lewis v. State, No. W86-73713-H(A) (Tex. Dist. Ct. Dallas Cnty. Feb. 10, 1993); *Ex parte* Lewis, No. 24,429-01 (Tex. Crim. App. Feb. 16, 1993); *Lethal Indifference*, Texas Defender Service (2002), 54–55.

67. Katie Wood, "Challenging Ghost-Written Habeas Orders," *Fulton County Daily Report* (GA), Nov. 25, 1992; Jefferson v. Zant, 431 S.E.2d 110, 112–13 (Ga. 1993); Jefferson v. Sellers, 250 F. Supp. 3d 1340, 1354–87 (N.D. Ga. 2017), *aff'd*, 941 F.3d 452 (11th Cir. 2019).

68. Cooper v. Harris, 137 S. Ct. 1455, 1465 (2017); Anderson v. Bessemer City, 470 U.S. 564.

69. Seth Freed Wessler, "Eugene Clemons May Be Ineligible for the Death Penalty. A Rigid Clinton-Era Law Could Force Him to Be Executed Anyway," ProPublica, May 28, 2021.

70. Jones v. Smith, 599 F. Supp. 1292, 1310 (S.D. Ala. 1984) (appending the Dec. 12, 1984, order of the Circuit Court of Mobile County).

71. Opinion and Order, Grayson v. State, No. CV 86–193 (Ala. Cir. Ct. Shelby County Jan. 19, 1993).

72. Bright and Keenan, "Judges and the Politics of Death"; Memorandum Opinion, State v. Singleton, No. CC-78-117 (Ala. Cir. Ct. Mobile Cnty. Dec. 26, 1986); Jones v. Davis, 906 F.2d 552 (11th Cir. 1990); Order and Opinion, State v. Singleton, No. CC-78-117 (Ala. Cir. Ct. Mobile Cnty. Nov. 27, 1990);

Order, Holladay v. State, No. CC-86-1057.60ST (Ala. Cir. Ct. Etowah Cnty. Dec. 5, 1991).

73. Hurst v. Florida, 577 U.S. 92 (2016).

74. Porter v. State, 723 So.2d 191 (Fla. 1998).

75. Michael L. Radelet, "Overriding Jury Sentencing Recommendations in Florida Capital Cases: An Update and Possible Half-Requiem," *Michigan State Law Review* (2011): 793–822, 797.

76. *The Death Penalty in Alabama: Judge Override*, Equal Justice Initiative (July 2011), 7, 14–16; Patrick Mulvaney and Katherine Chamblee, "Innocence and Override," *Yale Law Journal Forum* 126 (Aug. 8, 2016): 118–23, 120 n. 10.

77. Harris v. Alabama, 513 U.S. 504, 519–20 (1995) (Stevens, J., dissenting) (internal quotation marks and citations omitted).

78. Pub. L. No. 104-132, 110 Stat. 1214 (codified as amended in scattered sections of the U.S. Code).

79. See 28 U.S.C. § 2244(d).

80. 28 U.S.C. § 2254(d)(1).

81. Harrington v. Richter, 562 U.S. 86, 101 (2011) (quoting Yarborough v. Alvarado, 541 U.S. 652, 664 (2004)).

82. Burt v. Titlow, 571 U.S. 12, 15 (2013).

83. Shinn v. Ramirez, 142 S. Ct. 1718, 1734–38 (2022); ibid., 1749–50 (Sotomayor, J., dissenting).

84. Brown v. Davenport, 142 S. Ct. 1510 (2022); Davenport v. MacLaren, 964 F.3d 448, 467 (6th Cir. 2020).

85. Shinn v. Kayer, 141 S. Ct. 517, 524–25 (2020) (per curiam).

86. Dunn v. Reeves, 141 S. Ct. 2405, 2414–15 (2021) (per curiam) (Sotomayor, J., dissenting).

87. Ibid., 2411–12 (majority opinion).

88. Ibid., 2421 (Sotomayor, J., dissenting).

89. Bucklew v. Precythe, 139 S. Ct. 1112, 1133–34 (2019).

90. Ibid., 1146 (Sotomayor, J., dissenting).

91. Dunn v. Ray, 139 S. Ct. 661 (2019); ibid., 661 (Kagan, J., dissenting).

92. Murphy v. Collier, 139 S. Ct. 1475 (2019).

93. United States v. Higgs, 141 S. Ct. 645, 648 (2021) (Sotomayor, J., dissenting).

94. Ibid., 645–47 (Breyer, J., dissenting), 647–52 (Sotomayor, J., dissenting). See also Barr v. Purkey, 140 S. Ct. 2594, 2597–600 (2020) (Sotomayor, J.,

dissenting); Barr v. Lee, 140 S. Ct. 2590, 2591 (2020) (per curiam); Bernard v. United States, 141 S. Ct. 504, 505–6 (2020) (Sotomayor, J., dissenting); Bourgeois v. Watson, 141 S. Ct. 507, 507–9 (2020) (Sotomayor, J., dissenting).

95. Emma Schwartz, "Justice O'Connor's Wish: A Wand, Not a Gavel," *U.S. News & World Report*, Nov. 7, 2007; "Arizona Courts: The Historical Perspective," Arizona Judicial Branch; "Selection of Judges," Arizona Judicial Branch.

96. Sandra Day O'Connor, "Keynote Address," *Seattle University Law Review* 33 (2010): 559–67, 563–65; *The O'Connor Judicial Selection Plan*, Institute for the Advancement of the American Legal System.

97. A. G. Sulzberger, "Ouster of Iowa Judges Sends Signal to Bench," *New York Times*, Nov. 3, 2010.

98. Martin W. Healy, *A Guide to the Massachusetts Judicial Selection Process: The Making of a Judge*, 3rd ed. (2015), 1.

99. D.C. Code § 11–1526. See also *Judicial Performance Evaluation, District of Columbia*, Institute for the Advancement of the American Legal System.

100. Quoted in Robert W. Raven, "Does the Bar Have an Obligation to Help Ensure the Independence of the Judiciary?," *Judicature* 69, no. 2 (1985): 66–67, 115, 117–18, at 67.

101. O'Connor, "Keynote Address," 565–66.

102. Caperton v. A.T. Massey Coal Co., Inc., 556 U.S. at 884; Ward v. Village of Monroeville, 409 U.S. 57, 61–62 (1972).

103. Nevius v. Warden, 960 P.2d 805, 809–10 (Nev. 1988) (Springer, J., dissenting); Nevius v. Warden, 944 P.2d at 860 (Springer, J., dissenting).

104. Alan Johnson, "Justice French Won't Remove Herself from Case Despite Bias Allegations," *Columbus Dispatch*, Feb. 4, 2015; "Justice French: Court the 'Backstop' for GOP Legislation," *Columbus Dispatch*; State *ex rel.* Ohio Civ. Serv. Emps. Assn. v. State, 56 N.E.3d 913 (Ohio 2016).

105. Ohio v. Thompson, 23 N.E.3d 1096 (Ohio 2014); ibid. at 1158 (Pfeifer, J., joined by Lanzinger, J., concurring in part and dissenting in part); ibid. at 1159 (O'Neill, J., concurring in part and dissenting in part).

106. Levine and Cooke, "In States with Elected High Court Judges, a Harder Line on Capital Punishment."

107. Sheppard v. Maxwell, 384 U.S. 333 (1966).

108. Chambers v. Florida, 309 U.S. 227, 241 (1940).

5. The Whitewashed Jury

1. Duncan v. Louisiana, 391 U.S. 145, 156 (1968).

2. Thomas Ward Frampton, "For Cause: Rethinking Racial Exclusion and the American Jury," *Michigan Law Review* 118 no. 5 (2020): 785–839, 801–2; Foster v. Chatman, 578 U.S. 488, 492–93 (2016).

3. Trial Transcript at 2505, State v. Foster, No. 86-2218-2 (GA. Super. Ct. Floyd Cnty. May 1, 1987); Record at 551, State v. Foster, No. 86-2218-2 (Ga. Super. Ct. Floyd Cnty.) (Affidavit of Bobby Potts.)

4. Swain alleged "that there never has been a Negro on a petit jury in either a civil or criminal case in Talladega County." Swain v. Alabama, 380 U.S. 202, 223 (1965). The majority opinion cited this allegation but also said that there had not been a Black person on a jury since "about 1950." Ibid., 205, 226. The dissent stated that no Black person had served on a jury "within the memory of persons now living." Ibid., 231–32 (Goldberg, J., dissenting).

5. Ibid., 219–21.

6. Ibid., 220, 223–24.

7. Batson v. Kentucky, 476 U.S. 79, 104, 104 nn.3–4 (1986) (Marshall, J., concurring) (quoting *Dallas Morning News*, Mar. 9, 1986, p. 29, col. 1).

8. Edwards v. Thigpen, 682 F. Supp. 1374, 1375–77 (S.D. Miss. 1987), *aff'd*, Edwards v. Scroggy, 849 F.2d 204, 207–8 (5th Cir. 1988).

9. Bryan A. Stevenson and Ruth E. Friedman, "Deliberate Indifference: Judicial Tolerance of Racial Bias in Criminal Justice," *Washington and Lee Law Review* 51 (1994): 509–27, 520, 523 (citing Transcript of Postconviction Rec., Jefferson v State, CC-8-77 (Chambers County Cir. Ct. Jan. 25, 1989), 39–56, *rev'd on other grounds*, CR 92-0158 (Ala. Crim. App. 1994).

10. Harris v. Texas, 467 U.S. 1261, 1264 (1984) (Marshall, J., dissenting).

11. McCray v. New York, 461 U.S. 961, 964–65 (1983) (Marshall, J., dissenting).

12. Batson v. Kentucky, 476 U.S. at 83, 92–93, 99 (1986).

13. Ibid., 96–98.

14. Ibid., 105–6 (Marshall, J., concurring).

15. Foster v. Chatman, 578 U.S. 488 (2016), Joint Appendix at 17–20.

16. Exhibits 1, 2, 1A, and 2A admitted at hearing, Sept. 10–11, 1990, Transcript at 176–77, State v. Brooks, Indictments Nos. 3888, 54606, Super. Ct. Muscogee Cnty., Ga.; *Chattahoochee Judicial District: Buckle of the Death Belt: The Death Penalty in Microcosm*, Death Penalty Information Center (Jan. 1, 1991).

17. Foster v. Chatman, 578 U.S. 488, Joint Appendix at 42, 57.

18. Ibid., 45–47.

19. Foster v. Chatman, 578 U.S. at 507–8, Joint Appendix at 55–57.

20. Foster v. Chatman, 578 U.S. at 505–6, Joint Appendix at 58.

21. Bobby Ross Jr., "Why a Georgia Church Elder Is Making News at U.S. Supreme Court," *Christian Chronicle*, Nov. 18, 2015; Stephanie Mencimer, "Black Juror: Prosecutors Treated Me 'Like I Was a Criminal,'" *Mother Jones*, Nov. 5, 2015.

22. Foster v. Chatman, 578 U.S. 488, Joint Appendix at 62–63.

23. Ibid., 78–113; Foster v. Chatman, 578 U.S. at 508.

24. Foster v. State, 374 S.E.2d 188, 191–92 (Ga. 1988).

25. Foster v. Chatman, 578 U.S. at 493–95, 511.

26. Ibid., Joint Appendix at 195.

27. Foster v. Chatman, 578 U.S. at 502, 507–12.

28. Ibid., 504–6.

29. Ibid., 514.

30. R. Robin McDonald, "'I Would Avoid Blacks on This Jury': Will a Secret Memo See a Murder Case Overturned?," *Daily Report*, Aug. 11, 2017; R. Robin McDonald, "Brunswick DA Tosses Chua Murder Conviction in Wake of Secret Memo," *Daily Report*, Sept. 19, 2017.

31. Thomas Ward Frampton, "The Jim Crow Jury," *Vanderbilt Law Review* 71 (2018): 1593–654, 1601–5.

32. Strauder v. West Virginia, 100 U.S. 303, 310 (1879); Virginia v. Rives, 100 U.S. 313 (1879).

33. Benno C. Schmidt Jr., "Juries, Jurisdiction, and Race Discrimination: The Lost Promise of *Strauder v. West Virginia*," *Texas Law Review* 61 (1983): 1401–99, 1406, 1414, 1432–33; James Forman Jr., "Juries and Race in the Nineteenth Century," *Yale Law Journal* 113 (2004): 895–938, 915–34.

34. Morton Stavis, "A Century of Struggle for Black Enfranchisement in Mississippi: From the Civil War to the Congressional Challenge of 1965—and Beyond," *Mississippi Law Journal* 57 (1987): 591–676, 604–7, 607 n.57 (1987).

35. Williams v. Mississippi, 170 U.S. 213, 217 n.1, 219, 225 (1898); Douglas L. Colbert, "Challenging the Challenge: Thirteenth Amendment as a Prohibition Against the Racial Use of Peremptory Challenges," *Cornell Law Review* 76 (1990): 1–128, 76–77.

36. Colbert, "Challenging the Challenge," 78 (citing Eric Foner, *Recon-*

struction: America's Unfinished Revolution 1863–1877 (New York: Harper & Row, 1988), 595).

37. Franklin v. South Carolina, 218 U.S. 161, 168 (1910).

38. Castaneda v. Partida, 430 U.S. 482, 484, 491, 497 (1977); Peter W. Sperlich and Martin Jaspovice, "Grand Juries, Grand Jurors and the Constitution," *Hastings Constitutional Law Quarterly* 1 (1974): 63–95, 68; Charles R. DiSalvo, "The Key-Man System for Composing Jury Lists in West Virginia—the Story of Abuse, the Case for Reform," *West Virginia Law Review* 87 (1985): 219–69, 252–54; Norris v. Alabama, 294 U.S. 587, 588, 590 (1935); Carter v. Jury Commission of Greene County, 396 U.S. 320, 331, 335–37 (1970); Colbert, "Challenging the Challenge," 89 (citing Clarence Callendar, *The Selection of Jurors—A Comparative Study of the Methods of Selection and the Personnel of Juries in Philadelphia and Other Cities* (1942)), 10; Frampton, "For Cause," 809.

39. People v. Hines, 86 P.2d 92, 93 (Ca. 1939).

40. Norris v. Alabama, 294 U.S. at 593–94, 597–99.

41. Akins v. Texas, 325 U.S. 398, 399–407 (1945).

42. Avery v. Georgia, 345 U.S. 559, 561 (1953); Williams v. Georgia, 349 U.S. 375 (1955).

43. Castaneda v. Partida, 430 U.S. 482 (equal protection clause); Duren v. Missouri, 439 U.S. 357 (1979) (fair cross-section requirement of the Sixth Amendment); Turner v. Fouche, 396 U.S. 346, 567 (1970).

44. Taylor v Louisiana, 419 U.S. 522, 525 (1975). The Court had previously upheld a system in which women served only if they volunteered. Hoyt v. Florida, 368 U.S. 57 (1961).

45. Castaneda v. Partida, 430 U.S. at 495–96 (1977).

46. Paula L. Hannaford-Agor, "Systematic Negligence in Jury Operations: Why the Definition of Systematic Exclusion in Fair Cross Section Claims Must Be Expanded," *Drake Law Review* 59 (2011): 761–98, 767–68.

47. State v. Plain, 898 N.W.2d 801, 825 (Iowa 2017); *Illegal Racial Discrimination in Jury Selection: A Continuing Legacy*, Equal Justice Initiative (2010), 6, 35–36.

48. Amadeo v. Zant, 486 U.S. 214 (1988); Horton v. Zant, 941 F.2d 1449, 1458 (11th Cir. 1991).

49. 28 U.S.C. §§ 1861–69.

50. Hiroshi Fukurai and Edgar W. Butler, "Sources of Racial Disenfranchisement in the Jury and Jury Selection System," *National Black Law Journal* 13 (1994): 238–75.

51. Ibid., 250.

52. James M. Binnall, "Summonsing Criminal Desistance: Convicted Felons' Perspectives on Jury Service," *Law & Social Inquiry* 43 (2018): 4–27, 4; Brian C. Kalt, "The Exclusion of Felons from Jury Service," *American University Law Review* 53 (2003): 65–190, 67.

53. Smith v. Berghuis, 543 F.3d 326, 331, 340–41 (6th Cir. 2008), *rev'd*, 559 U.S. 314 (2010).

54. People v. Smith, 615 N.W.2d 1, 3 (Mich. 2000); Berghuis v. Smith, 559 U.S. 314 (2010).

55. Ballew v. Georgia, 435 U.S. 223, 236–37 (1978); Shari Seidman Diamond et al., "Achieving Diversity on the Jury: Jury Size and the Peremptory Challenge," *Journal of Empirical Legal Studies* 6, no. 3 (2009): 425–49, 442; Michael J. Saks and Mollie Weighner Marti, "A Meta-analysis of the Effects of Jury Size," *Law and Human Behavior* 21, no. 5 (1997): 451–67, 457.

56. State v. Dorsey, 74 So.3d 603, 635 (La. 2011).

57. Frampton, "For Cause," 794, 834; Ronald F. Wright et al., "The Jury Sunshine Project: Jury Selection Data as a Political Issue," *University of Illinois Law Review* (2018): 1407–42, 1426.

58. Aliza Plener Cover, "The Eighth Amendment's Lost Jurors: Death Qualification and Evolving Standards of Decency," *Indiana Law Journal* 92, no. 1 (2016): 113–56, 121.

59. Lockhart v. McCree, 476 U.S. 162, 173 (1986).

60. Cover, "The Eighth Amendment's Lost Jurors," 137.

61. *Illegal Racial Discrimination in Jury Selection*, Equal Justice Initiative, 6, 31; McGahee v. Alabama Department of Corrections, 560 F.3d 1252, 1257–59 (11th Cir. 2009).

62. McGahee v. Alabama Department of Corrections, 560 F.3d at 1266; Lee v. Commissioner, 726 F.3d 1172, 1224 (11th Cir. 2013).

63. Allen v. Hardy, 478 U.S. 255 (1986); ibid., 263–65 (Marshall, J., dissenting). See also Griffith v. Kentucky, 479 U.S. 314, 328 (1987) (holding that *Batson* applied to cases on direct review and those not yet final when *Batson* was decided).

64. Hernandez v. New York, 500 U.S. 352, 375 (1991) (O'Connor, J., concurring).

65. Purkett v. Elem, 514 U.S. 765, 766 (1995); Elem v. Purkett, 25 F.3d 679 (8th Cir. 1994).

66. Purkett v. Elem, 514 U.S. at 768–69; ibid., 775, 777–78 (Stevens, J., dissenting).

67. State v. Dorsey, 74 So.3d 603, 617–22 (La. 2011); State v. Duncan, 802 So.2d 533, 550–51 (La. 2001).

68. Ratliff v. State, 199 S.W.3d 79, 83 (Ark. 2004) (citing Jackson v. State, 954 S.W.2d 894, 895 (Ark. 1997)).

69. Norm Pattis, "Jury Selection Strategies Are Far from Color Blind," *Connecticut Law Tribune*, Nov. 3, 2015.

70. State v. Saintcalle, 309 P.3d 326, 371 (Wash. 2013) (Chambers, J., dissenting).

71. Mason v. United States, 170 A.3d 182, 185–87 (D.C. 2017).

72. See, e.g., United States v. Jones, 600 F.3d 985, 991 (8th Cir. 2010) (upholding as a race-neutral reason the belief by two prospective jurors that African Americans are treated unfairly in the criminal justice system).

73. People v. Bryant, 40 Cal. App. 5th 525, 546 (2019) (Humes, J., concurring).

74. Jeffrey Bellin and Junichi P. Semitsu, "Widening Batson's Net to Ensnare More Than the Unapologetically Bigoted or Painfully Unimaginative Attorney," *Cornell Law Review* 96 (2011): 1075–130, 1079.

75. David C. Baldus et al., "Statistical Proof of Racial Discrimination in the Use of Peremptory Challenges: The Impact and Promise of the *Miller-El* Line of Cases As Reflected in the Experience of One Philadelphia Capital Case," *Iowa Law Review* 97 (2012): 1425–65, 1446–65; Samantha Melamed, "Sentenced to Death 3 Times in 1989, Philly Exoneree Harold Wilson Dies at 61," *Philadelphia Inquirer*, May 29, 2019.

76. Wilson v. Beard, 426 F.3d 653, 670 (3d Cir. 2005); Post Conviction Relief Act Hearing at 2–3, Commonwealth v. Spence, No. 3311 (C.P. Phila. March 22, 2004), cited in Commonwealth v. Cook, 952 A.2d 594, 643 (Pa. 2008) (Saylor, J., dissenting); Commonwealth v. Basemore, Nos. 1762–65, 2001 WL 36125302 (C.P. Phila. Dec. 19, 2001), cited in Commonwealth v. Cook, 952 A.2d at 642–43 (Saylor, J., dissenting).

77. Commonwealth v. Cook, 952 A.2d at 585–604; Commonwealth v. Lark, 746 A.2d 585, 589–90 (Pa. 2000); Commonwealth v. Rollins, 738 A.2d 435, 433 n.10 (1999).

78. State v. Randall, 671 N.E.2d 60, 65–66 (Ill. App. Ct. 1996).

79. Nancy S. Marder, "Justice Stevens, the Peremptory Challenge, and the Jury," *Fordham Law Review* 74, no. 4 (2006): 1683–730, 1707 n.165; "Gold Earrings and Sunglasses," *Dallas Morning News*, Aug. 23, 2005.

80. Order Granting Motions for Appropriate Relief at 73–74, ¶¶ 68–72,

State v. Golphin, No. 97 CRS 42314-15 (N.C. Super. Ct. Cumberland Co. Dec. 13, 2012), *vacated sub nom.* State v. Augustine, 780 S.E.2d 552 (N.C. 2015).

81. Elisabeth Semel et al., *Whitewashing the Jury Box: How California Perpetuates the Discriminatory Exclusion of Black and Latinx Jurors*, Berkeley Law Death Penalty Clinic (June 2020), 49–50.

82. Davis v. Fisk Electric Co., 268 S.W.3d 508, 525 (Tex. 2008).

83. Order Granting Motions for Appropriate Relief at 153, ¶ 254, State v. Golphin, No. 97 CRS 42314–15 (N.C. Superior Ct. Cumberland Co. Dec. 13, 2012), *vacated sub nom.* State v. Augustine, 780 S.E.2d 552 (N.C. 2015); Catherine M. Grosso and Barbara O'Brien, "A Stubborn Legacy: The Overwhelming Importance of Race in Jury Selection in 173 Post-*Batson* North Carolina Capital Trials," *Iowa Law Review* 97 (2012): 1531–60.

84. Frampton, "The Jim Crow Jury," 1624–25; Wright et al., "The Jury Sunshine Project," 24–30; *Illegal Racial Discrimination in Jury Selection*, Equal Justice Initiative, 14.

85. State v. Robinson, 846 S.E.2d 711, 716 (N.C. 2020); People v. Rhoades, 453 P.3d 89, 139 (2019) (Liu, J., dissenting); Chamberlin v. Fisher, 885 F.3d 832, 846 (2018) (Costa, J., dissenting).

86. *Illegal Racial Discrimination in Jury Selection*, Equal Justice Initiative, 4.

87. State v. Saintcalle, 309 P.3d at 329; Tennyson v. State, No. PD-0304-18, 2018 WL 6332331, at *7 (Tex. Crim. App. Dec. 5, 2018) (Alcala, J., dissenting from denial of petition for review).

88. Rice v. Collins, 546 U.S. 333, 343 (2006) (Breyer, J., concurring) (citing Batson v. Kentucky, 476 U.S. 79, 106 (1986) (Marshall, J., concurring) and Miller-El v. Dretke, 545 U.S. 231, 267–68 (2005) (Breyer, J., concurring)); Davis v. Fisk Electric Co., 268 S.W.3d at 529 (Brister, J., concurring).

89. Andrews v. Shulsen, 485 U.S. 919, 920, 922 (1988) (Marshall, J., dissenting from denial of certiorari).

90. Peña–Rodriguez v. Colorado, 137 S. Ct. 855, 862, 869 (2017).

91. Bennett v. Stirling, 842 F.3d 319, 322 (4th Cir. 2016); Bennett v. Stirling, 170 F. Supp. 3d 851, 861–72 (D.S.C. 2016), *aff'd*, 842 F.3d 319. The court of appeals upheld the district court's ruling that the closing argument was improper and did not address the ruling regarding the juror.

92. Bill Rankin, "Supreme Court Declines to Hear 'Racist Juror' Appeal in Georgia Case," *Atlanta Journal-Constitution*, Mar. 18, 2019.

93. Tharpe v. Warden, 898 F.3d 1342, 1345–46 (11th Cir. 2018); Tharpe v. Ford, 139 S. Ct. 911, 913 (2019) (statement of Sotomayor, J., regarding the

denial of certiorari); Kate Brumback, "Georgia Inmate Who Came Close to Execution in 2017 Dies," AP News (Jan. 26, 2020).

94. Order Denying Third Application for Post-Conviction Relief and Related Motions for Discovery and Evidentiary Hearing, Jones v. State, No. PCD-2017-1313, at 3–4 (Okla. Crim. App. Sept. 28, 2018).

95. Peggy C. Davis, "Law as Microaggression," *Yale Law Journal* 98, no. 8 (1989): 1559–78, 1571; Mikah K. Thompson, "Bias on Trial: Toward an Open Discussion of Racial Stereotypes in the Courtroom, *Michigan State Law Review*, no. 5 (2018): 1243–308.

96. Turner v. Murray, 476 U.S. 28, 35–37 (1976); ibid., 43 (Brennan, J., concurring in part and dissenting in part).

97. State v. Saintcalle, 309 P.3d at 337 (citing *Illegal Racial Discrimination in Jury Selection*, Equal Justice Initiative, 6, 40–41); Samuel R. Sommers, "On Racial Diversity and Group Decision Making: Identifying Multiple Effects of Racial Composition on Jury Deliberations," *Journal of Personality and Social Psychology* 90, no. 4 (2006): 597–612, 597; Georgia v. McCollum, 505 U.S. 42, 68–69 (1992) (O'Connor, J., dissenting).

98. State v. Saintcalle, 309 P.3d at 337.

99. City of Seattle v. Erickson, 398 P.3d 1124, 1131 (Wash. 2017).

100. Wash. Ct. R., Gen. R. 37.

101. State v. Jefferson, 429 P.3d 467, 480 (Wash. 2018).

102. Batson v. Kentucky, 476 U.S. at 105–9 (Marshall, J., concurring); Rice v. Collins, 546 U.S. at 343 (Breyer, J., concurring) (citing Batson v. Kentucky, 476 U.S. 79, 106 (1986) (Marshall, J., concurring) and Miller-El v. Dretke, 545 U.S. 231, 267–68 (2005) (Breyer, J., concurring)); State v. Veal, 930 N.W.2d 319, 340–41 (Iowa 2019) (Wiggins, J., concurring in part and dissenting in part); State v. Holmes, 221 A.3d 407, 439–45 (Conn. 2019) (Mullins, J., concurring); Davis v. Fisk Electric Co., 268 S.W.3d at 529–31 (Brister, J., concurring).

103. State v. Saintcalle, 309 P.3d at 370 (González, J., concurring).

104. Michael O. Finkelstein and Bruce Levin, "Clear Choices and Guesswork in Peremptory Challenges in Federal Criminal Trials," *Journal of Royal Statistical Society, Series A* 160, no. 2 (1997): 275–88, 284–85; David C. Baldus et al., "The Use of Peremptory Challenges in Capital Murder Trials: A Legal and Empirical Analysis," *University of Pennsylvania Journal of Constitutional Law* 3 (2001): 3–170, 130; Paula L. Hannaford-Agor and Nicole L. Waters, *Examining Voir Dire in California*, Administrative Office of the Courts, Judicial Council of California (Aug. 2004), 45.

6. Courts of Profit

1. Shaila Dewan, "A Surreptitious Courtroom Video Prompts Changes in a Georgia Town," *New York Times*, Sept. 4, 2015.

2. Complaint, Edwards v. Red Hills Cmty. Prob., LLC, No. 1:15-CV-67 (M.D. Ga. Apr. 4, 2015); Carrie Teegardin, "Ticket Torment," *Atlanta Journal-Constitution*, Nov. 22, 2014.

3. Third Amended Complaint, Egana v. Blair's Bail Bonds, Inc., No. 2:17-cv-5899 (E.D. La. Dec. 12, 2018); Jessica Silver-Greenberg and Shaila Dewan, "When Bail Feels Less Like Freedom, More Like Extortion," *New York Times*, Mar. 31, 2018.

4. Williams v. Illinois, 399 U.S. 235 (1970).

5. Tate v. Short, 401 U.S. 395, 398 (1971).

6. Bearden v. Georgia, 461 U.S. 660 (1983).

7. Argersinger v. Hamlin, 407 U.S. 25 (1972).

8. *Profiting from Probation: America's "Offender-Funded" Probation Industry*, Human Rights Watch (Feb. 2014), 13 n.4.

9. Thomas Harvey et al., *ArchCity Defenders: Municipal Courts White Paper* (2014), 6.

10. *Investigation of the Ferguson Police Department*, Civil Rights Division, U.S. Department of Justice (2015), 14.

11. Harvey et al., *ArchCity Defenders*, 12.

12. *Public Safety – Municipal Courts*, Better Together (Oct. 2014), 7.

13. Ibid., 8.

14. See "Policing and Profit," *Harvard Law Review* 128, no. 6 (Apr. 2015): 1723–46.

15. Mike Maciag, "Addicted to Fines," *Governing*, Aug. 19, 2019.

16. William Glaberson, "In Tiny Courts of N.Y., Abuses of Law and Power," *New York Times*, Sept. 25, 2006; *Fines and Fees and Jail Time in New York Town and Village Justice Courts: The Unseen Violation of Constitutional and State Law*, The Fund for Modern Courts (Apr. 3, 2019), 1–2.

17. *Report of the Supreme Court Committee on Municipal Court Operations, Fines, and Fees*, New Jersey Courts (June 2018), 2; Kala Kachmar, "Former Monmouth County Municipal Judge Admits Ticket-Fixing for Revenue," *Asbury Park Press*, Feb. 2, 2018.

18. *2018 Mayor's Courts Summary*, Supreme Court of Ohio (Aug. 2019), 1; "Ohio's Mayor's Courts, Big Business," *Columbus Dispatch*, July 22, 2012; *The*

Outskirts of Hope: How Ohio's Debtors' Prisons Are Ruining Lives and Costing Communities, ACLU of Ohio (Apr. 2013).

19. "Collection of Court Costs & Fines in Adult Trial Courts," Supreme Court of Ohio, rev. Mar. 2022 (emphasis in original).

20. Al Baker and Ray Rivera, "Secret Tape Has Police Pressing Ticket Quotas," *New York Times*, Sept. 9, 2010; Marina Carver, "NYPD Officers Say They Had Stop-and-Frisk Quotas," CNN, Mar. 26, 2013; Joel Rubin and Catherine Saillant, "L.A. Approves $6-Million Settlement over Alleged Traffic Ticket Quotas," *Los Angeles Times*, Dec. 10, 2013; Randy Travis, "Douglasville Cops Offered BBQ If They Wrote Enough Traffic Tickets," Fox 5 Atlanta, Mar. 10, 2020.

21. *Investigation of the Ferguson Police Department*, Civil Rights Division, 11.

22. Ibid., 62, 68–69.

23. *Overcoming the Challenges and Creating a Regional Approach to Policing in St. Louis City and County*, Police Executive Research Forum (Apr. 30, 2015), 40–44.

24. Patrick Smith, "What Happens When Suburban Police Departments Don't Have Enough Money?," NPR, Jan. 22, 2018.

25. Casey Toner and Jared Rutecki, "113 Suburban Cop Shootings, Zero Discipline," WBEZ, Jan. 8, 2018.

26. Rebecca Goldstein, Michael W. Sances, and Hye Young You, "Exploitative Revenues, Law Enforcement, and the Quality of Government Service," *Urban Affairs Review* 56, no. 1 (2020): 5–31.

27. *Overcoming the Challenges*, Police Executive Research Forum, 41.

28. Andrea Bopp Stark and Geoffrey Walsh, *Clearing the Path to a New Beginning: A Guide to Discharging Criminal Justice Debt in Bankruptcy*, National Consumer Law Center (Oct. 2020), 7–8.

29. Joseph Shapiro, "As Court Fees Rise, the Poor Are Paying the Price," NPR, May 19, 2014; "State-By-State Court Fees," NPR, May 19, 2014.

30. North Carolina: Matthew Menendez et al., *The Steep Costs of Criminal Justice Fees and Fines: A Fiscal Analysis of Three States and Ten Counties*, Brennan Center for Justice (Nov. 21, 2019), 6. Georgia: *Final Report of the Senate Study Committee on Court Surcharges and Additional Fines*, [Georgia] Senate Research Office (2006), 4–5. Washington: Shapiro, "As Court Fees Rise, the Poor Are Paying the Price." Massachusetts: Wendy Sawyer, *Punishing Poverty: The High Cost of Probation Fees in Massachusetts*, Prison Policy Initiative (Dec. 8, 2016).

31. Alexes Harris et al., *Monetary Sanctions in the Criminal Justice System: A Review of Law and Policy in California, Georgia, Illinois, Minnesota, Missouri, New*

York, North Carolina, Texas, and Washington, Laura and John Arnold Foundation (Apr. 2017), 28–30, 53–54; Juliette Rihl, "A $25 Fine Can Wind Up Costing More Than $150. So Where Does the Rest of the Money Go?," PublicSource, Feb. 13, 2020; Menendez et al., *The Steep Costs of Criminal Justice Fees and Fines*, 6.

32. "Over the Years, Court Fines, Fees Have Replaced General Revenue Funds," KGOU, Feb. 9, 2015.

33. Complaint, Harrison v. Columbus, Ga., No. 4:16-cv-00329 (M.D. Ga. Oct. 5, 2016); Jessica Pishko, "She Didn't Want Her Boyfriend to Go to Jail. So They Sent Her to Jail Instead," *Cosmopolitan*, Apr. 13, 2017.

34. *New York's Ferguson Problem*, No Price on Justice (2020), 17.

35. R. Robin McDonald, "Grady County Is Asked to Repay Thousands in Illegal Court Fees," *Daily Report*, Aug. 9, 2013.

36. Complaint, *In re* Anderson, No. 15-2380-AS (Cir. Ct. Macomb Cnty. July 9, 2015); Shapiro, "As Court Fees Rise, the Poor Are Paying the Price"; Adam Ganucheau, "Judge Who Demanded Blood from Defendants Censured After Suspension," AL.com, Jan. 21, 2016.

37. Joseph Shapiro, "Jail Time for Unpaid Court Fines and Fees Can Create Cycle of Poverty," NPR, Feb. 9, 2015.

38. *The Outskirts of Hope*, ACLU of Ohio, 8–9, 16.

39. United States v. Bajakajian, 524 U.S. 321, 355 (Kennedy, J., dissenting).

40. *Fines, Fees, and Bail: Payments in the Criminal Justice System That Disproportionately Impact the Poor*, Council of Economic Advisers (Dec. 2015), 1.

41. Shapiro, "As Court Fees Rise, the Poor Are Paying the Price."

42. Anna Wolfe and Michelle Liu, "Want Out of Jail? First You Have to Take a Fast-Food Job," *Mississippi Today*, Jan. 9, 2020.

43. Carlos Campos, "Poverty Keeps Woman Jailed, Lawsuit Says," *Atlanta Journal-Constitution*, Sept. 19, 2006; Jim Tharpe, "Deal Frees 'Debtor Prison' Woman," *Atlanta Journal-Constitution*, Sept. 20, 2006.

44. *In Trouble: How the Promise of Diversion Clashes with the Reality of Poverty, Addiction, and Structural Racism in Alabama's Justice System*, Alabama Appleseed Center for Law & Justice (2020), 5.

45. Michael Kiefer, "Maricopa County Attorney Sued over Marijuana Diversion Program," *Arizona Republic*, Aug. 24, 2018.

46. Rebecca Burns, "Diversion Programs Say They Offer a Path away from Court, but Critics Say the Tolls Are Hefty," ProPublica, Nov. 13, 2018.

47. Alexes Harris, *A Pound of Flesh: Monetary Sanctions as Punishment for the Poor* (New York: Russell Sage Foundation, 2016), 3.

48. Gracie Bonds Staples, "How a $900 Court Fine Forced a Woman Out of Her Home," *Atlanta Journal-Constitution*, Apr. 3, 2020.

49. Mario Salas and Angela Ciolfi, *Driven by Dollars: A State-by-State Analysis of Driver's License Suspension Laws for Failure to Pay Court Debt*, Legal Aid Justice Center (Fall 2017), 1, 8–9; Meghan Keneally, "'It's Not America': 11 Million Go Without a License Because of Unpaid Fines," ABC News, Oct. 25, 2019.

50. Carrie Teegardin, "Bainbridge Settles Private Probation Suit Filed by Southern Center," *Atlanta Journal-Constitution*, Sept. 21, 2015; Kate Brumback, "Columbus Ends Fees for People Who Drop Abuse Allegations," Georgia Public Broadcasting, Oct. 13, 2017.

51. Joanna Weiss and Lisa Foster, "San Francisco's Justice System Gets a Little More Just," *Washington Post*, June 13, 2018; Jackie Botts, "Los Angeles County Eliminates Criminal Fees. Will California Follow?," CalMatters, Feb. 19, 2020; Andrew Sheeler, "New California Law Strikes Criminal Court Fees Charged by Sheriffs, Police," *Sacramento Bee*, Sept. 22, 2020; Erin B. Logan, "Courts in Most States Charge Juveniles to Exist Inside the Justice System. This Movement Wants to Change That," *Washington Post*, Aug. 10, 2018.

52. Thomas v. Haslam, 329 F. Supp. 3d 475 (M.D. Tenn. 2018); Thomas v. Lee, 776 Fed. Appx. 910 (6th Cir. 2019); Stinnie v. Holcomb, 355 F. Supp. 3d 514 (W.D. Va. 2018); Fowler v. Johnson, 2017 WL 6379676 (E.D. Mich. Dec. 14, 2017).

53. Yolanda Jones, "Shelby County DA's Office Won't Prosecute Many Revoked Driver's License Cases," *Daily Memphian*, Oct. 20, 2018; Megan Crepeau, "Cook County to Stop Prosecuting Some Traffic Offenses Because It Lacks Resources, Foxx's Office Says," *Chicago Tribune*, June 15, 2017.

54. "Maps," Free to Drive.

55. Michigan: "State Supreme Court Rules Curb 'Pay-or-Stay' Sentences," *Detroit News*, May 25, 2016; Miss. Code Ann. § 99-19-20 (2). Idaho: *Re* Petition for Writ of Prohibition, 489 P.3d 820 (Idaho 2021).

56. Colo. Rev. Stat. § 18-1.3-702 (2)-(5); "Fact Sheet: HB 1311—a Bill to End Debtors' Prisons in Colorado," ACLU of Colorado, Apr. 6, 2016; Colo. HB 16-1311; *Justice Derailed: A Case Study of Abusive and Unconstitutional Practices in Colorado City Courts*, ACLU of Colorado (Oct. 5, 2017), 9.

57. "State-by-State Court Fees," NPR; *Profiting from Probation*, Human Rights Watch, 2–3; Sarah Stillman, "Get Out of Jail, Inc.," *New Yorker*, June 23, 2014.

58. *Profiting from Probation*, Human Rights Watch, 39, 57–58.

59. Complaint, Edwards v. Red Hills Cmty. Prob., LLC, No. 1:15-CV-67; Carrie Teegardin, "Lives Upended as Judges Push Legal Limits," *Atlanta Journal-Constitution*, May 2, 2015; Teegardin, "Bainbridge Settles Private Probation Suit Filed by Southern Center."

60. *Profiting from Probation*, Human Rights Watch, 52.

61. "State-by-State Court Fees," NPR; *"Set Up to Fail": The Impact of Offender-Funded Private Probation on the Poor*, Human Rights Watch (Feb. 2018).

62. *Profiting from Probation*, Human Rights Watch, 37, 37 n.89.

63. Carrie Teegardin, "Council to Call for Probation Reforms," *Atlanta Journal-Constitution*, Jan. 22, 2015; *Profiting from Probation*, Human Rights Watch, 4.

64. Rhonda Cook, "Probation Company to Pay Georgians Forced to Take Drug Tests," *Atlanta Journal-Constitution*, Aug. 22, 2017.

65. *Profiting from Probation*, Human Rights Watch, 34–35.

66. Tony Messenger, "Warren County Woman Highlights Private Probation Abuses in Missouri," *St. Louis Post-Dispatch*, Feb. 14, 2020.

67. Nazish Dholakia, "The Steep Price of Probation in Missouri," Human Rights Watch, Feb. 20, 2018.

68. *"Set Up to Fail,"* Human Rights Watch, 72. Providence Community Corrections agreed in 2018 to a settlement prohibiting the incarceration of individuals for failure to pay court fines and fees without a determination of the individual's ability to pay. Order Granting Final Approval of Class Settlement and Plan of Allocation, Granting Motions for Attorney's Fees, Granting Permanent Injunction, and Dismissing Case, Rodriguez v. Providence Cmty. Corr., No. 3:15-cv-01048 (M.D. Tenn. July 5, 2018).

69. Stillman, "Get Out of Jail, Inc."

70. Whitworth v. State, 622 S.E.2d 21 (Ga. Ct. App. 2005); Terry Carter, "Privatized Probation Becomes a Spiral of Added Fees and Jail Time," *ABA Journal*, Oct. 1, 2014.

71. Stillman, "Get Out of Jail, Inc."

72. Walker v. City of Calhoun, 2016 WL 361612 (N.D. Ga. Jan. 28, 2016).

73. Bearden v. Georgia, 461 U.S. 660, 672–73 (1983).

74. People *ex rel.* Lobell v. McDonnell, 71 N.E.2d 423, 425 (N.Y. 1947).

75. Wendy Sawyer and Peter Wagner, *Mass Incarceration: The Whole Pie 2020*, Prison Policy Initiative (Mar. 24, 2020).

76. Letter to New York City Council Member Rory Lancman, City of New York Independent Budget Office, May 16, 2017; Ron Kuby, "No Back-

ing Down on Bail Now: The Law Remedies an Injustice That Persisted for Decades," *New York Daily News*, Jan. 28, 2020; *Broken Rules: How Pennsylvania Courts Use Cash Bail to Incarcerate People Before Trial*, ACLU of Pennsylvania (Dec. 2021), 8.

77. Silver-Greenberg and Dewan, "When Bail Feels Less Like Freedom."

78. *Selling Off Our Freedom: How Insurance Companies Have Taken Over Our Bail System*, Color of Change and ACLU Campaign for Smart Justice (May 2017), 7, 10.

79. Adam Liptak, "Illegal Globally, Bail for Profit Remains in U.S.," *New York Times*, Jan. 29, 2008.

80. Curtis Waltman, "Five Heartbreaking Examples of Why the Bail Bonds Industry Is Badly in Need of Reform," *MuckRock*, July 31, 2017.

81. *The Devil in the Details: Bail Bond Contracts in California*, UCLA School of Law Criminal Justice Reform Clinic (May 2017), 5.

82. Silver-Greenberg and Dewan, "When Bail Feels Less Like Freedom."

83. Amy E. Lerman, Ariel Lewis Green, and Patricio Dominguez, "Pleading for Justice: Bullpen Therapy, Pre-Trial Detention, and Plea Bargains in American Courts," *Crime & Delinquency* 68, no. 2 (2022): 159–82, 168–71.

84. Will Dobbie, Jacob Goldin, and Crystal S. Yang, "The Effects of Pretrial Detention on Conviction, Future Crime, and Employment: Evidence from Randomly Assigned Judges," *American Economic Review* 108, no. 2 (2018): 201–40, 204, 225; see also Lerman et al., "Pleading for Justice," 173.

85. Mary T. Phillips, *A Decade of Bail Research in New York City*, New York City Criminal Justice Agency (Aug. 2012), 117; Nick Petersen, "Do Detainees Plead Guilty Faster? A Survival Analysis of Pretrial Detention and the Timing of Guilty Pleas," *Criminal Justice Policy Review* 31, no. 7 (2020): 1015–35.

86. Pennsylvania: Tina L. Freiburger, Catherine D. Marcum, and Mari Pierce, "The Impact of Race on the Pretrial Decision," *American Journal of Criminal Justice* 35, nos. 1–2 (June 2010): 76–86. Kentucky: Brian P. Schaefer and Tom Hughes, "Examining Judicial Pretrial Release Decisions: The Influence of Risk Assessments and Race," *Criminology, Criminal Justice, Law & Society* 20, no. 2 (2019): 47–58. Miami and Philadelphia: David Arnold, Will Dobbie, and Crystal S. Yang, "Racial Bias in Bail Decisions," *Quarterly Journal of Economics* 133, no. 4 (Nov. 2018): 1885–932. Three federal districts: Cassia Spohn, "Race, Sex, and Pretrial Detention in Federal Court: Indirect Effects and Cumulative Disadvantage," *University of Kansas Law Review* 57, no. 4 (May 2009): 879–901. New York City: Besiki L. Kutateladze et al., "Cumulative Disadvantage: Examining Racial and Ethnic Disparity in Prosecution and Sentencing," *Criminology* 52, no. 3 (2014): 514–51.

87. Oren M. Gur, Michael Hollander, and Pauline Alvarado, *Prosecutor-Led Bail Reform: Year One*, [Philadelphia] District Attorney's Office (Feb. 2019).

88. *Washington, DC Pretrial Facts and Figures*, Pretrial Services Agency for the District of Columbia (Mar. 2018).

89. New Jersey: *Jan. 1–Dec. 31 2018 Criminal Justice Reform Report to the Governor and the Legislature*, New Jersey Courts (Apr. 2019). New York: Jesse McKinley and Vivian Wang, "New York State Budget Deal Brings Congestion Pricing, Plastic Bag Ban and Mansion Tax," *New York Times*, Mar. 31, 2019. Illinois: Cheryl Corley, "Illinois Becomes 1st State to Eliminate Cash Bail," NPR, Feb. 22, 2021.

90. *Selling Off Our Freedom*, Color of Change and ACLU Campaign for Smart Justice, 10.

91. ODonnell v. Harris County, 892 F.3d 147, 153–54 (5th Cir. 2018); ODonnell v. Harris County, 251 F. Supp. 3d 1052, 1130 (S.D. Texas 2017).

92. Brandon L. Garrett et al., *Monitoring Pretrial Reform in Harris County: Fourth Report of the Court-Appointed Monitor* (Apr. 18, 2022), vii.

93. Brangan v. Commonwealth, 80 N.E.3d 949 (Mass. 2017); *In re* Humphrey, 482 P.3d 1008 (Cal. 2021).

94. Joshua Page and Christine S. Scott-Hayward, "Bail and Pretrial Justice in the United States: A Field of Possibility," *Annual Review of Criminology* 5 (2022): 91–113, 105; Collette Richards and Drew Griffin, "States Are Trying to Change a System That Keeps Poor People in Jail. The Bail Industry Is Blocking Them," CNN, Aug. 30, 2019.

95. Alaska: James Brooks, "Gov. Dunleavy Signs Legislation to Repeal, Replace the Crime-Reform Measure SB 91," *Anchorage Daily News*, July 8, 2019. New York: "A Sad Last Gasp Against Criminal Justice Reform," *New York Times* (editorial), Nov. 17, 2019; Taryn A. Merkl, "New York's Latest Bail Law Changes Explained," Brennan Center for Justice, Apr. 16, 2020. California: Patrick McGreevy, "Prop. 25, Which Would Have Abolished California's Cash Bail System, Is Rejected by Voters," *Los Angeles Times*, Nov. 3, 2020; Tony Bizjak, Molly Sullivan, and Alexei Koseff, "How Will No Cash Bail Work in California? Here Are Answers to Common Questions," *Sacramento Bee*, Aug. 28, 2018.

96. E. Ann Carson, *Prisoners in 2016*, Bureau of Justice Statistics, U.S. Department of Justice (updated Aug. 7, 2018), 1.

97. Madison Pauly, "A Brief History of America's Private Prison Industry," *Mother Jones*, July/Aug. 2016.

98. Stephen Raher, *The Company Store: A Deeper Look at Prison Commissaries*, Prison Policy Initiative (May 2018); Peter Wagner and Alexi Jones, *State*

of Phone Justice: Local Jails, State Prisons and Private Phone Providers, Prison Policy Initiative (Feb. 2019); Daniel Wagner, "Prison Bankers Cash In on Captive Customers," Center for Public Integrity, Sept. 30, 2014; Beth Schwartzapfel, "How Bad Is Prison Health Care? Depends on Who's Watching," The Marshall Project, Feb. 26, 2018.

99. Stillman, "Get Out of Jail, Inc."

100. Scott Soriano, "Private Prison Firms Make Big Money in California," *Capitol Weekly*, Dec. 13, 2021; Joshua Holland, "Private Prison Companies Are Embracing Alternatives to Incarceration," *Nation*, Aug. 23, 2016.

101. *Form 10-K for the Fiscal Year Ended December 31, 2021*, The GEO Group, Inc. (2022); *Form 10-K for the Fiscal Year Ended December 31, 2021*, CoreCivic, Inc. (2022).

102. Andy Kroll, "This Is How Private Prison Companies Make Millions Even When Crime Rates Fall," *Mother Jones*, Sept. 19, 2013; Sharon Dolovich, "State Punishment and Private Prisons," *Duke Law Journal* 55, no. 3 (Dec. 2005): 437–546, 457–60.

103. James Salzer, "Audit Stirs Debate About Costs of Private and State Prisons in Georgia," *Atlanta Journal-Constitution*, Jan. 1, 2019; *Biennial Comparison of "Private Versus Public Provision of Services" Required per A.R.S. § 41-1609.01(K) (M)*, Arizona Department of Corrections (Dec. 21, 2011), 60–61.

104. Travis C. Pratt and Jeff Maahs, "Are Private Prisons More Cost-Effective Than Public Prisons? A Meta-analysis of Evaluation Research Studies," *Crime & Delinquency* 45, no. 3 (1999): 358–71; Brad W. Lundahl et al., "Prison Privatization: A Meta-analysis of Cost and Quality of Confinement Indicators," *Research on Social Work Practice* 19, no. 4 (July 2009): 383–94.

105. Florida: William D. Bales et al., "Recidivism of Public and Private State Prison Inmates in Florida," *Criminology & Public Policy* 4, no. 1 (Feb. 2005): 57–82. Oklahoma: Andrew L. Spivak and Susan F. Sharp, "Inmate Recidivism as a Measure of Private Prison Performance," *Crime & Delinquency* 54, no. 3 (2008): 482–508. Minnesota: Grant Duwe and Valerie Clark, "The Effects of Private Prison Confinement on Offender Recidivism: Evidence from Minnesota," *Criminal Justice Review* 38, no. 3 (Sept. 2013): 375–94, 385–86.

106. *Review of the Federal Bureau of Prisons' Monitoring of Contract Prisons*, Office of the Inspector General, U.S. Department of Justice (Aug. 2016); *How Private Prison Companies Increase Recidivism*, In the Public Interest (June 2016), 4–5.

107. Anita Mukherjee, "Impacts of Private Prison Contracting on Inmate Time Served and Recidivism," *American Economic Journal: Economic Policy* 13, no. 2 (May 2021): 408–38.

108. Timothy Williams, "Inside a Private Prison: Blood, Suicide and Poorly Paid Guards," *New York Times*, Apr. 3, 2018.

109. "Occupational Employment and Wage Statistics," U.S. Bureau of Labor Statistics, U.S. Department of Labor, retrieved Apr. 3, 2019, https://www.bls.gov/oes/home.htm; Williams, "Inside a Private Prison."

110. Megan Mumford, Diane Whitmore Schanzenbach, and Ryan Nunn, *The Economics of Private Prisons*, The Hamilton Project (Oct. 2016), 4.

111. Tennessee: Daniel Arkin, "Tennessee Audit Finds Rampant Understaffing, Other Issues at Prisons," NBC News, Nov. 14, 2017. Mississippi: "The GEO Group Must Address Workplace Violence Hazards as a Result of Corporate-Wide Settlement with U.S. Department of Labor," Occupational Safety and Health Administration, U.S. Department of Labor (press release), Feb. 27, 2014. Florida: Pat Beall, "'Parade of Horribles' in Private Prisons," *Palm Beach Post*, Nov. 3, 2013. Idaho: Rebecca Boone, "FBI Investigates 'Gladiator School' Prison Company," *Seattle Times*, Mar. 7, 2014.

112. *Gaming the System: How the Political Strategies of Private Prison Companies Promote Ineffective Incarceration Policies*, Justice Policy Institute (June 2011), 3.

113. Ciara O'Neill, "Private Prisons: Principally Profit-Oriented and Politically Pliable," National Institute on Money in Politics, June 7, 2018.

114. Timothy Williams and Richard A. Oppel Jr., "Escapes, Riots and Beatings. But States Can't Seem to Ditch Private Prisons," *New York Times*, Apr. 10, 2018; Amy Brittain and Drew Harwell, "Private-Prison Giant, Resurgent in Trump Era, Gathers at President's Resort," *Washington Post*, Oct. 25, 2017.

115. *Private Prisons in the United States*, The Sentencing Project (Oct. 2019).

116. Tara Tidwell Cullen, "ICE Released Its Most Comprehensive Immigration Detention Data Yet. It's Alarming," National Immigrant Justice Center, Mar. 13, 2018.

117. Casey Tolan, "Biden Vowed to Close Federal Private Prisons, but Prison Companies Are Finding Loopholes to Keep Them Open," CNN, Nov. 12, 2021.

7. The Madness of Measuring Mental Disorders

1. Rumbaugh v. Procunier, 753 F.2d 395, 415 (5th Cir. 1985) (Goldberg, J., dissenting).

2. Christine Montross, *Waiting for an Echo: The Madness of American Incarceration* (2021), 5–6.

3. *Ex Parte* Andre Lee Thomas, 2009 WL 693606, at *1 (Tex. Crim. App. Mar. 18, 2009) (Cochran, J., concurring).

4. Marc Bookman, "How Crazy Is Too Crazy to Be Executed?," *Mother Jones*, Feb. 12, 2013.

5. *Ex Parte* Andre Lee Thomas, 2009 WL 693606, at *2–3 (Cochran, J., concurring); Bookman, "How Crazy Is Too Crazy to Be Executed?"

6. *Ex Parte* Andre Lee Thomas, 2009 WL 693606, at *6 (Cochran, J., concurring).

7. Bookman, "How Crazy Is Too Crazy to Be Executed?"

8. William Blackstone, *Commentaries on the Law of England* (1765–69), Book 4, chap. 2, 24–25.

9. *ACLU National Survey*, Benenson Strategy Group (Oct. 5–11, 2017), 6; "Poll: Americans Oppose Death Penalty for Mentally Ill by 2–1," Death Penalty Information Center (press release), Dec. 1, 2014.

10. Jeremy Travis, Bruce Western, and Steve Redburn, eds., *The Growth of Incarceration in the United States: Exploring Causes and Consequences*, National Research Council (2014), 204–5; Jennifer Bronson and Marcus Berzofsky, *Indicators of Mental Health Problems Reported by Prisoners and Jail Inmates, 2011–12*, Bureau of Justice Statistics, U.S. Department of Justice (June 2017), 1, 3–16.

11. "Mentally Ill Prisoners Who Were Executed," Death Penalty Information Center.

12. Drope v. Missouri, 420 U.S. 162, 171 (1975).

13. Ford v. Wainwright, 477 U.S. 399 (1986).

14. Alisa Roth, *Insane: America's Criminal Treatment of Mental Illness* (New York: Basic Books, 2018), 2.

15. E. Fuller Torrey, "Deinstitutionalization: A Psychiatric 'Titanic,'" *Frontline*, May 10, 2005; Ana Swanson, "A Shocking Number of Mentally Ill Americans End Up in Prison Instead of Treatment," *Washington Post*, Apr. 30, 2015.

16. See, for example, *Improving Outcomes for People with Mental Illnesses Involved with New York City's Criminal Court and Corrections System*, Council of State Governments Justice Center (Dec. 2012), 3.

17. Wesley Lowery et al., "Distraught People, Deadly Results," *Washington Post*, June 30, 2015.

18. Ibid.; "Almost 1,000 Were Killed by Police Last Year. Here's What to Do About It" (editorial), *Washington Post*, Jan. 8, 2018; John Sullivan et al., "Four Years in a Row, Police Nationwide Fatally Shoot Nearly 1,000 People," *Washington Post*, Feb. 12, 2019; "Families Failed by a Broken Mental Health

Care System Often Have No One to Call but Police," Globe Spotlight Team, *Boston Globe*, July 6, 2016.

19. Alisa Roth, "A Worried Mom Wanted the Police to Take Her Mentally Ill Son to the Hospital. They Shot Him," *Vox*, May 30, 2018.

20. Alexi Jones and Wendy Sawyer, "Arrest, Release, Repeat: How Police and Jails Are Misused to Respond to Social Problems," Prison Policy Initiative, Aug. 2019; see also Bronson and Berzofsky, *Indicators of Mental Health Problems Reported by Prisoners and Jail Inmates, 2011–12.*

21. Julie E. Grachek, "The Insanity Defense in the Twenty-First Century: How Recent United States Supreme Court Case Law Can Improve the System," *Indiana Law Journal* 81, no. 4 (2006): 1479–501, 1487–88.

22. Dusky v. United States, 362 U.S. 402, 402 (1960).

23. Drope v. Missouri, 420 U.S. at 171.

24. Anthony G. Amsterdam and Randy Hertz, *Trial Manual 6 for the Defense of Criminal Cases*, vol. 1, American Law Institute (2017), 352.

25. Ake v. Oklahoma, 470 U.S. 68 (1985).

26. Ford v. Wainwright, 477 U.S. at 412 (quoting Solesbee v. Balkcom, 339 U.S. 9, 23 (1950) (Frankfurter, J., dissenting)).

27. Roth, *Insane*, 185.

28. Stephanie Mencimer, "We're Going to Execute a Man Who Subpoenaed Jesus While Representing Himself Wearing a Purple Cowboy Suit," *Mother Jones*, Oct. 15, 2014; Panetti v. Quarterman, 2008 WL 2338498, at *5, 6, 9, 15 (W.D. Tex. Mar. 26, 2008).

29. Panetti v. Quarterman, 551 U.S. 930, 936 (2007); Mencimer, "We're Going to Execute a Man Who Subpoenaed Jesus."

30. Panetti v. Quarterman, 551 U.S. at 937.

31. Godinez v. Moran, 509 U.S. 389, 391–92 (1993); ibid. at 410 (Blackmun, J., dissenting).

32. Faretta v. California, 422 U.S. 806, 835 (1975).

33. Godinez v. Moran, 509 U.S. at 391, 398–400.

34. Indiana v. Edwards, 554 U.S. 164, 179 (2008).

35. Ibid., 167, 174–78.

36. See Sonja E. Siennick et al., "Revisiting and Unpacking the Mental Illness and Solitary Confinement Relationship," *Justice Quarterly* 39, no. 4 (2021): 772–801; David Lovell, "Patterns of Disturbed Behavior in a Supermax Prison," *Criminal Justice and Behavior* 35, no. 8 (2008): 985–1004; Maureen L. O'Keefe and Marissa J. Schnell, "Offenders with Mental Illness in the Correc-

tional System," *Journal of Offender Rehabilitation* 45 (2007): 81–104; Peter Scharff Smith, "The Effects of Solitary Confinement on Prison Inmates: A Brief History and Review of the Literature," *Crime and Justice* 34, no. 1 (2006): 441–528, 471–97.

37. Jamie Fellner, "A Corrections Quandary: Mental Illness and Prison Rules," *Harvard Civil Rights–Civil Liberties Law Review* 41, no. 2 (2006): 391–412.

38. Roth, *Insane*, 117–28.

39. Ibid., 135.

40. Sandy Hodson, "Allegations of Abuse at Augusta State Medical Prison Grow," *Augusta Chronicle*, Sept. 3, 2017, updated Jan. 25, 2022; Bill Rankin, "Conditions for Mentally Ill Women at Fulton Jail Called 'Barbaric,'" *Atlanta Journal-Constitution*, Aug. 30, 2018; Bill Rankin, "Lawsuit: Conditions Horrific for Women at South Fulton County Jail," *Atlanta Journal-Constitution*, Apr. 10, 2019; Bill Rankin, "Judge to Fulton: Fix Repulsive Jail Conditions for Mentally Ill Women," *Atlanta Journal-Constitution*, July 23, 2019.

41. Ford v. Wainwright, 477 U.S. at 409.

42. Ibid., 422 (Powell, J., concurring in part and concurring in the judgment).

43. California v. Brown, 479 U.S. 538, 545 (1987) (O'Connor, J., concurring).

44. Bigby v. Dretke, 402 F.3d 551, 566 n.6, 571 (2005).

45. Ibid., 571.

46. Rumbaugh v. Procunier, 753 F.2d at 396–97, 402.

47. Ibid., 403, 409 (Goldberg, J., dissenting).

48. Marshall Frady, "Death in Arkansas," *New Yorker*, Feb. 22, 1993, 105, 122–23, 125, 128.

49. Marc Bookman, "13 Men Condemned to Die Despite Severe Mental Illness," *Mother Jones*, Feb. 12, 2013.

50. Ferguson v. Secretary, 716 F.3d 1315, 1340, 1342 (11th Cir. 2013).

51. Panetti v. Quarterman, 551 U.S. at 954–55.

52. Ibid., 958.

53. Panetti v. Quarterman, 2008 WL 2338498, at *37.

54. Panetti v. Davis, 863 F.3d 366, 378 (5th Cir. 2017).

55. Panetti v. Quarterman, 551 U.S. at 959.

56. Solesbee v. Balkcom, 339 U.S. 9, 23 (1950) (Frankfurter, J., dissenting).

57. Madison v. Alabama, 139 S. Ct. 718 (2019).

58. Steve Leifman and Tim Coffey, "Jail Diversion: The Miami Model," *CNS Spectrums* 25, no. 5 (Oct. 2020): 659–66, 662; John Buntin, "Miami's Model for Decriminalizing Mental Illness in America," *Governing*, July 29, 2015; Stephen Eide, "Keeping the Mentally Ill Out of Jail," *City Journal*, Autumn 2018; Daniel Rivero and Nadege Green, "How Miami-Dade's Mental Health Program Steers People to Treatment, Not Jail," *Health News Florida*, WUSF, Mar. 14, 2019.

59. Leifman and Coffey, "Jail Diversion: The Miami Model," 660, 662.

60. Ibid., 662–64.

61. Miami Center for Mental Health and Recovery, https://miamifounda tionformentalhealth.org/.

62. Michael Kimmelman, "How Houston Moved 25,000 People from the Streets into Homes of Their Own," *New York Times*, June 14, 2022.

63. Melvin Washington II, "Beyond Jails: Community-Based Strategies for Public Safety," Vera Institute of Justice, Nov. 2021, 4–5.

64. Evan M. Lowder, Candalyn B. Rade, and Sarah L. Desmarais, "Effectiveness of Mental Health Courts in Reducing Recidivism: A Meta-analysis," *Psychiatric Services* 69, no. 1 (2018): 15–22; *Mental Health Courts: An Overview*, Administrative Office of the [California] Courts (2012).

65. Joseph Blocher and Jacob D. Charles, "Firearms, Extreme Risk, and Legal Design: 'Red Flag' Laws and Due Process," *Virginia Law Review* 106, no. 6 (2020): 1285–344.

66. Steve Contorno, Leyla Santiago, and Denise Royal, "Florida's Red Flag Law, Championed by Republicans, Is Taking Guns from Thousands of People," CNN, June 1, 2022; Amber Phillips, "What Are Red-Flag Laws?," *Washington Post*, June 14, 2022.

67. Caitlin Owens, "'Red Flag' Laws Test Evidence That Mass Shootings Are Preventable," *Axios*, June 6, 2022.

68. Kristen Nelson, Tamara Brady, and Daniel King, "The 'Evil' Defendant and the 'Holdout' Juror: Unpacking the Myths of the Aurora Theater Shooting Case as We Ponder the Future of Capital Punishment in Colorado," *Denver Law Review* 93, no. 3 (2016): 595–633, 600–611.

69. "Kentucky Judge Sentences Man to Death for 1987 Slayings," Associated Press, Feb. 7, 2005.

70. Jeremy Pelzer, "Ohio Lawmakers Pass Legislation Banning Executions of the Seriously Mentally Ill," *Cleveland Plain Dealer*, Dec. 17, 2020; "Kentucky Becomes the Second State to Bar Imposing the Death Penalty on Those Diagnosed as Seriously Mentally Ill," Death Penalty Information Center (press release), Apr. 14, 2022.

8. An Excess of Punishment

1. Victor Hugo, *Les Misérables*, tr. Norman Denny (1982), 97.

2. Evans v. Muncy, 498 U.S. 927, 928 (1990) (Marshall, J., dissenting).

3. Evans v. Commonwealth, 284 S.E.2d 816, 818 (Va. 1981).

4. Evans v. Muncy, 498 U.S. at 929–31 (Marshall, J., dissenting) (emphasis in original).

5. State v. Woodson, 215 S.E.2d 607 (N.C. 1975); Woodson v. North Carolina, 428 U.S. 280, 283–84, 304 (1976).

6. "From Death Row to Preacher, Man Changed NC's Death Penalty Law Has Died," WRAL News, Oct. 8, 2018; "Death Row Inmate's Case Struck Down Old State Death Penalty," WCNC Charlotte, Nov. 20, 2009; "Former Prisoner's Case Changed N.C.'s Death Penalty Law," WRAL News, Nov. 17, 2009.

7. Amadeo v. Zant, 486 U.S. 214, 226 (1988).

8. Tony Amadeo, undated letter to Stephen Bright.

9. Horton v. Zant, 941 F.2d 1449 (11th Cir. 1991).

10. McCleskey v. Kemp, 481 U.S. 279, 329–32 (1987) (Brennan, J., dissenting) (quoting Georgia Penal Code of 1861); See also A. Leon Higginbotham Jr., *In the Matter of Color: Race and the American Legal Process: The Colonial Period* (Oxford: Oxford University Press, 1978), 38–47, 181–90, 193–99, 252–65.

11. *Reconstruction in America: Racial Violence After the Civil War, 1865–1876*, Equal Justice Initiative (2020), 7.

12. Douglas L. Colbert, "Challenging the Challenge: Thirteenth Amendment as a Prohibition Against the Racial Use of Peremptory Challenges," *Cornell Law Review* 76, no. 1 (1990): 1–128, 80; *Capital Punishment 1982*, Bureau of Justice Statistics, U.S. Department of Justice (Aug. 1984), 14, Table 1; *Historical Corrections: Statistics in the United States, 1850–1984*, Bureau of Justice Statistics, U.S. Department of Justice (Dec. 1986), 10, Table 2.1; "Lynchings: By Year and Race," Famous Trials, website edited by Douglas O. Linder, University of Missouri at Kansas City School of Law.

13. Douglas A. Blackmon, *Slavery by Another Name: The Re-enslavement of Black Americans from the Civil War to World War II* (New York: Anchor Books, 2008); David M. Oshinsky, *"Worse Than Slavery": Parchman Farm and the Ordeal of Jim Crow Justice* (New York: Free Press, 1996).

14. Oshinsky, *"Worse Than Slavery,"* 245. See also Gates v. Collier, 349 F. Supp. 881, 885–93 (N.D. Miss. 1972), *aff'd*, 501 F.2d 1291 (5th Cir. 1974).

15. Hutto v. Finney, 437 U.S. 678, 681–82 nn.3–5 (1978).

16. Toussaint v. McCarthy, 597 F. Supp. 1388, 1400 (N.D. Cal. 1984), *aff'd in relevant part*, 801 F.2d 1080 (9th Cir. 1986).

17. French v. Owens, 777 F.2d 1250, 1253 (7th Cir. 1985).

18. Donald A. Cabana, *Death at Midnight: The Confession of an Executioner* (Boston: Northeastern University Press, 1996), 20.

19. *Prisoners 1925–81*, Bureau of Justice Statistics, U.S. Department of Justice (Dec. 1982); George Hill and Paige M. Harrison, *Prisoners in Custody of State or Federal Correctional Authorities, 1977–98*, Bureau of Justice Statistics, U.S. Department of Justice (Sept. 2000); Heather C. West, William J. Sabol, and Sarah J. Greenman, *Prisoners in 2009*, Bureau of Justice Statistics, U.S. Department of Justice (Dec. 2010).

20. Marc Mauer, *Race to Incarcerate*, rev. ed. (New York: The New Press, 2006), 1–2.

21. *State and Local Expenditures on Corrections and Education*, Policy and Program Studies Service, U.S. Department of Education (July 2016), 18.

22. David Fathi, "Supermax Prisons: Cruel, Inhuman and Degrading," American Civil Liberties Union, July 9, 2010.

23. Prison Litigation Reform Act, Pub. L. No. 104-134, 110 Stat. 1321 (1996) (codified at 42 U.S.C. § 1997e and other sections of 18 and 42 U.S.C.); Andrea Fenster and Margo Schlanger, *Slamming the Courthouse Door: 25 Years of Evidence for Repealing the Prison Litigation Reform Act*, Prison Policy Initiative (Apr. 26, 2021).

24. Wendy Sawyer and Peter Wagner, *Mass Incarceration: The Whole Pie 2022*, Prison Policy Initiative (Mar. 14, 2022); Roy Walmsley, *World Prison Population List*, 12th ed., World Prison Brief, Institute for Criminal Policy Research (2018), 2.

25. Danielle Kaeble, *Probation and Parole in the United States, 2020*, Bureau of Justice Statistics, U.S. Department of Justice (Dec. 2021), 1.

26. Peter Wagner, "Incarceration Is Not an Equal Opportunity Punishment," Prison Policy Initiative, Aug. 28, 2012; Sarah K.S. Shannon et al., "The Growth, Scope, and Spatial Distribution of People with Felony Records in the United States, 1948–2010," *Demography* 54, no. 5 (2017): 1795–818, 1807.

27. *The Death Penalty in 2021: Year End Report*, Death Penalty Information Center (Dec. 16, 2021); *Facts About the Death Penalty*, Death Penalty Information Center (Oct. 20, 2022).

28. *Death Sentences and Executions 2019*, Amnesty International (2020).

29. Furman v. Georgia, 408 U.S. 238 (1972); Gregg v. Georgia, 428 U.S.

153 (1976); Proffitt v. Florida, 428 U.S. 242 (1976); Jurek v. Texas, 428 U.S. 262 (1976).

30. Woodson v. North Carolina, 428 U.S. 280; Roberts v. Louisiana, 428 U.S. 325 (1976); Coker v. Georgia, 433 U.S. 584 (1977); Eberheart v. Georgia, 433 U.S. 917 (1977); Kennedy v. Louisiana, 554 U.S. 407 (2008).

31. Atkins v. Virginia, 536 U.S. 304 (2002); Roper v. Simmons, 543 U.S. 551 (2005).

32. Atkins v. Virginia, 536 U.S. at 308 n.3 (citing the definitions of the American Association on Intellectual and Developmental Disabilities (then the American Association on Mental Retardation) and the American Psychiatric Association).

33. Cherry v. State, 959 So.2d 702 (Fla. 2007).

34. John H. Blume et al., "A Tale of Two (and Possibly Three) *Atkins*: Intellectual Disability and Capital Punishment Twelve Years After the Supreme Court's Creation of a Categorical Bar," *William & Mary Bill of Rights Journal* 23, no. 2 (Dec. 2014): 393–414, 412–13; Hall v. Florida, 572 U.S. 701 (2014).

35. *Ex parte* Briseño, 135 S.W.3d 1, 8–9 (Tex. Crim. App. 2004).

36. Brief of American Association on Intellectual and Developmental Disabilities as *Amicus Curiae* in Support of Petitioner, Chester v. Thaler, 568 U.S. 978 (2012) (No. 11-1391).

37. Andrew Cohen, "Of Mice and Men: The Execution of Marvin Wilson," *Atlantic*, Aug. 8, 2012.

38. Moore v. Texas, 137 S. Ct. 1039, 1044 (2017); *Ex parte* Moore, 548 S.W.3d 552 (Tex. Crim. App. 2018); Moore v. Texas, 139 S. Ct. 666 (2019); Jolie McCullough, "Bobby Moore's Death Sentence Is Changed to Life in Prison After Lengthy Court Fights over Intellectual Disability," *Texas Tribune*, Nov. 6, 2019; Jolie McCullough, "Bobby Moore's Supreme Court Case Changed How Texas Defines Intellectual Disabilities. After 40 Years in Prison, He's Just Been Granted Parole," *Texas Tribune*, June 8, 2020.

39. "Texas Court of Criminal Appeals Reverses Course, Takes a Second Foreign National with Intellectual Disability off Death Row," Death Penalty Information Center, Oct. 2, 2020.

40. Raulerson v. Warden, 928 F.3d 987, 1009, 1017–18 (11th Cir. 2019) (Jordan, J., concurring and dissenting); Lauren S. Lucas, "An Empirical Assessment of Georgia's Beyond a Reasonable Doubt Standard to Determine Intellectual Disability in Capital Cases," *Georgia State University Law Review* 33, no. 3 (Spring 2017): 553–607.

41. Affidavit of Thomas H. Sachy M.D., MSc., *In re* Hill, 715 F.3d 284, Appendix B (11th Cir. 2013) (Barkett, J., dissenting); Ed Pilkington, "Georgia

Executes Inmate Warren Hill After Supreme Court Refuses Stay," *Guardian*, Jan. 27, 2015.

42. Hill v. Schofield, 608 F.3d 1272, 1275 (11th Cir. 2010); Head v. Hill, 587 S.E.2d 613 (Ga. 2003).

43. Hill v. Schofield, 608 F.3d at 1283; Hill v. Humphrey, 662 F.3d 1335, 1347–61 (11th Cir. 2011).

44. *In re* Hill, 715 F.3d 284; ibid., 302 (Barkett, J., dissenting).

45. *Young v. State*, 860 S.E.2d 746, 768–76 (Ga. 2021).

46. Furman v. Georgia, 408 U.S. at 249–51, 257 (Douglas, J., concurring), 310 (Stewart, J., concurring), 364–65 (Marshall, J., concurring).

47. Gregg v. Georgia, 428 U.S. 153; Proffitt v. Florida, 428 U.S. 242; Jurek v. Texas, 428 U.S. 262.

48. Walton v. Arizona, 497 U.S. 639 (1990); Lewis v. Jeffers, 497 U.S. 764 (1990); Maynard v. Cartwright, 486 U.S. 356 (1988); Godfrey v. Georgia, 446 U.S. 420 (1980).

49. Tennard v. Dretke, 542 U.S. 274 (2004); Lockett v. Ohio, 438 U.S. 586 (1978).

50. *America's Top Five Deadliest Prosecutors: How Overzealous Personalities Drive the Death Penalty*, Fair Punishment Project (June 2016), 18; "Death Sentences in the United States Since 1977," Death Penalty Information Center.

51. Stephen B. Bright, "Discrimination, Death and Denial: The Tolerance of Racial Discrimination in Infliction of the Death Penalty," *Santa Clara Law Review* 35, no. 2 (1995): 433–83, 453–54.

52. Erica L. Smith and Alexia Cooper, *Homicide in the U.S. Known to Law Enforcement, 2011*, Bureau of Justice Statistics, U.S. Department of Justice (Dec. 2013), 4; *Facts About the Death Penalty*, Death Penalty Information Center (May 12, 2022).

53. McCleskey v. Kemp, 481 U.S. at 342 (Brennan, J., dissenting).

54. John Charles Bolger, "*McCleskey v. Kemp*: Field Notes from 1977–1991," *Northwestern University Law Review* 112, no. 6 (2018): 1637–88, 1660; David C. Baldus, George G. Woodworth, and Charles A. Pulaski Jr., *Equal Justice and the Death Penalty: A Legal and Empirical Analysis* (Boston: Northeastern University Press, 1990); Scott Phillips and Justin Marceau, "Whom the State Kills," *Harvard Civil Rights–Civil Liberties Law Review* 55, no. 2 (Summer 2020): 585–656, 587.

55. McCleskey v. Kemp, 481 U.S. at 321 (Brennan, J., dissenting).

56. Ibid., 296–97.

57. Batson v. Kentucky, 476 U.S. 79 (1986).

58. McCleskey v. Kemp, 481 U.S. at 297.

59. Ibid., 308–9; ibid., 333 (Brennan, J., dissenting).

60. Ibid., 312–13; ibid., 329 (Brennan, J., dissenting).

61. Scott E. Sundby, "The Loss of Constitutional Faith: *McCleskey v. Kemp* and the Dark Side of Procedure," *Ohio State Journal of Criminal Law* 10, no. 1 (Fall 2012): 5–35, 5; see also Kenneth Williams, "The Deregulation of the Death Penalty," *Santa Clara Law Review* 40, no. 3 (2000): 677–728, 708 n.219.

62. John C. Jeffries Jr., *Justice Lewis F. Powell, Jr.: A Biography* (New York: Fordham University Press, 2001), 451–52.

63. Lowell Dodge, *Death Penalty Sentencing: Research Indicates Pattern of Racial Disparities*, U.S. General Accounting Office (Feb. 1990), 4; Catherine M. Grosso et al., "Race Discrimination and the Death Penalty: An Empirical and Legal Overview," in *America's Experiment with Capital Punishment: Reflections on the Past, Present, and Future of the Ultimate Penal Sanction*, 3rd ed., ed. James R. Acker, Robert M. Bohm, and Charles S. Lanier (Durham, NC: Carolina Academic Press, 2014), 525–76, 538–40.

64. State v. Santiago, 122 A.3d 1, 14 (Conn. 2015).

65. State v. Gregory, 427 P.3d 621, 627, 633 (Wash. 2018).

66. "Innocence," Death Penalty Information Center; Ankur Desai and Brandon L. Garrett, "The State of the Death Penalty," *Notre Dame Law Review* 94, no. 3 (2019): 1255–312, 1258.

67. "Death Sentences in the United States Since 1977," Death Penalty Information Center; "Executions Overview," Death Penalty Information Center; Table 1, *Crime in the United States, 2018*, Criminal Justice Information Services Division, FBI (Fall 2019).

68. *Habeas Corpus Reform: Hearings Before the Comm. on the Judiciary*, 101st Cong., 1st & 2d Sess. 349 (1989–90).

69. Glossip v. Gross, 576 U.S. 863, 922–23 (2015) (Breyer, J., dissenting).

70. Tracy L. Snell, *Capital Punishment, 2000*, Bureau of Justice Statistics, U.S. Department of Justice (Dec. 2001); Tracy L. Snell, *Capital Punishment, 2020—Statistical Tables*, Bureau of Justice Statistics, U.S. Department of Justice (Dec. 2021), 1, 10, 23; Ashley Nellis, *No End in Sight: America's Enduring Reliance on Life Imprisonment*, The Sentencing Project (2021), 10, 15–17; Ashley Nellis, *Still Life: America's Increasing Use of Life and Long-Term Sentences*, The Sentencing Project (2017), 19; Marc Mauer and Ashley Nellis, *The Meaning of Life: The Case for Abolishing Life Sentences* (New York: The New Press, 2018), 15–16.

71. *A Living Death: Life Without Parole for Nonviolent Offenses*, American Civil Liberties Union (2013), 20.

72. Saul Elbein, "How Georgia's Criminal Justice Reform Law Almost Left Former Inmate Aron Tuff Behind," *Atlanta Magazine*, Apr. 24, 2019; Ivana Hrynkiw, "Two Men Sentenced for Drug Trafficking and No Chance at Parole Now Free," AL.com, June 6, 2020; Kathryn Casteel, "How Being a Passenger Almost Put a Man Behind Bars for Life in Alabama," Southern Poverty Law Center, May 7, 2020.

73. Nellis, *Still Life*, 10, 12.

74. *The Effects of Aging on Recidivism Among Federal Offenders*, U.S. Sentencing Commission (Dec. 2017), 23; Expanded Homicide Data Table 3, *Crime in the United States, 2018*, Criminal Justice Information Services Division, FBI (Fall 2019).

75. Harmelin v. Michigan, 501 U.S. 957, 994 (1991) (upholding life without parole for possession of more than 650 grams of cocaine).

76. Graham v. Florida, 560 U.S. 48, 53–57, 68 (2010) (quoting Roper v. Simmons, 543 U.S. 551, 569–70 (2005)).

77. Miller v. Alabama, 567 U.S. 460, 479 (2012).

78. Montgomery v. Louisiana, 577 U.S. 190, 208 (2016).

79. Josh Rovner, *Juvenile Life Without Parole: An Overview*, The Sentencing Project (May 2021), 3.

80. Montgomery v. Louisiana, 577 U.S. at 208.

81. Liliana Segura, "Henry Montgomery Paved the Way for Other Juvenile Lifers to Go Free. Now 72, He May Never Get the Same Chance," *The Intercept*, June 2, 2019.

82. Rovner, *Juvenile Life Without Parole*, 1, 4.

83. Jones v. Mississippi, 141 S. Ct. 1307, 1311 (2021); Kim Chandler, "Juvenile Lifer Who Set Precedent Sentenced to Life Again," Associated Press, Apr. 27, 2021.

84. Rummel v. Estelle, 445 U.S. 263, 276 (1980); ibid., 286 (Powell, J., dissenting).

85. Ewing v. California, 538 U.S. 11, 16 (2003); Nellis, *Still Life*, 7; Nellis, *No End in Sight*, 10.

86. Greg Krikorian, "More Blacks Imprisoned Under '3 Strikes,' Study Says," *Los Angeles Times*, Mar. 5, 1996.

87. Ewing v. California, 538 U.S. at 18–19, 30; ibid., 43–45 (Breyer, J., dissenting).

88. Lockyer v. Andrade, 538 U.S. 63 (2003).

89. Marc Mauer, "Long-Term Sentences: Time to Reconsider the Scale of Punishment," *UMKC Law Review* 87, no. 1 (Fall 2018): 113–31, 119; Jennifer Corbett, "Three Strikes Laws in Different States," LegalMatch, updated Mar. 1, 2021.

90. Ala. Code § 13A-5-9; Ivana Hrynkiw, "Man Gets Time Served After 36 Years in Prison for Bessemer Bakery Robbery," AL.com, Aug. 28, 2019.

91. State v. Bryant, 300 So.3d 392, 394 (La. 2020) (Johnson, C.J., dissenting).

92. Scott Ehlers, Vincent Schiraldi, and Eric Lotke, *Racial Divide: An Examination of the Impact of California's Three Strikes Law on African-Americans and Latinos*, Justice Policy Institute (Oct. 2004), 6.

93. Matthew S. Crow and Kathrine A. Johnson, "Race, Ethnicity, and Habitual-Offender Sentencing: A Multilevel Analysis of Individual and Contextual Threat," *Criminal Justice Policy Review* 19, no. 1 (Mar. 2008): 63–83.

94. Stephens v. State, 456 S.E.2d 560, 564 (Ga. 1995) (Thompson, J., concurring); ibid., 566–67 (Benham, P.J., dissenting).

95. Stephens v. State, 1995 WL 116292 (Ga. Mar. 17, 1995); Motion for Reconsideration on Behalf of the Appellee by the District Attorney of the Northeastern Judicial Circuit and, as Amicus Curiae, by the Attorney General and Undersigned District Attorneys, Stephens v. State, No. S94A1854, 1995 WL 17055014 (Ga. Mar. 27, 1995).

96. Stephens v. State, 456 S.E.2d at 563.

97. Nellis, *Still Life*, 10, 12; *A Living Death*, American Civil Liberties Union, 6.

98. *Cocaine and Federal Sentencing Policy*, U.S. Sentencing Commission (May 2007), 2–4.

99. Joseph J. Palamar et al., "Powder Cocaine and Crack Use in the United States: An Examination of Risk for Arrest and Socioeconomic Disparities in Use," *Drug and Alcohol Dependence* 149 (Apr. 2015): 108–16, 110–11; Jamie Fellner, "Race, Drugs, and Law Enforcement in the United States," *Stanford Law & Policy Review* 20, no. 2 (2009): 257–91, 266.

100. *Cocaine and Federal Sentencing Policy*, U.S. Sentencing Commission, 16.

101. United States v. Clary, 846 F. Supp. 768, 788, 790, 797 (E.D. Mo. 1994).

102. United States v. Clary, 34 F.3d 709, 713 (8th Cir. 1994).

103. Fair Sentencing Act of 2010, Pub. L. 111-220, 124 Stat. 2372.

104. M. Marit Rehavi and Sonja B. Starr, "Racial Disparity in Federal

Criminal Sentences," *Journal of Political Economy* 122, no. 6 (2014); 1320–54, 1323.

105. Wisconsin: Carlos Berdejó, "Criminalizing Race: Racial Disparities in Plea-Bargaining," *Boston College Law Review* 59, no. 4 (2018): 1187–249, 1216. New York City: Besiki L. Kutateladze et al., "Cumulative Disadvantage: Examining Racial and Ethnic Disparity in Prosecution and Sentencing," *Criminology* 52, no. 3 (2014): 514–51, 531. See also Dave Ress, "Blacks More Likely to Get Prison Time in Plea Deals, Hampton Roads Court Data Show," *Daily Press*, Mar. 17, 2016.

106. Josh Salman, Emily Le Coz, and Elizabeth Johnson, "Florida's Broken Sentencing System," *Herald-Tribune*, Dec. 12, 2016; Josh Salman, Emily Le Coz, and Elizabeth Johnson, "Tough on Crime," *Herald-Tribune*, Dec. 12, 2016.

107. Federal courts: *Demographic Differences in Sentencing: An Update to the 2012* Booker *Report*, U.S. Sentencing Commission (Nov. 2017), 2. Wisconsin: Berdejó, "Criminalizing Race," 1211. New York City: Kutateladze et al., "Cumulative Disadvantage, 532; Traci Burch, "Skin Color and the Criminal Justice System: Beyond Black-White Disparities in Sentencing," *Journal of Empirical Legal Studies* 12, no. 3 (Sept. 2015): 395–420. See also Stephen Demuth and Darrell Steffensmeier, "Ethnicity Effects on Sentence Outcomes in Large Urban Courts: Comparisons Among White, Black, and Hispanic Defendants," *Social Science Quarterly* 85, no. 4 (Dec. 2004): 994–1011; John Wooldredge et al., "Is the Impact of Cumulative Disadvantage on Sentencing Greater for Black Defendants?," *Criminology & Public Policy* 14, no. 2 (May 2015): 187–223.

108. Alexi Jones, "Stagnant Populations and Changing Demographics: What the New BJS Reports Tell Us About Correctional Populations," Prison Policy Initiative, May 5, 2020.

109. Kaeble, *Probation and Parole in the United States, 2020*, 1; Fiona Doherty, "Obey All Laws and Be Good: Probation and the Meaning of Recidivism," *Georgetown Law Journal* 104, no. 2 (Jan. 2016): 291–354, 337.

110. Ronald P. Corbett Jr., "The Burdens of Leniency: The Changing Face of Probation," *University of Minnesota Law Review* 99, no. 5 (May 2015): 1697–732, 1708–12; Doherty, "Obey All Laws and Be Good," 301–2, 305 & n.40, 307–8.

111. Ibid., 315.

112. Ibid., 316–19, 325–26, 334; Corbett, "The Burdens of Leniency," 1712.

113. Victor M. Rios, *Punished: Policing the Lives of Black and Latino Boys* (New York: New York University Press, 2011), 84–91.

114. *Confined and Costly: How Supervision Violations Are Filling Prisons and Burdening Budgets*, Council of State Governments Justice Center (June 18, 2019). The data include state-funded jails but not locally funded jails.

115. Sara Steen and Tara Opsal, "'Punishment on the Installment Plan': Individual-Level Predictors of Parole Revocation in Four States," *Prison Journal* 87, no. 3 (Sept. 2007): 344–66, 356; see also Jesse Jannetta et al., *Examining Racial and Ethnic Disparities in Probation Revocation: Summary Findings and Implications from a Multisite Study*, Urban Institute (Apr. 2014), 3.

116. Gagnon v. Scarpelli, 411 U.S. 778, 786 (1973).

117. Doherty, "Obey All Laws and Be Good," 322.

118. Wendy Sawyer, Alexi Jones, and Maddy Troilo, "Technical Violations, Immigration Detainers, and Other Bad Reasons to Keep People in Jail," Prison Policy Institute, Mar. 18, 2020.

119. Maura Ewing, "How Minor Probation Violations Can Lead to Major Jail Time," *Atlantic*, June 9, 2017; see also *Confined and Costly*, Council of State Governments Justice Center.

120. *States Can Shorten Probation and Protect Public Safety*, Pew Charitable Trusts (Dec. 2020).

121. Nellis, *No End in Sight*, 10.

122. Beth Schwartzapfel, "Life Without Parole," The Marshall Project, July 10, 2015.

123. Greenholtz v. Inmates of Neb. Penal and Corr. Complex, 442 U.S. 1, 7 (1979).

124. Ebony L. Ruhland et al., *The Continuing Leverage of Releasing Authorities: Findings from a National Survey*, Robina Institute of Criminal Law and Criminal Justice (2017), 17–18; Sarah French Russell, "Review for Release: Juvenile Offenders, State Parole Practices, and the Eighth Amendment," *Indiana Law Journal* 89, no. 1 (Winter 2014): 373–440, 400–405; Edward E. Rhine, Kelly Lyn Mitchell, and Kevin R. Reitz, *Levers of Change in Parole Release and Revocation*, Robina Institute of Criminal Law and Criminal Justice (2018), 19.

125. Greenholtz v. Inmates of Neb. Penal and Corr. Complex, 442 U.S. at 10; Edward E. Rhine, Joan Petersilia, and Kevin R. Reitz, "The Future of Parole Release," *Crime and Justice* 46 (2017): 279–338, 299.

126. Ruhland et al., *The Continuing Leverage of Releasing Authorities*, 27; Beth M. Huebner and Timothy S. Bynum, "The Role of Race and Ethnicity in Parole Decisions," *Criminology* 46, no. 4 (Nov. 2008): 907–38. See also

Richard Tewksbury and David Patrick Connor, "Predicting the Outcome of Parole Hearings," *Corrections Today*, June–July 2012.

127. Schwartzapfel, "Life Without Parole"; Rhine et al., "The Future of Parole Release," 314.

128. *Max Out: The Rise in Prison Inmates Released Without Supervision*, Pew Charitable Trusts (June 2014), 2–3; Huebner and Bynum, "The Role of Race and Ethnicity in Parole Decisions"; Michael Winerip, Michael Schwirtz, and Robert Gebeloff, "For Blacks Facing Parole in New York State, Signs of a Broken System," *New York Times*, Dec. 4, 2016.

129. Nazgol Ghandnoosh, *Delaying a Second Chance: The Declining Prospects for Parole on Life Sentences*, The Sentencing Project (2017), 3.

130. Herrera v. Collins, 506 U.S. 390, 412 (1993).

131. "Clemency," Death Penalty Information Center.

132. Brooke A. Masters, "Missteps on Road to Injustice," *Washington Post*, Dec. 1, 2000; "Earl Washington," Innocence Project.

133. Ken Armstrong and Steve Mills, "Ryan Suspends Death Penalty," *Chicago Tribune*, Jan. 31, 2000; Pam Belluck, "Class of Sleuths to Rescue on Death Row," *New York Times*, Feb. 5, 1999; *Innocence Protection Act of 2000: Hearing on H.R. 4167 Before the Subcomm. on Crime of the H. Comm. on the Judiciary*, 106th Cong. 71 (2000) (statement of Governor George Ryan); "Clemency for All," *Chicago Tribune*, Jan. 12, 2003.

134. Cara H. Drinan, "Clemency in a Time of Crisis," *Georgia State University Law Review* 28, no. 4 (Summer 2012): 1123–59, 1124; "Execution Database," Death Penalty Information Center; "Clemency," Death Penalty Information Center.

135. "A Nation of Second Chances: President Obama's Record on Clemency," The White House, President Barack Obama.

136. Conn. Bd. of Pardons v. Dumschat, 452 U.S. 458, 464 (1981).

137. Appellant's Brief, 1999 Westlaw 33732407, at 12–13 (quoting the record from the district court), Faulder v. Tex. Bd. of Pardons and Paroles, 178 F.3d 343 (5th Cir. 1999); ibid. (affirming the district court); Alan Berlow, "The Texas Clemency Memos," *Atlantic*, July–Aug. 2003.

138. Tamayo v. Perry, 553 Fed. Appx. 395, 402 (5th Cir. 2014); Faulder v. Tex. Bd. of Pardons and Paroles, 178 F.3d 343.

9. More Justice, Less Crime

1. Dietrich Bonhoeffer, *Letters and Papers from Prison*, ed. John W. de Gruchy (2015), 11–12.

2. Wendy Sawyer and Peter Wagner, *Mass Incarceration: The Whole Pie 2022*, Prison Policy Initiative (Mar. 14, 2022); Table 1, *Crime in the United States, 2018*, Criminal Justice Information Services Division, FBI (Fall 2019); Table 1, *Crime in the United States, 2008*, Criminal Justice Information Services Division, FBI (Sept. 2009).

3. Rachel E. Morgan and Alexandra Thompson, *Criminal Victimization, 2020—Supplemental Statistical Tables*, Bureau of Justice Statistics, U.S. Department of Justice (Feb. 2022); John Gramlich, "What the Data Says (and Doesn't Say) About Crime in the United States," Pew Research Center, Nov. 20, 2020; Don Stemen, *The Prison Paradox: More Incarceration Will Not Make Us Safer*, Vera Institute of Justice (July 2017).

4. Damon M. Petrich et al., "Custodial Sanctions and Reoffending: A Meta-analytic Review," *Crime and Justice* 50, no. 1 (2021): 353–424, 400–402.

5. Craig Haney, *Criminality in Context: The Psychological Foundations of Criminal Justice Reform* (Washington, DC: American Psychological Association, 2020), 3, 10.

6. Ibid., 55, 89–101, 142–43, 153–54, 249, 271.

7. Ibid., 110 (emphasis in original), 199.

8. Ibid., 366–70, 376; Melvin Washington II, *Beyond Jails: Community-Based Strategies for Public Safety*, Vera Institute of Justice (Nov. 16, 2021).

9. Sawyer and Wagner, *Mass Incarceration: The Whole Pie 2022*; *Treatment Approaches for Drug Addiction DrugFacts*, National Institute on Drug Abuse (Jan. 2019); "Drug Overdose Deaths in the U.S. Top 100,000 Annually," National Center for Health Statistics, Centers for Disease Control and Prevention (press release), Nov. 17, 2021; "U.S. Overdose Deaths in 2021 Increased Half as Much as in 2020—but Are Still Up 15%," National Center for Health Statistics, Centers for Disease Control and Prevention (press release), May 11, 2022; Nora D. Volkow et al., "Drug Use Disorders: Impact of a Public Health Rather Than a Criminal Justice Approach," *World Psychiatry* 16, no. 2 (June 2017): 213–14.

10. Ibid., 213.

11. Ari Davis et al., *A Year in Review: 2020 Gun Deaths in the U.S.*, Johns Hopkins Center for Gun Violence Solutions (Apr. 28, 2022), 11; Franklin E. Zimring and Gordon Hawkins, *Crime Is Not the Problem: Lethal Violence in America* (New York: Oxford University Press, 1997).

12. Scott R. Kegler et al., "*Vital Signs*: Changes in Firearm Homicide and Suicide Rates—United States, 2019–2020," *Morbidity and Mortality Weekly Report* 71, no. 19 (2022): 656–63, 656, 658, Table 1; John Woodrow Cox, *Children Under Fire: An American Crisis* (New York: HarperCollins, 2021).

13. *Gun Violence and COVID-19 in 2020: A Year of Colliding Crises*,

Everytown for Gun Safety (May 7, 2021); "Gun Violence Archive 2020," *Gun Violence Archive*; "#NotAnAccident Index," Everytown for Gun Safety; Davis et al., *A Year in Review: 2020*, 13.

14. J. David Goodman, "Texas Goes Permitless on Guns, and Police Face an Armed Public," *New York Times*, Oct. 26, 2022.

15. Davis et al., *A Year in Review: 2020*, 18.

16. Ibid., 9, 23.

17. Kegler et al., *"Vital Signs,"* 659–61; Davis et al., *A Year in Review: 2020*, 9–10; Thomas Abt, *Bleeding Out: The Devastating Consequences of Urban Violence—and a Bold New Plan for Peace in the Streets* (New York: Basic Books, 2019), 87–93; Charles C. Branas et al., "Citywide Cluster Randomized Trial to Restore Blighted Vacant Land and Its Effects on Violence, Crime, and Fear," *Proceedings of the National Academy of Sciences* 115, no. 12 (Mar. 20, 2018): 2946–51.

18. Bill Rankin, "Nathan Deal's Criminal Justice Reforms Leave Lasting Legacy," *Atlanta Journal-Constitution*, Dec. 21, 2018.

19. "An Overview of the First Step Act," Federal Bureau of Prisons; *The First Step Act of 2018: An Overview*, Congressional Research Service, Mar. 4, 2019.

20. Campbell Robertson, "Would You Let the Man Who Killed Your Sister Out of Prison?," *New York Times*, July 19, 2019; Nazgol Ghandnoosh, *A Second Look at Injustice*, The Sentencing Project (2021), 21.

21. Ghandnoosh, *A Second Look at Injustice*, 18–21, 24–25.

22. Danielle Sered, *Accounting for Violence: How to Increase Safety and Break Our Failed Reliance on Mass Incarceration*, Common Justice and Vera Institute for Justice (2017), 12–14.

23. Danielle Sered, *Until We Reckon: Violence, Mass Incarceration, and a Road to Repair* (New York: The New Press, 2019); "Common Justice Model," Common Justice.

24. Michelle Alexander, "Reckoning with Violence," *New York Times*, Mar. 3, 2019.

25. David B. Wilson, Ajima Olaghere, and Catherine S. Kimbrell, *Effectiveness of Restorative Justice Principles in Juvenile Justice: A Meta-analysis*, Office of Juvenile Justice and Delinquency Prevention, U.S. Department of Justice (2017), 27, 34–35; Heather Strang et al., *Restorative Justice Conferencing (RJC) Using Face-to-Face Meetings of Offenders and Victims: Effects on Offender Recidivism and Victim Satisfaction. A Systematic Review*, The Campbell Systematic Reviews

2013:12 (2013), 4–5. See also Lawrence W. Sherman and Heather Strang, *Restorative Justice: The Evidence*, The Smith Institute (2007).

26. Paul Tullis, "Can Forgiveness Play a Role in Criminal Justice?," *New York Times Magazine*, Jan. 4, 2013; Eli Hager, "They Agreed to Meet Their Mother's Killer. Then Tragedy Struck Again," The Marshall Project, July 21, 2020.

27. Woodson v. North Carolina, 428 U.S. 280, 304 (1976).

Index

About the Authors

Stephen B. Bright is a renowned death penalty lawyer and a professor at Yale Law School and the Georgetown University Law Center. He was director and later president of the Southern Center for Human Rights, where he tried capital cases before juries and argued four capital cases in the Supreme Court, winning all four. He received the American Bar Association's Thurgood Marshall Award. He lives in Lexington, Kentucky.

James Kwak is the author or co-author of four books, including *13 Bankers*, a *New York Times* bestseller. He is a fellow at the University of Connecticut School of Law, where he was the Jesse Root Professor of Law. He was previously the chairperson of the board of directors of the Southern Center for Human Rights. James lives in Amherst, Massachusetts, and is a freelance cellist.

Publishing in the Public Interest

Thank you for reading this book published by The New Press; we hope you enjoyed it. New Press books and authors play a crucial role in sparking conversations about the key political and social issues of our day.

We hope that you will stay in touch with us. Here are a few ways to keep up to date with our books, events, and the issues we cover:

- Sign up at www.thenewpress.com/subscribe to receive updates on New Press authors and issues and to be notified about local events
- www.facebook.com/newpressbooks
- www.twitter.com/thenewpress
- www.instagram.com/thenewpress

Please consider buying New Press books not only for yourself, but also for friends and family and to donate to schools, libraries, community centers, prison libraries, and other organizations involved with the issues our authors write about.

The New Press is a 501(c)(3) nonprofit organization; if you wish to support our work with a tax-deductible gift please visit www.thenewpress.com/donate or use the QR code below.